THE COMMERCIALIZATION OF INTIMATE LIFE

ARLIE RUSSELL HOCHSCHILD

THE COMMERCIALIZATION OF INTIMATE LIFE

Notes from Home and Work

UNIVERSITY OF
CALIFORNIA PRESS
Berkeley
Los Angeles
London

University of California Press
Berkeley and Los Angeles, California

University of California Press, Ltd.
London, England

© 2003 by Arlie Russell Hochschild

Hochschild, Arlie Russell
    The commercialization of intimate life : notes from home and
work / Arlie Russell Hochschild.
        p. cm.
    Includes bibliographical references and index.
    ISBN 0-520-21487-0 (alk. paper) — ISBN 0-520-21488-9
(pbk. : alk. paper)
        1. Interpersonal relations and culture.   2. Emotions—
Sociological aspects.   3. Social pressure.   4. Man-woman
relationships.   5. Self.   6. Family.   I. Title.

HM1106 .H63   2003
302—dc21   2002152224

Manufactured in the United States of America

12   11   10   09   08   07   06   05   04   03
10   9   8   7   6   5   4   3   2   1

The paper used in this publication meets the minimum
requirements of ANSI/NISO Z39.48–1992 (R 1997)
(*Permanence of Paper*).♾

For Ilse Jawetz

CONTENTS

ACKNOWLEDGMENTS

I am pleased to see these essays gathered between two covers. While each essay describes how I see things now, ideas breathe and grow, and I hope these do too. And so I offer them as works in progress. For the process of getting them this far, I owe many thanks all around. To my longtime friend Ann Swidler and to the late Michael Rogin, I owe thanks for looking with me into the early mists from which these ideas emerged. Thanks to Jerry Karabel and Mike Hout for help hunting down information of different sorts. I owe a great deal to the sage, perceptive advice of Tom Englehardt on the whole gestalt of these essays and for suggesting what didn't belong. For excellent research assistance, many thanks to Allison Pugh and Roberta Espinoza, and for their wonderful support and careful work, many thanks to UC Press editors Naomi Schneider and Sue Heinemann and copyeditor Kay Scheuer. For careful typing, and unpredictable giggle fits, many thanks to Bonnie Kwan.

I want to pay special tribute to Ilse Jawetz, with whom I've talked every weekday for nearly thirty years—about children, writing, Freud, Hitler, love, and all the harsh and gentle mysteries of life. Thank you so much for being my friend. I am the better for it.

And many thanks to my husband, Adam, who captured my heart at age twenty and has kept it with him ever since. He's lived with these ideas nearly as much as I, and has read these essays at various stages. He's said things about content, of course, but he's a real stickler for style too. To impress on me the dangers of using too many quotation marks, he commented in the margin of one early draft, "Oy!" "So" "many" "quotation marks" "around" "so" "many" "words" "makes" "the" "essay" "seem" "weird." Quotation marks, he sensibly pointed out, are a way of placing reservations on our use of a word, and we need to have a good reason for doing that. So, the few quotation marks in this book that have resisted his red upward-tilting deletion marks had to make a strong case in writer's court for their right to stay. I "thank" "him" "for" "his" "good" "advice," and send him love with no quotation marks.

Introduction

TWO SIDES OF AN IDEA

Lore has it that a person without a compass, tramping a long distance in the wilderness, will slowly veer sideways, make a circle, and end up where she began. When I first laid out these essays on the blue rug in my study, starting with the first essay I thought to include and ending with another I'd just drafted, there it was—that circle. In the center is the idea that love and care, the very basis of any social life, are a source of great confusion in America today. We do a caring act. But why do we do it? Are we motivated by personal desire or obligation, or by what blend of each? Are these motives anchored to family or something like it? To friendship or something like it? Are we motivated by civic pride, devotion to God, professional pride, or the desire for money? And what happens when the institutions to which these anchors are attached themselves change—as when, in the United States today, family bonds grow lighter or shift, the state withdraws support for the poor, companies cut benefits and reduce job security, or the care sector of the economy expands, recruiting from across the globe? What knots, disconnects, and surprises appear—apparently unrelated—in the daily expressions of love and care and in our feelings about those expressions? When a Thai nanny in Redwood City, California, tells me she loves the American children she cares for more than her own children back in Thailand, is this an example of a rich country "extracting" the ore of love from a poor country? And, if so, what social anchors for love and care do her children have?

Emotion, gender, family, capitalism, globalization—these are the topics. But I invite the reader to use the ideas in all of them to help figure out what affects the fate of love and care. That's the question at the center of the circle.

For, over the past twenty years, we have witnessed a growing care gap. Informal systems of kin care have grown more fragile, uncertain, and fragmented. Yet newer institutional forms of care are not universally in place or uniformly humane. The larger structure of American society has become less caring too. The class gap has widened. Large corporations increasingly hire and fire workers as market demand dictates.

1

All of this has altered the nature of the public world that American women, during this period, have entered in huge numbers. In 1900 less than a fifth of married women in the United States worked for pay; in 1950 about 40 percent did, and in 2000 close to 70 percent did.[1] Indeed, whether a husband is present or not, six out of ten mothers of two-year-olds and over half of mothers of one-year-olds are engaged in paid work. Nowadays the grandmothers, aunts, and neighbors to whom one might have turned for caring help are also working. Fathers haven't cut back their hours but, if anything, have expanded them, while a growing divorce rate has led many fathers to leave all care of their children to their ex-wives. So there are fewer hands at home. At the same time, many people can't find or afford good paid care. And neither the government nor private corporations are stepping forward to bridge the gap. On the contrary, in recent years both the state and capitalism have stepped back from previous commitments (the state through welfare reform, capitalism through the growth of the contingency labor force). Instead, both have tossed the care ball back to the private realm, where few are home to catch it. We have "dead-beat dads" it seems, in both the private and the public realms.[2]

All of this is bad news for care. Children and the elderly were far worse off in the America of 1690, 1890, and 1930, of course. Still, those who make the argument that "it used to be worse" sometimes do so in the spirit of emotionally bracing us to accept the tough news of today's world. I don't want to do that. We don't need to imagine an unrealistically idyllic past in order to recognize today's care gap as a care gap.

And it's one that has led to a curious outcome. On one hand, the work of caring for young and old seems to have moved down in honor and monetary reward, and become work to get out of, to pass on to someone who can't get a better job. On the other hand, care has moved up in ideological importance, as part of an intense and hazy quest to create a kinder, gentler family and nation. Ideologically, "care" went to heaven. Practically, it's gone to hell.

Indeed, despite escalation in public rhetoric about care, we are asking increasingly anxious questions about the practical realities of it. One set of questions focuses on the informal care offered by family and friends. Is a father or stepfather the "real dad" in a small child's life? Are the ex-husband's parents the primary grandparents of a child or does a child now look to the parents of a new husband? In what way does a long-hours dad share the care of his elderly mother with his siblings, his wife, the home health-care worker? Is a neighbor looking in on a twelve-year-old, or is the child old enough to stay alone until working parents come home? Given the new pressures at work, when can working parents make it home?

As we supplement or replace family care with paid care, how do we make it work in a humanly meaningful way? As the "artisanal" family becomes the postindustrial one, tasks formerly done inside are increasingly outsourced to specialists—childcare workers, eldercare aides, hospice workers, summer camp counselors, psychiatrists, and for the affluent, chauffeurs, family photo assemblers, and birthday party coordinators. Less and less do we produce care. More and more we consume it. Indeed, increasingly we "do" care by buying the right service or thing.

While many paid forms of care are vast improvements over the unpaid care of yesteryear, paid care raises challenging questions. Are we okay with the fact that baby may say his first word to the childcare worker, and grandma her last word to the nursing home aide? If we reserve for such moments some sense of private awe, how do we reconcile this with the demands of our workplaces, the equality of the sexes, and the very structure of honor in modern life? That's the basic question.

Many of the essays in this book try to capture and magnify moments in the circle around it. A child eavesdrops on a phone call in which a parent hires a babysitter. A man wants more thanks from his wife for doing the laundry. An advice book tells her to drop him. Private moments of confusion or conflict about care are often directly linked to contradictory social pressures in society at large. Sometimes these pressures originate in one place and show up in another, as in what doctors call "referred pain." Just as pain in a leg may originate in a slipped disk in our back, so too a painfully deteriorating bond between parent and child may link back to a company speed-up or government retrenchment. Increasingly we feel in our moments of detachment and neglect the referred pain of unfettered global capitalism itself.

ON THE PERSONAL SIDE

This, then, was my first discovery that my thoughts—over the years—have focused on various facets of care. But in thinking about these essays, I also began to wonder what hidden compass in my own personal life might account for my strong interest in care. And there I made a second discovery. Like many white middle-class women of my generation, I became a "migrant" in the 1960s from the emotional culture of my mother to that of my father. My mother was a full-time homemaker who raised my brother, Paul, and myself, volunteered for the PTA, and helped start a preschool program in Montgomery County, Maryland, all the while supporting my father's career as a government official and diplomat. It was she who deciphered some intention in our chaotic fingerpaintings, and she who reassured us that scary monsters go "back home" so we could sleep in peace at night. She gave us many gifts of love, but each with a touch of sadness.

When I was around ten I remember jumping off my school bus in the afternoon, dashing up the hill in front of our house, flinging open the front door, bounding up the stairs, knocking on my mother's bedroom door, and entering to find her lying in bed, mild in manner, pleased to see me, I think, but was it an effort to be pleased? I couldn't tell. She was the one in charge of me, and she seemed sad about it. When I remember my father, I picture him skip-stepping down a long flight of stairs in front of our house, whistling a jaunty tune, facing away from the house and from us. My father seemed the happy one, but he wasn't the "caring" one. So my mother was the sad caretaker and my father the happy non-caretaker, or so it seemed.

When I compared my mother to the stay-at-home moms of my girlfriends in the suburban world of Kensington, Maryland, in the 1950s, I felt very lucky. Jan's mother would ridicule Jan in front of me. Susan's mom, a heavy-set woman in a muumuu, would shuffle into the kitchen to tuck away a wine bottle, surprised Susan was home "so soon." Penny's mom was like a drill sergeant. No, I had it good.

But my best friend, Janet Thompson, had a wonderfully twinkly, welcoming mom who seemed to like being a mother. When I occasionally stayed for dinner, Janet's cute baby sister Betsy would set us all to laughing. Seated in her highchair, all messy, Betsy would authoritatively babble some baby joke of hers. Mrs. Thompson would laugh at Betsy's jokes without getting them, and that would seem funny in itself. Then she'd laugh inclusively, invitingly, and soon waves of tearful mirth rippled around the table. It was happy laughter—easy, spontaneous, infectious, a new emotional continent. And if I were to name a moment when I began to wonder about the connection between caring for children and having fun, and about the feeling of enjoyment itself, it would be those evenings at the Thompsons. But it took living in my house, with my slightly sad, meditative, highly intelligent mother to get the idea that I could think about feelings and not just feel them.

My mother's moods led her to see the world darkly, but the very darkness of her vision allowed her to penetrate other people's psychic defenses and predict events with uncanny accuracy. The white-coated, positivist social scientists whose dubious predictions I was to solemnly study in graduate school would have sold their objectivist souls to bottle her magic. She could tell that my grandmother would soon become sick, that my aunt might just burn down her house, that our peaceable dog would soon bite someone. She read emotions the way doctors read x-rays. So my father, brother, and I listened respectfully to her dark hunches, because there was usually something to them. My older brother and I fought incessantly, my father was preoccupied, and all my other relatives lived far away. So my mother was it, my center, my source of warmth and concern. All would be well, I thought, if only I could use my own magic to decipher her and cheer her up. And these became my twin missions.

I could cheer her up some, but it was harder to decipher her. I knew that my mother loved my father and he very much loved her. I would overhear them laughing and sensed in their teasing and joking a sensual connection. So, as a child, I concluded that mother wasn't sad about her husband, just about her motherhood. The German psychoanalyst Christa Rohde-Dachser speaks of the "female depressive solution"—the woman's renunciation of her own needs in order to focus exclusively on the urgent needs of others. Rohde-Dachser joins these two improbable words "solution" and "depressive," proposing the fascinating idea that one problem could be the solution to another. But when I was a young girl, my mother's depression didn't seem like a "solution" to anything. It was a void.

Meanwhile, armed with his confidence, clarity, ambition, and joy, my father daily set off to an office job somewhere that I imagined to be serious, interesting, and important. Early on, I developed the simple, mistaken, idea that staying home to care for children was sad and going to work was happy. Each had its own emotional weather. If my mother had had a career, I reasoned, she would have been happy, the way my father was. And so would I. So while as a young girl I prepared for motherhood, endlessly dressing and undressing Yonny, a large rubber doll, a gift from my grandmother, I also vowed that when I grew up I would make a beeline for that skip-step, happy-whistle career.

I don't want to lay too much on this. Many children of depressed mothers become waitresses, chiropractors, or roller-derby contestants, and not sociologists preoccupied with care. And there are many other reasons, beyond the scope of this introduction, why sociology as a way of seeing has felt so right to me. Needless to say, too, I by no means believe that it inherently depresses a person to care for another. On the contrary. I'm simply explaining why I haven't taken it for granted that care brings joy.

Like most women over the last three decades, I left that care-oriented world of my mother without quite departing and joined the career world of my father without really settling in. I inhabited both spheres but held citizenship in neither. Only with the collectively born insights of the women's movement of the 1960s and 1970s did I come to recognize an enormous problem in the *colonial arrangement* between the "metropolis" of my father's world and the native village of my mother's. Just as the low price of sugar rips off the Third World farmer who produces it while benefiting the First World consumer, so the undervalued labors of the homemaker enable her husband to have his more highly valued career. If happiness derives in part from feeling valued, it occurred to me, we need to create new supports for valuing care—through well-paid childcare or gender-free homemaking. In my own life I wanted to *be* that social support for my mother, and while escaping her life, I also secretly planned to rescue her by having my career for her. She encouraged this. But in the end, of course, it couldn't make her happy. Instead, it led me to write the essays in this book.

Some colleagues I respect consider it risky to link a personal journey to an intellectual interest because doing so reveals a personal "bias." If by "bias" we mean "a mental leaning or inclination"—which is one definition *Webster's New World Dictionary* suggests—then yes, it does. The self is an instrument of inquiry. In the end we have no other. To understand the childhood origins of an intellectual passion is to understand the possibilities and limitations of that instrument, the better to see what other instruments one needs to know the world. But such subjectivity—what, it turns out, *drives* us—does more than just that. It shapes what we expect and wish, and so it shapes how the world surprises us. As Maurice Merleau-Ponty observed, every time we *see*, we *compare*.[3] A wall is more or less white than another wall we can see or imagine. So, our subjectivity, with the wealth of comparisons it implants in us, transforms us into tourists of ourselves, visitors of the odd sights of everyday life. It removes the dull sense that anything at all is obvious. Every social scientist has his or her subjectivity; the question is how we use it.

In his essay "'Objectivity' in Social Science and Social Policy," Max Weber traced the "hair-line which separates science from faith."[4] We rightly rely on values, he suggested, to decide what it is we need to understand and to determine the purposes to which findings are put. In between these two stages, Weber posits a value-neutral middle stage of "finding the truth." Here he thought values were a source of bias. But in my own view, the urgent dilemmas of childhood set up a quest that inevitably backlights our findings, so we need to run our hunches through every kind of test. We need to continually question our values. But I don't see how we can "find this truth" without guidance from them.

And so it's been with me. During my first year of graduate school in sociology at the University of California, Berkeley, like so many other women students I pored through Betty Friedan's *The Feminine Mystique* and concluded that my mother had what Friedan calls the "problem with no name." Having herself come of age and earned a college degree in the "flaming twenties," my mother had settled down to married life in the mid-1930s and was still at it in the postwar 1950s. One social class up from Rosie the Riveter, she was educated to play a public role she never played. She felt stuck.

How could women such as my mother feel discontent, but misunderstand the powerful cultural source of it?[5] And how does the misrecognition of a feeling alter the authenticity of it? *Can* it do that? How does culture—through setting out "rules" of feeling—establish what we imagine we "should" and "shouldn't" feel? How do we reconcile what we think we *should* feel with what we think we *do* feel? And so began my quest into feelings and feeling rules.

I did not have those famed library "aha!" experiences first-year graduate students are supposed to undergo as they open up tomes by Weber, Durkheim, and Marx. But the power of their ideas came upon me gradually as I began to grapple with one or another face of the care gap, and it is reflected in the essays here. Weber's thinking is crucial to "The Commercial Spirit of Intimate Life and the Abduction of Feminism," Durkheim's to "Emotional Geography and the Flight Plan of Capitalism," and Marx's to "Love and Gold."

All along, I've been deeply influenced by Erving Goffman, whose many works—particularly *The Presentation of Self in Everyday Life, Asylums, Stigma,* and *Encounters,* as well as his essay "Footing" in *Forms of Talk* — reflected the poignant vulnerability of the marginal man and woman. But Goffman gave us actors without psyches. His characters had feelings—that's what I loved about them—but we couldn't know, from Goffman, where those feelings came from. And so, still mulling over my own mother's experience of caring for me and her own private "care gap," I turned to Freud, Darwin, Max Scheler, and the anthropologist George Foster among others for help in grasping the social aspect of emotion. I began to think more about a sociology of emotion. And it was through this lens of the sociology of emotion that I came to understand this greatest social revolution of our time—the one that so divided my life from my mother's—the revolution in the role of women.

Women like myself have very much wanted to be equal to men in public and private life. But this desire raises the question: *equal to what?* Equal in *what culture of care?* Like immigrants moving from country to city, many women have emigrated from the culture of our mothers to that of our fathers. But what of the language and love of that old mother culture, imperfect as it was, have we been able to keep and share with men? What have we left behind? Does what we have feel right? On what basis do we tell?

The immigrants I am describing here move between gender cultures that are powerfully linked to a sense of *self.* One sixty-five-year-old man I recently interviewed who had devoted much time, effort, and love to caring for an eighty-seven-year-old godmother said to me matter-of-factly, "If a man is caring for others, calling, shopping, visiting, it shows the world he has failed as a man." "Failed as a man?" I asked. "Yes," he replied with great feeling, "He *really has* failed as a man." If this man can't care for an elderly woman (as this man so movingly does) without giving up the sense that he is a "real" man, how can women who delegate to others the care of their children and parents feel like "real" women without suffering some ambivalence? Just as peasants having newly migrated to the city sift through their indigenous culture, keeping some elements, discarding others, so over the last decades of American life both sexes have been searching through old cultural markers of the "real self," and weighing the emotional price of each "keep" and each "drop." Care: we haven't worked it through yet.

For all the migrations in this gender-revolutionary century, care still remains largely in women's hands. "Women," according to Robert Putnam, "make 10–12 percent more long-distance calls to family and friends than men, are responsible for nearly three times as many greeting cards and gifts, and write two to four times as many personal letters. Women spend more time visiting with friends, though full-time work blurs this gender difference by trimming friendship time for both sexes. . . . Even in adolescence . . . women are more likely to express a sense of concern and responsibility for the welfare of others by doing volunteer work more frequently. Although American boys and girls in the 1990's used computers almost equally, boys were more likely to use them to play games; girls more to e-mail friends."[6]

But caring has become increasingly associated with "getting stuck" outside the main show. When in the mid-nineteenth century, men were drawn into market life and women remained outside it, female homemakers formed a moral brake on capitalism. Now American women are its latest recruits, offered membership in the public side of market society on the same harsh terms as those offered to American men. The result makes for a harshness of life that seems so normal to us we don't see it. We really need, I believe, a revolution in our society and in our thinking, one that rewards care as much as market success, one that strengthens a nonmarket public sphere—like the old village commons. For the very balance we strike between market and nonmarket forces is itself a stand on care. I mean these essays to open a door to this revolution.

I love to interview people, discover my ideas as I do it, and often reflect back on particular encounters months, years, even decades later. Virtually all the essays collected here reflect my recent thinking and so all of them go beyond what I have written in my other books. I've divided this book into five sections. The main points of focus are culture (part 1), emotion (part 2), family and work (part 3), care (part 4), and a personal essay touching on all of these (part 5). Each part gathers essays that focus on one facet in a larger portrait of personal life under American capitalism. Each facet is distinct, though some facets appear in the territory of others. I invite the reader to browse and read according to interest, or sample one essay in each part, and with any luck, one essay will point to another. Indeed, the reader will find overlaps. In a number of essays I describe women's move into paid work, remark on popular advice to women, and refer to Thorstein Veblen's 1914 essay *The Instinct for Workmanship and the Industrial Arts*. I've left these repetitions because they are touchstones to thinking that moves in each essay along different tracks, and because each time I tried to take them out it felt like I was unraveling a sweater.

These essays do not do full justice to the rich racial, ethnic, religious, and sexual diversity of women's experiences, or men's, but I hope that some of the ideas—the economy of gratitude, emotional labor, displaced love as a global commodity, to mention a few—will be useful in future work that explores that diversity. In the end, I offer these essays as so many lanterns to shed light on what's happening to care in everyday life under global capitalism.

Part One

A CULTURE OF PSYCHIC DIVESTMENT

1 THE COMMERCIAL SPIRIT OF INTIMATE LIFE AND THE ABDUCTION OF FEMINISM

Signs from Women's Advice Books

Praising and encouraging are very close to pushing, and when you do that you are trying again to take control of his life. Think about why you are lauding something he's done. Is it to help raise his self-esteem? That's manipulation. Is it so he will continue whatever behavior you're praising? That's manipulation. Is it so that he'll know how proud you are of him? That can be a burden for him to carry. Let him develop his own pride from his own accomplishments.

Robin Norwood, *Women Who Love Too Much* (1985)

Best-selling advice books for women published in the United States in the later part of the past century offer a glimpse into an important future trend in American popular culture. This trend is a curious, latter-day parallel to the very different cultural shift Max Weber describes in *The Protestant Ethic and the Spirit of Capitalism*. Just as Protestantism, according to Max Weber, "escaped from the cage" of the church to be transposed into an inspirational "spirit of capitalism" that drove men to make money and build capitalism, so feminism may be "escaping from the cage" of a social movement to buttress a commercial spirit of intimate life that was originally separate from and indeed alien to it.[1] Just as market conditions ripened the soil for capitalism, so a weakened family prepares the soil for a commercialized spirit of domestic life. Magnified moments in advice books tell this story.

The current cultural shift differs in the object of its ideas (love and not work), in the social sphere it most affects (the family and not the economy), and in the population most immediately influenced (women, not men). The cultural shift reflected in advice books concerns a more marginal ideology—feminism—and the commercial transmutation of it is a shift that is smaller, I hope, in scale. Like the earlier trend, this one represents the outcome of an ongoing cultural struggle, gives rise to countertrends, and is uneven in its effect. But the parallel is there.

To explore evidence of this shift, this parallel, let's turn to best-selling advice books for women published between 1970 and 1990 as a likely bellwether of trends in the popular ideas governing women's approach to intimate life.[2] For, like other commercial and professional conveyors of guidance, advice books are becoming more important while traditional spheres of authority, families and to a degree churches, are becoming less so. Thus, while the counsel of parents, grandparents, aunts and uncles, ministers, priests, and rabbis holds relatively less weight than it did a century ago, that of professional therapists, television talk show hosts, radio commentators, video producers, and magazine and advice book authors assumes relatively more weight.[3] While people turn increasingly to anonymous authorities, the emotional problems they wish to resolve are probably more perplexing than ever.

Like other commercially based advice-givers, the authors of advice books act as emotional investment counselors. They do readings of broad social conditions and recommend to readers of various types how, how much, and in whom to "invest" emotional attention. They recommend emotional practices—such as asking the reader to think of "praise" as "manipulation"—to cast doubt on the sincerity of one's own praise and to detach oneself from another person, as the advice book writer Robin Norwood recommends in this essay's epigraph. Writers also motivate their readers by hitching investment strategies to inspirational ideas and images buried in "magnified moments" inside the parable-like stories that make up much of these books.

Neither author nor reader, I imagine, is much aware that they are offering or receiving "emotional investment counseling." Rather, authors see themselves as giving, and readers see themselves as receiving, helpful advice. Sometimes it is. My basic point is that helping and being helped are matters of such overwhelming importance that any cultural shift that "thins out" the process through which we give care to one another or empties the content of help should make us stop and think about where we're going.

A CULTURAL COOLING: TRENDS AND COUNTERTRENDS

With these starting points, I propose that many best-selling advice books published in recent years have become cooler in their approach to intimate life. They reflect a cultural cooling. This does not mean that individuals need one another less, only that they are invited to *manage their needs more*. The trend also reflects a paradox. Earlier advice books were far more patriarchal, less based on open and equal communication, but, oddly, they often reflect more warmth. More recent advice books call for more open and more equal communication but propose cooler emotional strategies with which to engage those equal bonds. From the vantage point of the early feminist movement, modern advice books reaffirm one ideal (equality) but undermine another (emotionally rich social bonds).[4]

Two trends in the literature bear on this "cooling." One supports the observation of cooling but doesn't link it to advice books. The other analyzes advice books but doesn't focus on cooling. Christopher Lasch, Ann Swidler, Francesca Cancian, and Mary Evans, among others, argue that "commitment" is a diminishing part in people's idea of love.[5] Data from American national opinion polls document a decline over recent decades in commitment to long-term love. In their study of daytime soap opera heroes and heroines, Lee Harrington and Denise Bielby don't observe a shift away from the idea of lasting love, but they note a shift away from social practices that affirm it.[6]

Analyses of the advice literature, on the other hand, say little about this cooling. Commentators have instead critiqued the authoritarianism, privatism, and ideology of victimhood implicit in many advice books. In *I'm Dysfunctional, You're Dysfunctional,* Wendy Kaminer critiques advice books in the Recovery Movement (based on the twelve-step program of Alcoholics Anonymous) for appealing to individual choice while giving orders and taking it away. In *Self-Help Culture: Reading Women's Readings* Wendy Simonds rightly argues a second point, namely that self-oriented quick-fix books deflect attention from problems in the public sphere that cause people to need private help in the first place. In "Beware the Incest-Survivor Machine" Carol Tavris critiques the cult of victimhood many survivor books seem to promote.[7]

While there is much truth in all three critiques, I believe something else is also going on—a shift in the cultural premises about human attachment. Although there is much talk about the relative merit of this or that kind of family, current advice books take us down a weird cultural tunnel, which reveals the soil and root system that characterizes them all.

To get a good look at this soil, we can draw an imaginary line through the emotional core of each advice book by focusing on the best and worst "magnified moments" in it, the top and bottom of the personal experience the book portrays. This method works best with the therapeutic, interview, and autobiographical books.

Most books seem to have four parts. In one, the author establishes a tone of voice, a relationship to the reader, and connects the reader to a source of authority—the Bible, psychoanalysis, corporate expertise, Hollywood, or the school of hard knocks. In a second part the author didactically describes moral or social reality. "This is how men are," or "that's what the job market's like," they say, or "this is the rule" and how it bends under a variety of circumstances. In a third part the book describes concrete practices; for example, "With your boyfriend, listen, with your girlfriend, talk," or "Wear blue to a 'power breakfast meeting' at work." In a fourth and I believe most revealing part of the advice book, the author tells stories about personal experience. These stories are based on the lives of patients in an author's psychotherapeutic practice, interviewees, or the author's own life. Such stories tend to be either exemplary or cautionary. Exemplary stories tell the reader what to do and cautionary stories tell her what not to do.

Stories of both sorts contain magnified moments, episodes of heightened importance, either epiphanies, moments of intense glee or unusual insight, or moments in which things go intensely but meaningfully wrong. In either case, the moment stands out as metaphorically rich, unusually elaborate, and often echoes throughout the book.

One thing a magnified moment magnifies is the *feeling* a person holds up as ideal. It shows what a person, up until the experience began, *wanted* to feel. Thus there is an ideal expressed in the moment and there is culture within the ideal. Magnified moments reflect a feeling ideal both when a person joyously lives up to it or, in some spectacular way, does not. More than the descriptions of the author's authority or beliefs, more than the long didactic passages in advice books about what is or isn't true or right, magnified moments show the experience we wish. We can ask many questions about this experience. We may ask, for example: What is it precisely about a feeling that makes it seem wonderful or terrible? Against what ideal is it being compared? Who is on the scene during the moment? What relations are revealed, in reality or imagination? By interrogating the moment, so to speak, we ferret out the cultural premises that underlie it. About the advice to which these magnified moments lend support, we can ask many questions. About the experience, and the ideal against which it is measured, we may ask further questions. Does the advice support a general paradigm of trust or caution? Does it center on expressing one's emotional needs or marshaling strategic control over them? Is the book warm, in the sense of legitimizing a high degree of care and social support and offering scope for human needs? Or is it cool, in the sense of presuming the individual should get by with relatively little support and of presuming she or he has fewer needs?

DOORWAY DRAMA

We can draw one set of magnified moments from Marabel Morgan's *The Total Woman* (1973), an arch-reactionary traditional book (covertly addressed to modern readers) that is curiously warm. We can draw a very different set from Colette Dowling's *The Cinderella Complex* (1981), a modern advice book that is curiously cool.

From *The Total Woman:*

If your husband comes home at 6:00, bathe at 5.00. In preparing for your six o'clock date, lie back and let go of the tensions of the day. Think about that special man who's on his way home to you. . . . Rather than make your husband play hide-and-seek when he comes home tired, greet him at the door when he arrives. Make homecoming a happy time. Waltzing to the door in a cloud of powder and cologne is a great confidence builder. Not only can you respond to his advances, you will want to. . . . For an experiment, I put on pink baby-doll pajamas and white boots after my bubble bath. I must admit that I looked foolish and felt even more so. When I opened the door that night to greet Charlie, I was unprepared for his reaction. My quiet, reserved, non-excitable husband took one look, dropped his briefcase on the doorstep, and chased me around the dining room table. We were in stitches by the time he caught me, and breathless with that old feeling of romance. . . . Our little girls stood flat against the wall watching our escapade, giggling with delight. We all had a marvelous evening together, and Charlie forgot to mention the problems of the day.[8]

What did Marabel Morgan feel? First, she felt delight and surprise at Charlie's response. Charlie was surprised, of course, but then so was Marabel—at the very fact that her act succeeded. In some ways, Morgan's peak moment is the same as other peak moments in advice books to women. She feels central, appreciated, in the middle of an experience she wants to have. But in other ways her moment is very different. For one thing, it's "fun," and fun in a certain kind of way. It is sexually exciting within the context of the family. It is marital and family fun. She is breathless in her husband's arms—not in a lover's arms. And her two girls are nearby, "flat against the wall" and "giggling." Sexual excitement is marital and marital fun includes the kids.

In addition to Morgan's husband and daughters, present in fantasy are a community of women who are also working on their marriages. After they have tried out a certain move at home, Morgan tells us, one "Total Woman" class member often calls another the next morning to see how it went. Spanning across families, a mirror opposite to the women's movement, a community of Christian wives are "watching the show" in each other's homes.

Marabel Morgan's big moment doesn't occur naturally, as when one is suddenly overcome by a magnificent rainbow or sunset. It is not spontaneous. Her moment is a well-planned, choreographed act. Sometimes instead of dressing in pink pajamas, she dresses as a pixie or a pirate, or comes to the door totally nude wrapped in cellophane. Her magnified moment is not an occasion for self-realization or revealing communication, not the "high" of sudden self-honesty or intimate communication. The act and the delighted response form a stylized, premodern form of communication in themselves. Marabel puts on her baby-doll suit. Charlie sees she means to please him. He is pleased. She receives his pleasure. They have communicated. *That* is the high point. At the same time, Morgan's act paradoxically doubles as a shield against intimate communication. With doorway surprises, she advises her readers to "keep him off guard."[9] Whether she is pleasing Charlie or getting her way with him by working female wiles, whether she draws inspiration from the Bible or Hollywood, Marabel Morgan is approaching her husband in an old-fashioned way.

At bottom, the pink pajamas and the "Total Woman" homework and tests are proposed as a Christian fundamentalist solution to disintegrating marriages—a trend quickly mounting through the 1960s and 1970s when Morgan wrote. Throughout the book, there is a drum-beat reminder of divorce. Speaking of a woman who could not adapt to her husband's desire to travel, Morgan cautions, "Betty is now divorced. . . . Carl has since found someone else to enjoy his exciting new way of life with him. In your marriage it only makes sense for both of you to paddle in the same direction. Otherwise, you'll only go in circles—or like Carl, he may pull out and go downstream."[10] In addition to friendly women in the same boat, then, are anonymous rivals who can replace the wife in a fading marriage. In spirit, these female rivals are present in the magnified moment of *The Total Woman* too.

I should add one other social relationship on the scene—that between author and reader. The girl-to-girl back fence tone of voice, the open, conversational style with which Morgan tells her story, is itself a message. Morgan talks to the reader, not as priest to parishioner or therapist to patient, but as girlfriend to girlfriend. She does not offer the indisputable received wisdom of the ages concerning "the correct way" to conduct oneself in a given situation. Her advice is personal. Culturally, she seems to be saying, "You and I are on our own. This is what I did. Why don't you try?" Curiously, other American traditional-for-moderns eschew a voice of authority in favor of the voice of a friend. How or whether you save your marriage is up to you, they seem to say; I wish you luck.

In contrast to her best moment, Morgan's worst moments virtually all focus on the discord that results when she challenges her husband's authority. Already criticized by her husband for being "uptight," she describes the following bad moment:

> I prepared a very nice dinner the next day and determined to be a sweet wife. However, the bottom fell out for me. Over the mashed potatoes, Charlie announced casually that we would be going out the next evening with some business associates. With no malice I blurted out, "Oh no, we can't." And then I began to tell him of the plans I had already made. A terrible stony look passed over my husband's face. I braced myself. In icy tones, with obvious control, he asked, "Why do you challenge me on every decision I make?"[11]

Elsewhere, she talks about confronting her husband "eye ball to eye ball."[12] To Morgan, patriarchy is what keeps a woman a woman; otherwise, it seems, she'd act like a man—and fight. Like many traditional women, Morgan presumes men and women are adversaries. Patriarchy, for her, is the arrangement that ends the war with the following deal: the man gets the power, the woman gets the stable home. Morgan's big moment thus expresses a series of basic premises: (a) that men should lead, women should obey, (b) that women benefit from patriarchy, and (c) that it's a woman's job to keep marriage happy and it is mainly her fault if it's unhappy. These premises make up the cultural floorboard beneath magnified moments in *The Total Woman*.

The magnified moment reflects an anxiety and what Morgan imagines as a solution to it. The anxiety is that of women who fear "getting fired" from their marriages and becoming the displaced homemakers of tomorrow. Morgan proposes to beat the 1960s disintegration of the family, compete with the pool of newly displaced women (the other women out there). And she does this on her own home turf. She incorporates the sexual revolution (including its ideal of sexual variety) into the monogamous Christian marriage, and adds a little theater to a housewife's day.

While Morgan may seem to draw more from Hollywood than the Bible and feminine tradition, and she may seem more flamboyant than warm, her magnified moments place her as both traditional and warm. It is overwhelmingly clear that Morgan favors an authoritarian world in which men rule women and men have greater human worth. In those respects, Morgan carries the antiquated, tattered flag for patriarchy. At the same time, her simpleminded tips are all about moving forward and in, not backward and out of relationships. However antiquated, the ethic she affirms is communal. As an emotional investment counselor, she recommends that women invest their emotion work in the family.

THE NO-NEEDS MODERN

At the other end of the spectrum we find a moment from Colette Dowling's *The Cinderella Complex*:

> Powerful emotional experiences await those who are really living out their own scripts. A Chicago woman in her early forties who still lives with and loves her husband is also intensely involved with a man she works with. He too is married, so their time together is limited. They look forward to the business trips they manage to take together several times a year. On one of these, the woman decided after a few days that she wanted to go skiing. The man was not a skier and in any event had further work to do in Boston. "I decided that I should ski by myself," she told me [Dowling]. "I got on a bus in the middle of the afternoon and as we wound up into the Vermont mountains, it began to

snow. I remember sitting by myself on this greyhound bus, looking out the window and watching the lights come on in the little towns we passed through. I felt so good, so secure in the knowledge that I could be myself, do what I want—*and also be loved*—I started to cry."[13]

Marabel Morgan is greeting Charlie in pink baby-doll pajamas at dinner-time while her children watch. The "Chicago woman" leaves her husband for her lover, then leaves her lover to ride a Greyhound bus up a mountain alone. One is in the thick of family life, the other pretty far outside it. One is acting; the other enjoying, perhaps, the release from acting. Morgan values fun; Dowling, aliveness and self-understanding. Morgan is onstage, Dowling's Chicago woman is offstage. In their magnified moments, Morgan's husband is the audience while the Chicago woman's husband functions more as a stage.

The drama in the Chicago woman's magnified moment doesn't take place between herself and her husband, but between her desire to be attached and her desire to be independent. For Dowling's woman, the drama does not take place through the enactment of a social role but in an emotional space outside her regular life, beyond the labors of love. For even when she is offstage, away from her marriage, she's not working on her "intense affair." The focus moves to her feeling in the bus, the mountains, the snow, the anonymous context within which she feels attached but independent. She comes alive focusing inward—figuring out a troubled boundary between herself and anyone else.[14] Her feelings are in response to thinking about relationships, not in response to enacting them. If Morgan is inspired by her own success at breathing life into monogamous marriage, the Chicago woman is inspired, perhaps, by daring to challenge it.

Who is on the scene in the Chicago woman's epiphany? She's honest. But who is she honest with? Her husband? Her lover? Her children? A close friend? A community of women? It is really none of these. Elsewhere we discover a somewhat people-less career and the idea of exertion, excelling. Her exertion is private and internal, against her very dependency on others.

For Dowling we're our best when we are by ourselves facing the elements alone, as in the myth of the cowboy, the Jack London trapper in a forest, Hemingway's man and the sea. Others of Dowling's positive moments are stories about women being sprung free into professional success, erotic freedom, and autonomy.[15] In her final chapter she describes a scene from the life of Simone de Beauvoir, who broke her dependence on her life's partner, the philosopher Jean-Paul Sartre, through a series of fierce missions "climbing every peak, clambering down every gully . . . exploring every valley . . . around Marseilles, through challenging solitary ten hour hikes, 25 miles each day. . . . Simone de Beauvoir's hikes became both the method and the metaphor of her rebirth as an individual," Dowling says. She quotes de

Beauvoir: "Alone I walked the mists that hung over the summit of Sainte Victoire, and trod along the ridge of the Pilon de Roi, bracing myself against a violent wind which sent my beret spinning down into the valley below. . . . When I was clambering over rocks and mountains or sliding down screes, I would work out shortcuts, so that each expedition was a work of art in itself." Once she charged up a steep gorge, unable to go back the way she came, but, upon reaching a fault in the rock, was unable to jump across. Backtracking down the treacherous rocks, triumphantly she concludes, "*I knew that I could now rely on myself.*"[16]

In her most dreadful moment, Dowling feels the opposite of this. She begins the book with this passage:

> I am lying alone on the third floor of our house with a bad bout of the flu, trying to keep my illness from the others. The room feels large and cold and as the hours pass, strangely inhospitable. I begin to remember myself as a little girl, small, vulnerable, helpless. By the time night falls I am utterly miserable, not so sick with flu as with anxiety. "What am I doing here, so solitary, so unattached, so . . . floating?" I ask myself. How strange to be so disturbed, cut off from family, from my busy, demanding life . . . disconnected. More than air and energy and life itself what I want is to be safe, warm, taken care of.[17]

This desire to be "safe, warm, taken care of" forms the basis of the dreaded "Cinderella Complex," which, Dowling goes on to generalize, is the "chief force holding women down today."[18] Elsewhere in the book, Dowling points to the waste of brains when women don't have careers. She cites the Stanford Gifted Child Study of 600 California children with IQs above 135. She notes that most male geniuses have had high-level professional careers while most women geniuses have not. This isn't good for society, she says, or fair to women; in this, Dowling's advice book is clearly feminist and modern.

The Total Woman and *The Cinderella Complex* are guided by different inspirations. Morgan tries to have fun, she likes to act and feel exuberantly playful in the confines of a unitary patriarchal world. The dangerous feelings for her are anger, assertiveness, strivings outside the home, feelings that do not fit that patriarchal world. Dowling, on the other hand, strives to be honest with herself, to control and tame her needs in a sparsely populated and socially dispersed world. For her, the dangerous feeling is the desire to be "safe, warm, and taken care of." Indeed, her fear of being dependent on another person evokes the image of the American cowboy, alone, detached, roaming free with his horse. The American cowboy has long been a model for men struggling against the constraints of corporate capitalism. Now Dowling embraces this ideal for women. On the ashes of Cinderella, then, rises a postmodern cowgirl.

The two authors differ in their ideas about what is exciting: attaching yourself to a man or detaching yourself from him. They differ in their poli-

cies toward emotion management: one advises women to suppress any
assertion of will in the service of binding them to men; the other advises
women to suppress any feeling that would bind them to men too closely.
They differ in the place they accord autonomy in the ideal feminine self and
ultimately in their views about danger and safety in the world for women.

Although the advice books I've studied don't line up in the same rows on
all dimensions, if we sort them according to their views on the role of women,
roughly a third lean toward the "traditional" model. Examples are the humorous Erma Bombeck's *Motherhood: The Second Oldest Profession* (1983), her *The
Grass Is Always Greener over the Septic Tank* (1976), and James Dobson's *Parenting
Isn't for Cowards* (1987). Roughly two-thirds lean toward the modern model,
of which *The Cinderella Complex* is an especially individualistic example. We find
a lighter, more saucy version of it in Helen Gurley Brown's *Having It All*
(1982). Equally searching but less focused on autonomy are Susan Forward
and Joan Torres's *Men Who Hate Women and the Women Who Love Them* (1987),
Robin Norwood's *Women Who Love Too Much* (1985), Connell Cowan and
Melvyn Kinder's *Smart Women, Foolish Choices* (1985), and Barbara De Angelis's
Secrets about Men Every Woman Should Know (1990).

Most of these "modern" books whisper to the reader, "Let the emotional
investor beware." If Morgan counsels women to accumulate domestic capital and invest at home, Dowling cautions women to invest in the self as a solo
enterprise. Most advice books of the 1970s and 1980s are spin-offs or mixtures of these two investment strategies. Gaining the edge during this
period, then, is the postmodern cowgirl who devotes herself to the ascetic
practices of emotional control and expects to give and receive surprisingly
little love from other human beings.

A handful of books are warm moderns, emphasizing equality *and* social
attachment, sharing *and* commitment. Examples are the Boston Women's
Health Book Collective's *Ourselves and Our Children* (1978) and Harriet
Lerner's *The Dance of Anger* (1985). It is my impression—though I've not
taken a systematic look at women's advice books since 1990—that the supply of warm modern books has expanded, although not that much.

THE COOL MODERN AND THE COMMERCIAL SPIRIT OF INTIMATE LIFE

Cool modern advice books reveal a newly unfolding paradox that is reminiscent of an earlier paradox. In *The Protestant Ethic and the Spirit of
Capitalism,* Weber describes a set of beliefs held by a variety of Protestant
sects—a belief in ascetic self-control, frugality, hard work, and devotion to
a calling. He traces the way in which these *religious* ideas were adapted to a
material purpose. The idea of devotion to a calling came to mean devotion
to making money. The idea of self-control came to mean careful saving,

spending, and capital reinvestment. The Protestant Ethic "escaped the cage" to become part of a new hybrid "spirit of capitalism."

Comparing the origin of these motivational ideas and their ultimate destination, Weber made this significant comment:

> Today the spirit of religious asceticism—whether finally, who knows?—has escaped from the cage. But victorious capitalism, since it rests on mechanical foundations, needs its support no longer. The rosy blush of its laughing heir, the Enlightenment, seems also to be irretrievably fading and the idea of duty in one's calling prowls about in our lives like the ghost of dead religious beliefs.[19]

The original religious ideas jumped the churchyard fence to land in the marketplace. Luther and Calvin would have been aghast at the leap their ideas took. As Weber notes, wryly:

> . . . it is not to be understood that we expect to find any of the founders or representatives of these religious movements considering the promotion of what we have called the spirit of capitalism as in any sense the end of his life work. We cannot well maintain that the pursuit of worldly goods, conceived as an end in itself, was to any of them of positive ethical value.[20]

Work devoted to a calling as the religious fathers originally intended it was a task set by God, and it led to salvation. In Benjamin Franklin's capitalist hands (his 1736 advice book was called *Necessary Hints to Those Who Would Be Rich*), a calling led elsewhere.

Now, has another set of beliefs jumped another fence? Is a more marginal belief system, feminism, escaping from the cage of a social movement to buttress a commercial spirit of intimate life? The feminism represented, for example, by Charlotte Gilman or Lucretia Mott, or by the mid-1970s second-wave feminists whose thinking is reflected in the best-selling advice book *Our Bodies, Ourselves,* has "escaped the cage" into a commercial arena. Like Calvin, the feminist founders might have worried at the cultural trends weaving themselves around their core ideals. "Equality, yes," they might say were they alive today, "but why allow the worst of capitalist culture to establish the *cultural basis* of it?" "Autonomy, yes," they might say, "but the stand-alone cowgirl—why?"

The analogy, then, is this: Feminism is to the commercial spirit of intimate life as Protestantism is to the spirit of capitalism. The first legitimates the second. The second borrows from but also transforms the first. Just as certain prior conditions prepared the soil for the spirit of capitalism to take off—the decline of feudalism, the growth of cities, the rising middle class—so, too, certain prior conditions ripen the soil for the takeoff of the commercial spirit of intimate life. The preconditions now are a weakening of the family, the decline of the church, and loss of local community—traditional shields against the harsher effects of capitalism.

Given this backdrop, a commercial culture has moved in, silently borrowing from feminism an ideology that made way for women in public life. From feminism these books draw a belief in the equal worth of men and women. Modern books begin with the idea that women think too little of themselves. Their human needs are not met. The authors of these books genuinely seek, I believe, to uplift women, to raise women's worth in their own eyes and the eyes of others. This idea is what makes cool modern books *modern.* This idea of equality makes them a powerful challenge to Marabel Morgan; it's what makes her advice seem old-fashioned, invalid, silly.

What advice books blend with feminism, however, is a commercial spirit of intimate life. And here I move well beyond analogy. For, it seems also true that part of the *content* of the spirit of capitalism is being *displaced* onto intimate life; this is, in fact, partly what the commercial spirit of intimate life *is.* The ascetic self-discipline that the early capitalist applied to his bank account the twenty-first-century woman applies to her appetite, her body, her love. The devotion to a "calling," which the early capitalist applied to earning money, the latter-day woman applies to "having it all." The activism, the belief in working hard and aiming high, the desire to go for it, to be saved, to win, to succeed, which the early capitalists used to build capitalism in a rough-and-tumble marketplace, many advice books urge women to transfer to love in a rapidly changing courtship scene.

The commercial spirit of intimate life is made up of images that prepare the way for a paradigm of distrust. These are images of "me" and "you" and "us" that are psychologically defended and shallow. It is also made up of a way of relating to others associated with the paradigm, a spirit of instrumental detachment that fits the emptied slots where a deeper "me," "you," and "us" might be.

Cool modern books prepare the self for a commercial spirit of intimate life by offering as ideal a self well defended against getting hurt. In Dowling's worst magnified moment, she leaps away in fright from her own desire to be "safe, warm, comforted." She ardently seeks to develop the capacity to endure emotional isolation. Parallel to the image of the low-needs self is the image of the self that ministers to itself. Who helps the self? The answer is the self. In appendix 4 of *Women Who Love Too Much,* Robin Norwood offers private affirmations: "Twice daily, for three minutes each time, maintain eye contact with yourself in a mirror as you *say out loud,* '(your name), I love you and accept you exactly the way you are.'"[21] The heroic acts a self can perform, in this view, are to detach, to leave, and to depend on and need others less. The emotion work that matters is control of the feelings of fear, vulnerability, and the desire to be comforted. The ideal self doesn't need much, and what it does need it can get for itself.

Added to the idea of a curtailed "me" is the idea of a curtailed "you." So a no-needs me relates to a no-needs you, and a paradigm of caution is stationed between the two. A woman who loves a man may have a "need to control" or be a "man junkie."[22] In many cool modern books, the author prepares us for people out there who don't need our nurturance and for people who don't or can't nurture us. Norwood catalogs cases of women who love men who drink too much, men who beat them up, men who run around, men who use them and leave. Drawing a general picture of the dysfunctional man and relationship, she proposes a general *paradigm of caution*. If we accept the cases, she implies, we should accept the paradigm. If we take the position that some men hurt some women, a position many of us, including myself, would take, we find ourselves on a slippery slope sliding gradually down to a paradigm of caution.

While books like *Women Who Love Too Much* focus on therapy, ironically the actual process of healing is subtracted from the image of normal family or communal bonds. The women in Norwood's tales seem to live in a wider community strikingly barren of emotional support. Actual healing is reserved for a separate zone of paid professionals where people have Ph.D.s, M.D.s, M.A.s, accept money, and have special therapeutic identities. While psychotherapy is surely a help to many, it is no substitute for life itself. In the picture Norwood paints, there is little power of healing *outside* of therapy. In the stories Norwood tells, love doesn't heal. When you give it, it doesn't take. When another offers it, it may feel good but it's not good for you. In fact, in the second paragraph of her preface, Norwood declares that if "we try to become his [a loved one's] therapist, we are loving too much."[23] If the word "therapy" conveys the desire to help another to get to the root of a problem, this is a very deep subtraction from our idea of love and friendship. It thins and lightens our idea of love. We are invited to confine our trust to the thinner, once-a-week, "processed" concern of the professional. This may add to our expectations of therapy, but it lightens our expectations of lovers, family, and friends. Cool modern books put a value on this lightness. The idea of liberation and independence that early feminists applied to the right to vote, to learn, and to work, the cool moderns apply to the right to emotionally detach.

Given these images of "me" and "you," we are more prepared to accept the spirit of commercialism. This spirit instrumentalizes our idea of love. To be sure, nothing is new about instrumentalism. As *The Total Woman* shows, under patriarchy women learned to "catch their man in the right mood to ask for a new hat." They used flattery and feminine wiles.

The decline of patriarchy has not eliminated instrumentalism. It has recast it into a new, commercial mold. The people in stories similar to *The Cinderella Complex* and *Women Who Love Too Much* tell us to "stop acting,"[24] to value honesty and authenticity, and this is part of what makes them feel "modern." But ironically, what many are honest about is authentic instrumentalism. For example, Norwood tells readers honestly how to shop around for a less needy guy, preferably a man with nonalcoholic parents. Just as characters in Jane Austen's *Pride and Prejudice* shrewdly appraise the bank accounts and social lineage of their suitors, so Norwood urges women to consider their suitors' psychological capital. The difference is more than an update. Norwood's attempt to give her readers a "clear head" about love goes with a readiness to detach, to leave, to turn inward toward oneself. For Jane Austen, family and community are confining whereas, for Norwood, they are barely there at all.

Each cool modern book offers a slightly different version of the commercial culture. Some express a theme of production, others a theme of consumption. In *Having It All*, Helen Gurley Brown does both, by focusing on the production of the body she displays as a ware. In the nearly one-third of *Having It All* that she devotes to the female face and hair, she proposes a policy of "investment" in the bodily self.[25] Brown tells women what to do: Dye your hair. Get a face-lift. Diet. Dress frilly. These practices should be done neither in the spirit of a purification rite, nor in the spirit of devotion to a particular person, but to look good to an anonymous market of men within a thirty-yard radius. She helps women advertise themselves to a diversified market. The light office affairs she recommends are those of a sexual venture capitalist, a diversified, high-risk, high-opportunity portfolio.

In *Women Who Love Too Much*, Robin Norwood expresses more the theme of consumption. She advises women how to "spend" their nurturance in the relational marketplace. Although the language is therapeutic, the spirit is that of a shrewd investment counselor. Don't waste your love, Norwood warns, on a poor investment. In her cautionary tales, stories of unhappy patients who "loved too much," one woman after another "wastes" her love and lacks a return commensurate to her devotion and attention. "Divest," she cautions. "Cut your losses. Invest elsewhere."

In *The Cinderella Complex*, Colette Dowling takes yet a third tack. Instead of focusing on women who love too much, Dowling concentrates on women who need too much. Displacing the spirit of capitalism onto private life, cool modern advice books for women both reinforce and create a commercial culture of intimate life. As a result, we may have global warming, but we have a cultural cooling.

ASSIMILATING TO MALE RULES OF LOVE

The commercial spirit of intimate life is woven with a second cultural tendency—for women to assimilate to male rules of love. On one hand, cool modern advice books address women. Two-thirds are written by women and all of them address problems women have. Nearly all picture women on the covers. Further, even if authors don't claim to be feminist at the outset, they refer to "progress," "struggle," "independence," "equality"—code words for core ideas of "feminism." Many portray women as victims who need to be freed from oppressive situations in love or work.

Curiously, though, such books simultaneously recycle the feeling rules that once applied to middle-class men of the 1950s. In doing so, they illustrate a pattern common to many stratification systems—of the "bottom" emulating the top in order to gain access to greater respect, authority, and power. Insofar as imitation represents in part a magical solution to redistribution of respect and power, however, female emulation of male emotional folkways is useless. In addition, it means that women are encouraged to be cooler while men are not urged to become warmer. In this sense, advice books conserve the already capitalized male culture. They *conserve* the damage capitalism did to manhood instead of *critiquing* it, in the tradition set out a century ago by Charlotte Gilman.

In recycling male rules of love, modern advice books for women assert that it's a "feminine" practice to subordinate the importance of love, to delay falling in love until after consolidating a career, to separate love from sex, and for married women to have occasional affairs.

For one thing, these books propose that love should play an altogether less central role than it has had in the lives of women, and that women should rid themselves of ideas about the importance of love, "de-culturize" themselves in Bourdieu's terms, to unlearn the idea that "love to man is a thing apart, 'tis woman's whole existence." Love should also occur later in life than before. In the 1950s it was middle-class men who waited until they were occupationally prepared to "fall in love and settle down." Love that occurred earlier was "too early." Now this delay in the timing of love, and the emotion management needed to delay, are recommended to women as well. Wait, advice books for women now caution, until your late twenties or thirties, when you are trained in a career, until you are ready to fall in love.

Just as love has been more easily separated from sex for men, so these advice books of the 1980s suggest, love can be separated from sex for women. In *Having It All,* Helen Gurley Brown tells readers how to avoid getting "too" emotionally involved with the married men at the office they sleep with. In the past, if premarital and extramarital sex were not actually affirmed for men, they were understood as a manly flaw. Now, as Dowling's Chicago woman suggests, they are a womanly flaw too.

Thus, in the lesser role of love, in the separation of love from sex, in the delay in the "right time" to fall in love, and in the feminization of adultery, advice books of the 1980s propose to women the emotional rules that were part of the gendered cultural capital of white middle-class men of the 1950s. We've moved from living according to two emotional codes—one for men and another for women—to a unisex code based on the old code for men. We've also moved from a warmer code to a cooler one, aspects of which both fit with and exacerbate a move to lighter family bonds.

Many authors of advice books conceive of their books as feminist, but they are in reality an abduction of feminism. Many advice books see their readers as patients. But, could it be that it's the commercial spirit of intimate life that's really sick?

EXCEPTIONS AND COUNTERTRENDS

A look at advice books for men would surely offer a more cheerful picture, since while women have been moving toward a male norm, some men have moved the other way. But since the traditional male culture that progressive men are challenging is still associated with power and authority, I believe women's move in the direction of traditional male culture is far stronger than men's move in the opposite direction.

In the 1970s and 1980s, the books pushing a procommercial spirit seemed to be winning. In the 1990s, with the renewal of "family values"—a phrase that means all things to all people—the anticommercial ones seemed to gain ground. Hitting the best-seller list were such books as *Men Are from Mars, Women Are from Venus*,[26] which exaggerates the differences between men and women but offers practical tips on "inter-species" communication and commitment. In *A Woman's Worth*, Marianne Williamson proclaims women to be queens and goddesses, weirdly combining a moral social mobility—"the purpose of life as a woman is to ascend to the throne and rule with heart"[27]—a call for family and community, and a paradigm of distrust. While women are asked in a general way to love "our communities, our families, our friends," in the end the only love they can really count on, says Williamson, is God's.[28]

Meanwhile, a smaller-sales stream of books has continued the commercial spirit without a communal gloss. Joyce Vedral's *Get Rid of Him*, Susan Rabin's *How to Attract Anyone, Anytime, Anyplace*, an extension of her "flirtation seminars," press forward the psychological frontier of commercialism.[29] They complement the increasingly popular mail-order videocassettes on marital sex, often authoritatively introduced by Ph.D. psychologists in the spirit of a science class. While such videos legitimate the importance of female sexual pleasure, they also make an emotionally depleted clinical matter of it.

Both the countertrend and the continued drum beat of the commercial spirit of intimate life pose the question: Will the anticommercial books toss out feminism? Or will they stop the abduction of feminism, only to flatten and commercialize it? Or will they integrate it with a paradigm of trust?

In *The Second Shift*, I have argued that American families are strained by the fact that they serve as a shock absorber of a stalled gender revolution. The move of masses of women into the paid workforce has constituted a revolution. But the slower shift in ideas of "manhood," the resistance to sharing work at home, the rigid schedules at work make for a "stall" in this gender revolution.[30] It is a stall in the change of institutional arrangements of which men are the principal keepers. But if we are at the same time undergoing a cultural cooling, then we are faced with another, almost opposite, problem. It isn't simply that men are changing too slowly, but that, without quite realizing it, women are also changing in the opposite direction—in the sense of assimilating to old-time male rules—too fast. Instead of humanizing men, we are capitalizing women. If the concept of the stalled revolution raises the question of how to be equal, the concept of the commercial spirit of intimate life raises the question: Equal *on what terms*?

With an American divorce rate of 50 percent, and with 60 percent of marriages formed in the 1980s projected to end, two-thirds of them involving children, many young women today are the single mothers of tomorrow. Given this, we have to ask, isn't it *useful* for women to know how to meet their emotional needs on their own? Isn't it useful to have a defended "me" hoping to meet a defended "you"? Even if *The Cinderella Complex* is selling defective psychic armor—these days, sadly enough, we have to ask if we don't need it. Even defective armor, if it helps us get around in a cool world, can be useful. But after we've asked whether being cool is useful, we have to ask whether being cool is good. Is it the best we can do? If we think it's not, then we have to ask the question those advice books do not ask—how can we rewire the broader conditions that make us need the tough armor they provide? On that we could really use good advice.

2 THE COMMODITY FRONTIER

An advertisement appearing on the Internet on March 6, 2001, read as follows:

(p/t) Beautiful, smart, hostess, good masseuse—$400/week.
Hi there.
This is a strange job opening, and I feel silly posting it, but this is San Francisco, and I do have the need! This will be a very confidential search process.

I'm a mild-mannered millionaire businessman, intelligent, traveled, but shy, who is new to the area, and extremely inundated with invitations to parties, gatherings and social events. I'm looking to find a "personal assistant," of sorts. The job description would include, but not be limited to:

1. Being hostess to parties at my home ($40/hour)
2. Providing me with a soothing and sensual massage ($140/hour)
3. Coming to certain social events with me ($40/hour)
4. Traveling with me ($300 per day + all travel expenses)
5. Managing some of my home affairs (utilities, bill-paying, etc.) ($30/hour)

You must be between 22 and 32, in-shape, good-looking, articulate, sensual, attentive, bright and able to keep confidences. I don't expect more than 3 to 4 events a month, and up to 10 hours a week on massage, chores and other miscellaneous items, at the most. You must be unmarried, unattached, or have a very understanding partner!

I'm a bright, intelligent 30-year-old man, and I'm happy to discuss the reasons for my placing this ad with you on response of your email application. If you can, please include a picture of yourself, or a description of your likes, interests, and your ability to do the job.

NO professional escorts please! NO Sex involved!
Thank You.

You can email me at . . . [1]

In this ad, we are looking at a certain cultural edge beyond which the idea of paying for a service, to many people, becomes unnerving.[2] But what activities seem to us too personal to pay for or do for hire? What about a social context and culture persuade us to feel as we do about it?

To be sure, a transaction that seems perfectly acceptable to some people in one context often seems disturbing to others in another. Notions of agreeableness or credibility also change over time. Indeed, I wonder if

American culture is not in the midst of such a change now. A half century ago, we might have imagined a wealthy man buying a fancy home, car, and pleasant vacation for himself and his family. Now, we are asked to imagine the man buying the pleasant family, or at least the services associated with the fantasy of a family-like experience.

In this essay I explore some reactions to this ad, selecting from the treasure trove of Neil Smelser's extraordinary corpus of creative work, especially his work on the relationship between family and economy, and on the psychological function of myth. For together, these ideas help us develop another of his key insights—that "economic man" is a very cultural and emotionally complex being.

I used this ad as a cultural Rorschach test. What, I asked upper-division students at the University of California, Berkeley, is your response to this ad? As I show, their response was largely negative—ranging from anxious refusal ("he can't buy a wife") to condemnation ("he shouldn't buy a wife") to considerations of the emotional and moral flaws that might have led him to write the ad. They were not surprised at the ad, only disturbed by it.

So how did the ad disturb the students and why? After all, family history is replete with examples of family arrangements that share some characteristics with the commercial relationship proposed in this ad. In answer, I propose that students, like many others in American society today, face a contradiction between two social forces.

On one hand, they face a commodity frontier. While the market is creating ever more niches in the "mommy industry," the family is outsourcing more functions to be handled by it. Through this trend, the family is moving, top class first, from an artisanal family to a post-production family. And with this shift, personal tasks—especially those performed by women—are become monetized and to some degree impersonalized.[3]

On the other hand, the family—and especially the wife-mother within it—has, as a result, become a more powerful, condensed *symbol* for treasured qualities such as empathy, recognition, love—qualities that are quintessentially personal. The resulting strains between these two trends have led to a crisis of enchantment. Are we to hold onto the enchantment of the wife-mother in the familial sphere, or can purchases become enchanted too? Each "faith"—in family or marketplace—brings with it different implications for emotion management. Each is also undergirded by the mistaken assumption that family and market are separate cultural spheres.

RESPONSES TO THE AD: CULTURAL SENSITIVITIES TO THE COMMODITY FRONTIER

I distributed copies of the ad posted by the shy millionaire to seventy students in my class on the sociology of the family at the University of

California, Berkeley, in the spring of 2001 and asked them to comment. I also followed up the survey with conversations with some half-dozen students about why they answered as they did. While many came from Asian immigrant families and believed in the importance of strong family ties, quite a few were also heading for workaholic careers in Silicon Valley where outsourcing activities that meet domestic needs is fast becoming a fashionable, if controversial, way of life. So, while hardly typical of the views of educated American youth in general, the views of these students hint at a contradiction between economic trends that press for the outsourcing of family functions and a cultural fetishization of insourced functions.

Most students expressed a combination of sympathy ("he's afraid to go out and get a girlfriend" or "he's pathologically shy") and criticism or contempt ("he's selfish," "he's a loser," "he's a creep," "he's too socially conscious"). Others expressed fear ("this ad is scary"), anger ("what a jerk"), suspicion ("he's a shady character"), and disbelief ("this is unreal").

Perhaps the most eloquent response came from a young woman, a child of divorce who still believes in love. As she put it:

> It is a very sad commentary on the state of relationships today. Even family life is being directly sought in commodity trade. Forget the messy emotions. Just give me the underlying services and benefits money can buy. And what's the point of trying, when all it brings are pain, strife and divorce? Then the act of sexual interaction is relativized and commodified, but *not* as prostitution. Clearly the intrinsic value [of the sensual massage] to the buyer is much higher [$140 an hour] so we're not talking a shoulder rub. But even the beautiful intertwining of loving, caring, spiritually connected partners in love-making is reduced to mechanized, emotionless labor for hire. Is it any wonder there's so much smoldering rage in such a graceless age?

Another commented: "This takes the depersonalization of relationships to new heights." At the same time, most of the respondents said the ad was thinkable. It was plausible. It wasn't surprising. As one student put it, referring to the San Francisco Bay Area and Silicon Valley, it could happen, "at least around here." Referring to another website he had seen, one young man said, "Given the website www.2kforawife.com [a website advertising for a wife, no longer up as of July 2001], I'm not that surprised." A minority condoned the ad: "If he has the money to burn, by all means . . ." Or they anticipated that, given the high salary, *others* would respond to, if not quite condone, it. Indeed, a number of the students spoke of living in a culture in which market-home crossovers were unsurprising. As one put it: "My reaction is one of 'sure, this is normal.' My own reaction surprises me because I know years ago . . . I would have been shocked and angry. But now I am desensitized, and accept that relationships don't always happen in the nice, neat boxes I once thought they came in."

Only four out of seventy thought the ad was a hoax.[4]

HOW WAS THE AD DISTURBING?

For most of these young educated Californians, the ad seemed to strike a raw nerve. How did it do this? First of all, it disturbed many students that a familial role was shown to be divisible into slivers, a whole separated into parts, as the student quoted above referred to the "beautiful intertwining of loving, caring, spiritually connected partners in love-making." Second, it bothered the students that this taken-apart wife-mother role was associated with varying amounts of money. Traveling together was to be worth $300 a day; managing home affairs, $30 an hour. Both the divisibility and the commercialization were offensive. But perhaps they were doubly so because the separate tasks were then implicitly associated with more diffuse personal characteristics apparently unrelated to the tasks. As one person noted: "It seems like he's looking for a personal assistant [to do these tasks]. . . . Yet he is specific about the *kind of woman* he wants—he mentions the word 'sensual' more than once. She needs to be attractive, young, in shape, sensual, bright (all marriageable qualities). If he just wanted these tasks done, why couldn't an old, fat man do them?" Another observed that the millionaire wanted someone ready to hear confidences, someone available to travel, and thus orient her time around his, which, even more than looks and age, implies a diffuse "intertwined" relationship.

The students were also disturbed, perhaps, by what often comes with monetization—a cultural principle of giving that characterizes market deals—short-term tit-for-tat exchanges. Commercial exchanges often also provide a shortcut around other principles of giving—decadal or generational tit-for-tat exchange, or altruism. One person remarked, "The man wants a wife, but he doesn't want to be a husband." He wants to receive, but not to give—except in cash. In other words, by offering money as the totality of his side of the bargain, the man absolves himself of any moral responsibility to try to give emotionally in the future. As one put it, "For him, money took care of his side of the deal." The students did not congratulate the man on his monetary generosity, though they understood the sums he offered to be high. Indeed, one woman commented, "He is taking the easy way out. He doesn't want to have to deal with what a partner may need from him emotionally and physically. So he is just looking for the benefits without the work." Another said, "He's advertising for a sexless, no-needs wife. While I do not object to this on principle I do think it sad that he would have *no need to give* in a relationship. It seems lonely and false" (emphasis mine). A few others also pointed out that the man stood to lose, not gain, through his financial offer. As one person put it, "The man's losing the chance to give. He's cheating himself."

Students were also disturbed by a closely related issue: the absence of emotional engagement. Here they focused directly on his emotional capacity and need. One complained that the man was emotionally empty, detached, invulnerable: "He has a strong desire to be in total control." Another young woman remarked, "He must feel very unloved and unable to give love." They thought he *should feel* something for the woman who does what he has in mind. The man who posted the ad said he had a "need," another observed. But what is his "need" for these services? "I find it amusing," he said, "that [the man] calls this a need." In later conversation the student explained, "The man mentions luxury items he doesn't really need, but what he does need, emotionally, he's not asking for or setting it up to get." Another commented, "It is so fascinating to me the things men will do to avoid emotional attachment."

Not only was emotion missing, so was the commitment to think about or work on one's feelings in order to improve the relationship. As one put it, "He wants to hire someone to fulfill his needs but without the hassle." Another complained, "I was disgusted [that the man is buying] the grunt labor of a relationship." In a sense, the students were observing the absence of an implied inclination to pay any allegiance to familial feeling rules or to try to manage emotions in a way mindful of them. He was buying himself out of all this.

Finally, for some it was not the splintering of the wife-mother role or the commodification of each part that posed a problem so much as the fact that—partly because of these—the potentially enchanted experience of being together was *disenchanted*. For a couple to feel their relationship is enchanted, they must feel moved to imbue the world around them with a sense of magic that has, paradoxically, power over them, the magic now coming from outside. In an enchanted relationship, not only the relationship but the whole world feels magical. And it does so through no apparent will of one's own. The individual externalizes his or her locus of control. This sense of enchantment is similar to Freud's notion of "oceanic oneness," which some associate with religion, and all, Durkheim argues, associate with the sacred.

This dimension of experience is here curtained off—not as it impacts the worst part of a close relationship but as it impacts the best. As one student observed, "It almost seems like the man wants to pay a woman to do the fun things couples do together." He was disenchanting fun.

Or, rather, he was gaining apparent control over any obligation to have fun. He exempted himself from family feeling rules. He doesn't want to even *have to* have fun. He wants to feel free to have a relationship—impersonal or personal—as he wishes and on the terms he wishes. Money *liberates* him, as Georg Simmel observes. But as the respondents noted repeatedly, he is also using money to narrow the relational possibilities. In the end, they felt that the options he was free to choose among were themselves stripped of meaning (a) by the separation between exclusive sex expression, intimacy, and affection; (b) by the attachment of money to each part of what is imagined to be whole; (c) by a noncommittal stance toward the emotion work and feeling rules that often apply in intimate engagement; and (d) by the implicit disenchantment with the whole complex they associate with adult sexual-emotional love. In a sense he seemed to them as he would to Simmel, as if he were trapped by a supposed liberation. The man was creating for himself a context in which he would be called upon to employ a mechanism of ego defense—depersonalization.[5]

WHY WAS THE AD DISTURBING?

All of this says *how* the ad was disturbing but not *why*. Why, we can ask, did the students sound this alarm? The answer is not, after all, self-evident. History is replete with examples of family patterns that illustrate each of the various ways in which this ad offended them. For example, in traditional China and many parts of Africa and the Muslim world, polygamy challenges the idea of the unity of love with sexual exclusivity. In Europe, the tradition of maintaining a bourgeois marriage and a mistress—sometimes paid with allowances or gifts, though not through salary—also disrupts the expectation that marriage, intimacy, affection, sexual exclusivity, and often procreation will form parts of one whole. A more covert pattern combines a conventional marriage and children with an intense homosexual relationship, again separating parts of this whole.

In the realm of parenting, too, history provides many examples of differentiation. In upper-class households, no one holds their breath at the slicing and dicing of "a mother's role" into discrete paid positions—nanny, cook, chauffeur, therapist, tutor, camp counselor, to mention a few. In the antebellum South, slave women breastfed children, and sometimes served the head of household as concubines. In all these times and places, people felt no commitment to the feeling rules and forms of emotion work which uphold the ideal of the romantic love ethic and the enchantment created by it. So the question becomes why, given all this, did this ad hit a certain contemporary cultural nerve?

The answer, I suggest, is that the ad strikes at a flash point between an advancing commodity frontier, on one hand, and the hypersymbolized but structurally weakened core of the modern American family, on the other.

THE COMMODITY FRONTIER

The commodity frontier, Janus-faced, looks out on one side to the marketplace and on the other side to the family. On the market side it is a frontier for *companies* as they expand the number of market niches for goods and services covering activities that, in yesteryear, formed part of unpaid "family life." On the other side it is a frontier for *families* that feel the need or desire to consume such goods and services.

On the company side a growing supply of services is meeting a growing demand for "family" jobs. In a recent article in *Business Week*, Rochelle Sharpe notes, "Entrepreneurs are eager to respond to the time crunch, creating businesses unimaginable just a few years ago." These include "breast feeding consultants, baby-proofing agencies, emergency babysitting services, companies specializing in paying nanny taxes and others that install hidden cameras to spy on babysitters' behavior. People can hire bill payers, birthday party planners, kiddy taxi services, personal assistants, personal chefs, and, of course, household managers to oversee all the personnel."[6] One ad posted on the Internet includes in the list of available services "pet care, DMV registration, holiday decorating, personal gift selection, party planning, night life recommendations, personal/professional correspondence, and credit card charge disputes." The services of others are implied in the names of the agencies that offer them—Mary Poppins, Wives for Hire (in Hollywood), and Husbands for Rent (in Maine).[7] One agency, Jill of All Trades, organizes closets and packs up houses. Clients trust the assistant to sort through their belongings and throw the junk out. As one assistant commented, "People don't have time to look at their stuff. I know what's important."[8] Another Internet job description read as follows:

> Administrative assistant with corporate experience and a Martha Stewart edge to manage a family household. . . . A domestic interest is required and the ability to travel is necessary. Must enjoy kids! This is a unique position requiring both a warm-hearted and business-oriented individual.[9]

Not only do the qualities called for in the assistant cross the line between market and home; the result can cross a more human line as well. As the *Business Week* reporter Rochelle Sharpe describes: "Lynn Corsiglia, a human resources executive in California, remembers the disappointment in her daughter's eyes when the girl discovered that someone had been hired to help organize her birthday party. 'I realized that I blew the boundary,' she says." Lynn Corsiglia felt she had moved, one might say, to the cultural edge of the commodity frontier as her daughter defined that edge.[10]

This expansion of market services applies mainly to executives and professionals—both single men and single women, and "professional households without wives" as Saskia Sassen has called them.[11] Often faced with long hours at work, many employees see the solution not in sharing or neglecting wifely chores, but in hiring people to do them. With the increasing gap between the top 20 percent and bottom 20 percent of the income scale, more rich people can afford such services, and poorer and middle-class people are eager to fill jobs providing them. As their income rises, wealthy peo-ple—especially those in high-pressure careers—take advantage of the goods and services on this frontier, and many poor people aspire to do so.

The commodity frontier has impinged on Western domestic life for many centuries. It is doubtful that Queen Victoria clipped her own toenails or breast-fed her children. Indeed, in early modern Europe, it was common for urban upper-class parents to give their babies over to rural wet nurses to raise during the first years of life.[12] So the commodity frontier has a history as well as a future trajectory, and both are lodged in a local sense of what belongs where for life to seem right.

Still, within American and European culture in recent decades, the char-acter of the commodity frontier has changed. We can speak crudely of newer and older expressions of it. Relative to ours today, eighteenth- and nineteenth-century commodification of domestic life involved a greater cultural blur between service and server. An eighteenth-century white south-ern aristocrat who bought a slave bought the person, not the service—the very ultimate in commodification.[13] And the indentured servant differed from the slave only in degree. The millionaire's ad for a "beautiful, smart hostess, good masseuse," by contrast, strikes us as modern in that it is purely the services, classified and priced, that are up for purchase. The ad seems to tease apart many aspects of what was once one role. Structural differentia-tion between family and economy, a process Smelser traces in English his-tory, becomes here a cultural idea in a commercial context, which lends itself to an almost jazzlike improvisation. As in jazz, the ad plays with the idea of dividing and recombining, suggesting different versions of various combinations.[14]

Especially in their more recent incarnation, the commercial substitutes for family activities often turn out to be better than the real thing. Just as the French bakery often makes better bread than mother ever did, and the cleaning service cleans the house more thoroughly, so therapists may rec-ognize feelings more accurately, and childcare workers prove more even-tempered than parents. In a sense, capitalism isn't competing with itself, one company against another, but with the family, and particularly with the role of the wife and mother.

A cycle is set in motion. As the family becomes more minimal, it turns to the market to add what it needs and, by doing so, becomes yet more mini-mal. This logic also applies to the two functions Talcott Parsons thought would be left to the family when all the structural differentiation was said and done: socialization of children and adult personality stabilization.

To be sure, there is a countertrend as well. The cult of Martha Stewart appeals to the desire to resist the loss of family functions to the market-place—like the "do-it-yourself" movement, which of course creates a market niche of its own for the implements and knowledge needed to do it yourself.

Still, the prevailing direction is toward relinquishing family functions to the market realm. And various trends exacerbate this tendency. Most important is the movement of women into paid work. In 1950 less than a fifth of mothers with children under six worked in the labor force while a half century later, two-thirds of such mothers do. Their salary is also now vital to the family budget. Older female relatives who might in an earlier period have stayed home to care for their grandchildren, nephews, and nieces are now likely to be at work too.

In addition, work has recently been taking up more hours of the year. According to an International Labor Organization report, Americans now work two weeks longer each year than their counterparts in Japan, the vaunted long-work-hour capital of the world. And many of these long-hour workers are also trying to maintain a family life. Between 1989 and 1996, for example, middle-class married couples increased their annual work hours outside the home from 3,550 to 3,685, or more than three extra forty-hour weeks of work a year.[15]

Over the last half century, the American divorce rate has also increased to 50 percent, and a fifth of households with children are now headed by single mothers, most of whom get little financial help from their ex-husbands and most of whom work full-time outside the home.[16] Like the rising proportion of women who work outside the home, divorce also, in effect, reduces the number of helping hands at home—creating a need or desire for supplemental forms of care.

The state has done nothing to ease the burden at home. Indeed, the 1996 federal welfare reforms reduced aid to parents with dependent children, with the responsibility devolving on the states, which have in turn reduced aid, even for food stamps. Many states have also implemented cutbacks in public recreation and parks and library programs designed to help families care for children.

In addition to the depletion of both private and public resources for care, there is an increasing uncertainty associated with cultural ideas about the proper source of it. The traditional wife-mother role has given way to a variety of different arrangements—wives who are not mothers, mothers who are not wives, second wives and stepmothers, and lesbian mothers. And while these changes in the source of care are certainly not to be confused with a depletion of care, the changing culture itself gives rise to uncertainties about it. Will my father still be living with me and taking care of me fifteen years from now, or will he be taking care of a new family he has with a new wife? Will the lesbian partner of my mother be part of my life when I am older if my mother's parents don't accept her, or will it be my grandma I don't see? In addition to a real depletion in resources available for familial care, then, the shifting cultural landscape of care may account for some sense of anxiety about it.

Thus, as the market advances, as the family moves from a production to a consumption unit, as it faces a care deficit, as the cultural landscape of care shifts, individuals increasingly keep an anxious eye on what seems like the primary remaining symbol of abiding care—mother.

THE HEIGHTENED SYMBOLISM OF MOTHER

The more the commodity frontier erodes the territory surrounding the emotional role of the wife and mother, the more hypersymbolized the remaining sources of care seem to become. And the more the wife-mother functions as a symbolic cultural anchor to stay the ship against a powerful tide. The symbolic weight of "the family" is condensed and consolidated into the wife-mother, and increasingly now into the mother. In *A World of Their Own Making,* the historian John Gillis argues that the cultural meanings associated with security, support, and empathy—meanings that once adhered to an entire community—were in the course of industrialization gradually focused on the family.[17] Now we can add, within the family, these symbolic meanings have been increasingly directed toward the figure of the wife-mother.

The hypersymbolization of the mother is itself partly a response to the destabilization of the cultural as well as economic ground on which the family rests. As a highly dynamic system, capitalism destabilizes both the economy and the family.[18] The more shaky things outside the family seem, the more we seem to need to believe in an unshakable family and, failing that, an unshakable figure of mother-wife.

In addition, in the West, capitalism is usually paired with an ideology of secular individualism. As an understanding of life, secular individualism leads people to take personal credit for their economic highs and personal blame for the lows. It leads us to "personalize" social events. It provides an intra-punitive ideology to go with an extra-punitive economic system. The effect of the impact of destabilizing capitalism on one hand and inward-looking individualist ideology on the other is to *create a need* for a refuge, a haven in a heartless world, as Christopher Lasch has argued, where we imagine ourselves to be safe, comforted, healed. The harsher the environment outside the home, the more we yearn for a haven inside the home. Many Americans turn for comfort and safety to the church. But the great geographic mobility of Americans often erodes ties to any particular church as it does bonds to local neighborhoods and communities.[19] In addition, divorce not only creates a greater need for supportive community, it tends to reduce the size of that personal community, as Barry Wellman's research on networks suggests.[20]

Like other symbols, the symbol of mother is "efficient." It is not the family farm, local community, or even whole extended family that does the symbolic work. All the meanings associated with these are *condensed* into the symbol of one person, the mother, and secondarily the immediate family. As Smelser observes, Americans entertain a "romance" of family vacations, family homes, and family "rural bliss" and, along with the hypersymbolization of the mother, these have probably grown in tandem with the destabilizing forces to which they are a response.

In sum, the students may have seen in the millionaire's ad, and in the commodity frontier itself, an attack on a symbol that had become a symbolic "holding ground," while all else seemed increasingly up for grabs. The attack on this symbol invites a crisis of enchantment. For, to believe in the wife-mother figure, one must submit to a sense of enchantment, magic, even a sense of being in love as a source of meaning in and of itself. At the same time, through the enormous growth in advertisement, the commodity frontier chips away at just this enchantment too. Is it the mother who is enchanted, the student may be led to wonder, or is it the services that pick up where she leaves off? And through advertising, is the commodity frontier gradually borrowing or stealing the enchantment of what seems like an ever more necessary remaining anchor against a market tide?

COMMODITIES AND THE MYTH
OF THE AMERICAN FRONTIER

As Smelser has observed in his analysis of the myth of California, every myth has an element of both reality and unreality. In our mental life a myth is located somewhere between daydream and ideology.[21] We have a myth of the American frontier, and of course, there really was a western frontier. The very possibility that a young man on a New England farm could set out for a more fertile and extensive plot of land out west led his parents to be more lenient, the historian Philip Greven shows, in hopes of motivating him to stay.[22] Attached to this real geographic frontier is a larger set of meanings, perhaps, including the idea that one can always leave something worse for something better. One doesn't have to stay and live with frustration and ambivalence: one can freely seek one's fortune on the emotional frontier. American heroes from Daniel Boone and Paul Bunyan to the restless prairie cowboy analyzed by Erik Erikson start somewhere and end somewhere else. At the end of *Huckleberry Finn*, Huck says, "I reckon I got to light out for the Territory ahead of the rest, because Aunt Sally she's going to adopt me and sivilize me and I can't stand it."[23]

Myths grow and change, and as part of change, myths can extend themselves to other areas of life. And perhaps we have seen a symbolic transfer of the fantasy of liberation from a geographic frontier to a commodity frontier. For the geographic frontier the point of focus is a person's location on land. For the commodity frontier the point of focus is a location in a world of goods and services. Instead of "going somewhere," the individual "buys something." And buying something becomes a way of going somewhere.

In the past, the fantasy of a perfect purchase might more often have centered on some feature of external reality. One might have dreamed of buying a perfect house, on a perfect lot of land, signifying one's rise in social station. But today, as more elements of intimate and domestic life become objects of sale, the commodity frontier has taken on a more subjective cast. So the modern purchase is more likely to be sold to us by implying access to a "perfect" private self in a "perfect" private relationship. For example, a recent ad in the *New Yorker* for "Titan Club, an Exclusive Dating Service" asks:

> Who says you can't have it all? Titan Club is the first exclusive dating club for men of your stature. You already have power, prestige, status and success. But, if "at the end of the day" you realize "someone" is missing, let Titan Club help you find her. Titan Club women are intelligent, diverse, sexy and beautiful. With a 95% success rate, we are confident that you will find exactly what you are looking for in a relationship.[24]

The fantasy of the perfect relationship is linked to the fantasy of the perfect personality with whom one has this relationship. Consider an ad for KinderCare Learning Centers, a for-profit childcare chain: "You want your child to be active, tolerant, smart, loved, emotionally stable, self-aware, artistic, and get a two-hour nap. Anything else?"[25] The service will produce, it implies, the perfect child with whom a busy parent has a perfect relationship.

This sort of ad promises a great deal about ambivalence. It promises to get rid of it. If Titan promises "exactly what you are looking for in a relationship" and if KinderCare promises exactly the personality you want in your child, they also deliver a state of unambivalence. And this is the hidden appeal in the marketing associated with much modern commodification. Thus, the prevailing myth of the frontier, commodification, and the subjective realm have fused into one—a commodity frontier that is moving into the world of our private desires. And to do so it borrow or steals—only time will tell—from the sense of enchantment earlier reserved for the home.

A word more about ambivalence. One way we "go west" is to buy goods and services that promise a family-like experience. But in doing so, we also pursue the fantasy of a life free from ambivalence. But the very act of fleeing ambivalence also expresses ambivalence. For commercial substitutes for family life do not eliminate ambivalence. They express and legitimize it. To return to our example of the shy millionaire, we might say that he is trying to act on two impulses. On one hand, he seeks the perfect woman to be by his side for many different purposes. This is one side of the ambivalence. On the other hand, he seeks to avoid entanglement with her. That's the other side of the ambivalence. Indeed, the man may be curtailing his idea of what he "needs" in order to fit into the narrow window of what he can purchase.

THE RICOCHET OF THE COMMODITY IMAGES

The Frankfurt school of sociology and more recent scholars such as Juliet Schor and Robert Kuttner have criticized consumerism without focusing on the family. Family scholars such as William Goode or Steven Mintz and Susan Kellogg have focused on the family without attending much to consumerism. Indeed, with the exception of Viviana Zelizer, Christopher Lasch, and Jan Dizard and Howard Gadlin, few scholars have focused on the relationship between these two realms. Perhaps this is because the two realms, now spatially divided and functionally separated, are assumed to be culturally free of each other as well. And perhaps this is why we tend to dissociate our ideas about the family from our ideas about the commodity frontier.

But these two realms are not at all separate. Culturally speaking, they ricochet off each other continually. As a cultural idea, commodification bounces from marketplace to home and back again. We buy something at the store. We bring it home. We compare what we have at home with what we bought. That comparison leads us to reappraise what we have at home. We make something at home. We go to the store. We compare what we think of buying with what we make at home. The reappraisal works the other way. In this way, events on the "frontier" are continually having their effect back home and vice versa.

We like to think of home as a haven in a heartless world, a benign sphere safely separate from the dangerous and hostile world outside or—a related idea—we see the family as a place of emotional expressivity separate from the emotionless, depersonalized world of the marketplace. As Zelizer has so beautifully shown, we have clearly different images of each. At home we act out of love. We are not cold and impersonal like people in the marketplace. And contrariwise, in the market, we say, we judge people on professional grounds. We don't let personal loyalties interfere. Each image is used as a foil, as the negative, as the "not" of the other—as in the ego defense of splitting.

Yet in my research on a Fortune 500 company, reported in *The Time Bind*, I discovered a number of managers who said that they brought home management tips that helped them smoothly run their homes. And sometimes people described themselves using work imagery. One man, humorously, spoke of having a "total quality" marriage, and another, seriously, spoke of a good family as like a "high productivity team." One man even explained that he improved his marriage by realizing that his wife was his primary "customer."[26] The roles and relationships of the office became benchmarks for those at home. For example, one married mother of three described the following:

> I had my husband's parents and aunt and uncle for a week at our summer cabin. It's rather small, and it rained most of the week except for Saturday and Sunday. And my mother-in-law offered to help me make the meals and helped me clear the dishes. But you know the real work is in figuring out what to eat and shopping. And the nearest store was at some distance. And I began to resent their visit so much I could hardly stand it. You know *I don't run a bed and breakfast!*

This woman chose a market role—manager of a bed and breakfast—as a measuring rod to appraise the demands made on her as a kinswoman. She measured what she did as an *unpaid relative* against another picture of life as a *paid employee*. On the family side of the commodity frontier, she felt she was doing too much and had a right to resent it. On the market side, she imagined, she would have been fairly compensated. In this way, she was tacitly measuring the opportunity costs of not working. She carried the market world with her in her imagination, even as she was cooking in the cabin.[27]

Other overburdened wives whom I've interviewed have said to their husbands, "I'm not your maid." One very well-to-do grandmother said about spending "too much" time with her own grandchildren, "I'm not their babysitter, you know."[28]

In twenty-five years, it may come to pass that remarks made at home will refer to new hybrid roles—"I'm not your paid hostess/masseuse"—as if that role were as normal and ordinary as any other. Or even "I'm not your half-wife," as if it had attained the moral weight of "wife" on one hand or "secretary" on the other. The market changes our benchmarks.

Through this borrowing from one side to the other of the commodity frontier, society itself expresses ambivalence about the family. Indeed, commodification provides a way in which people individually manage to want and not want certain elements of family life. The existence of such market substitutes becomes a form of societal legitimation for this ambivalence.

To return to the shy millionaire, we can't know what crossed through the heads of those who replied to his ad. But we do know that five of the seventy students from my class at Berkeley confessed that they wanted to be among them. As one confided, "Since this [questionnaire] is anonymous, I feel like I'd like to respond to this ad. It's a good deal, I think [crossed out, and over it written "maybe"]." Another said, "I am almost tempted to apply to this ad, except I don't meet the qualifications." Yet another replied, "If it's real, I'd do it." A number of people disparaged the ad but predicted that some others in the class would happily answer it. "The worst part," said one, "is that someone who needed the money probably took him up on his offer." In his essay on ambivalence, Smelser points out that sometimes we're ambivalent about our inner fantasies and impulses, and sometimes we're ambivalent about the real world outside ourselves. The commodity frontier is real, and maybe it's a good sign if we feel ambivalent about it.

3 GENDER CODES AND THE PLAY OF IRONY

In his book *Gender Advertisements*, Erving Goffman shows us the "look" of women in modern American advertising. Through his five hundred or so photos of women and men in advertisements, he shows us women pictured like children on or near the floor, or in whining or begging postures. He shows us women in clowning or pouting poses and men not in such poses. He shows us how, like children, female models hold a man's hand from behind. Goffman points out how women models show more emotion than male models ("flood out," as he puts it), expressing emotion since they are not expected to be in charge of anything. He shows how women are depicted listening intently to men talk, or how women look at men who point authoritatively to some distant object. He shows a female model, winsome and wide-eyed, revealing a bashful knee-bend, choreographed with a strong, protective male. In the details of such looks and scenes, Goffman shows us latent rules for how to "look feminine." And these rules suggest to him an analogy: man is to woman as parent is to child. Men and women are implicitly unequal in the apparently natural way that parents and children are unequal. Goffman suggests that this simple, apparently nonideological "look" is a sly way of reaffirming patriarchy. So *Gender Advertisements* concerns what a gender display displays, and how a display reaffirms what it reaffirms. In his articulation of these points, Goffman is our most observant observer.

In what he shows us, we can note several points. First, as Goffman talks about them, the models portrayed in *Gender Advertisements* do not seem to consider and decide how to pose; they know intuitively. The woman in the little-girl-bashful-knee-bend pose in *Gender Advertisements* thus differs from Goffman's description of Preedy at the beach, a self-conscious fictional character in *The Presentation of Self in Everyday Life*. The female model seems to know what to do; she does not seem to consciously choose. On the other hand, Preedy, a vacationing Englishman on a summer beach in Spain, is a conscious and strategic actor. As Goffman describes:

> By devious handlings he gave any who wanted to look a chance to see the title of his book—a Spanish translation of Homer, classic, thus but not daring, cos-

mopolitan too—and then gathered together his beach-wrap and bag into a neat and resistant pile (Methodical and Sensible Preedy), rose slowly to stretch at ease his huge frame (Big Cat Preedy) and tossed aside his sandals (Carefree Preedy after all).[1]

The image of the bashful-knee-bend model differs from the image of the actor in Goffman's other writings too. There Goffman offers us a world of unbudgeable rules, silly but necessary. Indeed, he seems to take the rules' point of view while, mockingly it seems, offering us an actor who works tirelessly at getting around these rules. Curiously, in his analysis of gender Goffman did not use all of "Goffman." Many of his conceptual tools remained in his tool kit. So we might start by applying the Goffman-on-everything-else to the topic of gender as seen in advice books. For some of these books presume an actor like Preedy at the beach.

Both the bashful-knee-bend model and Preedy are examples drawn from white, or whitish, middle-class American life, and the question we need to ask is the degree to which examples drawn from other racial or ethnic groups and other social classes point to important variations on the same psychosocial theme or to different themes. In posing as they pose, Goffman's models seem to follow one body of tacit social rules about gender, not two or three, or some mix. He assumes the cultural hegemony of a certain version of patriarchy, and he takes it as his task to reveal this code to us through his analysis of display. His choice of topic—ads—makes it hard to discuss real people's doubt about, conflict over, or estrangement from a code.

Though *Gender Advertisements* was published in 1976, it seems to reflect the social quietude of an earlier era. But as women move into paid work in both the Western and non-Western worlds, the main story is not ritual affirmation and cultural reproduction, but rather one of cultural diversity, upheaval, and challenge. The question becomes: How do women choose from among many *competing* codes?[2] In this respect women of any class partake of the minority experience of handling multiple codes. For the mainstream code is not made up for them.

In *Gender Advertisements* Goffman confines himself to describing rules that apply to the actor's outer appearance and sets aside the task of describing rules that apply to inner feeling. Though many illustrations in his other works reflect feeling rules, as I call them, perhaps because Goffman resisted the idea of a feelingful self, the concept of feeling rules remained undertheorized.[3] But if we do presume a self with an interior life, we are led to explore gender codes that regulate the emotional bottom of that life fully as much as the interactional surface.

Finally, although Goffman was often drawn to study the strain between strong rules and fragile selves, he doesn't look for that strain here, though we may do so by following his own tracks. Drawing ideas from Goffman's other works, then, and from Ann Swidler, in this essay I look at popular advice books for women as Goffman looked at ads.[4]

But with one difference. As I see it, women do not intuitively fall into this or that way of being, like the models in *Gender Advertisements*. When faced with new challenges, often their "old" intuition doesn't work. And so they work on their old intuition to try and create a *new intuition*. They aren't exactly Preedys acting before an imagined audience, though surely Preedy describes part of the story. They are cultural artists at work. They draw from expressions of the cultural premises at hand—gender codes. They switch, mix, and "balance" codes, trying semiconsciously to seem "just so feminine" in one aspect of self in order to seem "just so masculine" in another. In doing this, they do not remain forever detached from their work. Like real artists, they bring their more essential selves with them, or try to. Here I depart from Goffman and move toward Freud. Does a code fit the essential self? Or doesn't it? Life is all about trying them out and finding out how a given aspect of a code *feels*. Irony is the tone we strike when we can't hang on and can't let go.

American advice books for women seem to draw from one of two arche-typal codes—traditional and egalitarian—though other codes abound. I'll describe each, then show how advice books invite women to draw elements from each, mixing and balancing codes in order to put together a feminine identity. These advice books do not portray how real women act feminine; they are users' manuals.

Traditional books draw on the late eighteenth-century parlor life of the American urban upper class and fit with, even as they express, the economic dependence of women on men. (It is this code that is visually reflected in *Gender Advertisements*.) The traditional code provides the social guidelines for the establishment of male superiority. It exaggerates differences in the appearance of men and women and establishes asymmetrical rules of inter-action; women should listen more attentively, defer to the judgment and authority of men, and in general enhance the self-esteem of men more than men do for women. The traditional code prescribes asymmetrical rules of deference and makes it proper for women to have less power than men. What power they do have, they also attain not through a position in the larger social order but through personal relations, especially within the family.

The second code is egalitarian, linked to women's movement into paid work and the cultural ideals of the feminist movement. It extends to women many social rules of the male work culture. It provides the social guidelines for establishing equality between the sexes and calls for rules of equal defer-ence. Women are expected to listen and enhance the status of men as much as they expect to be listened to and complimented by them. According to this second code, differences are deemphasized and women have equal power. The egalitarian code has at least two versions, one basing equality on old-time male terms and one basing it on old-time female terms. Perhaps most modern egalitarian codes now combine these two kinds of terms.

A rough sketch of the two codes is shown in chart 1. I've drawn most illustrations of the traditional code from Marabel Morgan's *The Total Woman* and illustrations of the modern code from Gloria Steinem's *Outrageous Acts and Everyday Rebellions* (which, while not an advice book, offers a lot of advice). To illustrate a mixing of these codes to create a modified traditional code of its own, I draw from Helen Gurley Brown's *Having It All*.

A code simply tells us what (look, interactional style) goes with what (kind of emotion management). Over time, relations between the parts, the character, the salience, the tightness and looseness of each part can change. So what feels to us like a coherent, agreed-upon gender code at one place and time can slowly shift, like parts in a slow-motion kaleidoscope, and form another basis for coherence. In order for a code to change, the circumstances holding it in place must change, and while globalization is currently bringing about changes we can hardly envision today, for the moment, in the West, these Western archetypes cohere. To adapt ourselves to new circumstances, what we often do with codes, as Ann Swidler rightly suggests, is *mix* them.

MIXING CODES

In daily life, the individual actor mixes one look with another, one interaction style or emotional ideal with another. Half-wittingly, she blends parts of the two codes, or alternates between them depending on the situation at hand. Advice books do the same thing, occasionally adding other cultural elements as well. For example, Marabel Morgan's *The Total Woman* draws from a traditional code, as it was known to mainly white middle-class urban women of the late nineteenth century. In both books, wives are advised to defer to the husband's authority with good grace, and to cultivate a separate domestic presence as the "sunshine of one's home." At the same time, writing in 1973, as a right-wing Christian answer to the sexual revolution of the 1960s, Morgan drew simultaneously on the Bible and *Playboy* and gained notoriety for advising women to greet their husbands at the front door in a series of costumes. She says:

> I have heard women complain, "My husband isn't satisfied with just me. He wants lots of women. What can I do?" You can be lots of different women to him. Costumes provide variety without him ever leaving home. I believe that every man needs excitement and high adventure at home. Never let him know what to expect when he opens the front door, make it a surprise package. You may be a smoldering sexpot or an All American fresh beauty. Be a pixie or a pirate, a cowgirl or a show girl. Keep him off guard.[5]

CHART 1 Gender Codes

	Traditional (Hierarchical)	Modern (One Form of Egalitarian)
Look	highly gender differentiated	less gender differentiated
Female dress	pastel colors	subdued "male" colors
	small patterns	bold patterns
	smooth materials, silk	rough materials
	lace, ruffles, frills	no frills
	sweet-sixteen look: informal dress or slacks for house and shopping, "ladylike" look for parties	career-woman look: business suits for work, "upper-class ladylike" look for parties
	high-heeled shoes	low heels
	long fingernails	short, plain nails
	long hair	short hair
Interactional style	dissimulation, wiles, "getting around men" through indirect means, crying, playing on male sympathy	direct dealing, no wiles, (wiles considered beneath modern woman, "sneaky")
Face	deferential to men, bashful, blush easily, downward glance	direct look, no blushing, open "assertive expression"
	face used as instrument for emotional expression, uses "eyes"	masked and open emotional expression
Body	take up as little room as possible, leaning posture, bashful knee-bend, head tilt	assume full size, erect posture, weight on both legs
Hand	"fish" handshake, modified version of presenting hand for ritual kiss	direct, businesslike grasp
Speech	hospitable to interruption, use of "female" vocabulary, e.g., "lovely"	discourages interruption, male vocabulary
Feeling rules	gender asymmetry in love, put love of man first; cultivate love, subordinate ambition	gender symmetry in love; both sexes rank love in same way
	suppress anger, or deal with it indirectly	not good to be "clinging vine"
	don't be "too" aggressive, active, or independent	don't be "too" passive, dependent
Emotion management	suppress initiative, try to fit "code" personality	suppress passivity, try to be assertive

In harnessing the notion of sexual variety from the 1960s to monogamous Christian marriage, Morgan ironically concedes more cultural territory than she intends. By fighting fire with fire, she accepts the otherwise
inhospitable ideal of sexual variety into the Christian home, creating with it
a new job and series of looks for the Christian wife. She thus adds to the idea
of being the "sunshine of one's home" the further idea of being playful,
entertaining, sexy. It's now a woman's job to make monogamy fun.

In turn, important aspects of Morgan's mix appear in Helen Gurley
Brown's 1982 *Having It All.* Brown reduces the range of contexts in which
Morgan's rules of female deference to males apply and expands the range of
contexts in which egalitarian ones do. She advises women on the match of
context to code. For example, in *Having It All,* a woman should be flattering,
wily, and submissive with her new love or husband, but assertive and unafraid
to be defeminized at work. Just as Morgan created a hybrid code out of the
Bible and Hollywood, so Brown made a hybrid out of Morgan and Wall Street.

THE PRINCIPLE OF BALANCING

Not only do advice books mix codes, adding in other elements of culture;
some advice books tell readers how to balance "masculine" with "feminine"
demeanor and feeling rules. Some advice books urge women to adopt
"masculine" manners. In *The Right Moves* Charlene Mitchell urges women to
remain detached, cool, businesslike, and for purposes of making conversation, to learn some football teams and scores. Other advice books urge
women to adopt "feminine" manners. In *Feminine Leadership: How to Succeed
without Being One of the Boys* Marilyn Loden urges women to use their "natural" intuition (as if the very use of this advice book didn't put the idea of
intuition in question), warmth, and motherly qualities to induce subordinates and co-workers to be loyal and dedicated. In *Having It All* Helen
Gurley Brown advises the female executive not to pace, speak dramatically,
or act important as she might imagine a man would do. But Brown's advice
otherwise leans to the "male" side: there is no mention of acting or feeling
motherly. Instead the package includes developing an iron will "like a man"
but a demeanor and comportment "like a woman."

Anticipating that her reader may worry about not feeling feminine
enough, Brown reassures her:

> Don't be afraid that success will de-feminize you. . . . Robin Smith, former
> president and general manager of the Book Club Division of Doubleday and
> Company, now president of Publishers' Clearing House, largest magazine sub-
> scription agency in the world, says, "When you become an executive, you do
> not raise your voice or get loud or masculine. You got where you got . . . by
> being rational. . . . These qualities are where your strengths lie. There is noth-
> ing masculine about them. You also get what you want by being stubborn—a
> very feminine trait."[6]

Avoid the superficial mannerisms of male authority, but adopt the less tangible traits associated with it. Apparently assuming that the reader takes rationality to be a male trait, Brown urges women to degender rationality, so that they can feel feminine but act rational.

Brown doesn't question the gender codes themselves. She sees determination as male, stubbornness as female. But she relabels determined behavior as stubborn. With this feminine "cover," she can now permit herself the authoritative stance she needs to get the job done. Ultra-femininity, like ultra-masculinity, may mask the underlying social principle of "balancing."

This strategy of "balancing" is one response to a conflict Brown assumes many heterosexual women readers face. On one hand, they want to be seen as "feminine" lest they be seen as unattractive or abnormal. On the other hand, many job-relevant traits are traditionally associated with masculinity. A woman who cultivates a "masculine" trait risks compromising her "femininity." So she resorts to a balancing strategy. She appears "more" feminine in one realm in order to permit herself male traits in another realm. Given that many traits required for economic survival are culturally defined as male and that women now form 46 percent of the labor force, given the almost infinite variety of ways in which a person may be defined as "masculine" or feminine," the potential tradeoffs are almost endless. And so a woman who wears very long fingernails, very fluffy blouses, and very high-heeled shoes may try in this way to make up for being a hyperaggressive saleswoman and hope to come out even. But balancing has limits.

SELF AND CODE: THE CASE OF FEMININE WILES

One controversy running through both traditional and egalitarian advice books is whether to use feminine wiles; authors on both sides feel obliged to take a position on the question. In nineteenth-century America, "feminine wiles" were an acknowledged if not much admired way in which a woman might get what she wanted indirectly when direct access to power was blocked to her. Wiles were traditional. As women gained power and influence based on education and occupation, wiles became discredited, though not entirely.

Marabel Morgan proposes crude wiles in assignments for her Total Woman Classes (classes that sprang up—like feminist consciousness-raising groups—to support women in their efforts to stay traditional). She says:

> In class one day, I gave the assignment for the girls to admire their husband's body that night. One girl went right to work on her homework. Her husband was shorter than she but quite handsome. . . . That evening while he was reading the paper, she sat down next to him on the sofa and began stroking his arm. After a bit she stopped at the biceps and squeezed. He unconsciously flexed his muscle and she said, "Oh, I never knew you were so muscular!"

More generally Morgan advises women to plan the "proper time and atmo-sphere" for bringing up requests: "Let him relax and give yourself time to judge his mood."[7]

But Morgan feels obliged to anticipate the reader's objection to wiles, and to the self-acknowledgment her advice forces on the practitioner—that she *is* acting, and lying about it. As Morgan notes:

> I heard one wife say "I feel guilty using feminine wiles on my husband. It seems dishonest. Why should I lie to build him up? I want to be honest but still meet his needs." . . . I am not advocating that you lie to give your husband a superficial ego boost. Even a fool will see through flattery. But I am saying he has a deep need for sincere admiration. Look for new parts to compliment as you see him with new eyes.[8]

Morgan "solves" the problem of dishonesty by moving from advice about surface acting—trying to seem sincere about a compliment—to advice about deep acting—how to try to actually *feel* sincere. She tells women how through self-exhortation they can talk themselves into believing the flattery they give their husbands. Gamely she urges, "Starting tonight, determine that you will admire your husband." "Think back," she says, "to those days when you were first convinced that he was the one." Once you believe the compliment, Morgan suggests, flattery isn't "wiles." She says, "Put your hus-band's tattered ego back together again at the end of each day. That's not using feminine wiles; that is the very nature of love."[9] The work shifts from manipulating her husband to manipulating herself. Morgan asks the reader to mean what she says when she is wily, to put her self behind her act.

Helen Gurley Brown takes another tack. Lightheartedly she advises, "Maybe there is nobody much in the world to tell him he is wonderful except you. It really doesn't matter if the flattery you heap on him is close to baloney—heap away . . . do this for me. . . . Oh, my God, I sound like Marabel Morgan."[10]

In a section entitled "More Things to Do in the Early Stages" (of courtship), Brown recommends:

> When you are in love with a man, you have to be careful not to bore him. . . . You're in the car and he's deep into a monologue about the Salt II Treaty. . . . You pass an apartment house where you used to live or a school attended as a teenager. I see no reason to stop the Salt II talkathon to point out the house or school unless he's an architect. Point them out another time when he's not so caught up with his subject.

She goes on, "Save your own need to talk for women friends. . . . It's much safer to call a girl friend who will keep your confidence. . . . Release your steam on her instead of on your tired husband." Brown further advises, "I think every woman needs four to six 'main people' in her life apart from her husband, plus about ten to twenty peripherals."[11]

A prospective girlfriend is advised to do thoughtful deeds. She should help her boyfriend's sister sell raffle tickets, wash his Porsche, and photocopy articles about him. She should impersonate a kind person. She should understand that these favors are "'acceptable' but necessary bullshit."[12]

This is more than ordinary advice. Brown is guiding the reader in how *to feel about* that advice. Do these acts, she seems to say. Accept them as necessary. But you don't have to feel like doing them. You can feel annoyed at having to use them.

Morgan urges her reader to take flattery seriously, to mean it or try to mean it. Brown urges a lighter, tongue-in-cheek approach. Brown invites the reader to object to her cynicism. As she says, "You don't like my calling this stuff bullshit, right? Okay, call it anything you like (and of course you're doing it because you love him) but just do it."[13] By putting the reader's "real" feeling in parentheses Brown reduces her advice to pragmatically motivated ploys. Apply these "girlie" means of flattery, she seems to say, but only because it works, not because you believe in it. Morgan invites the reader to *believe* in flattery, extra favors, and listening—and more generally, in the asymmetrical rules of interaction. But it is Brown who is the true Goffmanian stage-directing the female Preedy.

But in truth, both Morgan and Brown have written acting manuals. They differ only in the kind of acting they advocate. Morgan advocates deep acting through which to persuade ourselves of our act, to blend ourselves into the act. Brown advises surface acting, holding an alternate, cynical self apart from the act. Needless to say, many modern advice books condemn feminine wiles altogether, recommending that the reader put her "whole self" behind a style of interaction based on direct dealing. In *Smart Cookies Don't Crumble,* Sonya Friedman disparages another, more traditional author's advice about how to get a man to fall in love. She says:

> Mirror his gestures, Cabot [Tracey Cabot, the author of *How to Make a Man Fall in Love with You*] further advises us—this comforts him—and breathe as he breathes. She proceeds to let us in on how to acquire this secret. You can tell how quickly a man is breathing by watching his shoulders. Mark them with a point on the wall behind him and watch them go up and down. Then simply start breathing yourself in the same rhythm.

Friedman comments wryly, "Breathe as he breathes and you may soon be gasping for breath."[14]

Authors differ on how much to put the self behind other issues apart from feminine wiles. In her book *Outrageous Acts and Everyday Rebellions,* Gloria Steinem offers exercises on how to get men to listen to women as much as women listen to men, and how to feel about being "too uncomfortable" trying to urge men to listen more. How can women try to right an uneven gender balance in talk? By tape-recording dinner table conversations or meetings, and then playing the tape back to the group. She suggests joking to men who interrupt them by saying, "That's one," and promising some conspicuous act when the number of male interruptions gets to three. She also recommends that a woman monitor her own responses for a troubling self-censorship:

> Check the talk politics concealed in your own behavior. Does your anxiety level go up (and your hostess instincts quiver) when women are talking and men are listening, but not the reverse? For instance, men often seem to feel okay about "talking shop" for hours while women listen, but women seem able to talk in men's presence for only a short time before feeling anxious, apologizing, and encouraging the men to speak. If you start to feel wrongly uncomfortable about making males listen, try this exercise: keep on talking, and encourage your sisters to do the same. Honor men by treating them as honestly as you treat women. You will be allowing them to learn.[15]

Morgan tells her reader to feel like herself as she adoringly "over-listens." Steinem tells her reader to feel like herself when she quits the habit. Despite their diametrically opposed views on life, both differ from the more cynical Brown. If Morgan says, "Believe your act," and Brown says, "Don't bother," Steinem says, "Don't act."

FEELING RULES: LOVE AND GRATITUDE

Morgan and Brown both tell women to expect less caretaking from their husbands than they should expect to give. As Brown notes flippantly, "At my house there isn't much wife coddling during illness, but then nobody female is ever ill at our house so the unilateral sick-care plan works okay."[16] Morgan finds support in the Bible for the same uneven expectations. As she exclaims, "God ordained man to be the head of the family, its president and his wife to be the executive vice president . . . allowing your husband to be your president is just good business."[17] From this, Morgan derives an emotional "policy" spelled out in the formula for women: accept him, admire him, adapt to him, and appreciate him. The policy is based on the idea that men and women have different needs; as Morgan argues, "Women need to be loved; men need to be admired"[18]—a proposition Steinem flatly rejects.

In addition to Morgan's rules for love, she gives guidance on how grateful women should feel toward men. If a woman feels properly grateful to her husband, Morgan reasons, it will be easier to accept, admire, adapt to, and appreciate him. And to feel grateful, it helps to dwell on what she should be grateful for . . . Discussing how, after a quarrel, a woman can bring herself to apologize first, Morgan notes:

I'll tell you what helps me apologize quite sincerely. I say to myself—and I mean every word of it—you are lucky, very lucky your husband married you, my dear, that you now have a husband. Should your marriage end, there is no big storehouse of possible new husbands for you to get yourself one from, at your age. That bin is practically empty. The bin that he gets a new wife from is not empty.[19]

But even a die-hard traditionalist like Morgan pitches her appeal to the reader not on the grounds that womanly gratitude is its own raison d'être but on the grounds of a cool calculation about the availability of alternate spouses. What is owed and owing in gratitude, she presumes does not flow from the give-and-take of marriage but from the remarriage market well outside it. Given this marital and job market, Morgan reasons that women should feel more grateful to be married to men than men are to be married to them. So women should also feel more grateful for all the little events of married life.

Bearers of an egalitarian code advocate a very different, if sometimes equally crude, emotional policy. This modern code calls for a symmetry in what is owed and owing in love and gratitude. In this they differ from the traditional. But modern advice books themselves differ on whether both men and women should follow the formerly "feminine" rules of love or whether both should follow the formerly "masculine" ones. In *Smart Cookies Don't Crumble*, Sonya Friedman advocates that women feel less grateful, not that men feel more so. She warns women that "being grateful is a trap" and elaborates: "When you're grateful for little favors, you will always empower others to run your life. Instead empower yourself to get what you want. Staying with the man who begrudges love day after day ensures a diet of 'mouthfuls of humiliation.' Remaining at a job that limits your potential saps energy and stifles goal setting."[20]

No advice book takes women "all the way" to what might be imagined to be the "male" line on gratitude: to be the less grateful party. But many move quite far in that direction by criticizing women for being too loving, too giving, too obsessed with romance, too clinging or dependent—ways that they describe as "sick" or psychologically defective. Again, in "The Compassion Trap" Margaret Adams argues that the traditional rule governing women's marital love results in a life devoted to serving others, making others comfortable and cared for.[21] This, she cautions, requires women to renounce their own ambitions. As Friedman comments, it is "an obstacle to assertion. . . . All this sounds noble and altruistic, and it is—within reason. But remember, it's still a trap." Friedman goes on to give examples of this trap—a secretary who stays at a dead-end job because the boss tells her no one could take her place, a woman who keeps finding excuses for her boyfriend's refusal to commit himself to marriage, or the wife who blames job pressures and alcohol for her husband's unkind behavior toward her.[22] In other books as well, Robin Norwood's *Women Who Love Too Much* and Colette Dowling's *The Cinderella Complex,* the problem is the traditional female emotional code—not the traditional male's—that is said to make women unhappy. In essence, Friedman warns against Morgan's advice: "If you put others before you, they are often quite happy to move forward and leave you behind."[23]

Other egalitarians propose that men learn to love by the old female rules. As Shere Hite put it in her book *Women and Love,* "It's not that women love too much, it's that men love too little."[24] Here Hite calls for a cultural revolution I hope comes to pass.

Just as ads tell us about the latent rules for how to look and choreograph a scene with men and women, so popular advice books tell us about rules for how to act and feel. They presume that we can improve on intuition. Such books guide women in their "surface acting" (where they try to change how they outwardly appear) and in their "deep acting" (where they try to change how they actually feel). They guide the reader in surface acting by showing her how to appear and guide her in deep acting by showing her how to see and feel.

To Goffman, everyone is an actor, and everyone, he implies, acts equally. But these advice books suggest something else: some people act *more* than others. While everyone may be concerned to present a certain face to the world, and may do emotion work to fix a self to that face, we do not do that to an equal extent. The slave acts more than the master. More rides on being pleasing. To the extent that women are subordinate to men, they have to act more. It is more socially "expensive" for them to freely express frustration or annoyance. Even today women are less often steering the boat, are more often thrust into situations where they must quickly adapt to changes someone else initiates—to try to feel what five minutes ago they did not feel—and have, in addition, to make it seem as if "everything's fine." Especially to people who are permanently or temporarily subordinate, feeling rules and emotion work are matters of great moment. This may be why the bookstore shelves are not filled with books for men parallel to those of Morgan, Brown, and Friedman.

Advice books also tell their readers how to take their advice—ironically, cynically, lightly, seriously, joyfully, guiltily, resentfully. They invite a reader toward a certain relationship between self and rule, self and code. If the war between advice books is one small clue to the contemporary conflict over the changing roles of women, then one important way this war goes on is in the innuendo of irony, play, humor—the various frames placed on the old rules that make them unserious, pragmatic, or just a bit foolish. The right way to follow an old rule in a modern world, it would seem in books like Brown's, is to disaffiliate yourself from it, to feel distant from it. You may yet need to use feminine wiles, she seems to say, so feel that you can use them when you have to. But, there being no purpose or legitimacy to feminine wiles left, wink at them, throw them away, and reach for another advice book. Irony becomes a way of holding on and letting go.

As in an urbanizing society the peasant comes to the city and is forced to change, so women have entered a new set of social scenes at work and at home. Just as the urbanizing peasant wonders how to fit into city life without losing all his or her peasant ways, so urban women wonder how to adapt to the industrial world of work without losing all of their domestic culture. Just as some peasants become completely urbanized, others go back home, and still others become urban-villagers, so women assimilate or in varying degrees do not. As the world becomes more economically unified, the full diversity of its cultural codes will begin to show. Other versions of a traditional code will move into circulation. But in the new code mixing to come, they may be decorative to an ever more stabilized egalitarian code. And as for the contradictions? Irony will handle them.

4 LIGHT AND HEAVY

American and Japanese Advice Books for Women

WITH KAZUKO TANAKA

Nowadays husbands and wives, parents and children don't say "hello" to each other in the morning. Sometimes not only does the wife not prepare breakfast, she doesn't even get out of bed. If you think this is sex equality and that the man is a "tender husband" you're mistaken.

Soshitsu Sen, *What a Beautiful Woman* (1980)

In *What a Beautiful Woman,* a best-selling Japanese advice book in 1980, Soshitsu Sen casts a skeptical eye on the working wife who sleeps in. Like other best-selling advice books published between 1970 and 1990 in the United States and Japan, this one specifies a whole array of actions—or inactions—which, the author thinks, bring a woman honor or disgrace. It tells us about the amount of *cultural room* she has to move around in. We speak of *cultural* room because sometimes aspects of the culture itself—the gendered nature of the Japanese language, for example—can indirectly immobilize a woman. Similarly, the ambiance of shared reverence for past traditions, especially those which women themselves are asked to gladly affirm, can increase the social penalties for stepping out of line. At the same time, the degree of social support she expects can make each private move just a bit more collective. In the course of telling people what to do, both Japanese and American advice books drop many clues about their respective notions of cultural room.

So when we speak of "gender culture" we refer not simply to this or that attitude toward women in the United States or Japan but to certain qualities of each general culture as well. For example, like any other aspect of culture, gender culture is infused with (a) a sense of connection between the present and the past (cultural weight), (b) a connection to unknown others in one's culture (cultural stretch), and (c) a connection to others in one's immediate place in that culture (cultural embeddedness). Through stories, commentary, and exhortation, Japanese and American advice books reflect positions along each of these dimensions of culture. An advice book can, for example, imply a great deal of "cultural weight" by invoking serious and authoritative judgments connected to a distant and revered past, including, potentially, reverence for female ancestors. Or such commentary can seem "light" because of a failure to acknowledge or pay tribute to the past.

Advice books also imply a degree of cultural stretch. That is, they may or may not imply the awareness, tolerance, or acceptance of a variety of social patterns. So, we can ask: Are there a number of cultural possibilities described in a book, or even on the list of best-selling advice books available at any point in time? Is the advice available to the readers in one book likely to be diametrically opposed to that in another equally popular book?

Advice books imply a degree of cultural embeddedness as well. They point to the degree to which an individual is implicitly expected to *coordinate* her or his line of action with that of others. Soshitsu Sen's sleeping mother is clearly embedded in a social scene. But, we also want to know, is she portrayed as deciding a line of action on her own or in close coordination with others?

All three of these deep dimensions of general cultural life in Japan and the United States—weight, stretch, and embeddedness—shape the cultural compromises we come to think of as "advice" or "opinion." As these two modern capitalist giants induct women into their labor forces, how do they differ in their style of cultural incorporation? To turn the question around, which cultural qualities make it easy for feminists to start a gender revolution? And which qualities enable them to conclude the revolution by both entering the labor force on equal terms and establishing a high level of care for the young and old?

Drawing on the cultural pragmatism of Pierre Bourdieu, the frame analysis of Erving Goffman, and the notion of culture as a site of struggle from Randall Collins, we explore best-selling advice books for women published between 1970 and 1990 in Japan and the United States.[1] Both the courses of action women pursue and the cultural room they have to do so are the result of a certain cultural work which an entire population performs. It is as if husbands and wives, grandparents, teachers, and employers from different sectors of society all sat around an imaginary bargaining table hammering out agreements about the proper role of a wife, a husband, a mother, a father. For collectively such populations strike cultural deals, each contingent on a variety of conditions. Any free choice, they imply, takes place in the context of such a history of cultural deals. We can't see these cultural deals, of course, but advice books give us some feel for them.

Cultures are always in motion. But how is it they change? Randall Collins suggests that cultures change as a result of a Darwinian struggle between contending ideas. One cultural idea "wins" out over another. Collins is right, of course, but we need to add to this picture some understanding of how cultural differences are brokered. Indeed, we prefer to think of cultures as the result of continually renegotiated "deals." It is as if some people called out, "We want this cultural ideal" and others called out, "No, we want that cultural ideal." Then, cultural intermediaries—such as authors of advice books—step in, saying in effect, "I propose a compromise." For example, an author may seem to say, "Let's accept the abbreviation of certain rituals, since working mothers don't have time to do the full proper preparation, but let's keep the idea of motherly sacrifice. Let's take rituals more lightly, but motherliness more seriously." Advice books don't tell who accepts what deal, but they show what the current proposals are and the amount and nature of the cultural room they leave women.

In some ways cultural bargaining is similar to other forms of collective bargaining, and in many ways it is, of course, different. When representatives of labor and management bargain, they do so in a formal, institutional setting. Representatives appointed by management meet with representatives elected by workers, and each bargainer is accountable to a constituency. Arbitrators are brought in, final deals are legally binding. But in cultural bargaining, the players are figures in one or another arena of the mass media. Instead of constituencies to which they are accountable, parties speak to those who listen, buy, and read. Labor-management bargains forge the terms of a relationship between union and company. But cultural arbitrators make deals between husbands and wives, parents and children—and taken as a whole, men as one stratum and women as another.

In labor-management bargains, what is negotiated are bread-and-butter issues—wages, hours, and benefits. In the informal realm of culture, though, the elements bargained about are ideas about virtues and flaws, status and honor, the weight of the past, the stretch or embeddedness of a culture. Again, when labor and management bargain, the negotiation is formal and conscious. But cultural bargaining is relatively incoherent and unconscious. In the case of advice books, agreement is shown not by a raising of hands, but by a ring of the cash register. But just as labor-management bargains in one company set the pattern for a whole industry, so, we believe, best-selling advice books describe the dominant notions of the cultural room given to women and men.

Some cultural ideas reinforce patriarchy, while others weaken it, and many ideas seems neutral in effect. Cultural ideas about, for example, honor—itself an important Japanese concern—can be seen as negotiating positions. For instance, a writer may say, "Women can be honorably modern in one way (say, by working), but will have to remain honorably traditional in another (say, by showing deference to their husbands)." Thus, the deal can be: "women can work if they still act deferential to their husbands at home." The study of advice books, then, is the study of such cultural deals, and the success of each kind of book may offer us clues to their public acceptance.

JAPANESE AND AMERICAN CONTEXTS

Cultural room is created within a broad context, and while the Japanese and American contexts are similar in some ways, they very much differ in others. Both societies have a "past" in which most women were more subordinate to men than they are today. Much of the cultural negotiation in each society centers on how much of which past gender practices and beliefs is to be incorporated into the present. But in Japanese tradition the genders have been far more deeply divided, women far more subordinate, and the weight of that tradition far heavier.

In addition, while both Japan and the United States are capitalist giants, Japan, a homogeneous society of 127 million people, has emerged from agrarian feudalism recently and rapidly. Its women have emerged from being a virtual lower caste in each tier of a Confucian feudal hierarchy to being secondary participants in its modern economy. For the last fifty years, half of all Japanese women have worked outside the home—a rapidly growing number of them in large companies—and a small but growing number of these employees are mothers of small children. In the 1980s, when the books were published, Japanese women made up about a fifth of college and university students, and about 90 percent of junior college students. Yet the weight of Japanese culture—its language, customs, and rites—have much more sharply divided men from women than in the United States. In Japanese, the very character for "wife" symbolizes "inside house." A 1972 best-selling advice book by Minoru Hamao, the former tutor of the emperor and two princes, even went so far as to recommend separate textbooks for Japanese boys and girls.[2]

The Japanese have historically honored the *ie*, the male family line, and strongly attached womanly honor to maternal sacrifice to husband, in-laws, and children. Masahiro Yamada, a sociologist at the University of Tokyo, offers the startling thesis that Japan has built capitalism on the basis of this maternal sacrifice. Adult men, he suggests, transfer their dependence from a sacrificing mother to a demanding company and, like their mothers, sacrifice themselves to it, in the process building capitalism. If this is plausible, then perhaps this tradition of maternal sacrifice is the most salient point of cultural brokering reflected in Japanese advice books for women. But today the family to which a woman is to sacrifice herself is in the process of transformation. Today fewer parents than in the past arrange their children's marriages, and because it is less compulsory than in the past, far fewer people marry. Those who do marry more often live independent of their parents and, compared to previous generations, have fewer children. Although very low to begin with, the divorce rate has risen since the 1960s to a high of one out of four in the 1980s, and one in three in the 1990s.

A larger (276 million) and ethnically more plural society, the United States lacks a feudal past, save that which immigrants brought with them from Europe and Asia. In 1900 a fifth of women worked outside the home, mostly in a few "women's" jobs. Today two-thirds of American women work and at almost every kind of job. To be sure, over the last two hundred years, the bulk of American women have moved from being husband-helpers on small farms to being factory hands, domestic workers, and clerical and service workers, but, in contrast to their Japanese sisters, many more American women are branching into the "male" trades, professions, and management. More American women than men now graduate from both two- and four-year colleges.

American, compared with Japanese, family life began from a very different cultural starting point, though it has been proceeding in the same direction. Outside of certain small ethnic enclaves, marriages in the United States were never arranged. If the Japanese family was patrilineal and patrilocal, American families, as William Goode and Talcott Parsons have pointed out, have long been neo-local and decreasingly patrilineal. But given different starting points, family trends have pointed in the same direction—toward less marriage, later marriage, more divorce, and fewer children. In both cultures, too, women have been granted more autonomy.

How, then, does the texture of each culture—its weight, stretch, and notion of connectedness—alter the prospects for working mothers? What clues do advice books give us about this?

HOW CULTURE FEELS

From lists of best-selling nonfiction books in Japan and the United States, we selected fifteen Japanese and twenty-eight American books that by title, cover, and table of contents are directly addressed to women or to social issues of direct concern to women. We chose best-sellers in hardcover or paperback, trade and mass market, for the years 1970 through 1990. For ratings of the American books, we relied on listings published by *Publishers Weekly*. The criteria used by *Publishers Weekly* to determine a best-seller changed through the years, and we followed those changes. The American system for determining a best-seller was based on the number of books publishers shipped to bookstores. The Japanese system was based on a poll of owners of major bookstores. We excluded books focused on weight loss, smoking, alcoholism, personal grooming, financial planning, sexual technique, spiritualism, or moral uplift, but included a few other books, non-best-sellers for women and some best-sellers for men and for both sexes.

The authors of these books do not passively transmit culture, of course, but actively interpret it, mixing new with old as they try to help readers resolve issues of daily life. Their *way* of transmitting culture is thus itself a message. More of the Japanese books are written from a teacherly this-is-how-you-do-it stance while most of the American ones are posed in a more neighborly, "democratic" tone. Most Japanese advice books are also written by men, whereas most American advice books are written by women. Eight of the twelve Japanese authors (of the fifteen Japanese advice books, one author wrote three) are men. Of the twenty-eight American books, nineteen are by sole authors, and of those, fourteen are female and five are male.

Japanese advice books are predominantly books of morality (inner virtues) and manners (outward comportment). The authors tend to be reserved, seldom personal, almost never confessional. In one manners book by Kenju Suzuki, *How to Be Considerate of Others*, he instructs women in the intricate art of bowing, including the point of origin, the pacing, the depth, and the solemnity of the bow. In another book, *Tenderness Makes Women Beautiful*, Suzuki tells women to speak softly, to remember to nod during conversations, and to avoid wide strides, crossed legs, and sudden loud laughs that reveal the upper gums "like a horse" (the lower gums are fine).[3]

In contrast, most American advice books of the 1970s and 1980s are books of popular psychotherapy. Instead of morality and manners, they focus on feelings. In these books the authors often tell about their own fears, dependency, or marital troubles before describing their triumph over such adversities. Two American male authors, Connell Cowan and Melvyn Kinder, in their 1985 *Smart Women, Foolish Choices*, for example, advise women on how to recognize hidden dependency needs and how to end an "addiction to love." Only a few best-selling American advice books in this period are morality and manners books, though interestingly many nineteenth-century American advice books fit this description.

Compared with their American counterparts, Japanese advice books devote more space to collective life. For example, the 1970–71 best-selling three-volume *Introduction to Rites of Passage* by Yaeko Shiotsuki, a female writer, appreciatively details the rites, festivals, and celebrations she sadly fears are in decline. She indicates how the families of oldest sons should greet the families of younger sons or daughters to celebrate New Year's Day. She describes how to display dolls—the prince, the princess, three ladies-in-waiting, five male musicians—to celebrate Girl's Day, and how to display warrior dolls with weapons to celebrate Boy's Day. (Boy's Day was renamed "Children's Day" and made into a Japanese national holiday. Girl's Day remains a more minor holiday.) Shiotsuki is not among the most traditional of advice book writers; she proposes modifications in ceremonies—such as the traditional wedding—that leave the ceremonies seeming proper while adapting to modern, urban needs. She wrote her best-selling trilogy of ritual life in the early 1970s, when a full half of Japanese women, normally the main keepers of family ritual life, were in paid work. How was a woman to work eight hours outside the home and celebrate all the rites and festivals as their more leisured mothers and grandmothers had in the past? Shiotsuki offers a compromise, a deal. A woman should keep *appreciating* and *caring about* ritual celebrations, but she may cut back on the actual practice of them. Shiotsuki rejects the total abandonment of rituals or the cynical, detached, or mechanical enactment of them. To the extent that one curtails ritual life, she suggests, one will regret it. On the other hand, Shiotsuki is flexible about how much ritual preparation a busy mother can leave out. By affirming ritual life and avoiding the subject of women's need or desire to work, Shiotsuki tacitly harks back to the model of the upper-middle-class woman of the nineteenth-century Meiji era. In this way she resists the changes in women. But her compromise offers working women a way of bowing in both directions at once—getting along with their mothers-in-law and paying the rent.

Among American advice books, no equivalent to *Introduction to Rites of Passage* exists. Indeed, nothing comes close. The Japanese texts suggest a different organizing principle than do the American ones. Japanese authors write about the past as if it held great weight. They assume that people agree on the *gravitas* they feel inherent in tradition and disagree only on how much is worth preserving. American authors write about the past as if it were light, thin, easy to remember wrongly, malleable. So, not only do Japanese and American traditions differ in content, tradition itself *feels* different.

The Japanese books seem to fall naturally along a continuum of total affirmation of the past, partial incorporation of it, and total rejection of it. In a sense, for the Japanese authors, unlike the American ones, the basic question is how an author faces the past. Kenji Suzuki's *A Story of Womanliness* and Soshitsu Sen's *What a Beautiful Woman* affirm the past while *Introduction to Rites of Passage* adapts tradition to modern circumstance. Such books as *Woman's Capacity Depends on Language* by Kumiko Hirose, a female author, strongly reject tradition, especially certain traditional linguistic practices.

A different organizing principle arises for the American books. The orienting question is not "Do you or don't you accept the past?" but "How light or heavy does the past feel?" The nearest equivalent to *Introduction to Rites of Passage* would be Judith Martin's *Miss Manners' Guide to Rearing Perfect Children*, which is light in tone, and covertly cavalier about "tradition." Another American book on proper dress, *The Women's Dress for Success Book*, is by John Molloy, who describes himself as a "wardrobe engineer," and is based not on tradition, but on a scientific study of male executives' response to various colors, cuts, and textures of women workers' clothes.[4] Even the most traditional of American advice books of the 1970s and 1980s, Marabel

Morgan's 1973 *The Total Woman,* a fundamentalist Christian guide for housewives, feels curiously modern by contrast with its Japanese counterparts. Morgan makes a case for tradition not by claiming that tradition is "true" or "right" but by saying it is useful. So when American advice book writers discuss tradition it is either with humor, irony, or pragmatism.

In addition to the different "feel" of tradition in the two cultures, the content of Japanese advice books is clearly more patriarchal. The books advance virtues of beauty, motherliness, and deference, virtues that would make an exhausted working mother feel guilty. Of the fifteen best-selling Japanese advice books, nine are traditional, if by "traditional" we mean that the author openly opposes women's equality with men. Four are modern, in the sense of advocating women's equality with men, and two are mixtures of both. But of the twenty-eight best-selling American advice books, fifteen are modern, nine are traditional, and four are mixtures of both.

Taken as a whole, the largest group of Japanese advice books (8, or about half) deal with cultural practices and the moral virtues of women that shine through whatever they are doing. A smaller number cover heterosexual love (3), parent-child relations (3), and old age (1). The largest group of American advice books (15, or about half) deal with male-female love and marriage. Far fewer deal with womanly "virtues" (7), and those that do so focus on aspects of character from a psychological and not a moral point of view. As in Japan, about a fifth (6) of the books examine parent-child relations. None of the American best-selling books in this period focuses on old age.

Some traditional books, such as Soshitsu Sen's *What a Beautiful Woman,* extol the virtue of the woman who cares about how she looks. Sen describes a novelist's memory of his mother: "She had six children, so in the morning she was so busy. But none of these children ever saw her in a sloppy nightgown or dirty clothes. This is because she woke up earlier than the children. She opened the small window and under the window she began dissolving her face powder in water, and in one moment she applied the powder, combed her hair, and put on her kimono very neatly. So, in my mind, my mother is always beautiful."[5] In addition to beauty, traditional Japanese advice books stress modesty and deference. In *How to Discipline Girls* Minoru Hamao says mothers should defer to their husbands at all times in front of daughters. "My wife often tells my daughters, 'Since father is coming back soon, let's wait to eat.'" If he is late, Hamao's wife lets the children eat early and waits to eat later with him. "Not only in matters of eating, but in any important matter, my wife gives me the final decision. If my daughter wants money, her mother tells her . . . 'If Daddy says okay, I'll give it to you.'"[6]

Most important, to both her child and her husband, the Japanese wife should be motherly. Indeed, she should do many things for her husband that she does for her child. For example, in *A Story of Womanliness* Kenji

Suzuki proudly describes the solicitous way in which his wife picks out his underwear, socks, shirt, jacket, and handkerchief each day. Suzuki recounts an episode from his childhood when he scraped his knee. He recalls that a small girl approached him and "took out a handkerchief from the sleeve of her kimono, while asking me, 'Kenchan, are you all right?' and bandaged my wound. . . . This was my first experience of the tenderness of girls. . . . I wish my wound still hurt so Sacchan could come to my house." Then he adds, bitterly, "That was when girls were still tender."[7]

Modern Japanese advice books focus on women's independence and on what stands so implacably in the way of it: Japanese culture. Unlike American modern books, which see few cultural obstacles in the way of "having it all," modern advice books in Japan focus on custom. Perhaps the best example of this is the 1985 book *Women's Capacity Depends on Language*, by Kumiko Hirose, a well-known radio announcer at the Japanese Broadcasting Corporation. In her book Hirose describes her struggle to be heard by her listeners when she was paired with a male announcer: "I could not ask questions and guests on the program looked only at the male co-anchor. I became like a *tsuma*, a decoration at the side of the sashimi on the dinner plate."[8] Her struggle led her to call for a change in the way men and women speak Japanese. (We should note that Japanese men and women are taught to speak with different intonations, pitch, and vocabulary, so that women speak a deferential dialect of Japanese. The polite gender-neutral "I" [*Watashi*] usually used by women differs from the more aggressive "I" [*Ore*], used by men.) Hirose calls for a unisex Japanese language so that women may assume equal authority in public life—though she herself feels she can't use male language even at work. Given what seems natural to many women in Japan, and given her desire to bond with her listeners, Hirose feels she can't simply make the private choice to speak in the male language. She believes a change in the larger *culture* has to come first.

In a telling way, Hirose's struggle against Japanese culture and her personal success seem to her perfectly compatible with close motherly and daughterly bonds with family and friends. Hirose talks to her radio listeners as to friends and family, creating in this way a mock kin system. When she falls ill, fans write in. When they fall sick, she writes or sends gifts. She struggles against being a decorative *tsuma* in the male world of Japanese radio, but she does not strike out "on her own" as American advice books typically recommend. On the radio, she takes the role of a young woman receiving encouragement from an older woman. For example, when she was on the verge of quitting her Saturday afternoon program, Hirose recounts: "The most important reason I didn't quit was that I received a card from a middle-aged woman who said, 'When I was in the hospital I was deeply comforted to listen to you on the radio.' For me, who had almost become neurotic [over her struggle with male co-workers at the radio station], her words were like rays of sun." Again, she says of her listeners, "Your warmth helped heal me from my isolation and loneliness, so I will never let you feel lonely and isolated."[9]

Hirose also describes how she tried to gain support for her struggle at work from her skeptical mother-in-law. Seeing how hard she works, Hirose tells us, her mother encouraged Hirose to invite her mother-in-law to observe her life on the radio set and so appreciate her work. Hirose does not write about her family and friends as if they were incompatible with her fierce battle to win equality at work. She assumes they go together. But perhaps that calmly held assumption, along with the cultural space it seems to presume, is the basic advice here.

A few modern Japanese advice books focus on how to fit in work with childrearing. Kingsley Ward in *Letters of a Business Man to His Daughter,* the best-selling Japanese translation of a Canadian author, describes how his wife (though not he) took a leave from a high-powered executive job, when the children were small, to become a free-lance writer. He also tells about how she later became famous as a screenwriter for children's television programs. She adapted to her children's needs *and* she was a success.

Other modern books focus on a more active role for fathers. Kingsley Ward calls on young fathers to change diapers, drive children to the doctor, wash dishes, and shop, all in good spirit.[10] In Uzo Kayama's 1981 *This Love Forever: Yakadaisho's Diary of Childrearing,* the author, a famous actor who plays a daring adventurer, describes changing diapers at 3 A.M., throwing a ball, and playing train with his four tots. Though his wife, a homemaker, does more at home than he, his model is an advance over the stereotype of the Japanese salary man who, as the saying goes, comes home, sits down, and utters three words, "Dinner, bath, sleep." Kayama's book is similar to Bill Cosby's 1987 American best-seller, *Fatherhood.* Both are biographies of male media stars married to homemakers, and both celebrate active fathering from the safe distance of a primary breadwinner role.

There may be good news and bad in all this for the working mother in Japan. On one hand, tradition runs stronger there. In the eyes of most conservative Japanese advice book writers, the mother who goes out to work, even if she must, risks losing her womanliness, motherliness, and possibly her good manners. On the other hand, Hirose gives social support to her family and community and gratefully receives support too.

AMERICAN TRADITIONS: "HONK IF YOU LOVE JESUS"

In contrast to traditional advice books in Japan, traditional American books make light of tradition. For example, Dr. James Dobson's *Parenting Isn't for*

Cowards offers up a humorous poem about modern times. Quoting a poem, "Where Have All the Grandmas Gone?" he says:

> In the dim and distant past,
> When life's tempo wasn't fast
> Grandma used to rock and knit,
> Crochet, chat and baby-sit . . .
> But today she's in the gym,
> Exercising to keep slim,
> She's off touring with the bunch,
> Or taking clients out to lunch.[11]

Indeed, in contrast to best-selling Japanese traditionalists who strike a serious, nostalgic, or scolding tone, many best-selling American traditionalists are humorists. Erma Bombeck's three best-selling books, *Motherhood: The Second Oldest Profession, Aunt Erma's Cope Book,* and *The Grass Is Always Greener over the Septic Tank,* are not about the perfect, beautiful, motherly housewife, but about her comic opposite. Bombeck makes fun of being unbeautiful, noting that every time she sees her neck in a mirror, she's reminded that she hasn't made chicken soup in a while. She makes fun of being deferential to her husband. When her husband asks her if she married him because she loved him or because he could repair broken household appliances, she stares back in silence. Finally he says, "Okay, I'll fix the broken sink." She even makes fun of motherliness. At one point she writes in her diary, "I'm terribly concerned about what's his name." At another point she complains that "the high point of my day is taking knots out of shoestrings—with my teeth—that a kid has wet on all day long." When, after moving to the suburbs to raise their family, her husband questions why she needs her own car, she makes fun of the isolation of the suburban housewife, explaining: "I'll be able to go to the store, join a bowling league, have lunch downtown with the girls, volunteer. . . . I want to see the big, outside world. . . . I want to rotate my tires with the rest of the girls. Don't you understand? I want to honk if I love Jesus!"[12] Bombeck thus embraces the role of suburban homemaker not through serious nostalgia—as in the Japanese analogue—but by making fun of the role she embraces. Similarly, in *Love and Marriage,* Bill Cosby notes that he is the man of the house but that his wife, Camille, has "the keys to the house."[13] Among Japanese books, humor is more often located at the modern end of the continuum, as in Shusaku Endo's *Lazy Man's Guide to Love,* not at the more anxious traditional end of it.

Related to humor is the theme of fun. Traditional American advice books, like those by Morgan, Bombeck, and Cosby, make the case that traditionalism is good, not—as in Japan—because it is *right,* but because it is *fun.* Thus, the deepest rationale for tradition is not what it stands for in some objective sense, but how it feels.

Best-selling modern American advice books welcome the working mother. They prepare an emotional path for her. If the traditional American books assume an air of exchanging funny stories in the living room after dinner, the modern books put the reader on the psychoanalyst's couch for a serious review of her "issues." Often focused on troubles with men, books such as Cowan and Kinder's *Smart Women, Foolish Choices* or Robin Norwood's *Women Who Love Too Much* devote their serious tone not to reverence for the past but to a healing of the modern heart.

American modern advice books also give less honor, if not less attention, to the social support of family, friends, and co-workers. There is no analogue among the progressive American advice books to Kumiko Hirose's invitation to her mother-in-law to come and watch her in the studio. There is much less grateful mention of a mother or good friend. From time to time, American advice books refer to the support of a friend or a relative, but these are offered in passing, without appreciative mention of their helpfulness.

While Hirose, the Japanese newscaster, focuses on a moment during which she takes courage from an older female fan, in the American text the spotlight is on a heroic woman on her own. In Japanese advice books social bonds help a person achieve her goals; in American advice books social bonds seem to *get in the way*. Both American and Japanese advice book writers seem to assume that a woman needs cultural room to attain equality with men. But the American authors seem to assume she gets that room by going it alone. Japanese authors more often focus on the potential help to be found in allies within the family and community.

In addition to the different value placed on social attachments, there is a difference in the object of attachment. Of all American advice books, none is devoted exclusively to the topic of the elderly, and in most the elderly are mentioned little if at all. When old age is mentioned—as it is, for example, in Helen Gurley Brown's *Having It All*—it is not as an occasion to help others but as an aspect of self to avoid and disguise. In the Japanese best-seller *How to Grow Old Together,* Hajame Mizuno addresses the conflict between women's paid work outside the home and care of the elderly. He suggests that the elderly themselves should develop interests of their own. In addition, Mizuno notes that as they retire, men will have to learn to be more considerate of their wives: "It is said if you don't use your brain when you're old, the brain ages faster. If you stay at home without doing anything and say to your wife, 'Give me tobacco. Give me a light. Give me my newspapers'— if you act like this—your brain will age very fast and the final destination will be senility."[14] A Japanese popular saying about retired salary men is "You stick to your wife like wet fallen leaves to feet." Modern Japanese advice books say in essence, "Get your own tobacco, and help around the house." In America, as in Japan, it is mainly women who care for the elderly. But by avoiding the topic of old age, American advice books also avoid a basic problem for working mothers, and so fail to address the policies and workplace reforms they would need to combine work with care.

American advice books, modern and traditional alike, are generally silent about siblings, aunts, uncles, cousins, parents-in-law, neighbors, fellow congregants. They focus instead on one central man in a woman's life, how to find him, repair relations with him, and keep him. Perhaps that's because in America that one man has now become the emotional equivalent of a village. Considered as a whole, American advice books suggest two sides of American individualism. The good side of American individualism allows American women the cultural room to benefit from the opportunities of advanced capitalism. But the bad side leads Americans to see social support as entanglement and to stress individual over social solutions to its problems.

COMPARING CULTURAL STRETCH: CONTENT AND TONE

Japanese advice books reflect a far wider range of standpoints on the role of women than do their American counterparts. At the conservative extreme is *How to Discipline Girls,* by Minoru Hamao, the former tutor of the emperor and two princes. Hamao advises that "mothers should show respect for their husband's higher authority under all circumstances."[15] At the other extreme Kumiko Hirose, the radio announcer, denounces the authority differential built into male and female styles of speech. Among American advice books the extremes are much closer together. The emperor's former tutor and the radio announcer reflect a wider cultural stretch than, say, that between James Dobson's *Parenting Isn't for Cowards* and Cowan and Kinder's *Smart Women, Foolish Choices.* Paradoxically, advice books in the more culturally homogeneous Japan seem to express a wider range of viewpoints than those in the heterogeneous United States.

One possible reason for this may be that the 1970s and 1980s brought faster changes in Japan than they did in the United States, creating a wider gap between old and new. The range in tones of authority is also far wider among the Japanese than among the American advice books. Some authors write with a tone of stern command, as if to say, "I have the unquestioned right to tell you what to do." The advice of the emperor's former tutor, for example, takes the form of a hundred commands ("You should . . . ," "You should not . . ."). The rules are absolute; they do not depend on context. Hamao poses himself as the sole arbiter of the rules. In a preface to *How to Discipline Girls,* he notes, "This is for parents who raise girls and for young women about to marry and for women students. I want these people to read my book, and I also want critiques from teachers or other educators."[16] He invites no critiques from the girls themselves.

Other Japanese authors seem to write in the spirit of an older sister: "Why don't you try this? It might work." This range of tones is probably also due to the greater difference, in Japan, between the way female and male authors— at least conservative older males—grip authority. Between the early 1970s and the late 1980s, the gender gap in style of giving advice closed somewhat, leaving three types of voice—the old male authoritarian voice, the new male more democratic voice, and the new female democratic voice. In the American books, the old male authoritarian voice was missing.

Although most of the traditional Japanese books were written by men, it is not traditionalism that predicts the authoritarian tone. It's being male. A traditional *female* author, Yaeko Shiotsuki, author of *Introduction to Rites of Passage* and grand master of the Japanese tea ceremony, begins modestly: "When the editor encouraged me to write this book, I worried about my limited ability to write, but I decided to accept this opportunity and by consulting other professionals in the field, I was able to finally finish it."[17]

Feminist female Japanese authors such as Fumi Saimon and Kumiko Hirose adopt a more assertive but also more self-revealing, equalizing, and sisterly tone that makes them more like American female—and even American male—authors. For example, Saimon, a female humorist, ends her *Art of Loving*:

> Why could I write of love? . . . If a person is born a genius and can solve difficult equations at a glance and he writes about his experience passing an entrance exam for Tokyo University, then what use is it for most people? It's the same with love. If a woman just by walking down the street is approached by men who want to ask her to go to bed, or gets proposals from the very rich, or is sent words of love by artists, and writes about her experiences of love, this is useless to most girls (though it's very interesting just as a story). The regular person should be satisfied with falling in love once or twice in a life. . . . I myself have fallen in love from the bottom of my heart once or twice. And these are the treasures of my life. If you can experience true love, once or twice in life, this is a big success for the average person.[18]

American women authors do not differ much in tone from male authors. This is because the male authors base their authority, as women authors do, on professional expertise and personal experience. They also often appeal to the reader's desire to find an effective way of personally relating to members of the opposite sex and don't appeal to her desire to be morally correct. Instead of commanding, "You should, or you should not . . ." in *Smart Women, Foolish Choices*, Cowan and Kinder say, "Perhaps you are wondering who we are, and why we think we have something to say to smart women about their relationships with men. We are clinical psychologists who maintain individual practices of psychotherapy. . . . As men, we believe we understand how other men think, feel and react. We're going to tell you about strategies that work with men and . . . we will reveal insights and strategies that we hope will convince you that what now may appear to be a stand off between the sexes can instead be your opportunity to claim delightful, fulfilling experiences with men."[19] In making something as personal as their sex relevant to the credibility of their advice, Cowan and Kinder resemble such female writers as Robin Norwood (*Women Who Love Too Much*) or Susan Forward and Joan Torres (*Men Who Hate Women and the Women Who Love Them*).

Both sets of books offer a fascinating window onto a variety of cultural assumptions about the cultural room women have to live modern lives. Japanese advice books define cultural room in terms of what is virtuous or not virtuous (morality) or in terms of what are good or bad manners. American advice books define cultural room in terms of what one does or does not authentically feel.

In both cultures, beliefs and practices are the stuff of cultural collective bargaining. Advice books tell us what modernizing women and their allies and traditional men and their allies each bring to the imaginary cultural bargaining table. In this view, some customs are tools in the hands of those who uphold patriarchy. Other customs are tools in the hands of those pressing for equality. Some are useful to both or neither. Customs held lightly— for example, with humor—are worth less in tradeoffs than customs held sacred. The affirmation of a challenge to the prevailing culture in books such as these is part of a quiet struggle to establish favorable cultural terms for the working mother.

For Japanese women, the problem is to promote a gender revolution. To do this, they will have to challenge gender divisions that run deep. Japan's more communal ethos, we argue, is also partly a problem for Japanese working mothers, since it is mainly women who keep up the rituals that maintain this ethos. On the other hand, their more collective orientation helps protect Japanese women from falling into the trap of a stalled revolution in which women are individually emancipated in a society that leaves each woman to cope on her own. For American women, the problem is mainly getting out of a stall in the revolution, and for that they need a more communal approach than any of these do-it-yourself American books provide. Paradoxically, in order to start a gender revolution we need a "light" culture that gives women cultural room to move around, but in order to complete that revolution, we need to draw on the "heavier" culture of which social support is made.

Part Two

A FEELINGFUL SELF

5 THE CAPACITY TO FEEL

An image on the movie screen, a passage in a book, the look in an eye can move us deeply. But what in us is moved? How does culture help do the moving? How do sociologists understand the role culture plays? In this essay I look at what sociologists and psychoanalysts have to say before proposing in this and the following four essays a sociological way of seeing feeling.

By "emotion," I should say, I mean the awareness of bodily cooperation with an idea, thought, or attitude and the label attached to that awareness. By "feeling," I mean a milder emotion. So very basic are emotion and feeling to our social lives that it is remarkable how little attention sociologists have paid to them. Why would that be? It's not because the people we study do not take as real the "fact" that they feel. Nor is it because a person's job, sex, age, ethnic background, or religious experience is known to be unrelated to how he or she feels in certain situations. It is not, in other words, because we lack evidence. And it is not because sociologists in their work have completely ignored how actors feel. Ethnography, experimental social psychology, and qualitative sociology generally touch on the concepts of emotion and feeling in the process of explaining why people do what they do and think what they think. What we haven't done is put feelings front and center and think out a sociological way of seeing them.

Perhaps the main reason why not is that, as sociologists, we are members of the same society as the people we study. We share their feelings and values. Their culture divides thinking from feeling and defines thinking—cognition, intellect—as superior to feeling, and so does ours. Significantly the terms "emotional" and "sentimental" have come to connote excessive or degenerate forms of feeling. Through the prism of our rationalist culture, then, we are led to see emotion as an impediment to getting things done and to seeing the world as it really is.

But even if we do discredit emotion as a dimension of experience—and I do not—why would sociologists ignore it when they study plenty of other discredited things?[1] I believe the answer lies in the discipline's attempt to be recognized as a "real science," an attempt dating back to the naïve aspiration of Auguste Comte, the so-called father of sociology, to make sociology a social physics. For this misguided quest permits us to study only the most objective and measurable aspects of social life. This coincides with the values of the traditional "male" culture, to which academic women have, by exclusion, been somewhat less exposed. But if we are to bring sociology closer to reality, we will do it very poorly if we close an eye to feeling. We must open the other eye and think about what we see.

THREE IMAGES OF SELF

Much of social science seems to be based on two images of the self, which, like all such images, focus attention on certain aspects of life and away from others. The first image is of the *conscious, cognitive self*. According to this image, we consciously want something (e.g., money or status) and consciously calculate the merits of various means of getting it. For example, Erving Goffman takes us into the world of the presented self, and more particularly into the world of rational calculations that lead us to make each presentation. It is a world of Everyman as Con Man, a world of impressions managed and manipulated toward the end of an advantageous self-portrait. Consider Goffman's quote from Willard Waller: "It has been reported by many observers that a girl who is called to the telephone in the dormitories will often allow herself to be called several times, in order to give all the other girls ample opportunity to hear her paged."[2] Goffman shows us how much more we calculate than we think we do, but he neglects how much more we also *feel* in socially arranged ways than we think we do. We are not shown, for example, how a socially induced feeling, like anxiety or fear, may lead a girl in the dorm to compulsively calculate her advantages. Such calculation is surely not a constant feature of the consciousness of everyone. Outsiders and subordinates may be more concerned about looking, smiling, or talking in just the right way than are kings and queens, whose presentation of self rests peacefully upon unquestioned hereditary title.

Like many images, this one is not wrong, but it is only partly useful in its choice of what to highlight. It implies that we clearly know what we want, and it emphasizes the *having* of a goal (not the doubt or triumph attached to it) and the *use* of a means (not the guilt, apprehension, or glee attached to its use). Those who posit a model of a rational self generally don't deny that actors feel. But they imply that little is lost when feelings are ignored or tidily bunched under the terms "ends" and "means."

The second image, indebted to Sigmund Freud, is that of the *unconscious, emotional self*. Here we are guided by unconscious motivations and do or think things whose meanings are better understood by experts than ourselves. The self is said to be "driven" or "prompted" by a limited number of "instincts," "impulses," or "needs" to achieve, affiliate, or do any number of things that surface merely as ends or means. Philip Slater, for example, explores the world of unconscious affect, focusing on the subterranean channels through which energy emerges into behavior, nearly bypassing the actor's consciousness of feeling altogether.[3]

This image, like that of the conscious cognitive actor, does not *deny* affective consciousness. Images deny nothing. Rather a focus on conscious thinking, as with Goffman, and a focus on unconscious promptings, as with Freud and Slater, allow conscious feeling to fall into a no-man's-land in between. So we need a third image—that of the *sentient self,* a *self that is capable of feelings and aware of being so.* More than a bloodless calculator or blind expresser of uncontrolled emotions, the sentient self is aware of feeling as well as of the many cultural guideposts that shape it. In everyday life we are often aware of indicating to ourselves our subjective states ("I feel anxious today"), which in turn stand out against a taken-for-granted background stream of experience ("I'm not usually this anxious"). Further, we select and apply to these states a variety of labels (e.g., anxiety, malaise, uptightness) from among the emotion vocabularies available to us at a given time and place in the world.

Every sociological study focuses on a range of variation. In the study of the sentient self, we distinguish between one and another emotional state given the emotional vocabulary we have at hand. We explore what we *expect* to feel and *wanted* to feel. With clinical insight, we sometimes link these to unconscious goings-on beneath the conscious tip of the iceberg.

But we keep an eye out for patterns in the very terms we apply to emotional states and the "standing," so to speak, of each term. We can describe ourselves as "apathetic." But how bad is it to be apathetic? Is it always a problem? Is it ever normal or average? As Gordon Allport and H. S. Odbert observe, certain terms came into use in English only after the eighteenth century (e.g., depression, ennui, chagrin, apathy), and the modern sense of some older terms has become more subjective (e.g., constraint, embarrassment, disappointment). Such labels are not, as they note, "univocal symbols corresponding through the ages to fixed varieties of human disposition."[4] In addition, feelings—as people describe them to themselves and others—may vary in social ways. Just as certain behaviors (e.g., suicide, homicide, delinquency) are unevenly distributed across layers of society and the stream of time, so too we need to ask whether and why the various emotions, such as joy or depression, unfold in ways that reflect larger social patterns.

But are we not caught in a peculiar embarrassment by the elusiveness of our subject matter? For one thing, feelings relate to acts in many ways. So feelings are by no means a neat, clear predictor of actions. For example, William Kephart asked college students, "If a boy or girl had all the other qualities you desire, would you marry this person if you were not in love with him/her?" A total of 64 percent of the men, but only 24 percent of the women, said "no." For men and women, feeling in love appears to have a different tie to the *act* of marrying.[5]

There is another question, too: What if we think we are in love at one point, but later look back and declare that we were just infatuated? Or what if we think we're in love, but the beloved and our therapist don't agree? All this is no reason to flee to other questions that rest on more solid sociological ground. *This is sociological ground.* It's as solid as sociological ground ever really gets. If we want to pretend that we know what the actor's emotion "really is" (e.g., "It's really depression") and call what a person thinks it is "bias" ("I'm tired"), then part of our intellectual domain must still be precisely this "bias." For in ridding ourselves of the actor's own codification of feeling, and of his or her ignorance or linguistic habits, we rid ourselves of part of what is social about emotion. We eliminate from the start what we can then claim we do not find, a sociology of feeling and emotion. We are then left with inferences about instinct or motivation on one side and cognition on the other, because we haven't posed our question in a way that would lead to anything else.

If we start instead with the idea of a self capable of feeling, a sentient self, we then take an interest in a person's *own* definition of his or her feeling. We learn from this how the individual uses an "emotion vocabulary" and what social situations or rules call feelings forth or tuck them under. The image of a sentient self does not imply that there are no unconscious forces leading us to feel as we do. It does not imply that being emotional or emotionless in certain situations is "good" or "bad," "sick" or "healthy." It is often "rational," in the larger sense of being adaptive, to feel and very maladaptive not to feel. The business executive who felt terror at the sight, smell, or word of nearby smoke in the nearby World Trade Center and fled ended up better off than co-workers who tragically didn't feel afraid enough.

In *The Theory of Social and Economic Organization* Weber posits a model of social action based on a misguided set of categories—emotion-free rational action and emotional irrational action.[6] Here Weber confuses irrationality as it refers to thinking and doing with irrationality as it refers to feeling. He implies that emotion and feeling are not positively required for individuals both to really grasp what's going on and to pursue a rational course of action. He implies, too, that institutions don't need people who listen well to their feelings and those of others in order to adapt to their environment and act rationally. Weber thought emotions important, and deplored a "rationalistic bias" that might grow out of what he meant merely as a methodological device. But I do not get the sense that he saw how very necessary emotions were to making things run. Take his example of a theoretically posited course of rational action on the stock market. He treats deviations from rational behavior as something the sociologist might explain in terms of "irrational emotions" (e.g., panic). But, in the realm of emotion, the difference between the normal stock market and the sudden depression in stocks is the difference between stockbrokers in a state of elation and stockbrokers in a state of despair. It is highly questionable whether emotion enters into the life of stockbrokers only when there is panic or that emotion makes people act only in irrational ways.

Surely emotion and sentiment are active ingredients in *rational behavior* as well. A normal day at the stock market would amply show that feelings of excitement, anxiety, or glee are all part of a good, rational day's work. Weber mistakes actual emotionlessness for the prevailing norm of affective neutrality we suppose stockbrokers to have adopted for themselves. The image of the sentient self, on the other hand, guides our eye not only to exceptional waves of emotion, as in stock market panics, religious trances, and riotous crowds, but also to *normal emotions* in the office, factory, school, and home.

THINKING ABOUT FEELING

We need a sociological way of understanding emotion. The thinking we need is scattered around the social sciences and tucked into various approaches to the links between social structure and emotion.[7] In the first approach (associated with the image of the conscious, cognitive self), the social context and thinking about emotion are linked, but a focus on conscious feeling is missing. In the second approach (associated with the image of the unconscious self), unconscious emotional phenomena and social structure are linked but again conscious feeling is omitted. In the third approach, the relation between sentience and its labels is analyzed, but the social context disappears from view.[8]

The first approach to the sociology of emotion is to study what and how people *think* about emotion and feeling. This is the concern of attribution theorists who study actors' ideas about the causes of behavior.[9] Experimental psychologists have studied how actors use these ideas in their attributions of causality. The anthropologist Robert Levy also exemplifies this focus. Among Tahitians, he notes, the emotional response to the loss of someone dear is attributed to "illness." They link romantic love with extreme jealousy and consider both "crazy"—abnormal and bad.[10] In a somewhat related way Alan Blum and Peter McHugh focus not on emotion but on motive. A motive is, for them, a *way of conceiving of social action*. To the radical ethnomethodologist, the "way of conceiving of social action" is no small matter, since they believe that's all social action is.[11] Even if we accept this view of social action, we need to know the actor's view of his or her inner affective life—sentience—in order to learn the assumptions on which he or she is basing explanations for things. For example, in the study of sex roles it would be interesting to explore sex differences in the motives people give for why they do what they do. "I quit graduate school because I fell in love with your father" was, through the 1960s, a common and acceptable thing for a middle-class woman to say, while its counterpart for men ("I quit graduate school because I fell in love with your mother") was not. Today a woman saying this would be questioned, doubted, and put on the spot, and so would a man.

The second approach, corresponding to the unconscious emotional self, takes us to Freud and the applications of his thought to social science. While work by such diverse theorists as John Dollard, John Seeley, Philip Slater, Geoffrey Gorer, Margaret Mead, Erik Erikson, and Bronislaw Malinowski provides enriching integrations of what are—or were—fairly differentiated fields (psychoanalysis and sociology, say), it still often glosses over the sentient self.[12] This results in studies with a simultaneous focus on the unconscious and the social, with conscious feeling edged out now by two sides rather than one. Dollard, for example, uses the emotion word "frustration" to refer to observable *behavior* resulting from situations in which expected acts are prevented from occurring.[13] Between inducing situation and consequent behavior, Dollard gives only a casual glance at the individual's conscious experience of frustration, and at her or his response to that experience. The "it" of frustration that gets displaced from one issue to another, the "it" that is socially caused and in turn causes behavior, remains mysteriously out of view. We learn more from Dollard on the situational side than on the response side. His research nonetheless suggests how aggression—once we make clear what it *feels* like to the aggressive person—can be "displaced." (This is the central concern of the section of his essay called "Feeling and the Politics of Aim" and of the essay "Love and Gold" in part 4.)

The third approach, based on the image of the sentient self, leads us to map the inner world of feeling against the cultural world of labels. This is done either by holding experience constant and examining variations in labeling, or by holding labels constant and examining variation in experience, or by looking at the interrelationship, holding neither constant.[14] An example of the last approach is Robert Levy's study of what he called transschematic experience and cultural schema among Tahitians. In a list of 301 words describing feeling in the missionary dictionary, 47 referred to angry feelings and 27 to pleasurable states. To the Western eye, some feelings (e.g., anger, shame, fear) were well discriminated, while others (e.g., loneliness, depression, guilt) were poorly discriminated.

In the study of sex differences we might determine whether and how the same labels refer to different experiences for men and women. For example, Kephart found that college women reported more "infatuations" than did college men. He reasoned that for women looking back, "love affairs are related to infatuations . . . and are remembered merely as passing fancies."[15]

Because women are the upholders of the monogamous ideal, he reasoned, they tend to *relabel* or *re-remember* past love as "mere infatuation."

Associated, then, with the first image of the conscious cognitive self and the second image of the unconscious emotional self, we have two lines of inquiry that tend to bypass conscious feeling. But starting from an image of the sentient self, we have a line of inquiry that relates feelings to a rich array of cultural understanding of them. We can develop this line of inquiry in the direction of depth psychology (drawing from Dollard, Erikson, Freud, and Chodorow) and in a cognitive direction (drawing from Blum and McHugh). Sociologists have also pointed to the social causes and consequences of a great variety of emotions and sentiments.[16] On the causal side, authors such as the historian Herbert Moller and the philosopher C. S. Lewis in their studies of love deal with the grand historical picture, while others, such as Edward Gross and Anthony Stone in their study of embarrassment, deal with the immediate interactional setting.[17] On the consequence side, some writers such as the anthropologist George Foster in his classic study of envy analyze the customs and institutions that function to avert envy by devaluing, hiding, or symbolically sharing the envied object.[18] For Foster, inequality naturally causes envy, which is then averted through various social customs. In an equally classic essay on jealousy, Kingsley Davis questions the naturalness of sexual jealousy. Rejecting the position of the family historian Edward Westermarck, that adultery "naturally" arouses jealousy, which in turn causes monogamy, Davis suggests that the cause of jealousy lies in the expectations set up by the institution of monogamy, which then make adultery arouse jealousy. He focuses on the jealousy of men over their wives, who are conceived of as property. This property can be borrowed or lent without jealousy, as occurs in some traditional societies. It is only when their property is stolen or trespassed upon that men get jealous.[19]

Thus, feelings take on their meaning and full character only in relation to a specific time and place in the world. And each context has a normative, an expressive, and a political dimension.

The normative dimension of a context refers to our sense of what feels appropriate or right. It points our attention to the relation between feeling and feeling rules. So we might say, "This situation makes me happy, but I shouldn't feel this happy." Both feelings and feeling rules are socially induced, as is the potential conflict between the two. The expressive dimension of any context has to do with the relation between a person's feelings and other people's understanding of and response to those feelings, that is, with the issue of communication. Here we're dealing not with the wrongness of feelings, but with the inferred truth or falseness of them. The political dimension concerns the relation between a person's feelings and the target of those feelings. It focuses on the aiming of affect at those higher or lower, more or less powerful, than oneself. The first dimension tells us about judgments on feeling, the second about communication of feeling, and the third about the aiming of feeling. It is the image of the sentient self that draws our eye to these three aspects of feelings.

Feeling rules define what we imagine we should and shouldn't feel and would like to feel over a range of circumstances; they show how we judge feeling. Feeling rules differ from expression rules. A feeling rule governs how we feel whereas an expression rule governs how we express feeling. We can think of feeling rules as the underside of framing rules—rules governing how it is we see situations. Together, framing and feeling determine how it is we deeply *grasp* the situation before us. Feeling rules are also often deeply internalized, though this is obviously less the case for children, the insane, and the traumatized than for normal, emotionally healthy adults.

I explore feeling rules in the next essay ("Working on Feeling"), but let me flesh out the general idea here. When we judge a feeling as inappropriate, we actually apply one of three measuring rods we can see as *types* of appropriateness: (a) *clinical* appropriateness refers to what is expectable for normal, healthy persons (the person may think her/his anger "healthy" even if it's morally wrong); (b) *moral* appropriateness refers to what is morally legitimate (the person can get furious at a helpless child, but this may be morally inappropriate); (c) *social-situational* appropriateness refers to what is called for by the norms specific to the situation (e.g., to feel effervescent at a party). These three types of appropriateness correspond to the roles of the clinician, the minister, and the etiquette expert, and in practice these three senses of the term often—though not always—reinforce or fuse with each other.

Let's take the example of envy, the feeling of wanting what another has. Societies generate envy when they create winners and losers, and devalue losers for being losers.[20] While the moral injunction against envy applies to winners and losers alike, envy is unequally distributed among winners and losers. More of those who feel they are losers or think others think they are losers feel envy. So the socially induced feeling ("I envy you") and the socially established rule ("I shouldn't envy you") are at odds. This disjuncture might be strongest for the religious poor (for whom both envy and the prohibition against it are fostered) and weakest for the irreverent rich (for whom both might be less). I say "might" because the ultimate situation is always unique to the individual.[21]

The discrepancy between socially induced feelings of envy and envy rules may result in a number of social customs and institutional arrangements which handle this discrepancy. The anthropologist George Foster suggests that the experience of envy is a result of (a) notions about the limited or unlimited supply of desired "goods" (money, love, honor, security), (b) their distribution, and (c) the principle of equivalence (the tendency to equalize goods).[22] He suggests several social devices that deal with envy—

concealing or denying possession of that which is coveted and truly or symbolically sharing it. The great and recently increased extremes of wealth in the United States, the ethic of "equal opportunity," and individualism together create a general susceptibility to envy. Surely, the widespread popularity of TV game shows and "marry a millionaire" shows—programs that convey the idea "someone like me can get rich quick"—are a form of symbolic sharing. But how, we can wonder, do individuals pick up where culture leaves off?

Just as feelings are linked to rules in a normative context, so feelings are linked to expressions in a context of expression. Just as we appraise our experience in a context of rules, so too do we judge the emotional expressions of others in an expression context. In mapping rule to feeling, the actor judges whether a feeling is appropriate in the clinical, moral, or situational sense. In mapping *expression* to feeling, we judge whether the expression is true or false, partly or fully meant. We try to tell whether it corresponds to a "real" subjective experience. When I smile at you, I offer a sign of my inner feeling: say, liking. When you see me smile, in a flash, you make an inference, correct or not ("Does she really like me or is she just being polite? Is this expression fake or real?"). Quite apart from the judgment about the appropriateness of my liking or yours, there is the task of inferring from my smile what it is I really feel.

The many small decisions that lead us to discount or take seriously an expression rest on a variety of factors: our style of interpreting, our knowledge of another's smiling habits, our knowledge of events prior to the encounter, and so on. These elements also operate within a larger social context in which some expressions are by custom scarce and others abundant. The general "market" of expressions thus influences the value we impute to a particular smile as well as the probability of perceiving it as true or false.

We can see emotional expressions as a medium of exchange. The translation between expression and experience can be seen as analogous to the translation between a paper dollar bill and what it symbolizes.[23] Like paper money, many smiles and frowns are in circulation. They are symbolic with reference to certain taken-for-granted agreements as to which gesture goes with which meaning in which context. Like money, expressions work on a basis of trust that this expression (e.g., a clenched fist) corresponds to that range of inner experience (e.g., anger, exuberant bravado). So our trust in a gesture rests on a public trust in the general validity of such expressions, their general link to inner experience.

The more bureaucratized our society, the more standardized, commodified, and depersonalized are public displays of feeling, and the more discounting we do. The "have a nice day" buttons, the waiter's "hope you enjoy your meal," the receptionist's smile—all these are so abundant that we almost cease to imagine that they correspond to anything real. Still, such commercialized niceness is enormously important as a form of needed reassurance that in the midst of many strangers we are safely out of harm's way. Like the arable soil on the earth, public goodwill is life-sustaining, needs maintenance, and is vulnerable to erosion.

In a commercialized society, positive expression is more "inflated" than expression, say, of envy, anger, or resentment. There are more phony dollars in circulation. So a slight expression of anger is trusted to correspond to felt anger in a way not generally true for an expression of liking. Expressions of anger are more "serious" and more likely to be sensed as "true."[24]

Within the general market of expressions, there are particular markets associated with regional subpopulations or strata. Within the expression market for anger in southern Italy, for example, anger is "cheaper" than it is among Maine Yankees.[25] Moreover, sex-role socialization may render anger expressions more scarce and "serious" for women than for men. Daphne Bugental and her coauthors show that, compared with men, women are more likely to smile while angry or frustrated.[26] In his study of facial expressions, the psychologist Paul Eckman found women more likely to mask (quickly cover up) anger, while men more often mask fear.[27] A study of affect display in children's stories might show girls to be portrayed as more expressive of fear than of anger, while for boys the opposite is probably true. In any case, the translation from outer expression to inner feeling and vice versa is set against different expectations about anger expression in women from those for men.

Feelings are linked not only to rules (in normative contexts) and to expressions (in expression contexts), but also to sanctions (in political contexts). Here we can explore the relation between power[28] and sanction, on one hand, and the target of feeling and expression, on the other. Whereas the first two levels deal with conscious feeling and thought (the sentient and cognitive self), this third level deals with what is often unconscious feeling.

The relation between sanction and feeling varies for different feelings. Insofar as anger is deflected at all from its "rightful" target, for example, it tends to be deflected "down" into relative power vacuums. So anger is most likely to be aimed at people with less power and least likely to be aimed at people with more power. Anger runs in channels of least resistance. The pattern is clearest in the case of the *expression* of anger, but I think in a milder way it is there also for the very experience of anger.

This general pattern parallels the hierarchy of joking observed by Rose Coser. Analyzing conversations in which humor occurred during three months of staff meetings at a mental hospital, Coser concluded, "Those who were of higher status positions more frequently took the initiative to use humor. More significant, still, the butt of the joke, if he was present, was never in a higher authority position than the initiator."[29] Insofar as jokes with a "butt" are a benign cover for hostility, they reflect the pattern in this way.

Contrariwise, more positive feelings tend to run up the sociopolitical hill (e.g., kissing the hand of the pope, bowing before the queen, shaking hands with the president). Under the governance of socially organized fear, there is both the downward tendency of negative feelings and the upward tendency of positive ones toward powerful parental figures.[30] *When deflected*, anger and resentment tend to get deflected down. But, needless to say, not all anger is deflected down. Revolutions erupt. Ideologies that challenge the elite and ignite the masses grab hold. Still, much about American culture, at least, trains our channels of identification up and our disdain and anger down. And the powerful can buffer themselves (via doormen and secretaries) against *exposure* to hostility, a buffer that powerless people less often enjoy. While anger can be aimed up, and the rule against envy suspended, as in the case of revolution, it is astonishing how rarely this has occurred in the United States.[31] Here among the dispossessed the emotional aspect of "false-consciousness"—*feeling* content with an unjustly dealt fate—is more the rule than the exception. Why? How does the mass media or the political apparatus "organize" and channel discontent and inhibit challenge? Surely we have to understand the politics of aim to know.

This up- and downstream pattern has enormous consequences for the emotional worlds we inhabit. Those near the bottom of power hierarchies tend to bear a disproportionate amount of displaced anger. A woman, for example, receives not only her husband's frustration displaced from the office to home, but also the anger of other women who are similarly displaced upon. If a woman takes her anger down (to children) and occasionally across (to other women), she, by the same token, becomes the less powerful target of both men's and women's anger. The least powerful become the targets of a wide variety of hostility. In a sense, they become the *complaint clerks of society*. For those on the bottom rungs of the political ladder, the world more often feels a *hostile* place.

Contrariwise, powerful people not only get a disproportionate amount of money and prestige, they also enjoy more emotional rewards. For the dwellers at the top, the world more often feels like a *benign* place. The more hierarchies one is at the top of (class, race, gender), the more this is probably true. One reason people want power, honor, and glory is precisely because they want protection from hostility and exposure to awe and liking. Thus, powerful and powerless people enjoy different emotional as well as social and physical worlds.

All this has implications for the study of gender. We might quite seriously examine the proverbial case of the boss who blows up at the worker, the worker who blows up at his wife, the wife who gets angry at her children, and the children who kick the dog. The very first task would be to explore the conscious feelings of people at each juncture in this series of emotional waterfalls. The second task would be to determine what anger seems to be "displaced" and what not. Who, we can ask, gets how angry at whom and for what? When a slightly burned chicken draws a raging response from the husband, and when a child's small miscalculation about continence draws a storm of reaction from the mother, we can make a guess about displaced anger, the idea being that each is "really" angry or "also" angry at something else. But in order to develop such a guess, we would need to inspect the *background expectations* of both the people in the "anger-chain" and the sociologists studying them.

The "social" goes far deeper than our current images of self lead us to suppose. Social roles and relations do not simply reflect patterns of thought and action, leaving the realm of emotion and feeling untouched, timeless, and universal. No, there are social patterns to feeling *itself*. Our task, as sociologists, is to invent both a magnifying glass and a pair of binoculars that permit us to trace the many links between a world that shapes people's feeling and people who can feel.

6 WORKING ON FEELING

Why is the emotive experience of normal adults in daily life as orderly as it is? Why, generally speaking, do people feel gay at parties, sad at funerals, happy at weddings? This question leads us to examine not conventions of appearance or outward comportment, but conventions of *feeling*. Conventions of feeling become surprising only when we imagine, by contrast, what totally unpatterned, unpredictable emotive life might actually be like at parties, funerals, weddings, and in all of normal adult life. Indeed, when novelists set out to create poignant scenes they evoke the full weight of a feeling rule. In *Lie Down in Darkness*, for example, William Styron describes a confused and desperately unhappy bride on the "happy" day of her wedding:

> When she spoke the vows her lips parted not like all the brides he'd ever seen—exposing their clean, scrubbed teeth in a little eager puff of rapture— but rather with a kind of wry and somber resignation. It had been a brief shadow of a mood, just a flicker, but enough for him to tell her "I will" had seemed less an avowal than a confession, like the tired words of some sad, errant nun. Not any of her put-on gaiety could disguise this.[1]

Against the chaotic flow of feeling that emerges from real relationships are more abiding (though also changeable) rules of feeling. In a culture of freely chosen love matches, the bride *should* feel like saying "I will" with an "eager puff of rapture."

But what, then, is a feeling or emotion? I define "emotion" as bodily cooperation with an image, a thought, a memory—a cooperation of which the individual is usually aware. I will use the terms "emotion" and "feeling" interchangeably, although the term "emotion" denotes a state of being overcome that "feeling" does not. The term "emotion management" I use synonymously with "emotion work" and "deep acting."

What happens to these emotions? Erving Goffman suggests both the surprise to be explained and part of the explanation: "We find that participants will hold in check certain psychological states and attitudes, for after all, the very general rule that one enter into the prevailing mood in the encounter carries the understanding that contradictory feelings will be in abeyance. . . .

So generally, in fact, does one suppress unsuitable affect, that we need to look at offenses to this rule to be reminded of its usual operation."[2]

The key—and curiously bureaucratic—word here is "unsuitable." In light of the passage from William Styron above, we could also add "disturbing" or even, in the emotional sense, "dangerous." "So why is she at the altar at all? And why in this way?" we ask. And, from the viewpoint of the guests and surely the groom, what is wrong with how—beneath the put-on gaiety—she is really feeling? This very line of questioning suggests that we have in mind a right way for her to feel. How are we to understand such a thing?

We can take two possible approaches. One is to study the situation that would seem to cause her to feel as she does. The other is to study secondary acts performed *upon* the ongoing nonreflective stream of primary emotive experience, that is, how she is or isn't trying to alter her state of feeling. The first approach focuses on how social factors affect what people feel, the second on how social factors affect what people think and do about what they feel or sense they are going to feel (i.e., acts of assessment and management). Those who take the first approach might regard those who take the second as being "overly cognitive," while those who take the second approach see the "stimulate primary emotions" people as simplistic. But we need both approaches, and indeed the second, taken here, relies on some understanding of the first.[3]

If we take as our object of focus what it is people think or do about feelings, several questions emerge. What is an emotion? How responsive is emotion to deliberate attempts to suppress or evoke it? What are the links among social structure, ideology, feeling rules, and emotion management? To begin with, *are* there feeling rules? How do we *know* about them? How are these rules used as baselines in social exchanges? What in the nature of work and childrearing might account for different ways adults of varying social classes and ethnic or religious cultures manage their feelings?

TWO ACCOUNTS OF EMOTION AND FEELING

So what do we assume is true about emotion? There is the *organismic* account and there is the *interactive* account. They differ in what they imply about our capacity to manage emotion, and thus in what they imply about the importance of rules about managing it. According to the organismic view, the paramount questions concern the relation of emotion to biologically given *instinct* or *impulse.* In large part, biological factors account for the questions the organismic theorist poses. The early writings of Sigmund Freud, Charles Darwin, and, in some though not all respects, William James fit this model.[4] The concept "emotion" refers mainly to strips of experience in which there is no conflict between one and another aspect of self: the individual "floods out," is "overcome." The image that comes to mind is that of a sudden, automatic reflex syndrome—Darwin's instant snarl expression, Freud's tension discharge at a given breaking point of tension overload, James and Lange's notion of an instantaneous unmediated visceral reaction to a perceived stimulus, the perception of which is also unmediated by social influences.

In this first model, social factors enter in only in regard to how emotions are stimulated and expressed (and even here Darwin took the universalist position).[5] Social factors are not seen as an influence on how emotions are actively suppressed or evoked. Indeed, emotion is seen as fixed and universal, much like a knee-jerk reaction or a sneeze. In this view, one could as easily manage an emotion as one could manage a knee jerk or a sneeze. If the organismic theorist were to be presented with the concept of feeling rules, he or she would be hard put to elucidate what these rules impinge *on,* or what capacity of the self could *be called on* to try to obey a feeling rule. Recent attempts to link an organismic notion of emotion to social structure, such as Randall Collins's wonderfully bold attempt, suffer from the problems that were implicit in the organismic account to begin with. Collins, like Darwin, on whom he draws, sees emotions as capacities (or susceptibilities) within a person, to be automatically triggered, as Collins develops it, by one or another group in control of the ritual apparatus that does the triggering.[6] A wholly different avenue of social control, that of feeling rules, is bypassed because the individual's capacity to try to—or try not to—feel that to which the rule applies is not suggested by the organismic model with which Collins begins.

In the interactive account, social influences permeate emotion more insistently, more effectively, and at more junctures. In large part, sociopsychological factors account for the questions the interactive theorist poses. The writings of Hans Gerth and C. Wright Mills, Erving Goffman, Richard Lazarus, James Averill, Stanley Schachter, Jerome Singer, Thomas Kemper, Judith Katz, and aspects of late Freudian and neo-Freudian thought fit this model.[7] To invoke the Freudian vocabulary, the image here is not that of a runaway id, but of an ego and superego, acting in union, shaping and nagging the id, however ineffectively, temporarily, or consciously. Emotion is sometimes posited as a psychobiological means of adaptation—an analogue to other adaptive mechanisms, such as shivering when cold or perspiring when hot. But emotion differs from these other adaptive mechanisms, in that thinking, perceiving, and imagining—themselves subject to social influence—enter in.

As in the first model, social factors affect how emotions are elicited and expressed. But here we also notice how social factors guide the ways we *label,* interpret, and manage emotion. These actions *reflect back,* in turn, on that which is labeled, interpreted, and managed. They are, finally, intrinsic to what we call emotion.[8] Emotion, in this second school of thought, is seen as more deeply social. Lazarus's work in particular lends empirical weight to the interactive model. It shows how normal adults, like the university students on whom he conducted experiments, can control their emotions. Their capacity is far greater than what we expect from a small child, an insane adult, or an animal, from all of which Freud and Darwin drew inspiration. But since we're trying to understand the emotional experience of normal adults, we would do well to explore the model that fits them best—the interactive account.

If emotions and feelings can to some degree be managed, how might we get a conceptual grasp of the managing act from a social perspective? The interactive account of emotion leads us into a conceptual arena "between" the Goffmanian focus on consciously designed appearances, on the one hand, and the Freudian focus on unconscious intrapsychic events, on the other. The focus of A. H. Mead and Herbert Blumer on conscious, active, and responsive gestures might have been most fruitful had not their focus on deeds and thought almost entirely obscured the importance of feeling. The self as emotion manager is an idea that borrows from both sides—Goffman and Freud—but squares completely with neither. Here I sketch only the basic borrowings and departures—and these begin with Goffman.[9]

Erving Goffman Goffman catches an important irony: moment to moment, the individual is actively, consciously negotiating a personal and apparently unique course of action, but in the long run all the action often seems like passive acquiescence to some unconscious social convention. But the conserving of convention is not a passive business. We can extend and deepen Goffman's approach by showing how people not only try to conform outwardly, but do so inwardly as well. "When they issue uniforms, they issue skins," Goffman says. And, we can add, "two inches of flesh."[10] But how can we understand these two inches of flesh?[11]

Goffman maintains a studied disregard for the links between immediate social situations and macrostructure on one hand and individual personality on the other. If one is interested in drawing links among social structure, feeling rules, and emotion management, this studied disregard becomes a real problem.

Goffman's "situationism" is a brilliant achievement, one that must be understood as a development in the intellectual history of social psychology. Earlier in the century a number of classic works linked social structure to personality, or dominant institutions to typical identities, and thus also related findings in sociology and anthropology to those in psychology or psychoanalytic theory. These studies appeared in a number of fields—in anthropology (Ruth Benedict), in psychoanalysis (Erich Fromm, Karen Horney, and Erik Erikson), in sociology (David Riesman, Guy Swanson and Daniel Miller, and Gerth and Mills).[12]

Possibly in response to their work, Goffman proposed an intermediate level of conceptual elaboration, *between* social structure and personality. He focused one by one on situations, episodes, encounters. The emergent encounters he evoked were not only nearly divorced from social structure and from personality; he even seems to intend his situationism as an analytic substitute for these concepts.[13] Structure, he seems to say, can be not only transposed but reduced "in and down," while personality can be reduced "up and out" to the here-now, gone-then interactional moment. The resulting perspective removes the determinisms of institution and personality. It illuminates the room there is between them to slide around.

But each episode—a card game, a party, a greeting on the street—takes on the character of a government. It exacts from us certain "taxes" in the form of appearances we "pay" for the sake of sustaining the encounter. We are repaid in the currency of safety from disrepute.[14]

This model of the situation qua minigovernment illuminates something. But, to study how and why "participants . . . hold in check certain psychological states,"[15] we are forced out of the here-now, gone-then situationism and back, in part at least, to the social structure and personality model. We are led to appreciate the importance of Goffman's work, as it seems he didn't, *as the critical set of conceptual connecting tissues by which structure and personality, real in their own right, are more precisely joined.* For if we are to understand the origin and causes of change in feeling rules—this underside of ideology—we are forced back out of a study of the immediate situations in which they show up, to a study of such things as the changing relations between classes, sexes, races, and nations, in order to see why they're changing.

If we are to investigate the ways people try to manage feeling, we shall have to posit an actor capable of feeling, capable of assessing when a feeling is "inappropriate," and capable of trying to manage feeling. The problem is that the actor Goffman proposes does not seem to feel much, is not attuned to, does not monitor closely or assess, does not actively evoke, inhibit, shape—in a word, *work on*—feelings in a way an actor would have to do to accomplish what Goffman says is in fact accomplished in one encounter after another. We are left knowing about "suppressive work" as a *result* but knowing nothing of the *process* or techniques by which it is achieved. If we are to argue that social factors influence how we try to manage feelings, if we are to carry the social that far, we have to carry our analytic focus beyond the "black box" to which Goffman finally refers us.

The characters in Goffman's books actively manage outer impressions, but they do not actively manage inner feelings. The very topic, sociology of emotion, presupposes a human capacity for, if not the actual habit of, reflecting on and shaping inner feelings, a habit itself distributed variously across time, age, class, and locale. This variation would quickly drop from sight were we to adopt an exclusive focus on the actor's attentiveness to behavioral facade and assume a uniform passivity vis-à-vis feelings.

This skew in the theoretical actor is related to what, from my viewpoint, is another problem: Goffman's concept of acting. Goffman suggests that we spend a good deal of effort managing impressions—that is, acting. But he talks about only one sort of acting—the direct management of behavioral expression. His illustrations, however, actually point to *two* types of acting— the direct management of behavioral expression (e.g., the given-off sigh, the shoulder shrug), and the management of feeling from which expression can follow (e.g., the thought of a hopeless project). Someone playing the part of King Lear might go about his task in two ways. One actor, following the English school of acting, might focus on outward demeanor, the con- stellation of minute expressions that correspond to Lear's sense of impotent rage. This is the sort of acting Goffman theorizes about. Another actor, adhering to the American or Stanislavsky school of acting, might guide his memories and feelings in such a way as to elicit the corresponding expres- sions. The first technique we might call "surface acting," the second "deep acting." Goffman fails to distinguish the first from the second, and he obscures the importance of "deep acting." When this is obscured we are left with the impression that social factors pervade only the "social skin," the tried-for outer appearances of the individual. *We are left underestimating the power of social forces on our inner grip of ourselves.*

In sum, if we accept the interactive account of emotion and study the self as emotion manager, we can learn from Goffman about the link between social rule and feeling. But to elaborate this insight we need to relax the the- oretical strictures Goffman stoically imposes against a focus on social struc- ture and on personality.

Sigmund Freud The need to replace Goffman's "black-box psychology" with some theory of self, in the full sense of the term, might seem to lead to Freudian or neo-Freudian theory. Yet, here, as with Goffman, only some aspects of the Freudian model seem useful to my understanding of con- scious, deliberate efforts to suppress or evoke feeling.

Freud dealt with emotions, of course, but for him they were always secondary to *drive.* He proposed a general theory of sexual and aggressive drives. Anxiety, as a derivative of aggressive and sexual drives, was of para- mount importance, while a wide range of other emotions, including joy, jealousy, and depression, were given relatively little attention. He devel- oped, and many others have since elaborated, the concept of ego defense as a generally unconscious, involuntary means of avoiding painful or unpleas- ant affect. The notion of "inappropriate affect" is then used to point to aspects of the individual's ego functioning, not the social rules according to which a feeling is or is not deemed appropriate to a situation.

The emotion-management perspective is indebted to Freud for the general notion of what resources individuals of different sorts possess for accomplishing the task of emotion work and for the notion of unconscious involuntary emotion management. The emotion-management perspective differs from the Freudian model in its focus on the full range of emotions and feelings and its focus on conscious and deliberate efforts to shape feeling.

How do we understand inappropriate emotion? In David Shapiro's well-known work on "neurotic style," he gives an example:

> An obsessive-compulsive patient—a sober, technically minded and active man—*was usually conspicuously lacking in enthusiasm or excitement in circumstances that might seem to warrant them.* On one occasion, as he talked about a certain prospect of his, namely, the good chance of an important success in his work, his sober expression was momentarily interrupted by a smile. After a few more minutes of talking, during which he maintained his soberness only with difficulty, he began quite hesitantly to speak of certain hopes that he had only alluded to earlier. Then he broke into a grin. *Almost immediately, however, he regained his usual somewhat worried expression.* As he did this he said, "Of course, the outcome is by no means certain," and he said this in a tone that, if anything, would suggest the outcome was almost certain to be a failure. After ticking off several of the specific possibilities for a hitch, he finally seemed to be himself again, so to speak.[16]

What seems interesting here differs according to whether one takes the psychiatric or the emotion-management perspective. To the psychiatrist, which circumstances warrant which degree and type of feeling seems relatively unproblematic. A doctor intuitively knows what inappropriate affect is; one should be happy at occupational success. The main problem is not so much to discern the rich variety of kinds of misfit of feeling to situation as to cure the patient of whatever interferes with feeling that "right" feeling. From the emotion-management perspective, on the other hand, the warranting function of circumstances is a real problem. How does the psychiatrist decide what the patient should feel? The way he decides may well be the same for a psychiatrist as for a salesclerk or school disciplinarian. For, in a sense, we all act as lay psychiatrists using unexamined means of arriving at a determination about just *which* circumstances warrant *that much* feeling of *that sort*.

What the psychiatrist, the salesclerk, and the school disciplinarian share is a habit of comparing situation (e.g., high opportunity, associated with an accomplishment at work) with role (e.g., hopes, aspirations, expectations typical of, and expected from, those enacting the role). Social factors alter how we expect a person to play—or shall we say encounter—a role. If, for example, the patient were a "sober, technically minded and active" *woman*, and if the observer (rightly or wrongly) assumed or expected her to value family and personal ties over worldly success, ambivalence at the prospect of advance might seem perfectly appropriate. Lack of enthusiasm would have a warrant of that social sort. Again, if the patient were an antinuclear activist and his discovery had implications for nuclear energy, that would alter his hopes and aspirations and might warrant dismay. Or if an immigrant is, by virtue of enormous family sacrifice, sent off to succeed in America, his or her enthusiasm might be infused with a sense of indebtedness to those left back home.

We assess the "appropriateness" of a feeling by making a comparison between feeling and situation, not by examining the feeling in the abstract. This comparison lends the assessor a "normal" yardstick—a *socially* normal one—with which to factor out the personal meaning systems that may lead a worker to distort his view of "the" situation and feel inappropriately with regard to it. The psychiatrist holds constant the socially normal yardstick and focuses on what we have just factored out. The student of emotion management holds constant what is factored out and studies variations in socially normal yardsticks.

There is a second difference in what, from the two perspectives, seems interesting in the above example. From the emotion-management perspective, what is interesting is the character and direction of volition and consciousness. From the psychiatric perspective, what is of interest is pre-will and nonconsciousness. The man described is not doing emotion work, that is, making a conscious, intended *try* at altering feeling. Instead, he is controlling his enthusiasm by "being himself," by holding in Alfred Schutz's term a "natural attitude." He "no longer needs to struggle not to grin; he is not in a grinning mood."[17] In order to avoid affective deviance, some individuals may face a harder task than others, the task of consciously working on feelings in order to make up for "a natural attitude"— explainable in psychoanalytic terms—that gets them into trouble. The hysteric working in a tightly controlled bureaucratic setting may face the necessity for more emotion work than the obsessive-compulsive who naturally fits in just fine.

In sum, the emotion-management perspective fosters attention on how people try to feel, not, as for Goffman, on how people try to appear to feel. It leads us to attend to how people consciously feel and not, as for Freud, to how people feel unconsciously. The interactive account of emotion points to alternate theoretical junctures—between consciousness of feeling and consciousness of feeling rules, between feeling rules and emotion work, between feeling rules and social structure.

By "emotion work" I refer to the act of trying to change in degree or quality an emotion or feeling. To "work on" an emotion or feeling is, for our purposes, the same as "to manage" an emotion or to do "deep acting." Note that "emotion work" refers to the effort—the act of trying—and not to the outcome, which may or may not be successful. Failed acts of management still indicate what ideal formulations guide the effort, and on that account are no less interesting than emotion management that works.

The very notion of an attempt suggests an active stance vis-à-vis feeling. In my exploratory study respondents characterized their emotion work by a variety of active verb forms: "I *psyched myself up* . . . I *squashed* my anger down . . . I *tried hard* not to feel disappointed . . . I *made* myself have a good time . . . I *tried* to feel grateful . . . I *killed* the hope I had burning." There was also the actively passive form, as in "I *let myself* finally feel sad."

Emotion work differs from emotion "control" or "suppression." The latter two terms suggest an effort merely to stifle or prevent feeling. "Emotion work" refers more broadly to the act of evoking or shaping, as well as suppressing feeling. I avoid the term "manipulate" because it suggests a shallowness I do not want to imply. We can speak, then, of two broad types of emotion work: *evocation,* in which the cognitive focus is on a desired feeling that is initially absent, and *suppression,* in which the cognitive focus is on an undesired feeling that is initially present. One respondent, going out with a priest twenty years her senior, exemplifies the problems of evocative emotion work:

> Anyway, I started to try and make myself like him. I made myself focus on the way he talked, certain things he'd done in the past. . . . When I was with him I did like him, but I would go home and write in my journal how much I couldn't stand him. I kept changing my feeling and actually thought I really liked him while I was with him, but a couple of hours after he was gone, I reverted back to different feelings.[18]

Another respondent exemplifies the work not of working feeling up, but of working feeling down:

> Last summer I was going with a guy often, and I began to feel very strongly about him. I knew, though, that he had just broken up with a girl a year ago because she had gotten too serious about him, so I was afraid to show any emotion. I also was afraid of being hurt, so I attempted to change my feelings. *I talked myself into not caring about Mike* . . . but I must admit it didn't work for long. *To sustain this feeling I had to almost invent bad things about him and concentrate on them or continue to tell myself he didn't care. It was a hardening of emotions,* I'd say. It took a lot of work and was unpleasant, because I had to concentrate on anything I could find that was irritating about him.

Often emotion work is aided by setting up an emotion-work system—for example, telling friends all the worst faults of the person one wanted to fall out of love with and then going to those friends for reinforcement of this view of the ex-beloved. This suggests another point: emotion work can be done by the self upon the self, by the self upon others, and by others upon oneself.

In each case the individual is conscious of a moment of "pinch," or discrepancy, between what one does feel and what one wants to feel (which is, in turn, affected by what one thinks one ought to feel in such a situation). In response, the individual may try to eliminate the pinch by working on feeling. Both the sense of discrepancy and the response to it can vary in time. The managing act, for example, can be a five-minute stopgap measure, or it can be a decade-long effort suggested by the term "working through."

There are various techniques of emotion work. One is *cognitive:* the attempt to change images, ideas, or thoughts in the service of changing the feelings associated with them.[19] A second is *bodily:* the attempt to change somatic or other physical symptoms of emotion (e.g., trying to breathe slower, trying not to shake). Third, there is *expressive* emotion work: trying to change expressive gestures in the service of changing inner feeling (e.g., trying to smile or cry). This differs from simple display in that it is directed toward change in feeling. It differs from bodily emotion work in that the individual tries to alter or shape one or another of the classic public channels for the expression of feeling.

These three techniques are distinct theoretically, but often go together in practice. For example:

> I was a star halfback in high school. Before games I didn't feel the upsurge of adrenalin—in a word I wasn't "psyched up." (This was due to emotional difficulties I was experiencing and still experience—I was also an A student whose grades were dropping.) Having been in the past a fanatical, emotional, intense player, a "hitter" recognized by coaches as a very hard worker and a player with "desire," this was very upsetting. *I did everything I could to get myself* "*up.*" *I would try to be outwardly "rah rah" or get myself scared of my opponent—anything to get the adrenalin flowing.* I tried to look nervous and intense before games, so at least the coaches wouldn't catch on. . . . When actually I was mostly bored, or in any event, not "up." I recall before one game wishing I was in the stands watching my cousin play for his school, rather than "out here."

Emotion work becomes an object of awareness most often, perhaps, when the individual's feelings do not fit the situation, that is, when the latter does not account for or legitimate feelings in the situation. A situation (such as a funeral) often carries with it a proper definition of itself ("this is a time of facing loss"). This official frame carries with it a sense of what it is fitting to feel (sadness). It is when this tripartite consistency among situation, conventional frame, and feeling is somehow ruptured, as when the bereaved feels an irrepressible desire to laugh delightedly at the thought of an inheritance, that rule and management come into focus. It is then that the more normal flow of deep convention—the more normal fusion of situation, frame, and feeling—seems like an enormous accomplishment.

The smoothly warm airline hostess, the ever-cheerful secretary, the unirritated complaint clerk, the undisgusted proctologist, the teacher who likes every student equally, and Goffman's unflappable poker player may all have to engage in deep acting, an acting that goes well beyond the mere ordering of display. Work to make feeling and frame consistent with situation is work in which individuals continually and privately engage. But they do so in obeisance to rules not completely of their own making.

FEELING RULES

We feel. We try to feel. We want to try to feel. The social guidelines that direct how we want to try to feel may be describable as a set of socially shared, albeit often latent (not thought about unless probed at), rules. In what way, we may ask, are these rules themselves known and how are they developed?[20]

To begin with, let us consider several common forms of evidence for feeling rules. In common parlance, we often talk about our feelings or those of others as if rights and duties applied directly to them. For example, we speak of "having the right" to feel angry at someone. Or we say we "should feel more grateful" to a benefactor. We chide ourselves that a friend's misfortune, a relative's death, "should have hit us harder," or that another's good luck, or our own, should have inspired more joy. We know feeling rules, too, from how others react to what they infer from our emotive display. Someone may say to us, "You *shouldn't* feel so guilty: it wasn't your fault," or "You *don't have a right* to feel jealous, given our agreement." Another may simply declare an opinion as to the fit of feeling to situation and attach authority to his opinion. Others may question or call for an account of a particular feeling in a situation, whereas they do not ask for an accounting of some other situated feeling.[21] Claims and callings for an account can be seen as *rule reminders*. At other times, a person may, in addition, chide, tease, cajole, scold, shun—in a word, sanction—us for "misfeeling." Such sanctions are a clue to the rules they are meant to enforce.

Rights and duties set out the proprieties as to the *extent* (one can feel "too" angry or "not angry enough"), the *direction* (one can feel sad when one should feel happy), and the *duration* of a feeling, given the situation against which it is set. These rights and duties of feeling are a clue to the depth of social convention, to one final reach of social control.

There is a distinction, in theory at least, between a feeling rule as it is known by our sense of what we can *expect* to feel in a given situation and a rule as it is known by our sense of what we *should* feel in that situation. For example, one may realistically expect (knowing oneself and one's neighbor's parties) to feel bored at a large New Year's Eve party and at the same time acknowledge that it would be more fitting to feel exuberant.

In any given situation, we often invest what we expect to feel with idealization. To a remarkable extent these realizations vary socially, as is shown by a woman recalling her experiences as a "flower child":

> When I was living down south, I was involved with a group of people, friends. We used to spend most evenings after work or school together. We used to do a lot of drugs, acid, coke or just smoke dope, and we had this philosophy that we were very communal and did our best to share everything—clothes, money, food, and so on. I was involved with this one man—and thought I was "in love" with him. He in turn had told me that I was very important to him. Anyway, this one woman who was a very good friend of mine at one time and this man started having a sexual relationship, supposedly without my knowledge. I knew though and had a lot of mixed feelings about it. I thought intellectually that I had no claim to the man, and believed in fact that no one should ever try to *own* another person. I believed also that it was none of my business and I had no reason to worry about their relationship together, for it had nothing really to do with my friendship with either of them. I also believed in sharing. But I was horribly hurt, alone and lonely, depressed, and I couldn't shake the depression and on top of those feelings I felt guilty for having those possessively jealous feelings. And so I would continue going out with these people every night and try to suppress my feelings. My ego was shattered. I got to the point where I couldn't even laugh around them. So finally I confronted my friends and left for the summer and traveled with a new friend. I realized later what a heavy situation it was, and it took me a long time to get myself together and feel whole again.

Whether the convention calls for trying joyfully to possess, or trying casually not to, the individual compares and measures experience against an expectation that is often idealized. It is left for motivation ("what I want to feel") to mediate between feeling rule ("what I should feel") and emotion work ("what I try to feel"). Much of the time we live with a certain dissonance between "ought" and "want," and between "want" and "try to." But the attempts to reduce emotive dissonance are our periodic clues to rules of feeling.

A feeling rule shares some formal properties with other sorts of rules, such as rules of etiquette, rules of bodily comportment, and those of social interaction in general. A feeling rule is like these other kinds of rules in the following ways: It delineates a zone within which one has permission to be free of worry, guilt, or shame with regard to the situated feeling. A feeling rule sets down a metaphoric floor, walls, and ceiling, there being room for motion and play within boundaries. Like other rules, feeling rules can be obeyed halfheartedly or boldly broken, the latter at varying costs. A feeling rule can be in varying proportions external or internal. Feeling rules differ curiously from other types of rules in that they do not apply to action but to what is *often taken as a precursor to action*. Therefore they tend to be latent and resistant to formal codification.

Feeling rules reflect patterns of social membership. Some rules may be nearly universal, such as the rule that one should not enjoy killing or witnessing the killing of a human being.[22] Other rules are unique to particular social groups and can be used to distinguish among them as alternate governments or colonizers of individual internal events.

FRAMING RULES AND FEELING RULES: ISSUES IN IDEOLOGY

Rules for managing feeling are implicit in any ideological stance: they are the "bottom side" of ideology. Ideology has often been construed as a flatly cognitive framework, lacking implications for how we feel. Yet, drawing on Emile Durkheim, Clifford Geertz, and Erving Goffman, we can think of ideology as an interpretive framework that can be described in terms of framing rules and feeling rules.[23] By "framing rules" I refer to the rules according to which we ascribe definitions or meanings to situations. For example, a man who just got fired can see it as a result of personal failure or heartless capitalism. According to another, one can't. Framing and feeling rules mutually imply each other. They stand back to back.

It follows that when an individual changes an ideological stance, he or she drops old rules and assumes new ones for reacting to situations, cognitively and emotively. A sense of rights and duties applied to feelings in situations is also changed. One uses emotional sanctions differently and accepts different sanctioning from others. For example, feeling rules in American society have differed for men and women because of the assumption that their natures differ basically. The feminist movement brings with it a new set of rules for framing the work and family life of men and women: the same balance of priorities in work and family now ideally applies to men as to women. This carries with it implications for feeling. A woman can now as legitimately as a man become angry (as opposed to disappointed) over abuses at work, since her heart is supposed to be in that work and she has the right to hope for advancement as much as a man would. Or a man has the right to feel angry at the loss of custody if he has shown himself the fitter parent. Old-fashioned feelings are now as subject to new chidings and cajolings as are old-fashioned perspectives on the same array of situations.

One can defy an ideological stance not simply by maintaining an alternative frame on a situation but by maintaining an alternative set of feeling rights and obligations. One can defy an ideological stance by inappropriate affect and by refusing to perform the emotion management necessary to feel what, according to the official frame, it would seem fitting to feel. Deep acting is a *form of obeisance* to a given ideological stance and lax emotion management a clue to a lapsed ideology.

As some ideologies gain acceptance and others dwindle, contending sets of feeling rules rise and fall. Sets of feeling rules contend for a place in people's minds as a governing standard with which to compare the actual lived experience of, say, the first kiss, the abortion, the wedding, the birth, the first job, the first layoff, the divorce. What we call the changing climate of opinion partly involves a changed framing of the same sorts of events. For example, each of two mothers may feel guilty about leaving her small child at daycare while working all day. One mother, a feminist, may feel that she should not feel as guilty as she does. The second, a traditionalist, may feel that she should feel more guilty than she does.

Part of what we refer to as the psychological effects of "rapid social change," or unrest, is a change in the relation of feeling rule to feeling and a lack of clarity about what the rule actually is, owing to conflicts and contradictions between contending rules and between rules and feelings. Feelings are taken out of their conventional frames but not set into new ones. We may, like the marginal man, say, "I don't know how I should feel."

It remains to note that ideologies can function, as Randall Collins rightly notes, as weapons in the conflict between contending elites and social strata.[24] Collins suggests that elites try to gain access to the emotive life of adherents by gaining legitimate access to ritual, which for him is a form of emotive technology. Developing his view, we can add that elites, and indeed social groups in general, struggle to assert the legitimacy of their framing rules and their feeling rules. Not simply the evocation of emotion but the rules governing it become the objects of political struggle.

FEELING RULES AND SOCIAL EXCHANGE

Any gesture—a cool greeting, an appreciative laugh, the apology for an outburst—is measured against a prior sense of what is reasonably owed another, given the sort of bond involved. Against this background measure, some gestures will seem more than ample, others less. The exchange of gestures has in turn two aspects. It is an exchange of display acts—of surface acting—and an exchange of emotion work—of deep acting. In either case, rules (display rules or feeling rules), once agreed upon, *establish the worth of a gesture and are thus used in social exchange to measure the worth of emotional gestures.* Feeling rules thus establish the basis of worth to be ascribed to a range of gestures, including emotion work. Emotion work is a gesture in a social exchange; it has a function there and is not to be understood merely as a facet of personality.[25]

There seem to be two ways in which feeling rules come into play in social exchange. In the first, the individual takes the "owed" feeling to heart, takes

it seriously. For example, a young woman on the eve of her college graduation felt anxious and depressed but thought that she "ought to feel happy,"
and that she "owed this happiness" to her parents for making her graduation possible.

> To my parents and friends, graduation was a really big deal, especially for my
> parents, since I'm the oldest in the family. For some reason, however, I couldn't
> get excited about it. I had had a good time at college and all, but I was ready to
> get out and I knew it. Also, we had practiced the ceremony so many times that
> it had lost its meaning to me. I put on an act, though, and tried to act real emo-
> tional and hug my friends and cry, but I knew inside I didn't really feel it.[26]

The young graduate "paid" her parents, we might say, in surface acting dis-
sociated from her "real" definition of the situation. Going one step further,
she could pay them with a gesture of deep acting—of trying to feel. A most
generous gesture of all is the act of successful self-persuasion, of genuine
feeling and frame change, a deep acting that jells, that works, that becomes
what the emotion *is,* though it is nonetheless not a "natural" gift. The best
gift, the gift the parents wish for, is, of course, their daughter's real joy.

The second way feeling rules come into play in exchange is shown when
the individual does not take the affective convention seriously but instead
plays with it. For example, an airport observation: There are two airline
ticket agents, one experienced, one new on the job. The new agent is faced
with the task of rewriting a complex ticket (involving change of date, lower
fare, and credit of the difference between the previous and present fare to
be made toward an air travel card, etc.). The new ticket agent looks for the
"old hand," who is gone, while the customers in line shift postures and stare
intently at the new agent. The old hand finally reappears after ten minutes,
and the following conversation takes place: "I was looking for you. You're
supposed to be my instructor." Old hand: "Gee," with an ironic smile, "I am
really sorry, I feel *so* bad I wasn't here to help out" (they both laugh). The
inappropriate feeling (lack of guilt, or sympathy) can be played upon in a
way that says, "Don't take my nonpayment in emotion work or display work
personally. I don't want to work here. You can understand that." The laughter at an ironic distance from the affective convention suggests also an intimacy: we do not need these conventions to hold us together. We share our
defiance of them.

COMMODIFICATION OF FEELING

In the beginning I asked how feeling rules might vary in salience across
social classes. One possible approach to this question is via the connections
among social exchange, commodification of feeling, and the premium, in
many middle-class jobs, on the capacity to manage meanings.

Conventionalized feeling may come to assume the properties of a commodity. When deep gestures of exchange enter the market sector and are bought and sold as an aspect of labor power, feelings are commodified. When the manager gives the company his enthusiastic faith, when the airline stewardess gives her passengers her psyched-up but quasi-genuine reassuring warmth, what is sold as an aspect of labor power is deep acting.

But commodification of feeling may not have equal salience for people in every social class or occupational sector. When I speak of social class, it is not strictly income, education, or occupational status that I refer to, but to something roughly correlated to these—the on-the-job task of creating and sustaining appropriate meanings. The bank manager or the IBM executive may be required to sustain a definition of self, office, and organization as "up-and-coming" or "on the go," "caring," or "reliable," meanings most effectively sustained through acts upon feeling. Feeling rules are of utmost salience in jobs such as these; rule reminders and sanctions are more in play. It is not, as Erich Fromm and C. Wright Mills suggest, that the modern middle-class man "sells" his personality but that many jobs call for an appreciation of display rules, feeling rules, and a capacity for deep acting.

Working-class jobs more often call for the individual's external behavior and the products of it—a car part assembled, a truck delivered 500 miles away, a road repaired. The creation and the sustaining of meanings go on of course, but it is not what the boss pays for. Some working- or lower-class jobs do require emotion work—the jobs of prostitute, servant, nanny, and eldercare worker, for example. Such workers are especially important as a source of insight about emotion management. Being less rewarded for their work than their superiors, they are, perhaps, more detached from, and perceptive about it. Just as we can learn more about "appropriate situation-feeling fits" by studying misfits, we can probably understand commodification of feeling better from those who more often have to ask themselves: Is this what I *do* feel or what I *have* to feel?

Why, I asked, do we feel in ways appropriate to the situation as much of the time as we do? One answer is because we *try* to manage what we feel in accordance with latent rules. In order to elaborate this suggestion I considered first the responsiveness of emotion to acts of management as it is treated in the organismic and interactive account of emotion.

Still, occasionally emotions come over us like an uncontrollable flood. We feel overcome with grief, anger, or joy. Insofar as emotion is, as Darwin suggests, a substitute for action, or *action-manqué*, we may become enraged instead of killing, envious instead of stealing, depressed instead of dying. Or, yet again, emotion can be a prelude to action—and we become so enraged that we kill, so envious that we steal, so depressed that we die. Newspapers make a business of recording emotions of this sort. But the other half of the human story concerns how people calm down before they kill someone, how people want something but don't steal it, how people put the bottle of sleeping pills away and call a friend. Just how it is we hold, shape, and—to the extent we can—direct feeling is not what we read about in the newspaper. But it may be the really important news.

7 THE ECONOMY OF GRATITUDE

A person is usually grateful to receive a gift. But what is a gift? The question has two answers. In the conventional sense, a gift is an object or service freely given, even if it's expected—a Christmas present, for example. But in the emotional sense on which I focus here a gift must seem extra—something beyond what we normally expect.[1] The broader culture helps fix in the individual a mental baseline against which any action or object seems extra and thus like a gift. Changes in the broader culture also shift the many tiny mental baselines that undergird a person's sense of a gift. The sense of genuine giving and receiving is a part of love. So it is through the idea of a gift that we use culture to express love.

In *The Gift* Marcel Mauss explores how, in pre-state societies, one person gave gifts on behalf of his tribe or village to another who received them on behalf of his tribe or village—gifts in the first sense of the word. The Big Man of a Micronesian tribe might, for example, give a basket of cowry shells to the Big Man in another tribe as a gift from one group to the other. In such societies, the gift exchange functioned as a form of diplomacy and carried with it strong obligations to give, to receive, and to reciprocate. In modern society, the state takes on much of the function of gift exchange Mauss talks about. Gift giving, as we usually think about it, is between private individuals and gifts carry personal meanings. But my point is that, even in individualistic market societies, the personal meanings of gifts are surprisingly cultural.

Take modern marriage or its equivalent. In light of changing cultural ideas about manhood and womanhood, what does a wife expect from her husband? What does she take as a gift and so feel moved to feel grateful to him for? What does he want to be thanked for? What really feels to the husband like a gift from her? Is the gift she wants to give the one he wants to receive? Much depends on how cultural currents influence their "marital baseline"—what each partner consensually, if not consciously, expects of the other. Sometimes couples agree on the definition of a gift. But when strong cultural currents affect men and women differently, a marriage may contain two separate and conflicting baselines.

Here I draw on a study of married heterosexual couples, but the economy of gratitude, of course, very much operates in committed gay and lesbian, as well as unmarried heterosexual, relationships. While gender culture impacts gay and lesbian couples differently, it is very much there, if only as an element to suppress. And so, in different ways, it enters into their economics of gratitude as well.[2]

Take the example of housework in a two-job marriage. A husband does the laundry, makes the beds, washes the dishes. Relative to his father, his brother, and several men on the block this husband helps more at home. He also does more than he did ten years ago. All in all he feels he has done more than his wife could reasonably expect, and with good spirit. He feels he has given her a gift and that she should be grateful. But to his wife, the matter seems altogether different. In addition to her eight hours at the office, she does 80 percent of the housework. Relative to all she does, relative to what she wants to expect of him, what she feels she deserves, her husband's contribution seems welcome but not extra, not a gift. So his gift is "mis-received." For each partner sees this gift through different cultural prisms. By creating different prisms for men and women, larger social forces can reduce gratitude.

The economy of gratitude is Janus-faced. It faces outward to bewildering and rapid changes in the larger society and inward to the private meanings shared by two people. One way to grasp that often indecipherable link between social issues and private troubles, as C. Wright Mills put it, is to focus on the place where they meet—the economy of gratitude.

An economy of gratitude is a vital, nearly sacred, nearly bottom-most, largely implicit layer of an intimate bond. It is the summary of all *felt gifts*. Some marital economies thrive, others flounder. Crucial to a healthy economy of gratitude is a common interpretation of reality, such that what feels like a gift to one person feels like a gift to another. A common interpretation of reality in turn relies on a shared template of prior expectations, itself often born of shared history.

Gratitude is a form of appreciation. We appreciate many acts and objects that we take for granted. But we feel grateful for what seems to us extra. In the *Random House Dictionary of the English Language*, gratitude is synonymous with the term "indebted" or "obliged." But gratitude as used in this essay is different and more; for a person may be burdened with a surfeit of gifts that formally obliges him to return the favor—without wanting to and without gratitude. Gratitude, as I'm thinking of it here, involves warmth, thankfulness, and a desire to return the favor. According to Joel Davitz, gratitude adds to "thanks" the feeling of an "intense positive relationship with another person . . . a communion, a unity, a closeness, friendliness and freedom, mutual respect and interdependence."[3]

Let us start, then, at the beginning of a chain of social events—with a recent mass movement of women into the cash economy. In 1969, 38 percent of married mothers worked for pay; in 1996, 68 percent did so. In the 1950s and 1960s, relatively few mothers worked. Now 74 percent of mothers with children six to seventeen are in paid work, 59 percent of mothers of children six and under, and 55 percent of mothers with children one and under.

Women's movement into the cash economy has drastically changed their lives. Yet, at the same time, the traditional view that childrearing and housework are "women's work" strongly persists. The culture lags behind the economy, creating what William Ogburn has called a "culture lag."[4]

Because economic trends bear most directly on women, they change women more.[5] As a result, culturally speaking, men lag behind women in their adaptation to the new economic reality. For women the *economy* is the changing environment, while for men *women* are the changing environment. Women are adapting more quickly to changes in economic opportunity and need than men are adapting to changes in women. A culture lag in the wider society, then, echoes as a "gender lag" at home. There is a lag both in behavior and in attitude: while women have gone out to paid work, most men have not greatly increased their care of the home. But, perhaps even more important, men emotionally support this change in women less than do women.

In uniting men and women, marriage intimately unites people who've changed less with people who've changed more. Behind this difference in cultural position lies a difference in interests; by holding to old-fashioned views, men enjoy more power, and by embracing newer views, women do. So marriage becomes an intimate arena in which to negotiate a broader culture lag and its consequences. So modern marriage is often not a "haven in a heartless world," as Christopher Lasch suggests, but a major shock absorber of tensions created by wider trends bearing unevenly upon men and women.[6] These shocks are finally absorbed—and felt—as the "misreceiving" of a gift.

How, then, do various conditions influence how people attune themselves to gratitude in similar or divergent ways? How do divergences alter an economy of gratitude and so affect love? To answer these questions I draw from in-depth interviews with fifty-five two-job families with preschool children in the San Francisco Bay Area reported in my book *The Second Shift*. A fifth of the husbands fully shared housework and parenting, while most of the rest "helped out."[7]

THE RIPPLE EFFECT OF GENDER CODES

Gender culture is a matter of beliefs about manhood and womanhood, and of emotional anchors attached to these beliefs. Many discrete beliefs, such as "a woman's place is in the home," can be understood as positions on central cultural rules about gender honor. The traditional person in Anglo-Saxon, Hispanic, and Asian American cultures within the United States generally means to or does accord more honor to men than women, whereas the egalitarian accords (or aspires to accord) equal honor to both. But, for both, it matters *how* and *where* honor is won. The issue arises for each: Does honor won in one sphere "convert" to honor in another? The traditional holds to what we might call a gendered "honor conversion rule." According to this rule, a man's greater glory in the world of *work* can be *converted into honor at home*. A woman's cannot. The traditional, in other words, holds beliefs not just about how much honor women can enjoy but about the basis that honor should rest on. To gauge a man's honor, the traditional asks: What's his job? How high up is he in the company? How much does he earn? How honest and fine a man is he at work? He may be an attentive parent, generous with his time, imaginative in the games he plays with the children—but this doesn't add as much to his honor *as a man* as his performance at work. To gauge a woman's honor, the traditional asks: Is she married? To a good fellow? How many children? Are her children doing well? Is her home tidy? She may work outside the home, but any honor she earns there doesn't convert into honor *as a woman*.

According to the traditional code, a man's success at work reflects glory on his wife. Mr. Jones gets promoted at the bank, and his wife is held in higher esteem. It is not just that Mrs. Jones takes pride in Mr. Jones. In the eyes of others, her *own* status rises. But in a traditional community, Mrs. Jones's promotion at work can't enhance her husband's status. She can't give him that. This is because Mr. Jones's honor as a man is based on his capacity to provide for his wife, and through this he provides a rank for the whole family on the social-class ladder. So his wife's job, or public presence in general, counts only insofar as it adds to or detracts from that. And indeed, the more successful she is at work, the more she can detract from his honor as a man.

The egalitarian honor code is very different. Here, male and female honor are based equally on their roles in the public and private realm. Women can transfer their honor to men, just as men transfer theirs to women. By this new code, women can rank the family on the social-class ladder too.

The communities from which my couples were drawn differed widely, some generally favoring the working wife, others the homemaker. Most couples had friends who shared their values, but acquaintances who didn't. One man captured this sense of cultural pluralism:

> In some social circles, it's high status to have a professional wife. I would say it is more high status to have a wife who is a highly regarded professional than one who is home cooking dinner. Yet we have a dentist friend who refuses to let his wife work. After a while, they crossed us off their list because my wife gave his wife too many ideas.

Only a minority of San Francisco Bay Area couples in the early 1980s were pure traditionals. One such couple were Frank and Carmen Delacorte.[8] Frank was a serious, quiet thirty-year-old, high school–educated, El Salvadoran by origin and a cabinetmaker by trade. He felt that it was his job— and only his job—to provide for his family. Frank disliked the unskilled work he had recently been forced to do assembling boxes in a box factory, daily inhaling a glue he feared might be harmful. But still, he was proud to provide for his family.

His wife, Carmen, was a large, voluble, dark-haired woman who ran a day-care center in her home for the children of neighboring mothers who worked. She did it, she explained firmly, "to help Frank": "The only reason I'm working is that every time I go to the grocery store, the bill is twenty dollars more. I'm not working to develop myself or to discover my identity. No way."

Frank felt grateful that Carmen helped him do his job—without complaining. Consider the "not complaining." One evening Frank and Carmen had dinner with another couple, the wife of which resented having to work as a waitress because "the *man* should earn the money." To the discomfort of the Delacortes, the wife openly exposed her husband's vulnerability—he didn't earn enough to keep her at home.

A similar situation arose when Frank rode in a carpool with his foreman, an ardently outspoken traditional. As Frank hesitantly explained:

> We are talking about needing extra money and I told him about the business that Carmen has [taking children into her home] and I said: "You know, you've got a house. Your wife could have a business like Carmen's. It's not too bad." His attitude was "no! no! no! . . . I don't want anybody saying my wife is taking care of other people's children." He feels like he lives the way most people should live—the husband working, the wife at home.

In the Delacortes' world, the old code held: the wife of an adequate man shouldn't work. At the same time, the declining earning power of men's wages from the 1970s on meant that, whether they like it or not, men like Frank *needed* their wives to work. The culture of patriarchy persists, but recent trends are eroding its economic base. Meanwhile Frank just dodged the waitress's insult and got an indirect hit from his foreman with his strong "no! no! no! . . ." So, thank God, he thinks, that Carmen works *without complaint.*

For her part, Carmen feels *her* job is to care for the home and children; she expects Frank to do the outside chores and to help with the inside ones when she asks. Like most working mothers, totaling paid and unpaid work together, Carmen averaged fifteen hours more each week than Frank did— which added up to an extra month a year. But as a traditional, Carmen could not define her "double day" as a problem. Like a number of traditional women I interviewed for *The Second Shift,* Carmen found a way around her dilemma. She claimed incompetence. She did not drive, so Frank had to shop with her. She didn't have a mechanical sense, so Frank had to get money from the automated bank teller. In this way, Carmen got relief from the burdens and also clung to her ideal as a traditional woman. But she did so, as Erving Goffman would note, at the expense of her "moral character"—for now she seemed just a bit stupid. Instead of switching to a new gender code that would give her credit for doing paid work and Frank credit for doing unpaid work at home, Carmen continued to see her earning as "helping Frank out" and his shopping as "helping her out"—as gifts.

The Delacortes agreed on certain symbolic extras. Frank occasionally brought flowers to Carmen. Carmen sometimes troubled to bake an apple pie because it was Frank's favorite dessert. The roses and pies were their private extras, symbols of other private gifts.

Flowers from a man to a woman, and food from a woman to a man, are widely shared symbols of giving—ritual *gendered gifts*. Commercial advertising exploits these gender conventions even as it perpetuates and vastly extends them. The floral industry advertises roses as a man's gift of love to a woman. Pillsbury advertises its flour with "Nothin' says lovin' like something from the oven—and Pillsbury says it best." Frank felt Carmen baked the pie because she knew that he *personally*—not eight million viewers— loved a pie with tart apples and a crisp crust. Carmen felt Frank gave her roses because he knew *she*—not all American women—loved red roses with tall stems. Each drew on public conventions and commercials as the model for their personal ones. They were recent immigrants in the diversity of San Francisco, and maybe roses and pie made them feel more American.

So the Delacortes' economy of gratitude was archetypically traditional. Economic times strained their gender ideal, but Carmen had found a way of getting Frank to help at home without altering that ideal, and her method was also archetypical for traditionals. But they agreed on the terms. So what felt like a gift to the giver felt like a gift to the receiver. Seldom was a gift "mis-received." There was no cultural waste in their gift exchange, and this was one reason they enjoyed such a rich economy of gratitude.

Michael Sherman was a thoughtful, upper-middle-class engineer who in the eight years of his marriage, at his wife's urging, had converted from traditional to egalitarian gender rules. His wife, Adrienne, was a college professor. By the time their twins were born, their understanding was that both would give priority to the family and would take whatever cuts in income and career they had to. Adrienne was not helping Michael establish a place on the class ladder: her job mattered as much as his to that sense of place. When Michael bathed the twins, he was not helping Adrienne: he was doing what good fathers do. Adrienne was not grateful for Michael's help bathing the twins. She expected it. But Adrienne *was* grateful for something else—Michael was sticking his neck out, he felt, because, for men of their generation in their social circle egalitarian marriages were still rare. In that sense, she felt Michael *had* given her an "extra." Because she had struggled to establish the new terms in her marriage, and because the rules were new in her social circle and in the wider culture itself, then, Adrienne sensed the terms were fragile. Michael had some social support, but not from the people he wanted it from. His wife, her friends, some women friends of his thought he was "wonderful." But his parents, Adrienne's parents, some of his male acquaintances didn't comment. They thought Adrienne was bossy and Michael henpecked.

Michael himself suffered pangs of anxiety and frustration that he was lagging behind other men in his field married to women who took the load off them at home. But Michael didn't complain; he was doing this for himself as well as for Adrienne, and for this Adrienne was grateful.

For his part, Michael was grateful because, despite their egalitarianism, Adrienne had for six years in good spirit moved from city to city, disrupting a professional training precious to her, in order to follow him. Acquaintances had mistaken her for "just a supportive wife," and her academic mentor had questioned the seriousness of her purpose. Adrienne had swallowed her pride, and she'd done that for Michael.

Also, just as the need for a woman's wage challenged the old gender rules, so the wage gap between working men and women challenges the new rules. Although Adrienne wanted her husband to treat her work as *just as* important as his, her *salary* was *half* of his. This vital reality undermined her cultural claim to an equal part in the "class-making" of the family. Adrienne was grateful, then, when Michael disregarded the wage gap and honored her anyway.

So Adrienne was especially grateful to Michael for the little signs of deference he showed for contributions she was making at work. On one occasion Michael brought the children to a conference at which she was giving a talk. As she rose to give her talk, she spotted in the fifth row center her beaming husband and two squirming children. Years later, Adrienne's eyes moistened as she recalled this moment of seeing them there.

In the economies of gratitude in modern American marriage, the egalitarian woman is oddly similar to the traditional man. A new economic reality has undercut the cultural identity of each, making each grateful to her or his partner for treading lightly over the soft patches in it.

The Delacortes and the Shermans illustrate the tie between a cultural baseline, the definition of a gift, and gratitude. For the Delacortes, gratitude emerges along old cultural tracks; for the Shermans, along new ones.[9] For each, cultural thinking implies a language by which we "speak gratitude." In this sense, the Delacortes and Shermans speak in different tongues. Just as a meaning in one language is not understood in the other, so gifts spoken in one language of gratitude are not interchangeable with gifts spoken in another. Carmen Delacorte's gift of "noncomplaint" would be meaningless if set on the cultural baseline of a Michael Sherman. Adrienne would never complain she had to work; she was dying to work. Had she complained, Michael would have scratched his head in bewilderment, talked of Adrienne's "hang-up" with ambition, her "will to fail," and urged her to see a therapist. Nor could gifts cross the language barrier the other way. How could Michael's praise of his wife's public contributions seem a compliment to Carmen, who said she was "not working to develop myself or to discover my identity. No way"?

The Delacortes and Shermans describe two cultural poles between which most couples fall into a large, confusing cultural middle ground. Unlike Carmen Delacorte, most Bay Area mothers *want* to work, but like Adrienne Sherman, they aren't primary earners. Unlike Frank Delacorte, most men wholeheartedly support their wives' work, but unlike Michael Sherman, most didn't share the housework and childcare.

More important, most couples differ to some degree in their ideas about manhood and womanhood, and so differ in their understandings about gifts. The "language barrier" lies *between* husband and wife. The most common form of "mis-giving" occurs when the man offers a traditional gift—hard work at the office—but the woman wants to receive a modern one—sharing the work at home. Similarly, the woman offers a modern gift—more money—while the man hopes for a traditional gift—a happily home-cooked meal. As external conditions create a gender gap in the economy of gratitude, they disrupt the ordinary ways men and women express love.

Many marriages resemble the couple in O. Henry's story "The Gift of the Magi." In that story, Della and Jim are very poor but very much in love. At Christmas each wants to buy a fine gift for the other. Della has beautiful long brown hair, which hangs below her waist. Jim sells his favorite gold watch in order to buy a comb for Della's beautiful hair. At the same time, Della secretly cuts off and sells her hair in order to buy a chain for Jim's watch. Each makes a sacrifice for the other that makes them unable to receive a gift from the other. The poignance of the story lies not in the mix-up of the gifts itself, which is farcical. The poignance arises from our fear that each lover will *fail to appreciate* the sacrifice of the other. The story ends happily, however, as each finds out and gives thanks. Presently, new economic pressures and old gender codes are creating in marriage a social version of "The Gift of the Magi," and often the endings are not so happy.

In the O. Henry story, the lovers exchange gifts on Christmas, a ritual occasion set aside for gift exchange. Each gift is intended, planned, and an object, not an activity. The objects also fit current notions of gender—Della's hair seemed an emblem of female beauty and Jim's watch an emblem of male industry. Each wants to give the other what they know the other would treasure. The "mis-giving" is clearly linked to *external* circumstance—the timing and secrecy of each sacrifice.

But in the daily life of modern couples, little time is set aside for ritually heightened gift-giving. Domestic chores usually feel more like flat, neutral, necessary activities than gemlike offerings, each given explicitly to please the other. Yet curiously, in the course of these "flat" doings, flashes of feeling can spontaneously emerge: on one side, "He should love this . . ." or on the other, "God, what a sweetheart." These spontaneous flashes suggest the comparison between the Christmas Eve watch chain and a Saturday afternoon dog wash. And for modern couples, washing the dog is more the real stuff of economies of gratitude.

LIGHT AND HEAVY MEANINGS: GRATITUDE TO NURTURANCE

Sometimes a "mis-giving" stays light, in the sense that a missed exchange does not make one or another person feel unloved. At other times, it cuts dangerously deep into signs by which partners know they are loved. Consider a light "mis-giving" between Peter and Nina Loyola, married twelve years, the parents of two. Peter was a sensitive, articulate man who runs a bookstore. Nina, a tall, lively woman, was a rising star in the personnel division of a large and expanding company. Like the Delacortes, they began their courtship on traditional terms. But as Nina's company grew and opportunities for women with MBAs opened up, Nina was promoted and promoted again, until she began to earn three times Peter's salary.

Proud of her career, Nina was glad to contribute her salary to the family coffers. She was glad to enable Peter to do work he loved, running an innovative bookstore, rather than slogging away at a more lucrative job in real estate. As Nina commented, "My salary and benefits make it possible for Peter to take some risks, starting the store. I'm really glad he can do it." In essence, Nina said, "Here you are Peter; here's my gift to you."

Peter knew Nina meant her salary as a gift. But he couldn't accept it. Peter was glad to do work he loved and appreciated what her salary allowed—a down payment on a new home, a second car, and a private education for their eldest daughter. But, as much as he loved Nina, he couldn't quite say "thanks." That was because Nina was giving him the sort of gift he thought *he* should be giving *her.*

Peter felt *ashamed* that Nina earned so much more than he did. What was the source of this shame? Peter didn't compete with Nina, nor did he sense her competing with him. He genuinely appreciated Nina's talents and accomplishments. As he put it, "Not all women could do as well as my wife has." He also appreciated her physical appearance. "She's a good-looking woman," he volunteered. "I love seeing her in the morning, her hair washed and shiny, when she's all fresh for the day." He wanted his daughter to be "just like her."

Peter felt proud *for* and *of* Nina, but he couldn't share in her new status. He couldn't feel "given to" by her. So Nina could not give her new status *to* him. Indeed, her rise in status reduced his—not in Nina's eyes, but in the eyes of his relatives, neighbors, and old friends—especially the men. Through Peter, with Peter's consent, these imagined others discredited Nina's gift. For they judged *his* honor by the *old* code.

Far from receiving Nina's salary as a gift, they both treated it as a miserable secret to manage. They didn't tell Peter's parents—his father, Peter explained, " would die." Nor did they tell Nina's parents, because "she even out-earns her father." They didn't tell Peter's high school buddies back in his rural hometown in Southern California because "I'd never hear the end of it." Her salary was treated like a rotting fish. As Nina explained in a near whisper, "I was interviewed for an article in *Business Week*, and I had to call the reporter back and ask him please not to publish my salary. When he interviewed me, I was a little proud of saying what my salary was. Then I thought, 'I don't want that in there—because of Peter.'" The taboo on talk of Nina's salary extended to Peter and Nina themselves. As Nina noted, "After a while we stopped talking about my salary. We still don't."

Another matter diminished Nina's gift. Her salary might make her expect more help from Peter at home. As Nina reported:

> Occasionally I've wondered if [my salary] bothered him. Because if we're having a disagreement over something, he sometimes indicates he thinks I'm acting high and mighty, like "Who do you think you *are?*" I say, "You never used to say that." He says, "I do think you've gotten much more assertive [nervous giggle] than you used to be." I do think Peter might equate my assertiveness with my income. I don't know in my own mind if that has anything to do with it. Or if I was just tired of doing all the housework.

If Nina's greater salary meant Peter would have to do more work at home, well, what kind of a gift was that?

In the climate of opinion he sensed himself to be living in, Peter felt like a "one in a hundred" kind of man. For, as he said with great feeling, "Most men couldn't *take* it if their wives out-earned them this much!" They both felt Nina was lucky to be married to such an unusually understanding man. So the gift, as Peter saw it, was not from Nina to Peter, but from Peter to Nina. Nina, too, felt lucky because only with such an unusually understanding man could she be both successful at work and happily married.

Nina gave Peter the kind of gift it was a "man's place" to give a woman. Peter wanted to give Nina his own high salary and the choice of whether or not she should work. But Nina didn't need that choice. Given her skills and opportunities, she would always choose to work. Instead, Nina really wanted

Peter to share the housework and childcare. As it was, Nina had to ask and remind Peter to help. His participation was not a settled matter. Because she had to ask, Peter's help did not *feel* to Nina like much of a gift. Given Peter's shame about her salary, though, Nina did not want to push Peter about the housework. So she rarely asked, doing the lion's share of it herself. Nina *made up* for out-earning her husband by working a double day.[10] In this way, the old gender code reduced the value of new economic opportunity for women and introduced a power imbalance in their marital economy of gratitude. In the end, Peter benefited from Nina's salary. But he also benefited from a second order of gifts his wife owed him *because* she had given him the first gift—an apology expressed in housework.

Given how traditional most men are, the "new man" could make a fine marital bargaining chip out of his sympathy with the new code, or even his attempt at sympathy. Peter gave Nina an unusual amount of personal support for her motherhood and her career. What he did not give her was an acceptance of her career's public reflection on him. Curiously, Nina was "doing it all"—being the prime provider and housekeeper too—and feeling *grateful* as well. We have here the emotional underbelly of gender ideology—not, as we might imagine, in its more popular form of anger and resentment, but in its more common form of apology and gratitude.

Nina and Peter talked to each other in ways that reduced the importance of this mis-giving. They sidestepped the issue and exchanged many *other* gifts. Nina also came to sympathize with Peter's view of the matter, so that they formed a united cultural baseline, according to which Peter's mis-giving was not a marital problem, but only Nina's personal problem of "role conflict," her personal weariness from too much to do.

In other marriages, mis-givings run deeper. Seth Stein, for example, was a hard-driving internist who worked eleven hours a day, and, three days a week, twelve. "I finally arranged to come home at 6:30," he explained, "when I realized I had missed the first two years of my son's growing up." Officially Seth supported his wife Jessica's career. As he commented, "I've always known my wife was a career lady." He also believed that women in general had as much place in public life as men. But it was also clear that his outward rhetoric cloaked deep and different feelings on the matter. Seth was an egalitarian on the surface and a traditional underneath.[11] He acted and felt as though his work mattered far more than Jessica's. This was because the reputational talk of fellow doctors mattered dearly to Seth and to such doctors—themselves career believers. It did not matter how many times he read "The Three Little Pigs" to his son. For Jessica, he thought, it must be different.

But Jessica had earned her own way through medical school and now practiced as an internist. To a certain degree, Seth felt proud of his wife; he didn't want her to be a housewife, or even a secretary. But the egalitarian code stopped at midpoint; he resisted the rest of its logic. His wife would be a professional, like himself. But her work would not be as important to the family or to himself as his work was to her and the family.

Because his work took priority over hers, its rewards—*nurturance and relaxation*—took priority over hers too. As Seth drove home from a grueling day at the clinic, he fantasized a fresh cooked meal, wine, the children in bed, and from Jessica a mood of open appreciation of his work, of him. Much to Jessica's dismay, Seth sought no exit from his extraordinary hours and insisted on thinking of them as his gift to the family. In return, he wanted this gift—this homecoming—from her.

For her part, Jessica wanted Seth to share the work at home with her. Failing that, she wanted Seth to feel bad about not sharing. Even if his career could not permit it, she wanted Seth *to want to* share. Failing that, she wanted Seth to set aside his concern for his own work, so he could appreciate *her* parenting. In contrast to the traditional Carmen, Jessica most of all wanted Seth to *appreciate the sacrifice* she was making—time away from her career in order for him to go full steam ahead in his. As Seth explained:

> Jessica has been very disappointed about my inability to do more in terms of the childrearing and my not doing 50–50. She says I don't do 50–50, that I have left the childrearing to her. Her career has suffered. She cut twice as much time, instead of me cutting time back from my career. She complains that I'm not more like some imaginary other men or men she knows. Such a man does take time with his children because he wants to and knows how important it is. I don't do enough parenting. So she's disappointed in me for not doing my share. On the other hand, she understands the spot I'm in. So she holds it in, until she gets good and pissed and then she lets me have it.

Their gratitude clash extended to nurturance. I asked Seth what he was not getting from Jessica that he wanted. He answered ruefully:

> Nurturing. She don't take care of me enough. But the deal was so straightforward from day one that I'm not bitter. But when I do reflect on it, that's the thing I reflect on. I ain't got a wife taking care of me. Every once in a while I will be upset about it and long for someone who might be sitting around waiting to make me comfortable when I get home. Instead, Jessica needs her back massaged just as much as I do.

Seth could not make a *first claim* to nurturance. But he badly wanted that first claim, though he was not convinced he had the *right* to want it. This was the first point in the interview at which he broke into ungrammatical English, as if to distance himself from what he was saying, as if to say "someone less educated, someone not me is talking."

Jessica proposed a different bargain: "If you help me at home, I will feel grateful for *that* and love you." Through their different stances on the gender code, they created a deep fracture in their understanding about what was and was not a gift. Both felt they were thanklessly giving gifts that were continually lost on the other. As Seth finally put it, "I work, and I work and I work, and I come home to what? Nothing." As Jessica put it, "I'm making sacrifices he doesn't even see." Each felt short-changed. Disappointed and deprived of "gifts," each now resented the other. In another, yet more adversarial marriage, a similar husband explained miserably:

> I could dig a twenty-foot ditch and she would not notice. Barbara complains I am not doing my share. We get into arguments. We are both equally convinced that we are doing our share of chores around the house and Jude [their two-year-old]—in a sense—is considered a chore. One or the other of us is always thinking we're getting ripped off.

Surely part of the cause of the problem in marriages such as that of Seth and Jessica lies in some early injury to human character, an early sense of insufficiency that projects itself onto the daily details of adult life. But misgivings also seem to occur to couples for whom this does not apply. The larger problem lies in "The Gift of the Magi."

REFERENCE POINTS FOR GRATITUDE

We may trace gratitude to three sources: to current ideas about honor that derive from a *moral* frame of reference, to ideas about current realities that derive from a *pragmatic* frame of reference, and to precedents that derive from a *historical* frame of reference. In describing how gender codes have a ripple effect on marriage, we have already talked of a moral frame of reference. Let's turn now to the pragmatic and historical ones.

To apply a pragmatic frame of reference, we invoke ideas about how common or rare a desirable attitude or action is within a contemporary marketplace of ideas and actions. For example, women married to egalitarian husbands nearly always mentioned how lucky they were to have a husband so *unusually* supportive of their work, so unusually willing to share the load at home, so unusually good with the children. Compared with other women, such women felt they had it good. When men spoke of luck, which they did far less, it was usually relative to that of other men, not women.

These luck-comparisons fit a certain pattern. When a woman tried to persuade her husband to do more in the home, she compared her husband to other men who did more. Husbands compared themselves to other men who did less. Underlying both comparisons, however, was a question of the gender marketplace: What was the *going rate* for male housework? For pitching in with the childrearing? For support for a wife's work? For fidelity? Financial support?

Some working mothers also felt grateful for being shielded against the disapproval of kin or neighbors. Many told "shielding stories"—stories of being protected from the dishonor of breaking the old gender code. One working mother was protected by a maid from the critical eye of a watchful neighbor. Another was protected by a co-worker from the disapproval of a boss. Another had earned an advanced degree in nursing much against the advice of her mother, mother-in-law, and sister-in-law. Her husband sometimes shielded her against this hostile climate of opinion. As she recounted appreciatively:

> Once when I was at the library working on a lecture. my husband's mother dropped by and asked where I was. Evan told her I was out shopping for Joey's clothes. He covered for me. Otherwise she would have been very critical of me for leaving Evan and Joey on a weekend like that.

When the climate of opinion is so unfavorable to women's ambitions, some unusual husbandly support becomes an extra chip in the marital bargain. This husband offered more than the "going rate" of advantages a man could offer. So his wife felt lucky.

We may also invoke a historical frame of reference. Over all, more women than men among these Bay Area couples in the 1980s mentioned feeling "lucky" about some aspect of their work and family arrangement. They felt lucky to have a good babysitter, an understanding boss, a cooperative husband, a healthy child. A number said they were lucky because they needed so little sleep. In many ways, their husbands seemed objectively luckier. For only slightly longer hours, they earned two-thirds more. They did much less housework and enjoyed more leisure. Were they to divorce, they were less likely to become poor and more likely to remarry. How ironic, then, that women talked about luck and men did not. Why?[12]

Perhaps women unconsciously compared themselves favorably to yet more oppressed women of previous eras—their mothers and grandmothers, who had still fewer opportunities and rights than they. While many men have moved up the class ladder, men as a gender have lost certain privileges their fathers and grandfathers enjoyed. Relative to men in the past, they may feel unlucky. To put it another way: if life is divided into a female domestic realm and a male public realm, if the female realm is devalued relative to the male, and if over the last half century females have been entering the male realm and males are encouraged to enter the female realm, these changes are likely to feel to women like moving up and to men like moving down. So history, too, provides a reference point for gratitude.

We may receive a gift from a person and feel grateful or receive a gift from "life in general" and feel lucky. In either case the gift is a profoundly social affair. For to perceive a gift as a gift is to hold up a context against which we appraise the present moment. This context is partly moral: "How lucky I am compared to what the cultural code leads me to expect." It is partly pragmatic: "How lucky I am compared to what is available to me." It is partly historical: "How lucky I am compared to people of my kind in the past." We bring to bear these three frames of reference upon the ongoing stream of experience, and the comparison of frame to reality can produce a series of moments of gratitude.

This analysis of gratitude is not an alternative to an analysis based on power. It highlights just how deep inequalities of power go into emotional life. Power does not work *around* the feeling of gratitude; it works *through* it by establishing moral, pragmatic, and historical frames of reference which lower the expectations of women and raise those of men. Gratitude tells a similar story in relations between people of different races, social classes, and nations. In years to come we can, through them, look for the cultural ripple effects of globalization itself. Hundreds of moments in the gift exchange will tell the story.

Social trends alter the moral, pragmatic, and historical frames of reference couples bring to bear on all that happens to them. If marriage is the shock absorber of a strain between cultural and economic realities and between women's and men's viewpoints, then we need to understand "marital" problems in more broadly social ways. Certainly marriage is a union of two personalities: there's good chemistry and bad. But something fundamentally social bedevils many modern marriages as well. For marriage is also a joining of two—often different, usually shifting—stances toward gender. Stances toward gender, in turn, affect what feels like a gift and a token of love. Much of marital dialogue is trying to work out just how much a stint of housework, disapproval-shielding, or "taking it from the boys about your wife's higher salary" counts in the currency of gratitude.

The strain in modern marriage may have less to do with "personal hang-ups" than with the *ripple effect* of larger social trends upon the understanding of a gift. Daily realities strain the traditional economy of gratitude—because most women have to work and come to want to be valued for it. At the same time, the lower pay scales for women's jobs mean strains for egalitarian marriages. For traditional and egalitarian couples alike, then, the notion of a gift is in flux.

The happiest of the two-job marriages I observed shared a common understanding of what a gift would be, and their understanding also fit the current realities of their lives: even highly traditional men in happy marriages did not come home, sit at the dining room table, and feel they "would be grateful" and "would feel loved" only if dinner were waiting on it—for often it wasn't. Each found feasible equivalents for roses and apple pie. Happy egalitarian couples sought out the social support to fully internalize the new gender rules. Most important, they did not make do with less gratitude: they found a way to exchange more gifts on new terms and in this way solved the problem of "The Gift of the Magi."

8 TWO WAYS TO SEE LOVE

All of the nineteenth-century founders of sociology touched on the topic of emotion and some did more. Max Weber elucidated the anxious "spirit of capitalism," the magnetic draw of charisma, and questioned—though not from this viewpoint—"rationality." Emile Durkheim focused on the experience of "solidarity." Karl Marx explored alienation and, in his analysis of class conflict, implied much about resentment and anger. Georg Simmel examined love and friendship, and Max Scheler explored empathy and sympathy. In the twentieth century, Erving Goffman traced out the complex web of unconscious rules of acting that people use to get through the day. Goffman strongly implied, though he draws back from actually positing, the existence of feeling rules and the sort of person who would be able to take them into account. Current sociology is rich in works that are either theoretically relevant to or empirical descriptions of the full cornucopia of feelings and emotions. The sociology of emotion takes off from these early beginnings. As with any new body of work, it has generated lively debate and become quickly subdivided by area, theoretical approach, and methodology. So it is no easier to speak these days of a typical sociologist of emotion than it is to speak of a typical sociologist. Still, we can ask what it is like to see the world from the point of view of the sociologist of emotion.[1]

How does one convey this way of seeing? One way is to look very closely at a grain of sand and to compare the various worlds a person sees in it. Drawing from my book *The Managed Heart*, let us listen to one young woman's description of her wedding day:

> My marriage ceremony was chaotic and completely different than I imagined it would be. Unfortunately, we rehearsed at 8 o'clock the morning of the wedding. I had imagined that everyone would know what to do, but they didn't. That made me nervous. My sister didn't help me get dressed or flatter me and no one in the dressing room helped until I asked. I was depressed. I wanted to be so happy on our wedding day. . . . This is supposed to be the happiest day of one's life. I couldn't believe that some of my best friends couldn't make it to my wedding. So as I started out to the church thinking about all these

119

things, that I always thought would not happen at my wedding, going through my mind, I broke down and cried. But I thought to myself, "Be happy for the friends, the relatives, the presents." Finally, I said to myself, "Hey, [other] people aren't getting married, *you* are." From down the long aisle I saw my husband. We looked at each other's eyes. His love for me changed my whole being from that point on. When we joined arms, I was relieved. The tension was gone. From then on, it was beautiful. It was indescribable.[2]

From childhood on, we actually "rehearse" for our wedding. As Emile Durkheim notes in *The Elementary Forms of Religious Life,* rituals create for any social group a circle within which things come to seem extraordinary, amazing, sacred, and outside of which things seem ordinary, unremarkable, profane. In modern Western society, the marriage ceremony itself sacralizes the bond between bride and groom. The vows and rings bring everyone's shared attention to the same thing, making the couple feel enhanced by being part of and supported by a larger whole—a community of family and friends, society. Their love is held from the outside as well as the inside.

But this young woman's wedding was not doing its Durkheimian job. For one after another of her family and friends were falling away from their ceremonial roles. Only when the bride focused on herself—"Hey [other] people aren't getting married, *you* are"—and on her groom did she feel moved. She was coping with a de-ceremonialized ceremony, a Durkheimian rite in a non-Durkheimian ambiance. Nervous and disappointed, she realized that she must *remove herself from* the ceremony in order to feel her wedding as sacred and to feel herself personally transformed. Endings are important and the bride ends her story by describing how she locked into a mutual gaze with her husband and felt transformed by it. The discombobulated ceremony suggests a larger modern story: when the surrounding community does not surround a couple, each partner has to be like a whole community to the other. The Durkheimian circle remains magical but it shrinks.

What in our bride's tale might catch the psychoanalyst's eye? Christa Rohde-Dachser (a commentator on an earlier version of this essay given at the German Psychoanalytic Association in 1995)[3] offered this interpretation: The young bride held "narcissistic expectations of this day." She expected to feel central, elevated, enhanced, and was disappointed that these expectations weren't met. When faced with an inattentive sister, an absent friend, and bumbling bridesmaids, she grew anxious at having to adopt the "female depressive solution"—to abandon hope of fulfilling her own needs and to focus on the more urgent needs of others. But then she experienced a moment of "Oedipal triumph" ("People aren't getting married, *you* are"), a moment in which she leaves the "white desert" of her early development in which she watched her parents' sexual happiness from the sidelines. Now she may enjoy her own sexual gratification. Why, Rohde-

Dachser also asks, does the story end when it ends, at a moment of happy union? Is this a fusion of her narcissistic expectation with her Oedipal triumph—central and united forever—and do these form a denial of reality?

In looking at our bride in this way, the psychiatrist relies on the idea of personality structure, itself formed in the course of early psychosexual development within the immediate family. This is because psychoanalysis is a body of theory about *individual human development*. Since its focus is on those moments in human development when things go wrong, psychiatrists often dwell on extreme or pathological emotion and, as a practice, focus on healing emotional injuries. Culture enters in as the *medium* in which human development, injury and repair, takes place. The psychoanalyst might not ask how it is that a certain emotion—feeling "his love for me"—stands out from an array of expectable or appropriate feelings. She might rely on an intuitive notion of appropriate affect, based on a prior notion of a mentally healthy response to this situation in this culture at this time.

So how would a sociologist of emotion approach the same bride? Like the psychoanalyst, the sociologist of emotion notices the bride is anxious and connects her anxiety with the meanings she attaches to this event. The sociologist is not focusing on human development per se, injury or repair, but on the cultural and social *context* of individuals, healthy and injured alike. Part of that context is a *culture of emotion*. What did the bride expect or hope to feel before she felt what she felt? She tells us, "I wanted to be so happy on our wedding day. This is supposed to be the happiest day of one's life."

To expect or hope to feel a certain feeling, the bride had to have a *prior idea about what feelings are feelable.* She had to rely on a prior notion of what feelings were "on the cultural shelf," pre-acknowledged, pre-named, pre-articulated, culturally available to be felt. We can say that our bride intuitively matches her feeling to a nearest feeling in a collectively shared emotional dictionary. Let us picture this dictionary not as a small object outside herself, but as a giant cultural entity and her as a small being upon its pages.[4] Matching her feelings to the emotional dictionary, she discovers that some feelings are feelable and others are not. Were she to feel homosexual attraction and love in China, for example, she would discover that to many people, homosexual love isn't simply "bad," it is not in the dictionary. It does not exist.

Like other dictionaries, the emotional dictionary reflects agreement among the authorities, and does not recognize all local usages. It is also subject to gradual change over time. But it expresses the idea that within an emotional language group there are given emotional experiences, each with its own ontology. So, to begin with, the sociology of emotion asks: With what feelings in the cultural dictionary of her time and place is our bride matching her inner experience? Is her feeling of happiness on her wedding day a perfect match, a near match, a frightening mismatch? This powerful, unconscious process of matching inner experience to a cultural dictionary becomes for the sociologist of emotion a complex, mysterious, important part of the drama of this bride's inner life.

Second, what does the bride believe she *should* feel? She is matching her experience not only to a dictionary but to a bible. Our bride has ideals about *when* to feel excited, central, enhanced, and when not to. She has ideas about *whom* she should love and whom not, and about how deeply and in what ways she should love. She has ideas about what the indications of this love are, and *how important* this love should be to her. The poet Byron wrote, "Man's love is of man's life a thing apart, 'tis woman's whole existence." Does love loom larger for our bride than it does for her groom? Or does she now try to make love a smaller part of her life, as men in her culture have tried to do in the past? What are the new feeling rules about the place of love in a woman's life? How desirable or valued is the emotion of love or the state of attachment? To what set of cultural meanings is this couple's magical mutual gaze linked?

Cultures differ in the pictures they project of "perfect love."[5] According to the Western "romantic love ethic" of the industrial period, the individual is supposed to fall "head over heels" in love, to feel he or she is losing control. In German, *Romantische Liebe* has a slightly derogatory connotation that it lacks in the United States. In many parts of non-Western societies like India, romantic love is seen as a dangerous, chaotic emotion, which threatens to destabilize the devotion the married couple owes the son's parents, with whom they live in a joint household. On the basis of interviews with Hindu men on the subject of love, the sociologist Steve Derne found that Hindu men felt that "head over heels" romantic love could and did occur, but it inspired dread and guilt.[6] This dread, of course, mixes with and alters the feeling of love itself.

So people in different eras and places do not just feel the same old emotion and express it differently. They feel it differently. Love in a New England farming village of the 1790s, say, is not the same old love as in upper-class Beverly Hills, California, in 1995 or among working-class Catholic miners in Saarbrucken, Germany. Each culture has its unique emotional dictionary, which defines what is and isn't, and its emotional bible, which defines *should* and *shouldn't*. As aspects of "civilizing" culture, they determine our *stance toward* emotional experience. They shape the predispositions with which we interact with ourselves over time. Some feelings in the ongoing stream of emotional life we gladly acknowledge, welcome, foster. Others we grudgingly acknowledge, and still others the culture invites us to completely deny. And the dictionary, the bible, the stance alter to some extent what we feel.

Like other sociologists, the sociologist of emotion looks at the *social con-*

text of a feeling. Is the bride's mother divorced? Is her estranged father at the wedding? And the groom's family? Who of their friends appeared at the wedding and what marital stances do they bring with them? Who is present in fantasy? What were the histories of *their* "happiest days"? This context also lends meaning to the bride's feelings on her wedding day—as ground lends meaning to a figure, or a puzzle to a piece of it.

Given the current emotional dictionary and bible in use on the one hand and the social context on the other, each culture delivers to its members a unique paradox. The modern Western paradox of love seems to be this: As never before, the culture now invites a couple to aspire to a richly communicative, intimate, playful, sexually fulfilling love. But, at the same time, the social context itself warns against trusting such a love too much. Thus, the culture increasingly invites couples to "really let go" and trust fully. But it also cautions: "You're not really safe if you do. Your loved one could leave." Just as advertisements saturating American television evoke *la belle vie* in a declining economy that denies it to so many, so the new cultural permission for a rich, full, satisfying love life has risen just as new uncertainties subvert it.

Let me elaborate. On one hand, love is increasingly expected to be more expressive and emotionally fulfilling. Economic reasons for men and women to join lives have grown less important, and emotional reasons have grown more important. In addition, modern love has also become more pluralistic. What the Protestant Reformation did to the hegemony of the Catholic church, the sexual and emotional revolution of the last thirty years has done to romantic love.[7] The ideal of heterosexual romantic love is now a slightly smaller model of love within an expanding pantheon of valued loves, each with its supporting subculture. In the United States gay and lesbian lovers are beginning to enjoy open acknowledgment. Some unmarried heterosexual women look forward, if the right guy doesn't come along, to a series of exciting affairs with men, which they supplement with warm, abiding friendships with women. Some of this diversification of love expands the social categories of people eligible to experience romantic love, and some provides alternatives to it. On the whole, though, the ideal of romantic love seems to be retaining its powerful cultural hold by extending and adapting itself to more populations.

Paradoxically, while people feel freer to love as fully as they wish, they are less and less sure that love will last. The American divorce rate has risen from 20 percent at the turn of the twentieth century to 50 percent today and remains the highest in the world. The breakup rate for unmarried couples who live together is higher still. More women also bear and raise children on their own, and more women have no children.[8] Norms that used to apply to American teenagers in the 1950s—"going steady," breaking up, going steady again with another—now apply to adults.

These trends present our young bride with a tease. She is inspired by the image of a greater love, but sobered by its "incredible lightness of being."[9] The promise of expressive openness is undercut by the fear of loss. For in order to dare to share our innermost fears, it greatly helps to feel safe that our beloved—perhaps, in the last instance, a symbol of mother—isn't going to ditch us.

Faced with this paradox, our bride may try to manage her emotions in one of several ways. She might try to make love last by unconscious, "magical" means. In one study of responses to the "divorce culture," the sociologist Karla Hackstaff notes that some young lovers who had grown up in divorced homes unconsciously warded off the "evil eye" of divorce in their own love life by creating a First-Love-That-Fails and a Second-Love-That-Works.[10] Our bride could have met a perfectly nice boyfriend before she met her husband. But because she felt there was a divorce she was destined to suffer and eager to avoid, she projects onto a first lover "everything bad" and tries to detach herself from him. Then she meets a second young man, just like the first, onto whom she projects "everything good." With him, she tries to stay in love, the "divorce" now behind her. Through this unconscious magic, our bride makes her first marriage into a symbolic second one and clears away the danger of divorce.

Alternatively, the bride can try to adapt to the disquieting uncertainties of love by defending herself not against a dangerous bad-news guy but against her own need for anyone.[11] She tries to expect less, to care less. In an era of sexual and emotional laissez-faire, our bride becomes an emotional Spartan. She can don this emotional armor in many ways. In one study of a small sample of African American single women, Kim DaCosta found that the women tried to limit their trust of men, to dampen their fantasies of rich, emotional bonds with men, while simultaneously expanding their fantasies of great love for children. With children, they could dare to "fall in love" and displace onto the children, perhaps, the dependency needs they felt they couldn't afford to feel with men. Faced with the paradox of modern love, more young women may follow the emotional strategy of these African American women.[12]

Fear of loss itself is hardly new. Through the ages, people have lost loved ones to disease, to war, to rivals, and have guarded themselves against such loss. But when the defenses against uncertainty arise from the *culture of love itself,* when the cultural dictionary elaborates varieties of guarded loves and ex-loves—and when this culture of love is linked to capitalism—we need the best thinking we have to understand it.

The paradox of modern love may result from its bumpy ride on the runaway horse of capitalism. Capitalism is a culture as well as an economic system. As Anthony Giddens and others have argued, the economy, the state, and the mass media have become a vast, far-flung empire, which dwarfs, undermines, and "disembeds" local cultures. If we all live in a "village" of some sort, capitalism transforms and sometimes dissolves the ties that bind us to it. One way in which we disembed ourselves from our local culture is through the application of metaphors. In our collective unconscious, we may be applying the metaphor of "emotional capital," posing for ourselves a new set of questions. Can we speak of new emotional investment strategies? Do people think of emotion as that which they invest or divest so that the self is ever more lightly connected to feeling? Does emotion itself take on the properties of capital?[13] Is this emotional capital now more "mobile" across social territory than in previous eras? Can we speak of a deregulation of emotional life, so that it flows across new boundaries linked to notions of private profit? If so, how does this affect the emotion management of a young bride? Given that half the divorced fathers in one American study, five years after divorce, had not seen their children during the last year, we can also ask how such a capitalized emotional culture affects children.

I am not arguing that people enter relationships more lightly nowadays than they did thirty years ago, or that they think shallow connections are better than deep ones. I am suggesting that one important strategy of emotion management *is to develop the ability to limit emotional connection since this strategy adapts us to survival in a destabilizing culture of capitalism.*

Fleeting as they are, moments of emotion management tell a great deal about the self we develop when we live in such a capitalist culture. In the case of mild feelings, acts of self-control can help shape feeling itself. We may try to alter the expression of our feeling and in doing so actually alter the inward feeling (one kind of deep acting). We can verbally prompt ourselves to feel one emotion and not another (another kind of deep acting). Or we can try to enter into a different way of seeing the world (and yet another, "method acting").

Whatever the method of emotion management, the emotions managed are not independent of our management of them. Emotions always involve the body, but they are not sealed biological events. Both the act of "getting in touch with feeling" and the act of "trying to feel" become part of the process that makes the feeling we get in touch with what it *is*. In managing feeling, we partly create it.[14] Through how it makes us see relations, define experience, and manage feeling, the culture of capitalism insinuates its way into the very core of our being. Weaving together the tatters of a waning tradition, the bride seeks to enter a private emotional bubble, her happiest day. In this light, her wedding is both a holdover and an act of resistance. She wants this day to be the happiest day of her life, but the day is stubbornly lodged in a larger culture, which expresses the paradox of modern love. Ultimately, *this* may be the source of the bride's unease.

This paradox is itself a result of the disjuncture between old feeling rules (a former emotional dictionary-bible) and a newly emergent social context. But feeling rules change and so do social contexts. So as sociologists of emotion, we need to ask: What emotional dilemma are we trying to resolve in order to live the lives we want? By what dialectical interaction between rules and context is an emotional paradox produced? In light of these paradoxes, what emotional strategies come to make sense? Do we think a given emotional strategy, however "normal" it may seem, hurts or helps us?

In the end, perhaps the bride is fixing all her attention, her hopes, her sense of meaning on her groom because the rest of the wedding scene, that supposedly magical Durkheimian circle, has fallen apart. The groom himself becomes the worshipped totem and the bride the lone worshipper. This could intensify her love, as the culture prescribes. But it also exaggerates the demands put on each party to that love. If the wedding is any reflection of her other social ties, we can ask how the bride's love for the groom *is related to* her absence of connections to others. When the micro-Durkheimian circles of marriage are so fragile, maybe we need—paradoxically—more proper weddings in which sisters are sisterly and friends are true friends. For it may take a whole village to make love work, and a repair to that village to make it last.

9 PATHWAYS OF FEELING

Are there emotional strategies that *prepare the ground* for the behavioral strategies men and women pursue in combining work and family life?[1] If so, what are they? What are the emotional consequences of each? To find out, I interviewed fifty married couples, in which both partners worked at full-time jobs and also cared for children under the age of six. I talked with their babysitters and also observed in the homes of ten families. At least one spouse in each couple worked at a large multinational company in the San Francisco Bay Area.

GENDER IDEOLOGIES AND FEELING RULES

The gender ideologies of these men and women fell into three main types: traditional, egalitarian, and transitional. Implicit in each ideology were rules about *how one should feel* about one's work outside and inside the home. Traditional men and women felt a woman's place was in the home even though she might have to work outside it and that a man's place was at the workplace even though he might have to help at home. Many traditional women talked as if they were being gracious to help support the family, and they reserved some right to resent such helping since earning money wasn't their job. Correspondingly, traditional husbands felt that by doing house-work they were doing their wives a favor for which the wives should feel grateful. In addition, traditional women did not believe it was right to iden-tify with their paid jobs or to love their work too much even though in a guilty way some did. And traditional men did not wish to identify themselves too closely with women's work at home, though, again, some did.

The egalitarian man or woman felt that husbands and wives should share both the paid and unpaid work. The wife was supposed to identify with her work and to feel her career mattered as much as her husband's, though some egalitarian women didn't really feel theirs did. The egalitarian hus-band was supposed to feel that his role as householder and parent mattered as much as his wife's, although, again, some didn't feel theirs did.

The transitional man or woman adhered to a mix between the traditional

127

and the egalitarian ideology. Of the several types of transitional ideologies, I focus here on one type in which the couple believed it was good for the wife to work full-time outside the home but it was *also* her responsibility to do most of the work at home. She was supposed to have an identity outside the home, and it was her right to care about and enjoy her paid work. But she didn't have a right to feel angry at a husband who didn't help much, since her husband wasn't supposed to have an identity equivalent to hers inside the home. Nor, if he didn't help at home, did the transitional husband feel obliged to feel very much guilt. Those were the feeling rules.

Traditionals were a small minority among both men and women in the San Francisco Bay Area in the 1980s, and of the rest, more women were egalitarian and more men were transitional. Thus, men and women often applied different feeling rules to what they actually felt about work and home.

Quite apart from differences in the content of gender ideology and feeling rules, I began to be impressed by the different ways individuals *held* their beliefs. A few traditionalists railed passionately against the ERA, abortion, and the economic need for a wife to work, as if a vital moral order were endangered. Others stated the same beliefs matter-of-factly. A number of men also seemed to be egalitarian on top but traditional underneath. This led me to ask how *feelings infuse* ideologies, how actors care about their beliefs. Passionately? Nonchalantly? Angrily? Hopelessly? Fearfully?

The underlying feelings of some people seemed to reinforce their surface ideology, while those of others seemed to subvert it. Some underlying feelings seemed traceable to "cautionary tales"—important episodes from a person's past that carried meaning for the future. For example, one passionate traditionalist, an El Salvadoran daycare worker, Carmen Delacorte, married to a factory worker, spoke vehemently against the ERA, comparable worth, abortion rights, and anything that would detach a woman's identity from the home. Reinforcing her gender ideology was her urgent desire to avoid the terrible struggles of her mother, a single mother whose husband abandoned her and her baby (the young Carmen) because, as she put it, my mother was "too dominating." The message of this cautionary tale seemed to be: Submit to your man so he won't leave you. The gender ideology of some passionate egalitarians seemed fueled by a dread born of a different cautionary tale: a mother who lacked self-esteem, felt depressed, and became a "doormat" for her husband. There the idea was: Work, assert yourself, so you don't internally leave us.

Often the feeling behind a person's gender ideology seemed to derive from the interface between a searing experience from the past and an emerging situation in the present. For example, an African American forklift driver, a father of three, firmly resisted the entreaties of his wife, a billing clerk, to help with housework and childcare. Even if his wife worked full-time, he strongly felt housework wasn't a "man's" job. He felt more strongly about this than other men I interviewed who were in his situation and shared his point of view, and I wondered why. Then he described an early loss; when he was a three-year-old, his mother had left him in the care of his aunt, not to return until he was twenty. Now, he wanted to be sure his wife did her "job" of taking care of him. Both the daycare worker and the forklift driver suggest biographic clues to the emotional anchors of gender ideology.

In other cases, the underlying feeling seemed to subvert the surface ideology. Consider the example of John Livingston, a white businessman who had been living for some time on the brink of divorce and had sought marriage counseling only a few months before I interviewed him. He described a childhood of extreme neglect in an Irish working-class family, with a reclusive father and workaholic mother. His mother, a waitress during the week, had taken an extra job selling ice cream on weekends. He spoke of how much it meant to him now to be married and to "finally communicate with somebody."

Ideologically, John was an egalitarian. His mother had "always worked"; he had always expected his wife to work and was "all in favor of sharing" the provider and homemaker roles in his own marriage. But when their daughter Cary was born, his feeling rules became much harder to follow. After Cary's birth, John very distinctly felt his wife withdraw from him. As he put it, "I felt abandoned, you might say, and angry." When his wife returned to a demanding job, he resented and resisted it bitterly. As he explained:

> Maybe I was jealous of Cary because, for the six years before she was born, I was the most important person to Barbara. For several months while she was working those long hours, I would come home and spend most of the night with Cary, which was okay. But I *resented* Barbara not being there. I wanted a few minutes to myself. Then I felt Cary was being cheated by her not being here. And I wanted Barbara to spend more time with me! So I withdrew. I didn't want to complain, to make her feel guilty about working long hours. But I resented it.

John believed Barbara should be engrossed in her work, but at the same time he was furious that she was. His feeling rule clashed with his feeling. Since it was John's habit to withdraw when he was angry, he withdrew from his wife in all ways, including sexually. His wife grew upset at his withdrawal, creating a painful deadlock, which, through their long hours at work and caring for Cary (supermom and superdad strategies), they were each avoiding. In the end, they separated, divorced, and fought bitterly over the custody of Cary.

EMOTIONAL PATHWAYS OF GENDER STRATEGIES

We not only adopt ideologies and feeling rules about dividing the work at home, we pursue gender strategies—persistent lines of feeling and action through which we reconcile our gender ideology with arising situations. Thus, our acts of emotion management are not randomly distributed across situations and time; they are guided by an aim. This aim is to sustain a certain gendered ego ideal, to be, for example, a "cookies-and-milk mom" or an "aim-for-the-top career woman" or something else. And this aim also sustains a certain ideal balance of power and division of labor between husband and wife. If we understand ourselves not simply as people but as pursuers of gender strategies, and if we attune ourselves to the feeling rules that guide them, we can see a certain pattern in how feelings clash with rules and in which feelings need managing. Often our gender strategy corresponds to what we consider our "real self." Who—as a man or a woman—we are trying to be fits who we think we really are. We may also find our gender strategy curiously at odds with our "real self." Or we may be only vaguely aware or totally unaware of our gender strategies and of the conflicts they pose for our "true self."

A gender strategy is a "strategy of action" in Ann Swidler's sense of a conscious or unconscious plan for what to *do*. But a gender strategy is also a strategy about how to *feel*. When we actively evoke and suppress various feelings we also clear a preparatory emotional pathway for our actions. We try to change how we feel to fit how we must feel in order to pursue a given course of action.

In the way they divided housework and childcare and in the way they felt about it, the couples I studied reflected long-term gender strategies. A few working mothers had always shared the work at home with their husbands and tried to maintain the arrangement of stabilized equity. Those who had not always shared did one of two things. They pressed their husbands to do more work at home, or they didn't. Some wives who tried to get their husbands to do more at home pressed in an active, direct way—by persuasion, reminding, argument, or sometimes a you-share-this-work-or-else showdown (a strategy of active change). Other wives pressed their husbands in passive or indirect ways, "played dumb" or got "sick," forcing their husbands to take on a larger load at home. Some women increased the cost of not helping out by emotionally isolating their husbands or losing sexual interest in them because they were "too tired."

Other working mothers kept most of the responsibility and work of the home for themselves. They became "supermoms," working long hours at their jobs and keeping their children (who napped during the afternoon at daycare) up late at night to give them attention. Some working mothers reduced their time, effort, or commitment to their jobs, their housework, their children and husbands, managing their overload through some combination of cuts.

To prepare the way for her behavioral strategy, the working mother created a certain emotional pathway for it. She tried to feel what it would be useful to feel in order to follow her line of action. For example, a few women confronted—or almost confronted—their husbands with an ultimatum: "Either you share the responsibility for tasks at home with me or I leave." To go through with this showdown, the woman had to rivet her attention on the injustice of the unfair load she carried and dwell on its importance to her. She distanced herself from all she would otherwise feel for her husband and suspended her empathy for his situation. She steeled herself against his resistance. One working mother described how she approached her husband:

> I'd had it. I was wiped out. And he was getting his squash game in like before the baby came. So I steeled myself. I prepared myself. I told him, "This can't go on." . . . I figured if he couldn't show me that consideration, he didn't love me. I'd had it. I mean marriages end like this.

Other working mothers avoided steeling themselves by using indirect means, developing incompetencies at home and drawing their husbands into the work by "needing help" paying the bills or driving a car. Their task was to maintain self-esteem by distancing themselves from the helpless image they had cultivated. Working mothers who cut back on their hours of work often prepared themselves for this move beforehand by trying to suppress or alter their feelings about work and its meaning for their identity. Despite this anticipatory emotional work, one highly successful businesswoman with an M.B.A., who quit her job to consult part-time, felt naked in public without the status shield of her professional role. As she explained it, "I used to be so gung-ho at work. But I just decided I had to put that aside while my kids are young. It was much harder than I thought, though, especially when I'm walking in the supermarket and other people think I'm just a housewife. I want to shout at them, 'I have an M.B.A.! I have an M.B.A.!'"

Other working mothers clung to their work commitments but relinquished their former concern about how the house should look or meals should taste. Interpreting the look of the house as a personal reflection on themselves, traditional women felt embarrassed when the house looked messy. On the other hand, egalitarian women tried not to care how the house looked, some priding themselves on how little they noticed the mess, how dirt no longer "got to them," how far beyond embarrassment they were.

More important than cutting back on housework, working mothers sometimes also resolved their conflict by cutting back on the time and attention they gave their children. Under the tremendous pressure of the demands of work and family, they scaled down their ideas about what their children needed. One working mother described her feelings about putting her daughter in the care of a babysitter for ten hours a day at the age of three months:

She took long naps in the afternoon, but face it, ten hours is still a long day. When I started out, I told myself, "Don't feel guilty." But when I leave her off at my sister-in-law's, I see her perfect family—she's home all day with her children. They have a dog and a yard. I think about the fact that my mom stayed home all day with me. I wonder if I'm giving my child the foundation my mother gave me. Then I tell myself, "Don't feel guilty! Your guilt has do with you, not the baby. The baby is fine." At least I think the baby's fine.

In part the gender strategies of men paralleled those of women. In part they didn't because it was not, by tradition, men's role to do housework and childcare, and men did not so often find themselves doing more of it than their wives. So they did not so often pressure their wives to share the work at home. On the contrary, men were more often the target of such pressure, and their resistance took many forms—disaffiliation from the task at hand, needs reduction, making substitute offerings to the marriage, and selective encouragement of the wife's efforts. Some strategies went more against the emotional grain than others and took more emotional preparation. Perhaps the male strategy that took the most emotional preparation was that of "needs reduction." Some men conceded that sharing was fair but resisted increasing their labor at home by scaling down what they thought needed doing. One man explained that he never shopped because he "didn't need anything." He didn't need to shop for furniture (the couple had recently moved into a new apartment) because he didn't care about furnishing their apartment. He didn't cook dinner because cold cereal "was fine." His wife joined him in scaling down her notion of their needs, but only to a certain point, after which she gave up, furnished their apartment, cooked their meals, and resented doing so. While some men pretended to reduce their needs, others pursuing this strategy stood by the truth of their lowered notion of needs. They actually suppressed their desires for comfort. As one man described working two jobs and raising small children, "It's like being in the army. You set the comforts of home behind you."

EMOTIONAL CONSEQUENCES

Just as the emotional pathways for each line of action differ, so do the emotional consequences. Many working mothers who held egalitarian gender ideals but had husbands who refused to share housework felt they had the right to feel resentful and felt so. Not looking to their husbands for a solution to the double day, many traditional women did not feel they had the right to resent nonhelping husbands and so didn't resent them. Under the strain, however, they seemed more often to get sick, feel frustrated at life in general, or take a sacrificial stance. If career loomed large in their identity, women who felt forced to severely curtail their careers often had to manage loss of self-esteem and depression. Women who felt homemaking was important and who cut corners at home often felt a loss of self-esteem and guilt. In general, the combination of an actor's gender ideology and the actual result of the interplay of each partner's gender strategy seemed to determine how he or she felt.

One woman, Nancy Holt, had staged a "sharing showdown" (a strategy of active change) with her husband. The issue of how to divide the housework and childcare was thick with symbolic meanings to both and had escalated into the storm center of their marriage. For Nancy, her husband's refusal to share work at home recalled her own father: "Coming home, putting his feet up, and hollering at my mom to serve him. My biggest fear is of being treated like a servant. I've had bad dreams about it." For her husband, Evan, Nancy's insistence felt like a form of domination. He also suspected that Nancy's ardent desire to get him more involved in work at home was motivated by her own desire to do less of it. His alcoholic mother had rarely cared for her children; now he felt he had a wife who was getting out of caring for him too. The Holts fought bitterly over who should assume how much responsibility for their domestic lives and finally reached an impasse. Nancy wouldn't give up wanting Evan to do half the housework, and Evan wouldn't do half. Nancy realized she had to choose between living up to her gender ideals or staying married. Not only did they have small children and a network of concerned, Catholic, middle-class, family-oriented relatives, but, aside from this great thorn in their sides, they loved each other. So to save the marriage, Nancy backed off, adjusting to doing 90 percent of the work at home herself but resenting it.

Her "solution" presented Nancy with a problem—how to manage her resentment. As a feminist working the double day, she felt angry. But as a woman who wanted to stay married to a chauvinist, she had to find a way to manage her anger. She couldn't change her husband's viewpoint, and she couldn't banish her deep belief that a man should share. What she engaged in instead was a private program of anger management. She avoided resentment by dropping from view a series of connections between his refusal to share the load at home and all that this symbolized to her—her lack of worth in his eyes, his lack of consideration and even love for her. She held on to sharing as a general principle that should operate in the world at large but tucked it away as not relevant in her case.

She also encapsulated her anger by dividing the issue of housework from the emotion-loaded idea of equality. She "rezoned" this anger-inducing territory so that only if Evan did not walk the dogs would she feel indignant. Focusing more narrowly on the minor issue of the dogs, Nancy would not need to feel upset about the double day *in general*. Compartmentalizing her anger this way, she could still be a feminist—still believe that sharing goes with equality and equality goes with love—but this chain of associations now hinged more specifically and safely on just how lovingly Evan groomed, fed, and walked *the dogs.*

Another plank in Nancy's emotion-management program, one she shared with Evan, was to suppress any comparison between her hours of leisure and his. Like other women who didn't feel angry at combining full-time work with the lion's share of the housework, Nancy narrowed her comparison group to other working mothers, and avoided comparing herself with Evan and other working fathers. She talked about herself as more organized, energetic, and successful *than they.* Nancy and Evan also agreed on a different baseline comparison between Evan and other men. If Nancy compared Evan to her ideal of a liberated husband or to men she actually knew who did more work at home, then she grew angry that Evan did not do more. But if she confined her comparisons to Evan's father or her own father, or to Evan's choice of men to compare himself with, then she didn't get angry, because Evan did as much or more around the house than they did.

Nancy and Evan attributed their unequal contributions to the home to their different characters. As Evan phrased it, there seemed to be no problem of a leisure gap between them, only the continual, fascinating interaction of two personalities. "I have a lazy personality," he explained. "And I'm not well organized. I need to do things in my own time. That's the sort of person I am." Nancy, on the other hand, described herself as "compulsive" and "well organized." Now, six months after their blowup, when discussing why Evan didn't share the housework, Nancy said fatalistically—as she had not previously—"I was socialized to do the housework. Evan wasn't." Seeing Evan's nonparticipation engraved in childhood, beyond change, lent their resolution of the matter a certain inevitability and further buried the frightening anger each felt toward the other.

All this did not mean that Nancy ceased to care about equality between the sexes. On the contrary, she cut out magazine articles about how males advanced faster in social welfare (her field) than females. She complained about the wage gap between men and women and the deplorable state of daycare. She pushed her feminism onto a difference stage. Discrimination that was safely "out there" made her indignant, but not the not-sharing at home. She bent her beliefs around her dilemma.

Not all of these anger-avoiding ways of framing reality were Nancy's doing. Together, she and Evan developed an anger-avoidant myth. Some time after their blowup, I asked Nancy to go down a long list of household chores: packing lunches, emptying garbage . . . She interrupted me to explain with a broad wave of her hand, "I do the upstairs. Evan does the downstairs." "What is upstairs?" I asked. Matter-of-factly, Nancy explained that upstairs there is the living room, the dining room, the kitchen, two bedrooms, and two baths—basically the entire house. Downstairs is the garage, a place of storage and hobbies, Evan's hobbies. There was no trace of humor in her upstairs-downstairs view of sharing. Later I heard the same upstairs-downstairs formula from Evan. They seemed to have agreed on it. In this upstairs-downstairs account, the garage was elevated to the full moral and practical equivalent of the rest of the house. Evan was to look after the dog, the car, and the downstairs.

The "upstairs-downstairs" formulation seemed to me a family fiction, even a modest delusional system concealing an unequal division of labor, Nancy's indignation over that inequality, and their joint fear of Nancy's anger. It seemed to me that her anger was still there—not in the sense that she acknowledged that she was angry, but in the sense that long after the crisis, her talk about the second shift evoked strong words and a raised voice. She had managed her anger by mentally partitioning anger-evoking ideas, by avoiding bad thoughts, by refocusing her attention and sustaining the upstairs-downstairs myth. But her anger seemed to persist and leak into other areas of their family anyway. Yet the myth of the upstairs-downstairs became the apparent burial ground of the very idea of the conflict and anger. It became a family coverup that concealed a great unresolved issue in their marriage. Writ large, it concealed the conflict between an egalitarian ideology and its feeling rules, on the one hand, and a traditional marriage, on the other.

Many women like Nancy Holt are caught between their new gender ideology and an old reality, her "new" rules and his "old" feelings. In the absence of basic changes in men, male culture, and the structure of work that keep up with the rapid changes in women, female emotion management smoothes over the contradictions. Personal emotion work picks up where social transformation leaves off. In this case, emotion work is the cost women pay for the absence of change in men and in their circumstances. Since Nancy's resentment leaked out despite her emotion work, Evan paid an emotional price as well. Indeed, the most important cost of the absence of change in response to social pressures on men like Evan may be the harmful ambivalence it introduces into their wives' love for them. Among the working parents I studied, the more the husband shared the load at home, the happier the marriage.

In sum, the men and women in my study pursued gender strategies, created emotional pathways for them, and experienced the emotional consequences of them. The links between gender strategies, the emotional preparation for them, and the emotional consequences of them are sketched in chart 2.

Just as we can speak of gender strategies, so we can speak of race and class strategies. Given an individual's placement in the race or class hierarchy, we can ask which feeling rules will make sense to them and which ways of managing emotion will seem necessary. Many of us think of race, class, and gender as stratification systems and as part of the social landscape "out there."

CHART 2   Gender Ideology, Strategy, and Emotions

Gender Ideology	Egalitarian	Traditional
Attitude to work	When wives work full-time, men should share work at home. Sacrifice no more natural to women than to men.	Even if women work full-time, it is women's job to care for the home. Women's sacrificial stance a virtue.
Feeling rules	Men should want to share; no gratitude owed. Okay for women to enjoy status from work, identify with it. A man earns his own and his wife's respect when he identifies himself with activities at home.	Men have a right to expect gratitude for help. Only what a woman does at home matters; only what a man does at work matters.
Preferred gender strategies	Strategies of active change or maintenance of equality.	Strategies of maintenance of inequality. Some strategies of passive change.
Emotional pathways	Steel self for assertion, muster indignation.	Suppress personal needs, work ambitions.
Consequences in emotion management	Happier with marriage or, if husband resists sharing, management of disappointment and anger.	Indirect expression of discontent at strain. Numbness: "I don't know what I feel."

Partly they are out there. But we also inwardly orient ourselves to these structures. We check our available resources for the opportunities "for a person of my race" or "a person of my class." In light of our intuitive grasp of our location in a stratification system, certain ideologies and feeling rules gain appeal and certain strategies of action unfold. How does a person deal with racial antagonism or discrimination—assimilate, retreat, or affiliate with a separate subculture? To what extent do we alter our strategy and coordinate our emotion work to suit each different context?

In their essay "The Hero, the Sambo, and the Operator," Stephen Warner, David Wellman, and Lenore Weitzman point to certain "racial roles."[2] The Sambo works through avoidance of conflict, ingratiation, and avoidance of the expression of anger. The Operator detaches from others. The Hero confronts inequities directly and openly expresses his feelings about them. If we conceive of these as active stances toward stratification, we can explore the emotions that go with them.[3]

One emotional preparation minorities often use for integrating with the majority group is to develop a protective sixth sense, a special sensitivity to others that highlights or filters out messages others send "to me as a black, as a gay, as an elderly person, as a poor person." This social paranoia, as we might call it, allows us to guard against feeling hurt or humiliated and to reframe personal insults as "X's prejudice." It is the psychological equivalent of a status shield.

Indeed, the higher our status, generally speaking, the more protected we are from insult and humiliation and the less emotionally armed we need to be against them. The less powerful our status shield, the more we must prepare ourselves internally. In this sense, gender, ethnic, and class strategies share certain emotional features. In each case, our social footing depends on our context. Some women in my study moved from the office, where they enjoyed a status shield, to their home, where they did not.[4] A thirty-five-year-old working mother, who had been promoted from secretary to junior manager, said:

> I sit here [in the office] and I . . . meet with lawyers, and I tell consultants what to do like a mogul. I get on the bus. I get off the bus and I'm home. I drop that personality completely. The personality I have at work is not the personality I have at home. It's frustrating to have just finished a high-level meeting on an issue involving millions of dollars and two hours later have to say to my husband, "Will you turn off the light when you come out of the kitchen." He thinks that's my job. It's very difficult making the switch those first few hours. I steam inside. The weekend—I'm fine.

But a Chicana garment worker and mother of four complained of the reverse problem. At home, she felt like a proud authority figure to her four children, but at her sewing machine in a long row of other workers, she felt like a humble worker. She wanted to avoid having her children see her at work because she would be "too ashamed." These examples pose further questions: Who "goes up" and who "goes down" in status when they come home from work? How does this vary by race and class? Where, relatively speaking, does one feel proud, and where ashamed? What emotion work does it take to make the transition?

It is, in the end, through the pathways of feeling that we deal with—and hopefully change—the realities of stratification far outside ourselves.

Part Three

THE REFERRED PAIN OF A TROUBLED SOCIETY

10 FROM THE FRYING PAN INTO THE FIRE

An advertisement for Quaker Oats cereal in an issue of *Working Mother* magazine provides a small window on the interplay between consumption and the application of the idea of efficiency to private time in modern America.[1] In the ad, a mother, dressed in a business suit, affectionately hugs her smiling son. Beneath the image, we read: "Instant Quaker Oatmeal, for moms who have a lot of love but not a lot of time." The ad continues with a short story: "Nicky is a very picky eater. With Instant Quaker Oatmeal, I can give him a terrific hot breakfast in just 90 seconds. And I don't have to spend any time coaxing him to eat it!"

The ad then presents "facts" about mother and child: "Sherry Greenberg, with Nicky, age four and a half, Hometown: New York City, New York, Occupation: Music teacher, Favorite Flavor: Apples and Cinnamon." The designers of this ad, we could imagine, want us to feel we've been let in on an ordinary moment in a middle-class American morning. In this ordinary moment, Sherry Greenberg is living according to a closely scheduled, rapidly paced "adult" time, while Nicky is living according to a more dawdling, slowly paced "child" time. So the mother faces a dilemma. To meet her work deadline, she must get Nicky on "adult" time. But to be a good mother it is desirable to give her child a hot breakfast—"hot" being associated with devotion and love. To cook the hot breakfast, though, Sherry needs *time*. The ad suggests that it is the cereal itself that solves the problem. It conveys love because it is hot, but it permits efficiency because it's quickly made. The cereal would seem to reconcile an image of American motherhood of the 1950s with the female work role of 2000 and beyond.

The cereal also allows Sherry to avoid the unpleasant task of struggling with her child over scarce time. In the ad, Nicky's slow pace is implicitly attributed to his character ("Nicky is a very picky eater") and not to the fact that he is being harnessed to an accelerating pace of adult work time or protesting an adult speed-up by staging a "slowdown." By permitting the mother to avoid a fight with her son over time, the ad brilliantly evokes a common problem and proposes a commodity as a solution.

Attached to the culture of time shown in the ad is a key but hidden social logic. This modern working mother is portrayed as resembling Frederick Taylor, the famed efficiency expert of modern industry. The principle of efficiency is not located, here, at work in the person of the owner, the fore-man, or the worker. It is located in the worker-as-mother. We do not see a boss pressing the worker for more efficiency at the office. Instead, we see a mother pressing her son to eat more efficiently at home. This efficiency-seeking is transferred from man to woman, from workplace to home, and from adult to child. Nicky becomes his own task master, quickly gobbling his breakfast himself because it is so delicious. Frederick Taylor has leapt the fence from factory to home, adult to child, and jumped, it seems, into the cereal box itself. Frederick Taylor has become a commodity. It provides efficiency. Thus, the market reinforces the idea of efficiency twice—once at a locus of production, where the worker is pressed to work efficiently, and again, as a supplier of consumer goods, where it promises to deliver the very efficiency it also demands.

Quaker Oats cereal may be a paradigm for a growing variety of goods and services—frozen dinners, computer shopping services, cell phones,[2] and the like—that claim to save time for busy working parents. They often save time at home. But the ethic of "saving time" raises the question of what we want to save time for.[3] In the case above, the photo of the happy mother and child suggests that the mother is rushing her son through breakfast, not to race out to an all-absorbing job at a dot-com company, but to teach a few piano lessons. The picture doesn't challenge our idea of the primacy, even sacredness, of Nicky's home. So we don't much notice the sly insinuation of Frederick Taylor into the scene.

CONVENTIONAL VERSUS UNCONVENTIONAL WISDOM

If, through modern Western eyes, the Greenbergs of this ad were a normal family, we could imagine them feeling that family life superseded all other aspects of life. That is, according to modern conventional wisdom, a happy family life is an end in itself. Earning and spending money are the means for achieving this end. Home and community are primary; workplace and mall are secondary. When we go out to work, it's to put bread on the table for the family. When we shop at the mall, it's often to buy a Christmas, birthday, or house present "for the family." Put in other terms, we often see the home and the community as sacred, and the workplace and the mall as profane. We are who we are at home and in our communities. We do what we do at work and buy what we buy at the mall.

To be sure, we make exceptions for the odd workaholic here or shopa-holic there, but, as the terms imply, an overconcern with the profane realms of work and mall are, given this way of seeing things, off moral limits. Sherry

Greenberg fits right in. She is in her kitchen feeding her son. She has what one imagines to be a manageable job. It's just that she's wanting to hurry things along a bit.

Implicit in this conventional view of family life is the idea that our use of time is like a language. We speak through it. By either what we say we want to spend time doing or what we actually spend time doing, we say what it is we hold sacred. Maybe we don't think of it just this way, but we assume that each "spending time" or each statement of feeling about time ("I wish I could spend time") is a bow from the waist to what we hold dear. It is a form of worship. Again, Sherry Greenberg is symbolizing the importance of family. It's just that she's slightly on the edge of that conventional picture because she's in a hurry to get out of it. The Quaker Oats ad both appeals to this family-comes-first picture of life and subtly challenges it, by taking sides with her desire to feed Nicky "efficiently."

The subtle challenge of the ad points, I believe, to a larger contradiction underlying stories like that of the Greenbergs. Reflecting on my research on the Fortune 500 company I call Amerco, I'll try to explore it. Increasingly, our belief that family comes first conflicts with the emotional draw of both workplace and mall. Indeed, I would argue that a constellation of pressures is pushing men and women further into the world of workplace and mall. And television—a pipeline, after all, to the mall—is keeping them there. Family and community life have meanwhile become less central as places to talk and relate, and less the object of collective rituals.

Many of us respond to these twin trends, however, not by turning away from family and community, but by actually elevating them in moral importance. Family and community are not a realm in decline, as David Popenoe argues about the family and Robert Putnam argues for the community. To many people, both have become even more important morally. We encapsulate the idea of the cherished family.[4] We separate ideal from practice. We separate the idea of "spending time with X" from the idea of "believing in the importance of X." We don't link what we think with what we do. Or as one Amerco employee put it, using company language, "I don't walk the talk at home." This encapsulation of our family ideal allows us to accommodate to what is both a pragmatic necessity and a competing source of meaning—the religion of capitalism. I say pragmatic necessity, because most Americans, men and women alike, have to work for food and rent.

At the same time, a new cultural story is unfolding. It is not that capitalism is an unambiguous object of worship. After all, American capitalism is, in reality, a highly complex, internally diverse economic system for making, advertising, and selling things. But, without overstating the case, it seems true that capitalism is a cultural as well as an economic system and that the symbols and rituals of this cultural system compete with, however much they seem to serve, the symbols and rituals of community and family. This means that working long hours and spending a lot of money—instead of spending time together—have increasingly become *how* we say "I love you" at home. As Juliet Schor argues in *The Overspent American,* over the last twenty years, Americans have raised the bar on what feels like enough money to get along. In 1975, according to a Roper poll, 10 percent of people mentioned a second color TV as part of "the good life," and 28 percent did in 1991. A 1995 Merck Family Fund poll showed that 27 percent of people who earned $100,000 or more agreed with the statement, "I cannot afford to buy everything I really need." At the same time, between 1975 and 1991, the role of family in people's idea of "the good life" declined while the importance of having money increased. The importance of having a happy marriage to "the good life" declined from 84 percent in 1975 to 77 percent in 1991. Meanwhile having "a lot of money" went from 38 percent in 1975 to 55 percent in 1991.[5]

How much of a stretch is it, I wonder, to go from the trends Schor points out to Harvey Cox's daring thesis: that capitalism has become a religion? As Cox puts it:

> Just as a truly global market has emerged for the first time in human history, that market is functioning without moral guideposts and restraints, and it has become the most powerful institution of our age. Even nation-states can often do little to restrain or regulate it. More and more, the idea of "the market" is construed, not as a creation of culture ("made by human hands," as the Bible says about idols), but as the "natural" way things happen. For this reason, the "religion" the market generates often escapes criticism and evaluation or even notice. It becomes as invisible to those who live by it as was the religion of the preliterate Australians whom Durkheim studied, who described it as just "the way things are."[6]

Capitalism has, Cox suggests, its myth of origin, its legends of the fall, its doctrine of sin and redemption, its notion of sacrifice (state belt-tightening), and its hope of salvation through the free market system. Indeed, if in the Middle Ages the church provided people with a basic orientation to life, the multinational corporation's workplace, with its "mission statements," its urgent deadlines, its demands for peak performance and total quality, does so today. Paradoxically, what would seem like the most secular of systems (capitalism), organized around the most profane of activities (making a living, shopping), provides a sense of the sacred. So what began as a *means* to an end—capitalism the means, a good living as the end—has become an *end* itself. It's a case of mission drift writ large. The cathedrals of capitalism dominate our cities. Its ideology dominates our airwaves. It calls for sacrifice, through long hours of work, and offers its blessings, through commodities. When the terrorists struck the twin towers on 9/11, they were, perhaps, aiming at what they conceived of as a more powerful rival temple, another religion. Heartless as they were, they were correct to see capitalism, and the twin towers as its symbol, as a serious rival religion.

Like older religions, capitalism partly creates the anxieties to which it poses itself as a necessary answer. Like the fire-and-brimstone sermon that begins with "Man, the lowly sinner," and ends with "Only this church can redeem you," so the market ethos defines the poor or unemployed as "unworthy slackers" and offers work and a higher standard of living as a form of salvation. Capitalism is not, then, simply a system in the *service of* family and community; it *competes* with the family. When we separate our fantasy of family life, our ideas of being a "good mother and father" from our daily expressions of parenthood, our ideals live timelessly on while we worship at the biggest altar in town, with ten-hour days and long trips to the mall.

A constellation of forces seems to be pressing in the direction of the religion of capitalism. And while no one wants to go back to the "frying pan" of patriarchy, we need to look sharp about the fire of market individualism under capitalism. It is in the spirit of looking at that fire that we can examine several conditions that exacerbate the tendency to apply the principle of efficiency to private life.

The first factor is the inevitable—and on the whole I think beneficial—movement of women into the paid workforce.[7] Exacerbating this squeeze on time is the overall absence of government or workplace policies that foster the use of parental leave or shorter, more flexible hours. Over the last twenty years, workers have also been squeezed by a lengthening workweek. According to a recent International Labor Organization report on working hours, Americans are putting in longer hours than workers of any other industrialized nation. We now work two weeks longer each year than our counterparts in Japan, the vaunted long-work-hour capital of the world.[8] American married couples and single-parent families are also putting in more hours in the day and more weeks in the year than they did thirty years ago. Counting overtime and commuting time, a 1992 national sample of men averaged 48.8 hours of work, and women, 41.7. [9] Work patterns vary by social class, ethnicity, race, and the number and ages of children, of course. But, overall, between 1969 and 1996 the increase in American mothers' paid work combined with a shift toward single-parent families has led to an average decrease of 22 hours a week of parental time available (outside of paid work) to spend with children.[10] And the emotional draw of a work culture is sometimes strong enough to outcompete a weaker family culture (see "Emotional Geography and the Flight Plan of Capitalism," chapter 15).

THE OTHER SIDE OF THE MARKET RELIGION:
NOT WALKING THE TALK AT HOME

If capitalism began as a means but became an end in itself, then families and local communities must daily face a competing urgency system and a rival conception of time. Company deadlines compete with school plays. Holiday sales at the mall vie with hanging out at home. The company's schedule and rules have come, for workers, to define those of families. For the managers and production workers at Amerco, the company I studied for the *Time Bind,* the debut of a certain kind of product and its "product life cycle" came to prevail over personal anniversaries and school holidays. When family events did take precedence, they did so on company terms. As one woman explained, "My mother died and I went back to arrange for the funeral and all. I went for four days. The company gives us that for bereavement, and so that's the time I spent." In the early industrial period in Europe, whole workforces disappeared at festival time, or workers put an iron bar in the machinery, stopped the assembly line, and took a break. Company time did not always rule.

In response to the challenge of this competing urgency system, I've argued, many families separate their ideal of themselves as "a close family" from a life that in reality is more hurried, fragmented, crowded, and individualized than they would like. They develop the idea of a hypothetical family, the family they would be if only they had time. And then they deal with life in a contrary fashion.

Many Amerco employees came home from a long workday to fit many necessary activities into a limited amount of time. Although there were important exceptions, many workers tried to go through domestic chores rapidly if for no other reason than to clear some space in which to go slowly. They used many strategies to save time—they planned, delegated, did several things simultaneously. They packed one activity close up against the next, eliminating the framing around each event, periods of looking forward to or back upon an event, which might have heightened its emotional impact. A 2:00 to 2:45 play date, 2:45 to 3:15 shopping trip, 3:15 to 4:45 visit to Grandma, and so on. As one mother, a sales manager, said with satisfaction, "What makes me a good employee at work is what makes me able to do all I do at home; I'm a multitasker, but [with a laugh] at work I get paid for it."

With all these activities, family time could be called "hurried" or "crowded." But in fact many working parents took a sporting "have fun" attitude toward their hurried lives: "Let's see how fast we can do this! Come on, kids, let's go!" They brought their image of the family closer to the reality of it by saying, in effect, "We like it this way." They saw hassle as challenge. In other families, parents seemed to encourage children to develop schedules parallel to and as hectic as their own. For example, the average annual vacation time both at Amerco—and in the United States as a whole—is twelve days, while schoolchildren typically have summer holidays of three months. So one Amerco mother placed her eight-year-old son in a nearby summer program and explained to him, in a you're-going-to-love-this way, "You have your job to go to, too." She talked about her schedule as she might have talked about a strenuous hike. She was having fun roughing it with multitasking and chopped-up time.

Another way of resolving the contradiction between ideal and reality was to critique the fun ethic and say, in effect, "Family life isn't supposed to be fun. It's supposed to be a hassle, but we're in the hassle together, and why isn't that okay?" This often carried families over long stretches of time, but it prevented family members from giving full attention to each other. Time was hurried (not enough time allotted for an activity—15-minute baths, 20-minute dinners, for example). Or time was crowded (one or more people were doing more than one thing at a time). Or it was uncoordinated. Only two out of four people could make it to dinner, the ball game, the reunion. If there was not some chronic avoidance of a deep tension, families usually also took another approach. They *deferred* having a good time. Instead of saying, "This hassle is fun," they said, in effect, "This hassle isn't fun. But we'll have fun *later*." They waited for the weekend, for their vacation, for "quality time."

But the more a family deferred the chance for relaxed communication, the more anxious they sometimes became about it. One man told me: "My wife and I hadn't had time together for a long time, so we decided to take some 'marital quality time' by going out to a restaurant to eat dinner together. We had a nice dinner and afterwards went for a walk. We passed a toy store and my wife wanted to shop for a toy for our child. But I told her, 'No, you have a different quality time with our child. This is *our* quality time.' So we spent the rest of the evening arguing about whose quality time it was we were spending."

Another long-hours Amerco executive seemed to take this strategy of deferral to an extreme. When I asked him whether he wished he'd spent more time with his three daughters when they were growing up, he answered, "Put it this way, I'm pleased with how they turned out." This father loved his daughters, but he loved them as results. Or rather, his feeling was " I want my wife to enjoy the process of raising them. I'll enjoy that vicariously. What I will enjoy directly is the result, the young adults." So he didn't think family life should or shouldn't be fun while the kids were small and adolescent. That was his wife's specialty. He was deferring his real enjoyment until his daughters had grown up. Even Amerco parents who spent far more time with their children occasionally justified this time in terms of future results. They were pleased at how "old for their age" their children were, how "ahead," given a limited expenditure of parental time. Perhaps, most parents held a double perspective on their children—they cared about the child as he or she was growing up and about the child as he or she emerged in adulthood. Most oriented toward the family as a source of intrinsic pleasure were women and workers in the middle or lower ranks of the company; least oriented in this way were upper management or professional men—the congregation and the priests.

From the top to the bottom of the Amerco workforce, workers were forced to answer the challenge of capitalism—not simply as a system that gave them jobs, money, and stuff, but as a system that offered them a sense of purpose and guidance in a confusing time. They had to deal with the religion of capitalism, its grip on honor and sense of worth, its subtraction from—or absorption of—family and community life. We've emerged from an era in which most women had little or no paid work to a era in which most do. Are women jumping from the frying pan of patriarchy into the fire of capitalism? Just as the early industrial workforces took off at festival time, because they were not yet "disciplined" to capitalism, maybe postindustrial ones will work out their own way of living a balanced life. There could be a balance not just between the role of piano teacher, say, and mother, but between the unpaid *world* of home and community and the money *world* of work and mall. That may be the deeper issue underlying the ad for Quaker Oats cereal. For, our cultural soil is surreptitiously prepared for ads, like that for Quaker Oats cereal, that make you spend time buying one more thing that promises to save time—which increasingly we spend earning and buying.

11 THE COLONIZED COLONIZER

Cruelty and Kindness in Mother-Daughter Bonds

In a workshop titled "Gender, Context and Narrative" in Trivandrum, Kerala, India, in 1998, a gathering of Indian women—Hindu, Muslim, Sikh, Syrian Christian, most from the Brahmin caste but some from the matrilineal Nayar, and others from the Ezhava and Pulaya—told stories of their grandmothers, their mothers, and themselves. These were unusually detailed, heartfelt stories. During this all-India workshop and during the five months I lived in Kerala as a Fulbright scholar, I came to know and admire the women who shared them.[1]

The stories of these three generations both compress many centuries of history and express a paradox of the colonized colonizer. The grandmothers of most of the narrators grew up in the strict seclusion of Hindu feudalism. Most of the granddaughters have become prominent figures in the academic and literary life of modern India. So the stories focus on the "great leap forward" from illiterate, secluded grandmothers to highly educated, publicly prominent granddaughters. They focus on the enormous discontinuities created by this great leap forward and also on the strong connections it failed to shake. What struck me, as an American listener, was the harshness of patriarchal custom—seclusion, widow penance, suttee—as well as the fact that it so often fell to older women to impose it on younger ones and the extraordinary power of compassion, or at least obligation, through which daughters continued their relations to their mothers.

It was as if patriarchal fathers subcontracted to their wives the job of keeping patriarchy going, much on the model of "indirect rule" under colonialism. Yet as small girls, the mothers had themselves suffered greatly from severe restrictions. A mother who dutifully upheld her family's honor had to enforce rules she knew all too well, from her own experience, hurt her daughter. She faced the difficult choice between being good (dutifully upholding family honor) and being kind (sparing her daughter from hurtful practices). So how did this colonial arrangement shape the relation between mother and daughter? What did it do to love?

The reality of a mother-child relation is wondrously hard to know. We have here the accounts of the daughters, which surely differ from those of the

149

mothers and grandmothers. These accounts are their personal truths. Their truths may be myths, but myths that they tell us ring true to them. Would such stories differ from those of a culturally attuned psychiatrist who came to know all three generations? We don't know. And about any ultimate meanings we are left to guess. Still, we have much to go on.

Let us take the story of Radharani, a Calcutta-bred Brahmin who lived between 1903 and 1989, as this is told to us by her daughter, the well-known Bengali poet and novelist Nabaneeta Sen. Like many Hindu girls of her generation, Radharani had an arranged marriage at age twelve. Unfortunately shortly after her marriage, her husband died of the Asiatic flu and she was returned to her parents' home as a very young and, as they say, "inauspicious" widow (a potential cause of family misfortune). Radharani's mother, Narayani, oversaw all the rites of young Radharani's widowhood. As Sen writes:

> Narayani took off all her jewelry, chopped off her thick long locks, enforcing a widow's close crop, made her wear the borderless white cloth and forced her to [dress] in the widow's chador [long cloth] around herself. From now on she was to eat a proper widow's diet, *havishyanna*, only once a day. Radharani was to eat . . . for the rest of her life what is usually eaten only by those practicing austerity during the formal mourning period after a death. And what did Radharani eat on the fasting days, like the *ekadasi*? She ate nothing and she drank nothing. What if she cheated while taking her bath and quietly gulped down a few drops of bath water on a hot summer's day? To stop that, she was always accompanied into the bathroom by an invigilator, like a sister or a maid who would keep a careful eye on her penance.[2]

In what spirit did Narayani impose these restrictions on her daughter? Did she admonish her daughter not to drink water regretfully and lovingly, or meanly and harshly? We don't know. But Nabaneeta Sen tells us that Narayani was "not being cruel." As a devout Hindu, she felt she was helping her daughter toward a better life in her next incarnation. And as a rule-abiding householder, she was reaffirming the honor of both the family and the girl by helping her daughter atone for her husband's death and uphold the powerful taboo against widow remarriage.

Radharani loved to read, and her mother now forbade her to read because her reading was taken as a "cause" of her husband's death. "By reading books, she was told, she had voluntarily courted widowhood. It was no one else's fault but her own that her young husband had to die," Sen writes. Insofar as Narayani upheld this interpretation, she was also participating in a common way of thinking at the time. So in the eyes of most of her kin, it seems she wasn't being cruel.

Still, it is not hard to imagine that Radharani felt that her *mother* and not simply the custom was cruel. As Sen writes, Radharani "realized that she was alone: she was an outsider in her parental home." Narayani finally sent her young daughter Radharani, head shaven, shorn of jewelry, back to her more urbane and broad-minded in-laws' home, where she was welcomed with kindness, allowed to read, talk with literary guests, and ultimately go out to meetings. It was perhaps the comparison between her strict, withholding mother and her nourishing mother-in-law that allowed her to acknowledge both her mother and the feudal customs of Hindu widowhood *as* cruel. As Radharani grew into a young adult, she published poems in major literary magazines and became a nationally recognized poet.

At age twenty-eight she even broke the strong taboo on widow remarriage and secretly remarried. For her new in-laws, this was the first widow remarriage in the joint family. So great was the stigma of widow remarriage that, Sen writes, "Although Mrinallna [the new mother-in-law] was broadminded, in view of the social stigma attached to widow remarriage, [she] decided to leave the family home together with her son and daughter-in-law, and moved to a country house so that the future of the unmarried girls in the joint family would not be affected [by the polluting influence of a remarried widow]."[3]

The context of Radharani's life was similar to that of other Brahmin women in Calcutta as late as the early twentieth century. Under Indian Hindu patriarchy of this period, grandfathers, fathers, and sons were supposed to rule over grandmothers, mothers, and daughters. To be sure, there were regional, class, religious, and caste variations on this theme. But from feudal times through a series of invasions from the north, British colonialism, Partition, and early nation-building, the vast majority of Indian Hindu families were patrilineal, patrilocal, and patriarchal, as they are to a lesser degree today. This meant that for much of its history, in a society that looked to its past, women were at every caste level a subcaste. The birth of a girl was greeted with much less joy than that of a boy. Indeed, in northern rural areas, girls were fed less well than boys, taken to the doctor less often, and occasionally allowed to sicken and die—a practice that exists in some regions today. Even among the rich, women were typically not educated beyond the elementary grades and were married off—married "off" was the phrase—before puberty. The Hindu marriage ceremony even describes the husband as a "god" whom his wife should worship. Having "too much education" or even traveling abroad made a girl less marriageable and increased the dowry her father had to pay a prospective suitor. Sons could have several wives and remarry. Girls like Radharani often became young brides to much older men, sometimes second wives, and were early widowed and confined for the rest of their lives. The custom of suttee—a widow burning to death on her husband's funeral pyre—was not apparent in the lives of grandmothers described here, though when Radharani became a widow in 1916 it had not yet been banned.

Material arrangements underlay the lowly status of women such as

Radharani. A girl grew up as the child who would leave home for the house of her husband's extended family, the boy as the child who would stay. The eldest boy, not the oldest girl, was also valued as the future caretaker of his aged parents. According to the dowry system (which remains in effect today), the parents of the bride pay the groom's family a sum of money. So for new parents, a baby girl meant they would eventually lose money; a baby boy meant they would gain money.

There also seemed no way out. In the early part of the twentieth century, marriage was compulsory. The rare girl who refused marriage was, like a widow, "inauspicious." (Such beliefs are still widespread today. One woman, a lively and brilliant Bombay professional, told me she had resisted marriage in order to be able to have a career, since it was commonly assumed that she could not have both. When her mother became fatally ill, relatives scolded her, saying that her refusal to marry had "caused" her mother's death.)

Given this set of constrictive customs why, the modern reader may ask, didn't women rebel and bring their daughters along with them? After all, while both men and women thought of women as "burdens" (and, as women were early forbidden to work, in the financial sense they were), it was also true that men were burdens on women. They had to be fed, served, cleaned up after, catered to. And paradoxically, while women were seen as *weak*, they—like Radharani—had to be supremely *strong* to endure the customs that symbolized their helpless dependence. So why, we can ask, would a mother like Narayani consent with such apparent wholeheartedness to patriarchal customs that so hurt her daughter?

The social anthropologist Marvin Harris has suggested that the basis for this strong devaluation of women is, at bottom, population control.[4] Girls grow up to be women who have babies, and when the environment can't sustain a large population, one way of reducing the population is to discourage the survival of girls. While somewhat plausible, this explanation speaks to the issue of how a custom has a function for the larger society, but not to how a custom is emotionally embraced by women themselves.

The question here is whether within the bosom of this strong, pervasive, patriarchal culture, women ever questioned or resisted the customs that, to modern eyes, suppressed them. The answer from these narratives is yes, some did, but most did not. Indeed, a good number like Narayani staunchly defended patriarchal customs such as the harsh rites of widow penance. Why?

One reason seems to be that while all women were subordinate to all men, older women got a piece of the power pie. As a well-married bride and a mother of sons, a woman earned honor, and as mother-in-law to the young brides of her sons, she held great but narrowly focused power over younger kinswomen. The wife of the oldest son in a joint household also had authority over the wives of younger sons, and first wives over second and third ones. Low as they were on the totem pole, women were permitted enough authority and honor to develop a stake in it.

Women were also discouraged from rebelling against patriarchal customs because they were schooled in a notion of *honor* according to which their subordination was rewarding to them as well as other members of the household. As Leela Dube notes in *Women and Kinship,* while Indian women lacked status in the wider society, they had both honor and power within the household. Indeed, throughout the discussion of these narratives in the Kerala workshop, and in other discussions on the subject I had in India, the phrase recurred: "status in the household." This is a phrase foreign to American ears, used as we are to our small, neo-local, bilateral nuclear family, which minimizes age and sex differences. In the Indian culture that forms a backdrop to these narratives, an elder son had higher status than a younger one. The wife of an oldest son had higher status than the wife of a younger son. The first wife had higher status than the third. The first son of a second or third wife had lower status than the first son of a first, and so on. One had a status within the household. So even if one lacked status *as a woman,* a mother such as Narayani could have status *as a mother.* And in traditional Indian society, the household was the main entity within which to have any status at all.

Another reason women didn't rebel is because they were taught to keep silent about suffering. Indeed, they lived in what Leela Gulati calls a "culture of silence."[5] This is not a minor, mannerly avoidance of certain topics, but an honorable resolve to keep real pain to oneself. Men and women alike thought it was women's lot to suffer. In her narrative Leela Gulati describes her mother, Saras, a Brahmin from Tamil Nader, who was, like Radharani, harshly dealt with by her mother, Seetha. Saras suffered greatly but stoically told no one. Forced to leave school at age twelve to enter an arranged marriage with a much older man, Saras became miserably stranded between an angry mother who hastened to marry her off and aloof in-laws unwilling to welcome her. From neither her parents nor her in-laws did Saras receive enough love or resources to live on. But, according to Gulati, her new husband "*had no inkling*" that she was suffering. So, in addition to the inertia of custom and power sharing with men, the honor attached to silent stoicism seemed to keep mothers like Seetha and Narayani upholding customs that hurt their daughters.

But given this context, we can now wonder: What did Narayani *feel* about her daughter Radharani? What did Radharani *feel* toward her mother, Narayani? How did patriarchy shape *their relationship?* Both are now dead. Their story is related to us by Nabaneeta Sen, a granddaughter who, she notes, did not love or feel loved by her grandmother Narayani. So the story we have reflects an openly stated vantage point. Sen recalls that her grandmother Narayani was the mother of twelve but doted only on her sons and "hated girl children in general." As she explains, "On festive occasions, she sent new cloths and sweets to her grandsons, but not to her granddaughters. She advocated education for the sons and grandsons, but not for the daughters and granddaughters. . . . [My grandmother] was not fond of me. In fact, she was not fond of any of her granddaughters with the sole exception of Padmadidi [Sen's elder sister], the firstborn of her first son."[6]

We can't, alas, know exactly how Narayani felt about her daughter, but we can come to appreciate some of the huge cultural obstacles to mother-daughter love. For woven into the relation between Narayani and Radharani is a paradox writ larger in colonialism itself. In *The Colonizer and the Colonized* the Tunisian author Albert Memmi reflects on the ways in which colonized people internalize the values of colonialism, become its lieutenants, enforce its rules, embrace its ideals, and uphold its code of silence. The colonizer gets the colonized to do the psychological dirty work of colonizing—to disdain, for example, the "lazy natives."

A glance at history reveals other versions of the colonized colonizer, which find expression outside the family. The Germans appointed Jewish *kapos* to help control Jewish prisoners in the concentration camps. The Soviets appointed *preduki* to do the same in the gulag. Top British and Dutch colonial officials trained natives to serve as police, lower-ranking soldiers, and minor officials, and it was through these lower officials that tough orders from on high were carried out. At the same time, the "lieutenants" in all these systems may *also* have wanted to rescue other colonized people—for few knew better than they did the painful costs of the system they upheld.

Memmi focuses on this pattern of indirect rule as it impacts a male general citizenry, and not as it impacts relations within a family or as it impacts women. But the lives of women in traditional India describe a parallel paradox, which strikes far closer to home. Under patriarchy, fathers and grandfathers often left it to their wives to enforce restrictions on girls. It was not Radharani's father, for example, who cut off his daughter's hair, confined her, and forbade her to drink water on hot days. Through the subcontracted power women wield over other women, through their acceptance of prevailing ideas about honor, through the stoical silence of daughters, the colonized colonize.

But colonizers often feel two ways about colonization. For Indian mothers in these narratives were *both* prison wardens of patriarchy *and* co-conspirators helping their daughter-prisoners to escape; some were more one, some more the other. Though Sen's Narayani and Gulati's Seetha passed on the hardships they had suffered, other mothers—many the same mothers—planned their daughters' great escape. These mothers said, in effect, "These rules are rigged against us, so I sympathize with your discontent. I couldn't escape, but I will help you do so."

A woman could split her ambivalence—prison warden vs. accomplice to the escape—any number of ways. But for all of these ways it may be useful to conceptualize the ambivalence as transgenerational. Three people can split a shared ambivalence between generations—a grandmother acting out one side of the conflict and a mother and daughter the other side. Indeed, Nabaneeta Sen's grandmother, Narayani, as we've seen, seemed to apply the cruel rules cruelly. But Radharani, whose hair was shorn and diet restricted, vowed to liberate her own young daughter from such customs. As a new mother, Radharani wrote a loving poem for *anna prasam,* the day of her baby daughter's rice-eating ceremony, the day she was named. Radharani's poem to Nabaneeta read:

Unspoilt and tender like freshly opened petals,
Our darling baby girl, forever smiling, forever matchless,
Sparkling with the purity of a morning-showered flower,
You've stepped into our home and lit it up with joy.
In you lie all our auspicious hopes,
In you is fulfilled the love that conquers pain,
My priceless jewel churned out of life's
Tears and laughter,
You've opened up in my heart a deathless
spring beyond words,
The ideals that I had cherished all through,
the boundless desires and visions that remain,
Unfulfilled and find no meaning in my life,
My auspicious girl, may it all bear fruit in yours.[7]

How, we can ask, could a girl who had been treated so harshly by her own mother be so loving to her daughter? Even allowing for the convention of flowery writing, we can perhaps speak of a mother's identification with her daughter coupled with the mission of compensation. "What I have wanted in my life," she says, "May you have in yours." But further, "may your life and your achievements make up for what was missing from my life as a young girl." We can only guess, but it is plausible to imagine that the extreme altruism in Radharani's poem was nourished by her own fairy-godmother-like mother-in-law. Yet the urgency of her wish seems at the same time to convey a command: "Make all my suffering worthwhile. Succeed."

As Nabaneeta Sen explains, "She wanted to live through me, who was less than a year old, and had shown no signs of the expected brilliance." From Sen's point of view, her mother wanted "too much." Sen says of her mother, "She was too strong for me. . . . She pushed too hard." As she further reflects,

My mother was my best friend and she was also my worst enemy. I am what I am today because of her, and what I am not, what I could not be, is also because of her. I meekly resisted her overpowering ambition by not being ambitious at all. I followed her dreams but not with my heart and soul. I applied myself with the minimum effort because I took my career as something that was dear to my mother and did not try to excel. In this way I was resisting Ma's will, denying her what she desired, by not trying for it. Now when I come to think of it all, I feel sorry for both of us.[8]

Ironically, Radharani, victim of her mother, the harsh lieutenant of patriarchy, became a lieutenant in the struggle for the liberation of her daughter. In taking up this other side too rigidly, she ambivalently embraced the paradox of the colonized colonizer. The mother—in this case, Nabaneeta Sen's mother, Radharani—suffers. Now, as a grown woman, Radharani is in a position to mete out punishment herself to her daughter. But does she? Or does her own suffering take the form of *sacrifice?* Does the mother forge a *renunciatory identification* with her daughter, a form of "altruistic surrender" so well described by Anna Freud?[9] If so, then perhaps Radharani came to own her suffering. It becomes hers. She does not try to pass it on. She herself takes on the cost of it to the detriment of her physical and mental health.

Or does the mother's suffering take the form of narcissistic sacrifice? Here the mother's suffering also becomes a sacrifice to others, but without renunciation of herself. She suffers "for" her daughter. She will not pass it on. But her own sacrifice will be compensated by the world. In particular, she will be compensated by the daughter's extraordinary success or devotion. So the mother says to the daughter, in effect, "My good wishes are yours *if* you are gifted, *if* you perform, *if* you bring honor to the family." In this case we can speak of narcissistically ambivalent, or contingent, altruism—altruism with a hidden price.

Alternatively, Radharani could have converted her own early suffering into a form of revenge on her daughter. This may, indeed, be what Radharani's own mother did to her. Here the mother does not "hold" her suffering. She passes it onto her daughter so as to rid herself of it.

In each case, the mother-daughter relationship carries the emotional burden of the syndrome of the colonized colonizer. In each case, the same culture is received, held, passed on in ways that reflect distinctly different emotional bargains. None of these three ways of addressing suffering—through renunciatory, narcissistic, or sadistic identification—could be said to be what we might today consider a "healthy" way of dealing with suffering. If feudal India's "culture of silence" guided mothers toward renunciation, women of Sen's generation question the very traditions that made women's suffering necessary in the first place. And they call for a new female self, which, when forced to suffer for whatever reason, can draw on strength based on a different cultural idea. If the long-suffering Indian mother of former times took pride in the strength to endure suffering and turned a blind eye to the ways in which mothers passed on their suffering to daughters, the new Indian feminist vision of the self calls for the strength it takes to create a kinder culture, and the strength it takes not to pass suffering on.

Radharani seems to have greeted the birth of her "auspicious" daughter Nabaneeta with both kindness and demands. Sen received her mother's blessings with a set of instructions about how to use them. For her part, Nabaneeta accepted her mother's gift ambivalently. She got a Ph.D. at age twenty-five and wrote well-received books. She fulfilled one side of the bargain. But at the same time she routinely sabotaged herself. As she writes, "Without the strong self-destructive force that makes me leave things to the last minute, lose important papers, forget important appointments, miss deadlines, forfeit offers and ignore opportunities, I would be living a different life today."[10] Some amount of such self-sabotage is normal enough. But maybe Nabaneeta's self-sabotage is part of an inaudible conversation across three generations of women about sacrifice in the crucible of the paradox of the colonized colonizer.

Other narratives presented at this workshop suggest that surviving this crucible is an extraordinary achievement. A good example of this achievement comes not from a mother but from a childless great-aunt. As Vina Majumdar, now a professor of English, tells it, her great-aunt Pishima as a thirteen-year-old girl ran away from an arranged marriage, returning to her parental home, where she remained single and devoted herself to the cause of education for all the girls in the family and community. Illiterate herself, Pishima obstinately insisted that Vina's mother be allowed to take lessons from a *dewar* (husband's younger brother), though by custom this was strictly forbidden. One by one, Pishima wrested the consent of all the parents of school-age girls in the neighborhood and personally escorted them, towel on her head against the rain, to and from school.[11]

If in some families, the grandmother acted the tough patriarch toward her daughter while the daughter, once grown, strongly supported her own daughter's autonomy, probably in most cases mothers expressed both sets of feelings at once, as if to say both "I will imprison you as I was imprisoned" *and* "I was born in jail, but I'll help set you free." Prita Desai describes just such a case. Her mother, Kusum, was born of Anavil Brahmins in south Gujarat. About her mother, Desai said, "I should view her as a Hindu *nari* (woman), her childhood dominated by her father and her youth and old age by her husband." Kusum had, Desai writes, "the makings of a modern woman but her wings were clipped by matrimony at the age of 15 years. When Kusum was a child, she was sent to school escorted by a beloved elder brother. Schooling ended when she finished seventh standard. Conservative attitudes toward co-education and the need to restrict a growing girl's movements grounded her early." This set up a conflict, which expressed itself in a message to her daughter which amounted to this: "These hurtful customs need to change. But, still, don't live in a way very different from how I have lived." Desai saw her mother as a "feminist . . . who quietly passed on the message that a woman had an identity, a will, and needed a space of her own." But Kusum also made it clear that instead of the four daughters she had, she had badly wished for four sons.[12]

Just as every human relationship is unique, so, too, is every form of ambivalence in the colonized-colonizer syndrome, and every daughter's response. For both Nabaneeta Sen and Prita Desai matters of personal chemistry and relations with other family members, matters that went well beyond patriarchy, influenced them.

But whichever side of the paradox came to prevail, it was usually daughters, and not sons, who took care of their mothers in old age. This was not the tradition, but it was often the truth. Sushil Narulla recounts the story of her Sikh family at the time of Partition. Mothers and grandmothers, she says, lovingly cared for their sons and grandsons, but in their final years received care from their daughters and granddaughters. Narulla describes her grandmother Ammaji, who lit the fire and cooked delicious meals with trembling hands and would, in summers, go from bed to bed kissing all her nine grandchildren while they slept. But when the family moved to better housing, none of her sons or grandsons took her in. Instead, her three daughters took turns looking after her. "In the end, what remained for the mother were the fraught bonds with her daughters." Poignantly, Prita Desai describes nursing her aged mother as she drifted into death, a mother about whom she says, "Deep within me remained the feeling that she hated and disliked me for a long time."[13]

Fathers did not live out the same paradox with their sons that mothers lived out with their daughters. For fathers, upholding family honor did not so fundamentally conflict with love and identification with a son as it did for mothers in relation to daughters. Fathers also faced the paradox differently with their daughters. For fathers, family honor was also pitted against what we now see as human kindness, but, as the stories suggest, many fathers didn't see it that way. A good number of grandfathers were described as tyrannical. The paternal grandfather of one narrator threw food in her grandmother's face because she served it too late. Perhaps most of the fathers in these stories were neither especially cruel nor highly supportive of their wives and daughters. Most wished for boy children but accepted and loved their girl children. Most men understandably felt that patriarchy served them well, and a female culture of silence sheltered men from realizing just how much patriarchy caused women pain.

For women, however, the need to be both the colonized and colonizer infused whole female lines of mothers and daughters. Traditional Indian mothers and daughters shared this paradox with their counterparts elsewhere. Upper-class women of feudal China bound the feet of their daughters so they would not be called "big foot" and disparaged as unmarriageable. African mothers advocated, and female relatives often performed, clitoridectomies on young girls to make them marriageable. American mothers often passed on oppressive norms of beauty modeled on Hollywood movie stars—thin, blond, and ever young. In each case, mothers were enlisted as lieutenants to carry out edicts of which they were not themselves the ultimate authors. But as victims of the same system, many mothers at the same time guided their daughters to the trap door—through a revolutionary shift in ideas about women.

In India, China, Africa, the United States, one thing is the same: whatever form it takes, patriarchy is not simply a set of *external* rules governing property, name, or behavior detached from women's inner lives.[14] No, the mother-daughter bond, like the family itself, is a shock absorber of social strains that originate far outside it. Through the pattern of the colonized colonizer, the Indian families in these stories absorbed the strains created by feudal patriarchy. Those strains are diminishing while others, due to newer trends, may be growing. For modernization, capitalism, and globalization are now undermining patriarchy and so, too, undermining the cultural legitimacy of subcontracting patriarchy. Certainly great changes have taken place in the lives of the Indian women who attended the workshop. In her family, Radharani's daughter, Nabaneeta Sen, was the first woman to freely choose her husband, attend a coeducational college, get a Ph.D., go abroad to study, drive a car, hold a paid job, have an inter-caste marriage, and divorce. For others the trends are in the same direction.

But something else beyond the decline of patriarchy and the backlash against that decline is happening now. Moving to replace the status system that underlay the colonized colonizer is a more impersonal market-driven basis for distributing status and honor. In the modern world, the Narayanis will measure their honor not by the size of a daughter's dowry or adherence to renunciatory rules, but by her education, her occupational rank, and her power of the purse. Status will derive less from the rapidly shrinking household and more from one's rank in school and at work. As the extended household gives way to smaller, conjugal households, there may be altogether less "status production," as Hanna Papenek has called it, in families and local communities, and less localism altogether.[15] Insofar as patriarchy depended on the watchful eyes of kin to keep going, the pressure may be off the subcontractors, and off the mother-daughter relation itself.

Or rather, *both* the coming trend and the going trend act on modern Indian women simultaneously. One thing that most struck me during my stay in Trivandrum, in fact, was the way in which modern ways of thinking harmoniously coexisted—like multiple Hindu gods—with traditional ways of thinking. More and more women were getting educated and getting jobs (given the high unemployment in Kerala, often abroad). So a modern thing

was happening. At the same time, Kerala was witnessing a renaissance—
indeed an expansion—in traditional "Devi worship" (worship of a local
female goddess). In 1997 a million female worshippers crowded into
Trivandrum, setting up small improvised brick fireplaces along miles and
miles of road to cook a sacred spiced cereal to honor Devi and to see her
"speak" through the rolling boil of the cereal. Friends invited me to par-
ticipate, and when I asked other women on my street what they were asking the Devi to give them, the answer often included both modern aspirations—"to do well in my exams, to find a good position in the hospital or
bank"—and traditional ones—"to get a large dowry, to arrange a good marriage, to have a male child."[16]

Even if the new does not replace the old, modernization, capitalism, and
globalization are introducing new issues and the family stands ready as a
shock absorber of them. For the family is Janus-faced. It turns one face to
the outer world, its notion of good and bad, high and low, sacred and profane, and its system of power. And it turns a second face to the inner world
of its members, their wishes, fantasies, and feelings. And now the family is
turning its external face to newer social trends. For example, a combination
of financial need and global opportunity has led many Filipina and other
Third World women to leave their children in the care of relatives, to take
jobs as nannies and maids in the United States, Italy, and Spain (see "Love
and Gold," chapter 14 in this book). The family absorbs globalization
through the migration of mothers, powerfully altering the relationship
they have to both their daughters and sons.

The paradox of the colonized colonizer is thus a metaphor for the
impact of a wide range of cultural and economic trends upon the family. It
points our attention to all the social contradictions that bear upon the family and which the emotional ties within it come to compress and express.
And the metaphor attunes us to the small heroisms, however flawed, of the
Radharanis and Pishimas of the world, who deflect rather than pass down
the troubles they have known.

12 THE FRACTURED FAMILY

In Silicon Valley, where peach orchards have disappeared and electronics factories have sprouted in their stead, where low-paying jobs have replaced high-paying jobs, where neighbors are new and the singles clubs full, we meet, in Judith Stacey's 1990 book, *Brave New Families*, a woman named Pam Gama. We meet her first as the young bride of a striving drafter and ten years later as a struggling single mother of three (ages eleven, nine, and six) working odd jobs and taking classes on the side. We next meet her one precarious remarriage later, and finally as a postfeminist, reborn Christian at the altar of the Global Ministry's Church, where she exchanges vows, again, of lasting love.

Those who have studied the family have very different responses to an odyssey like Pam's. To clarify these differences it is interesting to compare Stacey's view with those of David Popenoe (*Disturbing the Nest*) and Steven Mintz and Susan Kellogg (*Domestic Revolution*). They all agree that it's a modern story. They all think it's a sad story. After that, these authors differ on central questions: Is the family in permanent decline? Does the greater freedom and power of women inherently weaken it? Should we be nostalgic for more stable times? Can we honor a diversity of types of family and also push for stronger family bonds? If so, how do we do it?

In his 1963 classic, *World Revolution and Family Patterns*, William Goode describes a worldwide trend toward urban industrial life on one hand and independent "conjugal families" on the other. Stripped of ties of authority to a wider kin circle, able to move more easily with shifts in economic opportunity, the conjugal family fit the new industrial order. Sooner in some cultures, later in others, Goode correctly claims, it came to prevail.

But for how long? The three books just mentioned show that the conjugal family has grown fragile. All of them lack the reassuring tone of Mary Jo Bane's 1976 *Here to Stay*, though they avoid the shrill alarm of Christopher Lasch's 1977 *Haven in a Heartless World*, two books that mark the boundaries of the 1970s response to unsettling news on the domestic front. Updating Goode, all three books claim that we've entered a third stage of family history, but they differ on what this stage means for both human happiness and political action.

161

Stacey argues that the "modern family" (a term she uses to refer narrowly to a stable marriage between a breadwinner and a homemaker) is giving way to a collection of diverse, often fragile domestic arrangements that comprise the "postmodern family"—single mothers, blended families, cohabiting couples, lesbian and gay partners, communes, and two-job families. She describes the "modern" family as patriarchal, culturally predominant, and stable, and she describes the "postmodern" one as largely nonpatriarchal, diverse, and unstable. She treats these two sets of characteristics as fixed packages. The postmodern family, Stacey says, fits with the postmodern economy and with postfeminism, the three "posts." Loosely illustrating this thesis are twenty-eight lively oral histories of the mostly white and working-class kin and friends of two women living in Santa Clara County in the 1980s, Dotty Lewison and Pam Gama.

Like Emile Zola's nineteenth-century *Germinal,* the history of Dotty Lewison's family is a grim catalog of everything that can go wrong. Lou Lewison beats his wife, Dotty. When Dotty isn't protecting the children from Lou, she's beating them herself or taking off. One daughter has a sexually abused child whom she neglects. A son drinks and fights and dies driving his car 120 miles an hour after a quarrel with his wife. Another son is arrested with a hundred hypodermic needles and PCP. Another daughter attempts suicide when her husband impregnates a new lover. And so it goes.

Dotty and Pam both marry young. Each separates from her husband fairly young too. One divorces and one reunites, and each has one child who marries happily and many others who don't. In each generation, midlife women try to heal the hurts of ex-spouses, children, and the original kin and friends, and to add a new spouse, step-siblings, friends, and kin—an important and difficult work too blandly called "blending" the family.

These portraits of two topsy-turvy working-class families in Santa Clara County in the 1980s are "deeply revealing," Stacey says, of what we can expect when the irreversible "three posts" are "here to stay" in every other class and place. She mentions some long- and short-term trends propelling us toward a model of family like that of Dotty or Pam. The long-term trend, the one William Goode tracked, is the loss of wider kin control over couples. Stacey describes this, rightly I think, as the "vulnerable linchpin" of the modern family, the premise of "enduring a voluntary commitment" two people make independent of the wishes of their kin.

Shorter-term economic trends also weaken the family: the loss of union-protected jobs that allowed a man to support his wife and children, and the growth of low-wage service jobs that wives and husbands now take to make up for the lost pay. Another is decades of appalling government neglect obscured by Republican pro-family rhetoric. Stacey also claims that feminism "provided ideological support for divorce and for the soaring rates of female-headed households." This is the only feminist position on the family she mentions, and at one point she describes feminism as "being in remission," as if it were a cancer.

These economic and ideological forces, Stacey says, came first to African American and white working-class families, whose women are the postmodern "pioneers." Many women are good at pulling broken families together, as Pam Gama eventually did, according to Stacey. This is mainly women's work because the postmodern family is basically a woman's place, from which men watchfully come and go.

In a final bugle call, for me unexpected and inexplicable, Stacey writes, "The family is not here to stay. Nor should we wish it were. On the contrary I believe that all democratic people, whatever their kinship preferences, should work to hasten its demise . . . the 'family' distorts and devalues a rich variety of kinship stories . . . there is bad faith in the popular lament over the demise of the family." Ironically, Stacey embraces the postmodern family in the name of democracy, while every one of her informants, whose stories are so sensitively told, strongly votes against it. At one point Pam Gama says, "A rock bottom commitment is so important. Otherwise you don't know what's going to happen if you're not as beautiful as you used to be or you lose a job or you get sick." Pam Gama and Dotty Lewison know that postmodernism can hurt. Stacey conveys the pain through her informants' stories, but she doesn't take it to heart.

She rightly admires the heroism of many working-class women like Pam Gama, who can blend a post-divorce family, make friends with her ex-husband and his girlfriend, or pull off a good Thanksgiving again. But we can't generalize from Pam. Colleen Leahy Johnson's research on middle-class divorced couples and their parents, for example, shows that two-thirds of divorcees do not maintain cordial ties with ex-spouses or their relatives.

Underlying Stacey's welcome of the postmodern family is an implicit choice: either we're worried about the family, want to reinstall patriarchy, and devalue gay or nonmarried partnerships, *or* we value democracy and diversity without really worrying if families last. Pam Gama, reborn Christian, picks one side, and Judith Stacey, postmodern feminist, picks the other. I put down the book wondering: where's the third choice?

HIDDEN INJURIES OF POSTMODERN CHILDHOOD

David Popenoe would draw very different conclusions from Stacey's evidence. Indeed, Stacey's evidence lends far more support to Popenoe's argument than it does to her own, and much of his evidence goes better with her conclusions. Relying on national statistics from a half-dozen countries and carefully detailing secondary sources on attitudes and family patterns, Popenoe posits a "global family trend" from an "extended" family at one pole to a nuclear family (as Goode did), and extends it to a "postnuclear family" (as Stacey does). He details the cases of two countries that are "behind" the United States in his evolutionary scheme, Switzerland and New Zealand, and one that he thinks is ahead, Sweden. Although he says this is a historical-comparative study, Popenoe starts with an evolutionary schema and picks illustrations for it from here and there, which is another project entirely.

Popenoe argues that in all modern societies families are in "decline" in five senses of the word: (a) families are less directed toward collective goals; (b) they carry out fewer traditional functions, such as procreation, control of sexuality, and socialization of the young; (c) they have lost power to other institutions such as the state and school; (d) they are smaller and less stable; and (e) individual commitments to family are weaker.

Once the family becomes weaker in these ways, he reasons, new, looser norms emerge that weaken it further. The more it has become normal to have sex before marriage, for example, the less sense it makes to marry after children are born. Since the rate of breakup is greater among cohabiting than married couples, mothers in such relationships are less likely to stay with fathers, and children are less likely to grow up in intact homes. Once established, divorce increases, since people who divorce are more likely to divorce again, creating more divorced people, many with children. Popenoe's foremost concern, he says, is the well-being of children, and in the postmodern family, he thinks, children are worse off.

Examining Sweden today as a preview of the American future, he sees a high rate of family dissolution, a high and rising rate of single-parent families, and serial monogamy as a norm. The rates of divorce and single parenthood are not actually more extreme in Sweden than in the United States, although he doesn't make this clear. Swedes do marry less, marry later, and cohabit more. But their birth rate is the second highest in Western Europe, after Ireland's, and higher than ours.

Popenoe fears that the trends he thinks he sees in Sweden weaken the family. Take serial monogamy. Some have argued, Popenoe says, that mate-switching is a measure of family strength, not weakness. "Look how much people still value the family; when one unit breaks up they quickly form another," he quotes. Popenoe counters, without cracking a smile, "This is like arguing that high residential mobility is an indicator of community cohesion; since people are moving to other communities they apparently continue to favor community life. In fact, community cohesion is highest in those communities where people have lived the longest."

Compared to their counterparts three generations ago, Popenoe notes, Swedish children have fewer siblings, fewer joint activities with their families, a diminished amount of time with parents, fewer family-centered routines at bedtime, mealtime, birthdays, and holidays, less regular contact with relatives (except for grandparents, who live longer than their counterparts in the past), less contact with neighbors (as neighborhoods are emptied of adults during the day), and more fear and anxiety that their parents may break up. More and more, children live in their own separate world, which lacks connections to the past, for which afternoons of video games and television provide a debased substitute. Parents may be healthier, better educated, richer, even more psychologically sophisticated than a hundred years ago, he says, but children are worse off.

In *Second Chances,* a fifteen-year longitudinal study of sixty middle-class divorced families in California, Judith Wallerstein finds support for Popenoe's claim that an era of unstable marriage can hurt children.[1] On one hand, half the men and two-thirds of the women in her study felt more content with the quality of their lives after divorce. At the same time, only one in ten children felt the same way. Within ten years, half the children had gone through a parent's second divorce and half grew up in continuously angry families. Only one in eight saw both parents remarry happily. Typically, one parent successfully remarried and the other either divorced again or never remarried. Incredibly, half of the women and a third of the men were still intensely angry at their ex-spouses ten years after the divorce.

Although the children Wallerstein studied graduated from high schools where 85 percent of the student population went on to college, only half of the children who were Wallerstein's subjects in *Second Chances* did so. Indeed, Wallerstein concluded that 60 percent were on a "downward educational course compared with their fathers." Over a third of the children in the study who were in their twenties seemed to be drifting aimlessly through life. Three out of four children felt rejected by their fathers. Wallerstein does not compare children of divorce with a matched sample of children from intact marriages, so we don't know how many children from intact families share these characteristics. But if children from intact homes feel similarly rejected and aimless, we have even more cause for concern for the family's future.

In the end, Popenoe concludes that we should strengthen the family by reversing the trends that have weakened it. But here we run into surprises. Popenoe does not believe that the family has been weakened by poverty or insecurity, as others so often suggest. The richer Sweden has become, he points out, the weaker the family. In the United States, too, it was during the more prosperous decades of the 1960s and 1970s that the divorce rate rose and in the least prosperous, the 1930s, that it fell.

Popenoe also believes that more government help will weaken rather than strengthen the family. Sweden, a favorite liberal model of enlightenment, is the world leader in public child welfare, but, he also argues, the world leader in family decline. For the couple planning a family, the state guarantees a pregnancy leave at 90 percent salary for a maximum of fifty days, and fathers are guaranteed a two-week leave at almost full salary. The state offers a nine-month parental leave at nearly full pay, another three months at minimum pay, and an optional six months at no pay. Sweden has waged a massive campaign to convince fathers to use the leave (a quarter of fathers now use it) and subsidized research on the fathers who don't. It offers free parent education courses, and if asked to do so, employers must offer to subtract up to two hours from the workday for parents of children under eight. Sick-child leave is available at nearly full salary to parents of children up to the age of twelve, and a portion of the leave may be used to help children with adjustment problems at school. The Swedes passed a law condemning physical punishment and humiliating treatment of children and established the first ombudsman for children. The Swedish state supports many social workers, psychologists, physicians, and educators who help families with children.

Popenoe thinks this pro-family state actually has weakened the Swedish family. It has done so inadvertently, he thinks, by usurping functions traditionally located within the family, and inspiring the idea among parents that "the state offers a service. My taxes pay for it. I might as well use it instead of doing the job myself."

But is this true? If "too much" welfare weakens the family, we might expect a stingier government to promote a stronger family. This is not what we find. Like Stacey, Popenoe doesn't pay close attention to his own evidence. The United States is the only major industrial nation that still lacks guaranteed unpaid parental leave, and when Popenoe wrote his book—before Clinton signed the Family and Medical Leave Act—the United States lacked a sick-child leave policy, indeed lacked any family policy at all. So the American family might be thought to prosper more, according to Popenoe's theory, than the Swedish family. But no: the United States, not Sweden, holds the world record for marital breakup (in 1982 it was 5.03 divorces per 1,000 persons versus 2.49 in Sweden). The U.S. rate of teen pregnancy is also higher (the pregnancy rate for fifteen- to nineteen-year-olds is 96 per 1,000 in the United States and only 35 per 1,000 in Sweden). Half of American divorced fathers lose regular contact with their eleven- to sixteen-year-old children whereas less than a third in Sweden do. In all these ways we are in far deeper trouble than the Swedes.

Yet Popenoe is making the confusing case for family decline in Sweden, as the model we are "about" to adopt, though American families, further back on his evolutionary scale, are actually worse off. The problem is that Popenoe throws together rates of divorce, abandonment by fathers, and teen pregnancy (which to most people indicate trouble), with trends toward later age at marriage, smaller families, and more cohabitation (which indicate change but not necessarily trouble), and he labels all of these indicators of "decline."

All these trends count as decline for him, I think, because he has only one particular type of family in mind—a heterosexual married couple, with the father working and the mother staying home with their two kids. Two-job families don't count as good or strong families because, he presumes, women's economic independence prevents them from "pursuing joint goals." Like Stacey, Popenoe blames feminism for the decline of the family. As he rightly observes, feminism is widely accepted in Sweden, at least by women. But Popenoe makes the additional claim that the resulting higher expectations women have of men have weakened the family. Among residents of Stockholm seeking marriage counseling in 1980, he notes, "conflicts related to sex roles" ranked second as a problem in marriage. Another study of Swedish divorce found that one of the two most common reasons after poor sex life was "problems related to work inside and outside the home." So the more women want men to share childrearing and house care, Popenoe reasons, the bigger the strain, and the weaker the family.

But is the problem that working mothers want more help at home, or is the problem that they aren't getting it? If Popenoe had done a truly comparative study he would have compared Sweden and the United States with other industrial societies that have many women doing paid work but do not have feminism. A good example is Russia (where I lived for six months in 1992). Neither in the state nor in the popular mind has feminism established itself; eyes glaze over at the mere mention of the word. Adding paid work to home work, Soviet women average seventy hours a week and Soviet men forty-two. With the exception of an outspoken and discredited few, no one publicly defines this gap as a problem. Echoing what Francine du Plessix Gray reports in her book *Soviet Women*, the refrain I hear from Russian women is "We do it because we're stronger." If, as Popenoe believes, women's high expectations are a main cause of family decline, Soviet families should be islands of everlasting peace. In fact, though we lack good statistics, Russian marriages seem to be almost as fragile as ours and more fragile than those in Sweden.

The clue to family tension is not to be found, I believe, in prosperity, government aid, or feminism in any of these countries, nor is it to be linked to the sheer fact that many mothers work for pay outside the home. If working women were the cause of family tension, we would have to explain why, despite large structural obstacles, many two-job parents in all three countries have happy, stable marriages. For a large part of the answer, I think we have to look at something Stacey and Popenoe ignore: the culture and the social world of men. In some sense, we have recently raised our cultural expectations of fathers while the growing instability of economic and marital life have made those ideals harder to live up to.

THE DADDY HIERARCHY

The cultural preferences of many Americans are probably expressed in a conversation between children described in *Sweet Summer,* a memoir by

Bebe Moore Campbell. In it, she tells of four African American girls grow-ing up in the urban middle class of the 1950s. Their fathers had divorced their mothers, but to varying degrees the girls were still daddies' girls. Comparing their fathers to an image of a "good dad" in a "good family" in their time and place, they located them as higher or lower on a "daddy hier-archy." The children presumed the involvement of their mothers and so declined to arrange a hierarchy of mothers. At the top of the girls' list was the daddy of a little white girl who spent time with her and built her a beau-tiful dollhouse. In the middle were daddies present but preoccupied with repairing broken cars or daddies who loved their children but spanked them too hard. At the bottom were "dead-beat dads" who disappeared from their children's lives altogether.

Certain trends have pushed forward the ideal of the involved dollhouse-building dad. Since the 1970s inflation and the globalization of capitalism have reduced male wages, creating a need for women to contribute to the family income. At the same time, a declining birth rate, higher rates of female education, and the industrialization of housework have created opportunities for women to work. This has created a *need* for men to par-ticipate more actively at home. Especially for middle-class wives who've invested in higher education and want to work at jobs they enjoy, the ideal of the "new man" is in. And among intact families, to some extent he is here. In Michael Lamb's 1986 review of large-scale quantitative studies on father-ing, he distinguishes between *engagement* (for example, feeding the child, playing catch), *accessibility* (cooking in the kitchen while the child plays in the next room), and *responsibility* (being the one who makes sure the child gets what he or she needs). When wives go out to work, Lamb finds, men become more engaged and accessible but not more responsible for their children.[2] In two out of three ways, men are doing more at home than they have in the past.

But at the same time another trend points in an opposite direction. The rising rates of divorce and of unwed pregnancies are related to *weakening* bonds between fathers and children. Although fathers have long deserted families under the guise of seeking work or migrating, or under no guise at all, the modern scale of this is surely new. Half of all marriages now end in divorce and 60 percent of them involve children. In his large-scale study of children of divorce, Frank Furstenberg found that nearly half of the chil-dren had virtually no contact with the noncustodial parent (90 percent of whom were fathers) within the past year. One out of six had seen him as reg-ularly as once a week.[3] The proportion of children living with two parents has declined from 85 percent in 1970 to 72 percent in 1991. Fathers who lose touch with their children often retreat into what Judith Wallerstein poignantly calls phantom relationships with them, putting a child's photo on an office desk, and thinking, "My child can call me any time he wants."[4]

Such fathers imagine a relationship at one end that a child does not feel is being offered at the other.

In addition, based on the National Survey of Children, James Peterson and Nicholas Zill were able to compare the relationship of children (aged twelve to sixteen) with their parents as this varied according to different types of family situations. Even among children living with both biological or adoptive parents, a scant 55 percent had positive relations with both parents. Of children living only with their mothers, 25 percent had good relations with both parents. Of children living with just their fathers, 36 percent had good relations with both parents, perhaps because the mothers stayed more involved.[5]

Parallel to the rise in divorce is a rise in the rate of out-of-wedlock pregnancies, largely though not exclusively associated with the growth of poverty. The percentage of children born to unwed parents increased from 5 percent in 1958 to 18 percent in 1978 to 28 percent in 1988 and 38 percent in 2000.[6] The vast majority of unwed mothers know the identity of the father, and many cohabit with them, but the breakup rate is higher for cohabiting than for married couples, and fewer than a fifth of unwed mothers report receiving child support for the year after the breakup.[7]

There is a social-class pattern here. The new ideal of the nurturant father seems to be spreading from the middle class *down*, while the economic insecurity familiar to the lower class and undermining stable family ties seems to be spreading *up*. As the culture in which capitalism has made the deepest inroads, the United States may prove to be the handwriting on the wall for other countries, even as the 1950s African American childhood of *Sweet Summer* has foretold the future of many white children in America today.

Not only the culture of men, but a sense of the full array of social class and ethnic vantage points on family life is missing in both Stacey's and Popenoe's analyses. Popenoe's notion of decline, in particular, also presupposes that we imagine the particular history of a certain racial and class group. Instead of doing a comparative analysis, he has selected certain white middle-class societies—New Zealand, Switzerland—to illustrate his evolutionary story. So the "family in decline" turns out to be the one that white middle-class people had. In defining his topic, he sidesteps the issue of ethnic diversity, evoking a nostalgia for an undisturbed nest many African Americans and Chicanos never had.

The missing story of ethnic diversity in all its richness is found in Steven Mintz and Susan Kellogg's *Domestic Revolutions*. A descriptive rather than a "thesis" book, it offers a thorough, carefully documented, vividly written social history of the three hundred years of American family life. The authors trace white Anglo-Saxon families, as well as Dutch, French, German, Irish, Swedish, Swiss, and other European immigrant families, from 1920 forward; drawing on the most recent scholarship, they describe Native American families and African American families from slavery to the present. The emerging picture of the past—fourteen-hour workdays in factories and mines, children of all social classes fostered out for long periods as apprentices or servants, families torn by slavery, death a common visitor, endless toil and trouble, harsh punishment of children—while not contradicting Popenoe, puts a quick end to the nostalgia his description of the peaceful New Zealand middle class might inspire as an image of "where we've come from."

But just because family life has been rough before doesn't mean it has to be just as rough today. Judith Stacey gives us powerful evidence of families in crisis but ends up giving the crisis a hip new name and quixotically welcoming it. Popenoe recognizes the problem but, hesitating to say it openly, implies that to provide children a good life, women should go back to what they were doing in New Zealand in 1950. Both conceive of the family as a passive victim of history; neither envisions a happy realistic future. Curiously it is Mintz and Kellogg, the pragmatic historians, who, noting many earlier crises to which the family adapted, conclude that the "future of the family ultimately depends on whether we take the steps necessary to help the institution adapt to the unique conditions of our time." History, as they see it, has provided a series of challenges to the family—colonization, the industrial revolution, enslavement, immigration, the depression, wars. And they see the family as a spunky little institution, which has rolled with one punch after another.

Now we have another challenge—the entrance of most women into the labor force. To stabilize the family, both the workplace and the family need to change. To start with, we can work out a way of thinking about the family that both honors our diversity and also strengthens bonds between parents and children, and parents with each other, whoever they are. Mintz and Kellogg get it right when they say, "Nor do we need to worry obsessively about the increasing diversity of family arrangements, since ethnic, religious and economic diversity has always been a characteristic of American family life." Instead of dwelling on the question of whether or not the family will survive, they conclude, "We would do better as a society to confront the concrete problems that face families today."

We might turn to one major trend of our time that has indeed disturbed many nests and acknowledge that we are living in a time of a stalled revolution, a time in which women have changed much faster than the men they live with or the institutions in which both sexes work. This stalled revolution has marginalized family life and turned it into a "second shift." To resolve this tension, we could renew a feminism that has been there quietly all along, and that calls for honoring the work of nurturance and getting men into the act. We could strengthen a coalition between organizations such as the National Organization for Women, the Women's Legal Defense Council, and the Children's Defense Fund. This coalition might find a receptive audience among women such as Pam Gama and Dotty Lewison and their war-torn kin. Just as Stacey sees the isolated housewife as a source of revolt against the wage-earner/housewife marriage, so Popenoe, perhaps rightly, sees children as a potential source of revolt against the postmodern family. This would not be a revolt, I think, against alternatives to lasting marriage, but a *revolt against the larger conditions* that have made divorce the happier alternative for so many.

We could also enact family-friendly reforms. Indeed, I believe the Swedish programs of paid paternal leave, sick-child leave, and other supports for working parents should remain our model and primary goal. We need to extend these reforms with a comprehensive program of job training or retraining for the economically dispossessed. Parental leave is of little use if we lack decently paid, secure jobs from which to take those leaves.

We need to enlarge our image of what a family is and honor all the families we have, especially single-parent and gay families. That means pressing for the legitimacy of gay marriage and working on the same underlying societal conditions to make those marriages happy and lasting, too. We should get clear that working to increase the chances for commitment between adults and loving respect for children does not mean being antigay any more than being gay means you have to oppose the family.

Finally, we need to reduce the isolation of the elderly, and not simply for *their* sake. In the end, what I learned from David Popenoe is that a benevolent state and a prosperous economy are not enough to strengthen commitment between adults and increase the welfare of children. We will also need to strengthen social supports for these relations. This can be done in many ways, but one support for young parents may be found in strengthening bonds to their own older parents. Here we chart a path through what Third World visitors inevitably say is the saddest part of our postindustrial wilderness: the isolation of the old in America.

Many older people spend their days watching too much television in exurban retirement communities or midtown hotels in large cities and, like divorced fathers, retire into "phantom relations" with their young. We lament their isolation because, after all, the old need the young. But these days the opposite is more true. It is the young who need the old, to help them through the bad moments of marriage and parenthood and complete a larger circle of meaning. And it may be the old who need persuading. By the time Pam Gama is a great-grandmother, her children and their children may well have walked the same rocky road she has. What a pity, then, that we still seem stuck with a false choice—between stable tradition and unstable modernity—and that our government isn't taking a clue from Sweden on how to help stabilize all the many kinds of modern nest.

13 CHILDREN AS EAVESDROPPERS

In his classic novel about the Follet family in Knoxville, Tennessee, in 1915, James Agee describes how six-year-old Rufus and his younger sister Catherine secretly sit on the staircase overhearing a conversation between their recently bereaved mother and Father Jackson, the unpleasant priest who is paying their mother a mysterious visit.

> Taking great care not to creak, they stole up to the middle of the stairs. They could hear no words, only the tilt and shape of voices; their mother's, still so curiously shrouded, so submissive, so gentle, it seemed to ask questions and to accept answers. The man's voice was subdued and gentle but rang very strongly with the knowledge that it was right and that no other voice could be quite as right; it seemed to say unpleasant things as if it felt they were kind things to say, or as if it did not care whether or not they were kind because in any case they were right, it seemed to make statements, to give information, to counter questions with replies which were beyond argument or even discussion and to try to give comfort whether what it was saying could give comfort or not. Now and again their mother's way of questioning sounded to the children as if she wondered whether something could be fair, could possibly be true, could be so cruel, but whenever such tones came into their mother's voice the man's voice became still more ringing and overbearing, or still more desirous to comfort, or both, and their mother's next voice was always very soft.[1]

From the pattern of the two tones of voice the two children are trying to discover the purpose and character of this relationship. They are engaged in family life, but they are also studying it. They listen to the content of talk, of course, and also use their ears as tuning forks to gauge the emotional tenor of adult talk.

Children often observe their parents when they themselves are not being watched or talked to. In *Sweet Summer*, Bebe Moore Campbell describes ten-year-old Bebe seated on the front steps of her home in Philadelphia in the 1970s watching her mother lean into the car in which her father is sitting, ready to take Bebe for a long summer's visit to her grandmother in the South. Her parents are divorced, but Bebe watches to see how they cooperate in their care of her. She sees her mother lean into the car apparently discussing amicably the details of her upcoming trip, and notices that her parents don't touch. They don't have to be lovers or friends, she concludes, to cooperate in their care of her.[2]

Although parents often imagine they are most parental when they give full attention to their children during "quality time," children watch and listen during "quantity time" too. What do they eavesdrop on? Conversations of every sort, of course, but especially those in which the children learn about *their own place in their parents' world.*

I began to grasp the importance of eavesdropping while mulling over my field notes on two young girls I came to know as part of a larger research project on the families of employees of Amerco, a Fortune 500 company, reported in *The Time Bind*.[3] The parents of both children worked long hours. But one child fell into what I called a "time bind syndrome," while the other did not. For the family in the time bind syndrome, the story was this: The parents worked long hours. The child resented the parents' long work hours and was angry and difficult at dinner time; this made it all the harder for parents to come home, after a long day—for now they came home not only to a child who was hungry and tired but to one who was resentful as well. The parents then became tempted—unconsciously perhaps—to avoid this resentment by working just a bit longer.

For the second family, not caught in the time bind syndrome, the child had ceased to look to the parents as exclusive caregivers, did not seem to resent their absence, and didn't make it hard for them to reenter family life. So the parents came home less braced for trouble, more relaxed, and able to enjoy their child.

The difference between the two children's response to roughly the same long hours of parental work led me to wonder what accounted for the difference. It wasn't sheer hours of work, which in both cases were too long by everyone's account. So what was it? I see many possible answers, but here explore one that is often overlooked—the child's own research on the parents' relationships to paid caregivers. I focus, then, on two issues—*how* children learn and *what* they learn about their care. While I can't provide especially rich data on eavesdropping, I hope to make the case that we need to know more about it.

PICKING UP THE GIST OF DEEP STRUCTURE

Eavesdropping is discussed only glancingly in the literature on the socialization of children, child development, and sociology of childhood, and in the growing literature on work and family life, so let me say a word first about how it might fit in. The first three sets of literature take as their task the development of a theory of the child. Much of literature on work and family, on the other hand, really focuses on parents. What we don't know much about from any of this writing is how children come to understand the relationships between people who care for them.

Eavesdropping is a commonly acknowledged part of everyone's—and especially the sociologist's—life. It allows us to gather information not intended for us and quite possibly secret. But oddly, we seldom picture eavesdropping as part of socialization. When we think of a child "being socialized," we usually imagine a parent telling a child what to do: "Johnny, brush your teeth." We picture direct, frontal, face-to-face, voice-to-voice contact. Or, following R. D. Laing's theory of attribution, we think of a parent telling a child how she is. A parent might say, for example, "Sally, you are a hardworking girl," and by such an attribution make the child identify with "hard work" and so motivate the child to work hard.[4] Or we think of a parent exemplifying a social pattern that the child observes: "This is how we put on our boots." The very term "socialization of" suggests a process done to and not by children. As Barrie Thorne, Jean Briggs, Gary Fine and K. L. Sandstrom, and Barry Mayall have all emphasized, children have their own perceptions about what adults want for and from them. They pick what information they want to learn and make from it their own picture of what's going on. In the course of putting together their own picture of reality, children look over their parents' shoulders, at the wider scene. Like the little sociologists they are, kids see their parents *in context*.[5]

Socialization goes on when the child is in direct contact with an adult and also when she or he isn't. It is not made up of messages a parent *sends*, but of those a child *receives*—gleans, intercepts, or, like Rufus and Catherine, softly steals. Thus, socializing messages include not only gestures and statements about the direct relationship between parent and child ("I love you") or the parent's characterization of the child ("You are a good boy"), but also *indirect statements passed over the child's head* about the nature of his care ("I've got coverage 'til 5:00" or "It's your turn" or "Betty [a grandmother] fell through again for Friday night").

The cultural spotlight is trained on the nuclear family, where the action is supposed to be. But children learn about the *tilt* of the cultural spotlight, among other things, partly by exploring the world outside the family, too—babysitters, neighbors, relatives, childcare center staff. And what does the child researcher want to know? First, the child wants to know: *Is the person taking care of me now going to take care of me later?* Will this babysitter last? Is Aunt Alice going to come to our house often and regularly? How long will I stay in summer camp? Second, the child wants to know: *What is the relationship between one caregiver and another?* Are my parents more afraid of my third-grade teacher or is my third-grade teacher more afraid of my parents? Does the babysitter resent, envy, love, or just feel a tepid liking for my mother? Is she attached to my dad or only to my mom? Third, *what does that lead my caretaker to feel about me?* Does Aunt Alice like taking care of me, or is she bored with me? Is she nice to me but resentful on the phone to my mom? What does that resentment have to do with me, and what does it have to do with my aunt's relation to my mom? These are the kinds of questions that allow a child to guess how loving or predictable her or his world is. In a sense, this essay takes a child's viewpoint on the important research by Lynet Uttal, Cameron Macdonald, and Julia Wrigley on the adult relations between parents and those who care for their children.[6]

TWO CHILDREN, ONE TIME BIND SYNDROME

While spending time with their families over the course of three summers in the early 1990s, I became acquainted with two little girls, Janey King and Hunter Escala. When I first met them, both girls were four years old and both daughters of two-job couples who worked at Amerco, a company I researched to find out how workers were responding to family-friendly policies. The two girls had much in common. Both had loving, happily married parents who spoke appreciatively and knowledgeably about their children. Their parents also worked the same long hours for the same company in the same town during the same period of time. But the two children responded to their parents' work hours in completely different ways.

Janey King was the younger of two children born to a fast-rising company executive, Vicky King, and her husband, Kevin, a dentist.[7] Janey's parents both worked long hours, and when I met Janey during the first summer I was there, she was spending from 7:00 A.M. to 5:00 P.M. weekdays in a summer program and sometimes also spending between 5:00 P.M. and 7:00 P.M. with a warm, highly competent college student named Cammy.

Many evenings Janey and her mother fell into what I came to call a "time bind syndrome." The company was exerting steady pressure on Janey's mother to meet its production goals, catching her up in its strong company culture, and extending her work hours. Janey's father was less successful at his work, which was, in truth, less demanding, but as a matter of pride he put in the same long hours his wife did. Their work hours were also not overlapping but simultaneous.

In response to her parents' long hours, Janey grew resentful, cranky, offish, and demanding—mainly in the presence of her mother. She refused to report on the events of her day or show interest in anyone else's. This made 6:00 P.M. to 8:00 P.M. into a "witching hour," as Janey's mother humorously put it, and created a "third shift" for her, coping with Janey's resentment at her long day. Janey's crankiness exacerbated the strains of reentry and made it covertly a little tempting to extend time at the office. This was the time bind syndrome.

In another household in another part of town, four-year-old Hunter Escala responded to a working-class version of the same long workday in a very different way. Hunter was the second of three children born to Italian American factory workers. Her mother, Deb, worked a rotating swing shift with some overtime, as her own parents had before her. Hunter's father, Mario, worked steady day shifts plus overtime, and boasted of being a "60-hour-a-week man." The three children were cared for at various times by a kindly neighbor, their two grandmothers, their father's cousin, and assorted other relatives who lived in town.

When her parents returned home from work, Hunter seemed excited to see them, and this was the general report her parents gave of the interactions with her at the various endings of their workday, 3:00 P.M., 4:30 P.M., 5:00 P.M. and other times. In fact, because her parents' schedules were continually changing, it was hard for Hunter to know from week to week when homecomings were, and she often asked to be told when each parent would be home. But Hunter did not appear to lock into an adversarial campaign, as Janey King did, to win more time from her mother or father. Instead, she seemed to run around in a pack with her brother and sister, alternately appealing for attention to her mother, her father, and her older sister, Gina, who seemed to both nurture Hunter and boss her around.

Why, we may wonder, did Janey and Hunter respond so differently to situations that seem similar—at least with regard to parental time? Let's consider some possible explanations for this difference. First, we could have here two children of different temperaments, Janey more high-strung and insecure and Hunter more relaxed and self-assured. Or maybe Janey had the ego strength to challenge her mother and Hunter didn't dare, but instead defended against her need for her mother and father by diversifying her affections. Perhaps so, but I doubt that either of these explanations is the end of the matter. The difference between Janey and Hunter could also be due to the fact that Janey was insufficiently attached to her mother and that her mother, Vicky King, was overly preoccupied with her job, working as she did in a strong, absorptive work culture. Maybe Vicky was not what D. W. Winnicott has called a "good enough" mother.[8] Actually, though, Janey's mother spoke knowledgeably, warmly, and frequently about Janey. She knew a great deal about Janey's life, that of her friends, and her favorite activities, and spoke with sensitivity about the issues that troubled her. Vicky didn't seem depressed or angry. She loved her work and that seemed to rub off at home. Friends and co-workers spoke admiringly of her as a mother. If anything, it was Deb Escala, Hunter's mother, who seemed a bit tired and depressed.

Maybe the participation of the two fathers was the more critical factor. If so, the results are confusing—because Janey, who expressed more unhappiness, seemed to get somewhat more attention from her father, Kevin King, a dentist who took great pride in his identity as an involved father, while Hunter Escala's dad, a good-natured factory worker, wanted to get out of the house to play baseball at the slightest excuse, although he was very involved with the children when he was with them. In different ways both fathers were involved. Janey's dad engaged her in long conversations while Hunter's dad roughhoused with her and her sister and brother on the lawn out back. Janey's father was deliberate, thoughtful, even-tempered, and project-oriented, although it wasn't clear he had much fun being with Janey. Though less reliable, Mario Escala was more emotionally expressive and playful with Hunter. I find it hard to trace a pattern here between father-hoods and the time bind syndrome.

How about the children's relations to their siblings? Janey had one sibling; Hunter had two. So Hunter had to share parental attention with one more child than Janey did, even though she accepted her parents' long hours with greater equanimity. We might have expected Hunter to show signs of the middle-child malaise so pronounced in parental folklore, but here again we would seem to be wrong.

Can we also speak of a class- and sibling-related effect here? Janey's older brother worked hard at his schoolwork, came home with A's and B's on his report card, and was encouraged—as Annette Lareau's research suggests tends to be true for upper-middle-class children in general—to focus on individual achievements.[9] Meanwhile Hunter's siblings were more encouraged to form strong relations with kith and kin and less stimulated to focus on individual achievements. Along with gender, class background may help account for the fact that Hunter's sister was a "little mama" while Janey's older brother was not a "little daddy."

Social class can—and I think did—affect the girls in another way too. In her classic work *Worlds of Pain*, Lillian Breslow Rubin observed that the grown children of working-class parents forgave their parents for child-hoods far harsher than those of middle-class children, who complained more openly.[10] Maybe Hunter had already concluded that her parents had it hard and forgivingly concluded "they're doing their best," while Janey King, comparing herself to children of upper-middle-class stay-at-home moms, concluded her mother was not doing her best.

Social class may enter in yet again through the relative importance of extended kin ties. In Spotted Deer, the fairly rural company town I studied, an employee's occupational rank was strongly linked to the geographic proximity of kin. The company recruited its managers and professionals from a national pool of applicants, but recruited its unskilled workers from the local community. This meant that most managers lived *far* from their kin, and most factory workers lived *close* to their kin. Indeed, Janey King, the manager's daughter, was cared for by a paid babysitter and by the personnel at the Amerco childcare center. Janey's mother had moved far away from her parents and siblings, and the couple was estranged from Kevin King's nearby but dominating and disapproving father and mother. Hunter Escala, the factory workers' daughter, was cared for by a neighboring babysitter, two sets of grandparents—primarily the grandmothers—and a female cousin of Mario's. Janey's social setting reminded me of William Whyte's *The Organization Man,* with organization women added. Hunter's ambiance recalled scenes from Herbert Gans's *The Urban Villagers.*[11] In both cases, mothers organized and coordinated a series of caretakers. But Janey's care was forged more through market bonds, Hunter's more by kin bonds, although these were undergirded by private payments as well.

There is some truth in each of these pieces of the puzzle. But there is one additional piece: the *children's observation* of their parents' negotiations about their care. In the course of my fieldwork, I noticed children noticing their parents making deals about their care. They overheard phone conversations and listened to their parents talk to each other, to babysitters, to kinspeople, or to friends about care. This eavesdropping is a child's version of Erving Goffman's "glimpsed world," the world one catches the gist of as one hurries by. But the deals children glimpse in passing are the deals that hold their world together and show what they themselves *mean* to others in that world.[12]

In *The Private Worlds of Dying Children,* Myra Bluebond-Langer observes how terminally ill children learn from seeing nurses, doctors, the hospital, and the surrounding scene all that their parents cannot bring themselves to say directly.[13] Healthy children do the same. Janey and Hunter were trying to figure out their culture of care. How many people could their parents rely on to care for them? (How large was their culture of care?) How often would a care provider not appear, and how many anxious phone calls would ensue? (How reliable was their culture of care?) Do the people who care for them know and like each other? (How coherent was it?) Are care providers paid or not? And if so, what are the differences in power and status? (Is care market- or kin-based and what emotional difference does that make?)

The girls were also gauging their personal *footing* in that culture of care. Who feels grudgingly obliged to care for them and who strongly wants to? What was the *feeling tone* associated with each deal made over the child's head? Do adults offer care out of a sense of duty or what Carol Stack has called "kinscription"?[14] Or do they give it mainly out of desire? Or exactly in *what measure,* duty and desire? Do childcare workers offer care out of a sense of professional obligation and need for money? If so, how does professionalism go with a desire to care? What, if anything, is expected in return? These questions define the scope of the research of small children.

JANEY AND HUNTER

I interviewed both parents and others who cared for the children in each family and spent time observing each family during the week and on weekends. I also talked for some time to each child, although not about eavesdropping. In the course of my time with them I observed several episodes of eavesdropping, and Hunter eavesdropped on my interviews with her mother.

Spotted Deer was not a town in Sweden or Norway where childcare has long been a guaranteed right, readily available and publicly subsidized. Both the Kings and the Escalas made many anxious phone calls and visits to people concerning childcare. So both children got the message that child-care didn't happen automatically. It was a problem.

Beyond this, there were differences between the two homes in systems of care and in the ways parents arranged it. While her parents worked, Janey was cared for by providers at her childcare center and by Cammy, a college student taking some time off. Hunter's care came mainly from relatives. In one conversation I saw Janey overhear her mother speak glowingly of Cammy, "Cammy is great. She's got great people skills, and she's wonderful with the kids. I'd like to get her a job at Amerco." Vicky had searched, Janey knew, far and wide to get Cammy. Now that she employed Cammy, she was also offering extra kindnesses, including helping Cammy think about a future career with Amerco. But how did this conversation seem from Janey's point of view? First of all, Janey's mom didn't say, "Cammy is great. She's just the person to take care of Janey." The world of Janey's care was shown to be a sideshow next to the main attraction of Amerco. Someone of real talent, the kind of talent her mother admired, shouldn't be taking care of a kid. And from this conversation, Janey might also conclude that, friendly as Cammy was, Cammy wasn't going to be caring for her forever. Also, Janey knew that her mother paid Cammy to take care of her and that this was probably Cammy's motive for taking the job. With Cammy a temporary per-son in Janey's life, and her father a permanent but distracted one, Janey's mother became the main show in town. So she complained to her mother.

By way of contrast, Hunter overheard talk about her paternal grand-mother, someone with whom she had a long-term relationship, but with whom her mother had strong differences in the philosophy of childrearing. Hunter was showing her doll how to scramble an egg and putting the doll to bed near the couch her mother, Deb, and I were sitting on as I inter-viewed Deb. At one point in this adult conversation, Hunter looked up, interested, though she said nothing. Deb was confiding reservations about letting Hunter stay in her grandmother's care. "Grandma lets Hunter eat candy before meals and doesn't break it up soon enough when [Hunter's older sister] teases her." Hunter could probably surmise that her mother and grandmother disagreed on these issues but that the bond between them was not on the line. The deal about sweets might change, but the deal about Grandma's care would last.

So why was Hunter more content with her parents' work schedule than Janey was with hers? Maybe Hunter felt surrounded by her two grandmoth-ers, a series of aunts, and a friend-babysitter next door, all of whom seemed

permanent and in whose worlds she felt central. Part of being in this network was overhearing gossip, complaints, and endless stories about the people in it. Like Janey's parents, Hunter's parents paid her babysitter, but the
sitter lived across the street and was a friend. There was more of a village
community feel *behind* the deal of pay for service. Not so for Janey.

When a child eavesdrops on conversations about deals parents make concerning her care, the child learns specific facts (Mommy is going to get
Cammy a different job, Grandma gives me too much candy). But the child
also gets the gist of a deep structure of care— by which I mean the tacit
"social wiring" of care. There are many different kinds of care, and like an
adult, a child can distinguish between market care and kin-friend care, and
all different kinds of each. Children can discern market care that is kin-like,
and kin care that is market-like. They can tell the difference between market care by a neighboring friend and market care by an esteemed professional, or market care by "the only one I could find." They can distinguish
nonmarket care by a resentful, overburdened relative from nonmarket care
by kin as a loving friend.

Over the last thirty years, the proportion of preschool children in paid care
has increased while the proportion cared for by relatives has declined. So in
the future, more children are likely to be in Janey's situation and fewer in
Hunter's. Paid care generally differs from unpaid care, but often in strange
and complex ways.[15] In paid care, a parent pays for a specific service to be ren-
dered within a relatively short period of time. In kin-friend care, a parent may
ask a favor and expect a favor in return—but within a vague, tacit, extended
time frame. In market care, the limits of the exchange are up front and clear.
In market care, the acts of care are less fraught with intensely important meanings; in kin-friend care, they are far more so. When a parent complains about
paid care, the complaint refers to expectations established by professional
standards or by a formal understanding as to what a person deserves in
exchange for a certain fee. ("This isn't what I paid for.") When a parent asks
a relative to babysit a child, the request appeals to a prior web of obligations,
and a complaint refers to the assumptions a person makes about it. ("That's
not being a good sister.") Similarly, if a friend cares for a child, a complaint
might refer to a prior notion of what a friend should want to give. ("That isn't
how she should act after all we've been through together.") In real life, a child
senses many kinds of relationship between parent and provider which combine different threads of each type of arrangement. When children eavesdrop
on adult conversations, they are picking up scraps of evidence from which
they draw a complex mental picture—not just of their two parents personally,
though surely these loom large—but of the deeper structure of care.

For their part, parents don't take "market" and "kin" arrangements ready-
made. They actively shape them.[16] For example, Hunter's parents culturally
expanded their friendship with Melody, their babysitter. They paid Melody

just as Janey's parents paid Cammy. But Hunter's parents "friendified" this market bond. Melody had long lived across the street from the Escalas. She was a neighbor and mother of Hunter's pal long before she took Hunter into her family daycare. So it didn't seem a big step to exchange gifts at Christmas and share birthdays, Easter egg hunts, and Halloween junkets. The Escalas didn't celebrate Melody's birthday, but they crossed the street to celebrate Melody's daughter's birthday. In the grammar of these exchanges, the Escalas were saying, "You're like kin to us."[17] By contrast, the King family treated Cammy as a college student and future professional, someone who was great with kids for now but who was just passing through.

So Janey found herself spending long hours with a babysitter she knew to be temporary, and this she knew by eavesdropping on enough conversations to get the gist of the whole scene, as Rufus and Catherine Follet did overhearing their mother talk to Father Jackson. With an emotionally absent father, a highly individuated and competitive sibling, and a very nice but clearly temporary babysitter, Janey concluded that Mom was it, and Mom wasn't there. Hence the time bind syndrome. Had Janey had a whole scene that was structurally organized more like Hunter's, with a maternalized sister, a kinified babysitter, and kinspeople on all sides, perhaps Janey would have experienced her mother's absence with a greater sense of confidence that her world was intact and she was central in it. She would have seen a social wiring that promised her stable though diverse sources of what counted to her as real care.

If, as the saying goes, it takes a whole village to raise a child, we can ask what kinds of villages these two children lived in. In modern America, children like Janey and Hunter increasingly live in contexts that are villages in function but not in structure. This was more true for Janey than for Hunter. Janey's daycare teacher, her playmates at daycare, her babysitter, her brother, her parents, her swimming teacher, her grandmother and grandfather, and the child of her grandparents' neighbor, all these people functioned as her village. But most of these villagers didn't know each other or cohere as a community. Janey did not live in a self-contained, cohesive, Durkheimian tribe, she lived in an urban village. Hunter's "village" had more pieces, but they fit more coherently and stably together.

In the end, while children may be playing a video game, watching TV, or reading a comic, they are also doing something else: eavesdropping. Like Rufus and Catherine, Janey and Hunter caught scraps of overheard talk, picking up the gist of a deeper web of relationships on which their care was based. No matter how jolly a caretaker or engrossing the video game, children are often hard at work psyching out the deep structure of care. And this offers a lesson for parents struggling to free themselves of a time bind syndrome. Part of the answer clearly lies in shorter, more flexible hours. But part of it lies in how we weave—and children read—our cultures of care.

Part Four

THE ECOLOGY OF CARE

In the basement bedroom of her employer's home in Washington, D.C., Rowena Bautista keeps four pictures on her dresser: two of her own children, back in Camiling, a Philippine farming village, and two of children she has cared for as a nanny in the United States. The pictures of her own children, Clinton and Princela, are from five years ago. As she recently told *Wall Street Journal* reporter Robert Frank, the photos "remind me how much I've missed."[1] She has missed the last two Christmases, and on her last visit home, her son Clinton, now eight, refused to touch his mother. "Why," he asked, "did you come back?"

The daughter of a teacher and an engineer, Rowena Bautista worked three years toward an engineering degree before she quit and went abroad for work and adventure. A few years later, during her travels, she fell in love with a Ghanaian construction worker, had two children with him, and returned to the Philippines with them. Unable to find a job in the Philippines, the father of her children went to Korea in search of work and, over time, he faded from his children's lives.

Rowena again traveled north, joining the growing ranks of Third World mothers who work abroad for long periods of time because they cannot make ends meet at home. She left her children with her mother, hired a nanny to help out at home, and flew to Washington, D.C., where she took a job as a nanny for the same pay that a small-town doctor would make in the Philippines. Of the 792,000 legal household workers in the United States, 40 percent were born abroad, like Rowena. Of Filipino migrants, 70 percent, like Rowena, are women.

Rowena calls Noa, the American child she tends, "my baby." One of Noa's first words was "Ena," short for Rowena. And Noa has started babbling in Tagalog, the language Rowena spoke in the Philippines. Rowena lifts Noa from her crib mornings at 7:00 A.M., takes her to the library, pushes her on the swing at the playground, and curls up with her for naps. As Rowena explained to Frank, "I give Noa what I can't give to my children." In turn, the American child gives Rowena what she doesn't get at home. As Rowena puts it, "She makes me feel like a mother."

Rowena's own children live in a four-bedroom house with her parents and twelve other family members—eight of them children, some of whom also have mothers who work abroad. The central figure in the children's lives—the person they call "Mama"—is Grandma, Rowena's mother. But Grandma works surprisingly long hours as a teacher—from 7:00 A.M. to 9:00 P.M. As Rowena tells her story to Frank, she says little about her father, the children's grandfather (men are discouraged from participating actively in childrearing in the Philippines). And Rowena's father is not much involved with his grandchildren. So she has hired Anna de la Cruz, who arrives daily at 8:00 A.M. to cook, clean, and care for the children. Meanwhile, Anna de la Cruz leaves her teenage son in the care of her eighty-year-old mother-in-law.

Rowena's life reflects an important and growing global trend: the importation of care and love from poor countries to rich ones. For some time now, promising and highly trained professionals have been moving from ill-equipped hospitals, impoverished schools, antiquated banks, and other beleaguered workplaces of the Third World to better opportunities and higher pay in the First World. As rich nations become richer and poor nations become poorer, this one-way flow of talent and training continuously widens the gap between the two. But in addition to this brain drain, there is now a parallel but more hidden and wrenching trend, as women who normally care for the young, the old, and the sick in their own poor countries move to care for the young, the old, and the sick in rich countries, whether as maids and nannies or as daycare and nursing-home aides. It's a care drain.

The movement of care workers from south to north is not altogether new. What is unprecedented, however, is the scope and speed of women's migration to these jobs. Many factors contribute to the growing feminization of migration. One is the growing split between the global rich and poor. In 1949 Harry S. Truman declared in his inaugural speech that the Southern Hemisphere—encompassing the postcolonial nations of Africa, Asia, and Latin America—was underdeveloped, and that it was the role of the North to help the South "catch up." But in the years since then, the gap between North and South has only widened. In 1960, for example, the nations of the North were twenty times richer than those of the South. By 1980, that gap had more than doubled, and the North was forty-six times richer than the South. In fact, according to a United Nations Development Program study, sixty countries are *worse off* in 1999 than they were in 1980.[2] Multinational corporations are the "muscle and brains" behind the new global system with its growing inequality, as William Greider points out, and the 500 largest such corporations (168 in Europe, 157 in the United States, and 119 in Japan) have in the last twenty years increased their sales seven-fold.[3]

As a result of this polarization, the middle class of the Third World now earns less than the poor of the First World. Before the domestic workers Rhacel Parreñas interviewed in the 1990s migrated from the Philippines to the United States and Italy, they had averaged $176 a month, often as teachers, nurses, and administrative and clerical workers. But by doing less skilled—though no less difficult—work as nannies, maids, and care-service workers, they can earn $200 a month in Singapore, $410 a month in Hong Kong, $700 a month in Italy, or $1,400 a month in Los Angeles. To take one example, as a fifth-grade dropout in Colombo, Sri Lanka, a woman could earn $30 a month plus room and board as a housemaid, or she could earn $30 a month as a salesgirl in a shop, without food or lodging. But as a nanny in Athens she could earn $500 a month, plus room and board.

The remittances these women send home provide food and shelter for their families and often a nest egg with which to start a small business. Of the $750 Rowena Bautista earns each month in the United States, she mails $400 home for her children's food, clothes, and schooling, and $50 to Anna de la Cruz, who shares some of that with her mother-in-law and her children. As Rowena's story demonstrates, one way to respond to the gap between rich and poor countries is to close it privately—by moving to a better-paying job.

Even as the gap between the globe's rich and poor grows wider, the globe itself—its capital, cultural images, consumer tastes, and peoples—becomes more integrated. Thanks to the spread of Western, and especially American, movies and television programs, the people of the poor South now know a great deal about the rich North. But what they learn about the North is what people *have*, in what often seems like a material striptease.

Certainly, rising inequality and the lure of northern prosperity have contributed to what Stephen Castles and Mark Miller call a "globalization of migration."[4] For men and women alike, migration has become a private solution to a public problem. Since 1945 and especially since the mid-1980s, a small but growing proportion of the world's population has been migrating. They come from and go to more different countries. Migration is by no means an inexorable process, but, as Castles and Miller observe, "Migrations are growing in volume in all major regions at the present time."[5] The International Organization for Migration estimates that 120 million people moved from one country to another, legally or illegally, in 1994. Of this group, about 2 percent of the world's population, 15 to 23 million, are refugees and asylum seekers. Of the rest, some move to join family members who have previously migrated. But most move to find work.

As a number of studies show, most migration takes place through personal contact with networks of migrants composed of relatives and friends and relatives and friends of relatives and friends. One migrant inducts another. Whole networks and neighborhoods leave to work abroad, bringing back stories, money, know-how, and contacts. Just as men form networks along which information about jobs is passed, so one domestic worker in New York, Dubai, or Paris passes on information to female relatives or friends about how to arrange papers, travel, find a job, and settle.

Today, half of all the world's migrants are women. In Sri Lanka, one out of every ten citizens—a majority of them women—works abroad. That figure excludes returnees who have worked abroad in the past. As Castles and Miller explain:

> Women play an increasing role in all regions and all types of migration. In the past, most labor migrations and many refugee movements were male dominated, and women were often dealt with under the category of family reunion. Since the 1960s, women have played a major role in labor migration. Today women workers form the majority in movements as diverse as those of Cape Verdians to Italy, Filipinos to the Middle East and Thais to Japan.[6]

Of these female workers, a great many migrate to fill domestic jobs. Demand for domestic servants has risen both in developed countries, where it had nearly vanished, and in fast-growing economies such as Hong Kong and Singapore, where, write Castles and Miller, "immigrant servants—from the Philippines, Indonesia, Thailand, Korea and Sri Lanka—allow women in the richer economies to take up new employment opportunities."[7]

Vastly more middle-class women in the First World do paid work now than in the past. They work longer hours for more months a year and more years. So they need help caring for the family.[8] In the United States in 1950, 15 percent of mothers of children aged six and under did paid work while 65 percent of such women do today. Seventy-two percent of all American women now work. Among them are the grandmothers and sisters who thirty years ago might have stayed home to care for the children of relatives. Just as Third World grandmothers may be doing paid care work abroad in the Third World, so more grandmothers are working in the First World too—another reason First World families are looking outside the family for good care.

Women who want to succeed in a professional or managerial job in the First World thus face strong pressures at work. Most careers are still based on a well-known (male) pattern: doing professional work, competing with fellow professionals, getting credit for work, building a reputation, doing it while you are young, hoarding scarce time, and minimizing family work by finding someone else to do it. In the past, the professional was a man; the "someone else" was his wife. The wife oversaw the family, itself a flexible, preindustrial institution concerned with human experiences the workplace excluded: birth, childrearing, sickness, death. Today, a growing "care industry" has stepped into the traditional wife's role, creating a very real demand for migrant women.

But if First World middle-class women are building careers that are molded according to the old male model, by putting in long hours at demanding jobs, their nannies and other domestic workers suffer a greatly exaggerated version of the same thing. Two women working for pay is a good idea. But two working mothers giving their all to work is a good idea gone haywire. In the end, both First and Third World women are small players in a larger economic game whose rules they have not written.

The trends outlined above—global polarization, increasing contact, and the growth of transcontinental female networks—have caused more women to migrate. They have also changed women's motives for migrating. Fewer women move for "family reunification," and more move in search of work. And when they find work, it is often within the growing "care sector," which, according to the economist Nancy Folbre, now encompasses 20 percent of all American jobs.[9]

A good number of the women who migrate to fill these positions seem to be single mothers. After all, about a fifth of the world's households are headed by women: 24 percent in the industrial world, 19 percent in Africa, 18 percent in Latin America and the Caribbean, and 13 percent in Asia and the Pacific. Some such women are on their own because their husbands have left them or because they have escaped abusive marriages. In addition to these single mothers, there is also a shadow group of "almost" single mothers, only nominally married to men who are alcoholics, gamblers, or just too worn down by the hardships of life to make a go of it. For example, one Filipina nanny now working in California was married to a man whose small business collapsed as a result of overseas competition. He could find no well-paid job abroad that he found acceptable, so he urged his wife to "go and earn good money" as a lap dancer in a café in Japan. With that money, he hoped to restart his business. Appalled by his proposal, she separated from him to become a nanny in the United States.

Many, if not most, women migrants have children. The average age of women migrants into the United States is twenty-nine, and most come from countries, such as the Philippines and Sri Lanka, where female identity centers on motherhood and where the birth rate is high. Often migrants, especially the undocumented ones, cannot bring their children with them. Most mothers try to leave their children in the care of grandmothers, aunts, and fathers, in roughly that order. An orphanage is a last resort. A number of nannies working in rich countries hire nannies to care for their own children back home either as solo caretakers or as aides to the female relatives left in charge back home. Carmen Ronquillo, for example, migrated from the Philippines to Rome to work as a maid for an architect and single mother of two. She left behind her husband, two teenagers—and a maid.[10]

Whatever arrangements these mothers make for their children, however, most feel the separation acutely, expressing remorse to the researchers who interview them. One migrant mother who left her two-month-old baby in the care of a relative told researcher Rhacel Parreñas, "The first two years I felt like I was going crazy. You have to believe me when I say that it was like I was having intense psychological problems. I would catch myself gazing at nothing, thinking about my child." Recounted another migrant nanny through tears, "When I saw my children again, I thought, 'Oh children do grow up even without their mother.' I left my youngest when she was only five years old. She was already nine when I saw her again, but she still wanted me to carry her."[11]

Many more migrant female workers than migrant male workers stay in their adopted countries—in fact, most do. In staying, these mothers remain separated from their children, a choice freighted, for many, with a terrible sadness. Some migrant nannies, isolated in their employers' homes and faced with what is often depressing work, find solace in lavishing their affluent charges with the love and care they wish they could provide their own children. In an interview with Parreñas, Vicky Diaz, a college-educated schoolteacher who left behind five children in the Philippines, said, "The only thing you can do is to give all your love to the child [in your care]. In my absence from my children, the most I could do with my situation was to give all my love to that child."[12] Without intending it, she has taken part in a global heart transplant.

As much as these mothers suffer, their children suffer more. And there are a lot of them. An estimated 30 percent of Filipino children—some eight million—live in households where at least one parent has gone overseas. These children have counterparts in Africa, India, Sri Lanka, Latin America, and the former Soviet Union. How are these children doing? Not very well, according to a survey Manila's Scalabrini Migration Center conducted with more than seven hundred children in 1996. Compared to their classmates, the children of migrant workers more frequently fell ill; they were more likely to express anger, confusion, and apathy; and they performed particularly poorly in school. Other studies of this population show a rise in delinquency and child suicide.[13] When such children were asked whether they would also migrate when they grew up, leaving their own children in the care of others, they all said no.

Faced with these facts, one senses some sort of injustice at work, linking the emotional deprivation of these children with the surfeit of affection their First World counterparts enjoy. In her study of native-born women of color who do domestic work, Sau-Ling Wong argues that the time and energy these workers devote to the children of their employers is diverted from their own children.[14] But time and energy are not all that's involved; so, too, is love. In this sense, we can speak about love as an unfairly distributed resource—extracted from one place and enjoyed somewhere else.

Is love really a "resource" to which a child has a right? Certainly the United Nations Declaration on the Rights of the Child asserts all children's right to an "atmosphere of happiness, love, and understanding." Yet in some ways, this claim is hard to make. The more we love and are loved, the more deeply we can love. Love is not fixed in the same way that most material resources are fixed. Put another way, if love is a resource, it's a renewable resource; it creates more of itself. And yet Rowena Bautista can't be in two places at once. Her day has only so many hours. It may also be true that the more love she gives to Noa, the less she gives to her own three children back in the Philippines. Noa in the First World gets more love, and Clinton and Princela in the Third World get less. In this sense, love does appear scarce and limited, like a mineral extracted from the earth.

Perhaps, then, feelings *are* distributable resources, but they behave somewhat differently from either scarce or renewable material resources. According to Freud, we don't "withdraw" and "invest" feeling but rather displace or redirect it. The process is an unconscious one, whereby we don't actually give up a feeling of, say, love or hate, so much as we find a new object for it—in the case of sexual feeling, a more appropriate object than the original one, whom Freud presumed to be our opposite-sex parent. While Freud applied the idea of displacement mainly to relationships within the nuclear family, it seems only a small stretch to apply it to relationships like Rowena's to Noa. As Rowena told Frank, the *Wall Street Journal* reporter, "I give Noa what I can't give my children."

Understandably, First World parents welcome and even invite nannies to redirect their love in this manner. The way some employers describe it, a nanny's love of her employer's child is a natural product of her more loving Third World culture, with its warm family ties, strong community life, and long tradition of patient maternal love of children. In hiring a nanny, many such employers implicitly hope to import a poor country's "native culture," thereby replenishing their own, rich country's depleted culture of care. They import the benefits of Third World "family values." Says the director of a co-op nursery in the San Francisco Bay Area, "This may be odd to say, but the teacher's aides we hire from Mexico and Guatemala know how to love a child better than the middle-class white parents. They are more relaxed, patient, and joyful. They enjoy the kids more. These professional parents are pressured for time and anxious to develop their kids' talents. I tell the parents that they can really learn how to love from the Latinas and the Filipinas."

When asked why Anglo mothers should relate to children so differently than do Filipina teacher's aides, the nursery director speculated, "The Filipinas are brought up in a more relaxed, loving environment. They aren't as rich as we are, but they aren't so pressured for time, so materialistic, so anxious. They have a more loving, family-oriented culture." One mother, an American lawyer, expressed a similar view:

Carmen just enjoys my son. She doesn't worry whether . . . he's learning his letters, or whether he'll get into a good preschool. She just enjoys him. And actually, with anxious busy parents like us, that's really what Thomas needs. I love my son more than anyone in this world. But at this stage Carmen is better for him.

Filipina nannies I have interviewed in California paint a very different picture of the love they share with their First World charges. Theirs is not an import of happy peasant mothering but a love that partly develops on American shores, informed by an American ideology of mother-child bonding and fostered by intense loneliness and longing for their own children. If love is a precious resource, it is not one simply extracted from the Third World and implanted in the First. Rather, it is "assembled" here from elements that come from both here and there.

For María Gutierrez, who cares for the eight-month-old baby of two hardworking professionals (a lawyer and a doctor, born in the Philippines but now living in San Jose, California), loneliness and long work hours feed a love for her employers' child. "I love Ana more than my own two children. Yes, more! It's strange, I know. But I have time to be with her. I'm paid. I am lonely here. I work ten hours a day, with one day off. I don't know any neighbors on the block. And so this child gives me what I need."

Not only that, but she is able to provide her employer's child with a different sort of attention and nurturance than she could deliver to her own children. "I'm more patient," she explains, "more relaxed. I put the child first. My kids, I treated them the way my mother treated me."

I asked her how her mother had treated her and she replied:

My mother grew up in a farming family. It was a hard life. My mother wasn't warm to me. She didn't touch me or say, "I love you." She didn't think she should do that. Before I was born she had lost four babies—two in miscarriage and two died as babies. I think she was afraid to love me as a baby because she thought I might die too. Then she put me to work as a "little mother" caring for my four younger brothers and sisters. I didn't have time to play.

Fortunately, an older woman who lived next door took an affectionate interest in María, often feeding her and even taking her in overnight when she was sick. María felt closer to this woman's relatives than she did to her biological aunts and cousins. She had been, in some measure, informally adopted—a practice she describes as common in the Philippine countryside and even in some towns during the 1960s and 1970s.

In a sense, María experienced a premodern childhood, marked by high infant mortality, child labor, and an absence of sentimentality, set within a culture of strong family commitment and community support. Reminiscent of fifteenth-century France, as Philippe Ariès describes it in *Centuries of*

Childhood, this was a childhood before the romanticization of the child and before the modern middle-class ideology of intensive mothering.[15] Sentiment wasn't the point; commitment was.

María's commitment to her own children, aged twelve and thirteen when she left to work abroad, bears the mark of that upbringing. Through all of their anger and tears, María sends remittances and calls, come hell or high water. The commitment is there. The sentiment, she has to work at. When she calls home now, María says, "I tell my daughter 'I love you.' At first it sounded fake. But after a while it became natural. And now she says it back. It's strange, but I think I learned that it was okay to say that from being in the United States."

María's story points to a paradox. On the one hand, the First World extracts love from the Third World. But what is being extracted is partly produced here: the leisure, the money, the ideology of the child, the intense loneliness and yearning for one's own children. In María's case, a premodern childhood in the Philippines, a postmodern ideology of mothering and childhood in the United States, and the loneliness of migration blend to produce the love she gives to her employers' child. That love is also a product of the nanny's freedom from the time pressure and school anxiety parents feel in a culture that lacks a social safety net—one where both parent and child have to "make it" at work because no state policy, community, or marital tie is reliable enough to sustain them. In that sense, the love María gives as a nanny does not suffer from the disabling effects of the American version of late capitalism.

If all this is true—if, in fact, the nanny's love is something at least partially produced by the conditions under which it is given—is María's love of a First World child really being extracted from her own Third World children? Yes, because her daily presence has been removed, and with it the daily expression of her love. It is, of course, the nanny herself who is doing the extracting. Still, if her children suffer the loss of her affection, she suffers with them. This, indeed, is globalization's pound of flesh.

Curiously, the suffering of migrant women and their children is rarely visible to the First World beneficiaries of nanny love. Noa's mother focuses on her daughter's relationship with Rowena. Ana's mother focuses on her daughter's relationship with María. Rowena loves Noa, María loves Ana. That's all there is to it. The nanny's love is a thing in itself. It is unique, private—fetishized. Marx talked about the fetishization of things, not feelings. When we make a fetish of an object—an SUV, for example—we see that object as independent of its context. We disregard, he would argue, the men who harvested the rubber latex, the assembly-line workers who bolted on the tires, and so on. Just as we mentally isolate our idea of an object from the human scene within which it was made, so, too, we unwittingly separate the love between nanny and child from the global capitalist order of love to which it very much belongs.

The notion of extracting resources from the Third World in order to enrich the First World is hardly new. It harks back to imperialism in its most literal form: the nineteenth-century extraction of gold, ivory, and rubber from the Third World. That openly coercive, male-centered imperialism, which persists today, was always paralleled by a quieter imperialism in which women were more central. Today, as love and care become the "new gold," the female part of the story has grown in prominence. In both cases, through the death or displacement of their parents, Third World children pay the price.

Imperialism in its classic form involved the North's plunder of physical resources from the South. Its main protagonists were virtually all men: explorers, kings, missionaries, soldiers, and the local men who were forced at gunpoint to harvest wild rubber latex and the like. European states lent their legitimacy to these endeavors, and an ideology emerged to support them: "the white man's burden" in Britain and *la mission civilisatrice* in France, both of which emphasized the benefits of colonization for the colonized.

The brutality of that era's imperialism is not to be minimized, even as we compare the extraction of material resources from the Third World of that time to the extraction of emotional resources today. Today's North does not extract love from the South by force: there are no colonial officers in tan helmets, no invading armies, no ships bearing arms sailing off to the colonies. Instead, we see a benign scene of Third World women pushing baby carriages, elder-care workers patiently walking, arms linked, with elderly clients on streets or sitting beside them in First World parks.

Today, coercion operates differently. While the sex trade and some domestic service are brutally enforced, in the main the new emotional imperialism does not issue from the barrel of a gun. Women choose to migrate for domestic work. But they choose it because economic pressures all but coerce them to. That yawning gap between rich and poor countries is itself a form of coercion, pushing Third World mothers to seek work in the First for lack of options closer to home. But given the prevailing free-market ideology, migration is viewed as a "personal choice." Its consequences are seen as "personal problems." In this sense, migration creates not a white man's burden but, through a series of invisible links, a dark child's burden.

Some children of migrant mothers in the Philippines, Sri Lanka, Mexico, and elsewhere may be well cared for by loving kin in their communities. We need to know more than we do if we are to find out how such children are really doing. But if we discover that they aren't doing well, how are we to respond? I can think of three possible approaches. First, we might say that all women everywhere should stay home and take care of their own families. The problem with Rowena is not migration but neglect of her traditional role. A second approach might be to deny that a problem exists: The care drain is an inevitable outcome of globalization, which is itself good for the world. A supply of labor has met a demand—what's the problem? If the first approach condemns global migration, the second celebrates it. Neither acknowledges its human costs.

According to a third approach—the one I take—loving, paid childcare with reasonable hours is a very good thing. And globalization brings with it new opportunities, such as a nanny's access to good pay. But it also introduces painful new emotional realities for Third World children. We need to embrace the needs of Third World societies, including their children. We need to develop a global sense of ethics to match emerging global economic realities. If we go out to buy a pair of Nike shoes, we want to know how low the wage and how long the hours were for the Third World worker who made them. Likewise, if Rowena is taking care of a two-year-old six thousand miles from her home, we should want to know what is happening to her own children.

If we take this third approach, what should we or others in the Third World do? One obvious course would be to develop the Philippine and other Third World economies to such a degree that their citizens can earn as much money inside their countries as outside them. Then the Rowenas of the world could support their children in jobs they'd find at home. While such an obvious solution would seem ideal—if not easily achieved—Douglas Massey, a specialist in migration, points to some unexpected problems, at least in the short run. In Massey's view, it is not underdevelopment that sends migrants like Rowena off to the First World but development itself. The higher the percentage of women working in local manufacturing, he finds, the greater the chance that any one woman will leave on a first, undocumented trip abroad.[16] Perhaps these women's horizons broaden. Perhaps they meet others who have gone abroad. Perhaps they come to want better jobs and more goods. Whatever the original motive, the more people in one's community migrate, the more likely one is to migrate too.

If development creates migration, and if we favor some form of development, we need to find more humane responses to the migration such development is likely to cause. For those women who migrate in order to flee abusive husbands, one part of the answer would be to create solutions to that problem closer to home—domestic-violence shelters in these women's home countries, for instance. Another might be to find ways to make it easier for migrating nannies to bring their children with them. Or as a last resort, employers could be required to finance a nanny's regular visits home.

A more basic solution, of course, is to raise the value of caring work itself, so that whoever does it gets more rewards for it. Care, in this case, would no longer be such a "pass-on" job. And now here's the rub: the value of the labor of raising a child—always low relative to the value of other kinds of labor—has, under the impact of globalization, sunk lower still. Children matter to their parents immeasurably, of course, but the labor of raising them does not earn much credit in the eyes of the world. When middle-class housewives raised children as an unpaid, full-time role, the work was dignified by its aura of middle-classness. That was the one upside to the otherwise confining cult of middle-class, nineteenth- and early-twentieth-century American womanhood. But when the unpaid work of raising a child became the paid work of childcare workers, its low market value revealed the abidingly low value of caring work generally—and further lowered it.

The low value placed on caring work results neither from an absence of a need for it nor from the simplicity or ease of doing it. Rather, the declining value of childcare results from a cultural politics of inequality. It can be compared with the declining value of basic food crops relative to manufactured goods on the international market. Though clearly more necessary to life, crops such as wheat and rice fetch low and declining prices, while manufactured goods are more highly valued. Just as the market price of primary produce keeps the Third World low in the community of nations, so the low market value of care keeps the status of the women who do it—and, ultimately, all women—low.

One excellent way to raise the value of care is to involve fathers in it. If men shared the care of family members worldwide, care would spread laterally instead of being passed down a social-class ladder. In Norway, for example, all employed men are eligible for a year's paternity leave at 90 percent pay. Some 80 percent of Norwegian men now take over a month of parental leave. In this way, Norway is a model to the world. For, indeed, it is men who have for the most part stepped aside from caring work, and it is with them that the pass-it-on pattern truly begins.

In all developed societies, women work at paid jobs. According to the International Labor Organization, half of the world's women between ages fifteen and sixty-four do paid work. Between 1960 and 1980, sixty-nine out of eighty-eight countries surveyed showed a growing proportion of women in paid work. Since 1950, the rate of increase has skyrocketed in the United States, while remaining high in Scandinavia and the United Kingdom and moderate in France and Germany. If we want developed societies with women doctors, political leaders, teachers, bus drivers, and computer programmers, we will need qualified people to give loving care to their children. And there is no reason why every society should not enjoy such loving paid childcare. It may even be true that Rowena Bautista or María Gutierrez are the people to provide it, so long as their own children either come with them or otherwise receive all the care they need. In the end, the 1959 Article 9 of the United Nations Declaration on the Rights of the Child— which the United States alone has yet to sign—states an important goal for both Clinton and Princela Bautista and for feminism. It says we need to value care as our most precious resource, and to notice where it comes from and ends up. For, these days, the personal is global.

15 EMOTIONAL GEOGRAPHY AND THE FLIGHT PLAN OF CAPITALISM

Over the last two decades, American workers have increasingly divided into a majority who work too many hours and a minority with no work at all. This split hurts families at both extremes, but I focus here on the growing scarcity of time among the long-hours majority. For many of them, a speed-up at the office and factory has marginalized life at home, so that the very term "work-family balance" seems to many a bland slogan with little bearing on real life. Drawing on my research at Amerco, a Fortune 500 company, I argue that a company's "family-friendly" policy goes only as deep as the emotional geography of the workplace and home, the drawn and redrawn boundaries between the sacred and the profane.

For about a fifth of the employees I talked to at Amerco in the early and mid 1990s, family life had become like "work" and work had become more like "home." The latest advances in corporate engineering had, for them, increased the magnetic draw of work, while strain and fracture had reduced the draw of family. I also found exceptions to this cultural reversal, variations within it, and countertendencies against it. But new "company towns" are now growing up in America modeled on this cultural reversal—towns that offer a curious form of socialism for the professionals and managers of multinational corporations and capitalism for everyone else. As they show, it is not simply individual priorities we need to balance but *whole social worlds*.

Three factors are creating the current speed-up in work and family life in the United States. (By the term "family," I refer to adults who raise children—committed unmarried couples, same-sex couples, single mothers, two-job couples, and wage-earner-housewife couples.) First of all, increasing numbers of mothers now work outside the home. As I noted in the introduction, in 1900 less than a fifth of American women worked for pay and less than 10 percent of married women did. By 2000 two-thirds of women worked for pay, and mothers outnumbered nonmothers. Indeed, over half of mothers of children one year old and younger now work for pay. Second, according to a 1999 International Labor Organization report, workers are putting in longer hours than did their counterparts a decade ago, and longer than their counterparts in Japan today (see chapter 10).[1] Third,

Americans work in jobs that generally lack flexibility, and in many, if not most, workplaces the very model of "a job" and "career" is based on the image of a traditional man whose wife cares for the children at home. Many women now work on jobs that fit this mold. Compared to the 1970s, mothers now take less time off for the birth of a child and are more likely to work through the summer. They are more likely to work continuously until they retire at age sixty-five. So they increasingly fit the profile of year-round, life-long paid workers, a profile that has long characterized traditional men. Meanwhile, working fathers have not reduced their hours but, if anything, expanded them. So more parents are in a time bind.

Not all working parents with more free time will spend it at home being nice to children or elderly relatives, starting street theater and poetry readings, or growing organic vegetables in community gardens. But without a chance for more time at home, the issue of how to use it well or enjoy it does not arise at all.

So how are we to think about this time bind? If we explore recent writing, we can discern three stances toward it.

One is a *cool modern* stance, according to which the speed-up has become "normal," even fashionable. Decline in time at home does not "marginalize" family life, proponents say, it makes it different—maybe even better. Like many other popular self-help books addressed to the busy working mother, *The Superwoman Syndrome* (1984) by Marjorie Schaevitz offers tips on how to fend off appeals for help from neighbors, relatives, friends, and how to stop feeling guilty about one's mothering. It instructs the mother how to measure out "quality time" frugally and abandons as hopeless the project of getting men more involved at home. Such books call for no changes in the workplace, no changes in the culture, and no change in men. For the cool modern, *the solution to rationalization at work is rationalization at home.* Tacitly such books accept what others of us consider the corrosive effects of global capitalism on family life and on the very notion of what people need to be happy.

A second stance toward the work-family speed-up is *traditional* in that it calls for women's permanent return to the home, or *quasi-traditional* in that it acquiesces to a secondary role and lower-rank mommy track for women at work.[2] Those who take this stance believe that the work-family speed-up is a problem, but they deny the fact that most women now have to work, want to work, and embrace the concept of gender equity. They think of men and women as different in essential ways and add to this idea essential notions of time: "industrial" time for men and "family" time for women.[3]

Those who take a third, *warm modern* stance see the speed-up as a problem but also hold to an egalitarian ideal (at home and work). They advocate a shorter working week, such as workers enjoy in Norway and France, and company-based family-friendly policies. What are these family-friendly reforms?

- flextime: a workday with flexible starting and quitting times, but usually 40 hours of work and the opportunity to "bank" hours at one time and reclaim them later
- flexplace: home-based work, such as telecommuting
- regular or permanent part-time: less than full-time work with full or pro-rated benefits and promotional opportunities in proportion to one's skill and contribution
- job sharing: two people voluntarily sharing one job with benefits and salary pro-rated
- compressed working week: four 10-hour days with three days off, or three 12-hour days with four days off
- paid parental leave
- family obligations as a consideration in the allocation of shift work and required overtime

Potentially, a movement for shorter hours and this range of family-friendly reforms could spread work, increase worker control over hours, and create a "warm modern" world for women to be equal within. But as political goals in America over the last fifty years, work sharing and a shorter working week have "died and gone to heaven," where they live on as hopeless utopian ideals.

But are some companies offering these reforms? And if so, are they for real? And are working parents pressing for them? The good news is that more and more American companies are offering their workers family-friendly alternative work schedules. According to one 1991 study, 88 percent of 188 companies surveyed offer part-time work, 77 percent offer flextime of some sort, 48 percent offer job sharing, 35 percent offer some form of flexplace, and 20 percent offer a compressed working week.[4] The bad news is that in most companies the interested worker must seek and receive the approval of a supervisor or department head. More important still, most policies do not apply to lower-level workers whose conditions of work are covered by union contracts. So a new Faustian bargain—I'll give you family-friendly policies if you accept job insecurity—has begun to cast a pall on the whole project.

In this context, even if offered them, few workers are actually taking advantage of such policies. One study of 384 companies notes that only 9 companies reported even one father who took an official unpaid leave at the birth of his child.[5] Few are on temporary or permanent part-time. Still fewer share a job. Of workers with children ages twelve and under, only 4 percent of men and 13 percent of women worked less than 40 hours a week.[6] Among the 26,000 employees at Amerco, the average working week ranged from 45 to 55 hours. Managers and factory workers often worked 50 or 60 hours a week while clerical workers tended to work a more normal, 40-hour week. Everyone agreed the company was a "pretty workaholic place."

Why weren't workers trying to get more time off? Perhaps they shied away from applying for leaves or shortening their hours because they couldn't afford to earn less. This certainly explains why many young parents continue to work long hours. But it doesn't explain why the wealthiest workers, the managers and professionals, are among the least interested in additional time off. Even among the company's factory workers, who in 1993 averaged between $11 and $12 an hour, and who routinely competed for optional overtime, two 40-hour-a-week paychecks with no overtime work were enough, they said, to support the family. Still, that overtime looked pretty good.

Perhaps employees shied away from shorter-hour schedules because they were afraid of having their names higher on the list of workers who might be laid off in a period of economic downturn. This was not an idle fear. Through the 1980s a third of America's largest companies experienced some layoffs, though this did not happen to managers or clerical workers at Amerco. By union contract, production workers were assured that layoffs, should they occur, would be made according to seniority and not according to any other criteria—such as how many hours an employee had worked. Yet the workaholism went on. Also, employees in the most profitable sectors of the company showed no greater tendency to ask for shorter or more flexible hours for family reasons than employees in the least profitable sectors.

Is it, then, that workers who could afford shorter hours didn't *know* about the company's family-friendly policies? No. All of the 130 working parents I spoke with had heard about alternative schedules and knew where they could find out more.

Perhaps, then, managers responsible for implementing family-friendly polices were actually sabotaging them. Even though company policy allowed flexibility, a worker had to get his boss's okay. And the head of the engineering division of the company told me flatly, "My policy on flextime is that there is no flextime." Other apparently permissive division heads oversaw supervisors who were also tough on this issue. But even managers known to be cooperative had few employees asking for alternative schedules.

Workers could also ask for time off, but get it "off the books." To some extent, this indeed happened. New fathers would take a few days to a week of sick leave for the birth of a baby instead of filing for "parental leave," which they feared would mark them as unserious workers. Yet even counting informal leaves, most women managers returned to full-time 40- to 55-hour work schedules fairly soon after their six weeks of paid maternity leave. Most women secretaries returned after six months, and most women production workers returned after six weeks. Most new fathers took a few days off at most. Even "off the books," working parents were having a hard time spending much time at home.

More important than all these factors seemed to be a company speed-up in response to global competition. In the early 1990s workers each year spoke of working longer hours than they had the year before. When asked why, they explained that the company was trying to "reduce costs," in part by asking employees to do more than whatever they were doing before.

But the sheer existence of a company speed-up doesn't explain why employees weren't trying to resist it, why there wasn't much backtalk. Parents were eager to tell me how their families came first, how they were clear about that. (And national polls, too, show that next to a belief in God, Americans most strongly believe in "the family.") But practices that might express this belief—such as sharing breakfast and dinner—were shifting in the opposite direction. In the minds of many parents of young children, warm modern intentions seemed casually fused with cool modern practices. In some ways, those within the work-family speed-up didn't seem to be trying to slow down. What about their experience might be making this true?

BEHIND THE MISSING CULTURE OF RESISTANCE

In order to catch the full answer, we need to draw on a variety of perspectives in and outside the "work-family" field. The mainstream literature in the work-family field in the United States is both helpful and unhelpful. Rapidly expanding, mildly optimistic, policy-oriented, quantitative, the voluminous research by Ellen Galinsky and Dana Friedman of the Families and Work Institute provides some of the best survey data we have on workers' attitudes toward work and family life and corporate thinking and action on family-friendly reforms.[7] But this line of research doesn't question the construction of the social worlds that shape how people feel about their families, and the researchers don't dig deep into the paradoxes their own data reflect.

A second literature keeps a vigil on the deinstitutionalization of the *family* from either a declinist or an adaptationist viewpoint.[8] But by focusing on the family, this line of inquiry misses the symbiotic—even parasitic—relationship between work and family. That research which does focus on the relation of family to work is based on unquestioned assumptions about what families and workplaces feel like and mean.[9]

A third literature is devoted to "corporate culture."[10] Recent, growing, and relevant, this literature is wide-ranging and theoretically fruitful, but rarely do authors focus on work-family balance, emotional culture, or gender.[11]

Surrounding these literatures are works that help us to see the issue of work-family balance in its larger context. Highlighting as it does the small ways in which big "structures" change, Anthony Giddens's concept of "structuration" elucidates what we might call "familization," and "workization."[12] In this spirit of "liquefying" concepts, turning nouns into verbs, we may speak of ritualizing and de-ritualizing, sacralizing and de-sacralizing, moments in family and work life. We can see the recent history of work and family life as a history of these underlying processes. At the moment, work is becoming a little more ritualized and sacred, especially for "valued workers," while the family is becoming less so. But, depending on the logic of capitalism, and on the strength of the resistance to it, rituals and a sense of the sacred can also flow the other way.

Instead of thinking of the workplace or the family as unyielding thing-like structures, Giddens suggests that we see structures as fluid and change-able. For structures to change, there must be changes in what people do and, I would add, what they feel. For structures come with—and also "are"—emotional cultures.[13] A change in structure requires a change in emotional culture. What we lack, so far, is a vocabulary for describing this culture, and what follows is a crude attempt to create one. An emotional culture is a set of rituals, beliefs about feelings, and rules governing feeling that induce emotional focus and even a sense of the "sacred." This sense of the sacred selects and favors some social bonds over others. It selects and rese-lects relationships into a core or periphery of family life.

Thus, families have a more or less *sacred core* of private rituals and shared meanings, which vary enormously across time and space. In some families what is most sacred is sexuality and marital communication (back rubs, pillow talk, sex), and in other families the "sacred" is reserved for parental bonds (bedtime cuddles with children, bathtime, collective meals, parental talk about children). In addition, families have secondary zones of less important daily, weekly, seasonal rituals which back up the core rituals. These rituals stand against a profane outer layer of family life in which members might describe themselves as "doing nothing in particular" (doing chores, watching television, sleeping)—the character and boundaries of the sacred and profane aspects of family life are clearly in the eye of the beholder. But a sense of what is sacred—held apart as central in importance—is strongly linked to the temporal practices that set off one activity from another.

In the context of the work-family speed-up, many people speak of actively managing, investing, and saving time in order to spend it. They also speak of guarding or defending time in order to "be" in it. In an attempt to more actively control their schedules, many working parents turned on the phone machine at dinner time, set aside cell phones, and turned off computers. So one temporal practice turned out to be turning a switch, or resisting the impulse to lift a receiver or go to the computer. And even the very way people talked about time was itself a temporal practice that did or didn't guard a sacred core of family life.

Families had different patterns of sacredness. Some had highly pro-tected, thick cores of coordinated collective time and meager "skirts" of peripheral time in which people hung out in any old way. Other families had porous cores barely demarcated from casual, individualized, interruptible time hanging out. In either case, when they made sacredness, they made time. In the intermediate and peripheral zones of family life, very occasionally people spoke of "having time on their hands" or "doing nothing." This was time they felt they could give up because it was free. Yet sometimes people set aside periods of "doing nothing," which themselves felt sacred. They often spoke as if they had pulled up the drawbridge to the castle, in order to "do nothing" in it. And pulling up the drawbridge was an act of devotion.

But what people devote themselves *to* has changed. As the historian John Gillis notes, it is fairly recently that the family has become a discrete private realm with a ritual life separate from that of the community.[14] But the current time bind *privatizes the family* still further. By forcing families to cut out what is least important, the speed-up thins out ties that bind it to society. So under the press of the speed-up, families may be forced to give up their peripheral ties with neighbors, Brownie troops, distant relatives, bonds that had all along been sustained by "extra" time.

Both the family and workplace are linked to supportive realms. For the family, this includes neighborhood, church, and school. For the workplace, it includes such things as the bars, restaurants, conference halls, hotels, the commuter-van friendship network. A loss of supportive structure around the family may result in a gain for the workplace, and vice versa. The rise of what Jerry Useem calls "the new company town" has brought gyms, singles clubs, breast cancer support groups, and Bible study groups—civic life itself— under the social umbrella of the workplace.[15] At the same time, over the last twenty years the number of families eating evening meals together has dropped by 10 percent.[16] Families are less likely to receive visitors at home and less likely to visit others. Even time spent talking at home has declined. In sum, as family life becomes de-ritualized, in certain sectors of the economy cultural engineers are busy adding ritual to work.

At a certain point, change in enough personal stories can be described as a change in culture, and I believe many families at Amerco were at this turning point when I interviewed them. Pulled toward work by one set of forces and propelled from the family by another set, a growing number may be unwittingly altering the twin cultures of work and family.[17] As the cultural shield surrounding work has grown stronger, the supportive cultural shield surrounding the family has weakened. These twin processes—one going on at home and another at work—apply unevenly across the social-class spectrum. The pull toward work is stronger at the top of the occupational ladder, and the marginalization of family life is more pronounced at the bottom. Indeed, the picture I am drawing is one within a *wide array* of work and family "structurations" resulting from various combinations of social forces.

While this "reversal" of home and work did not simply happen *to* the people I interviewed, it would be a big mistake to see it as something they chose or wished for. Most workers in this and other studies say they *value* family life above everything else. Work is what they do. Family is why they live. So, I believe the logic I am describing proceeds despite and not because of the powerful intentions and deepest wishes of those in its grip.

When I entered the field, I assumed that working parents would want more time at home. I imagined that they experienced home as a place where they could relax, feel emotionally sheltered and appreciated for who they "really are." I imagined home to feel to the weary worker like the place where he or she could take off a uniform, put on a bathrobe, have a beer, exhale—a picture summed up in the image of the worker coming in the door saying, "Hi, honey, I'm home!" To be sure, home life has its emergencies and strains, but I imagined that home was the place people thought about when they thought about rest, safety, and appreciation. Given this, they would want to maximize time at home. I also assumed that these working parents, especially those who were low-paid factory or service workers, would not feel particularly relaxed, safe, or appreciated at work, at least not more so than at home.

When I interviewed workers at the company, however, a picture emerged that partly belied this model of family life. For example, one thirty-year-old factory shift supervisor, a remarried mother of two, described her return home after work in this way:

> I walk in the door and the minute I turn the key in the lock my oldest daughter is there. Granted she needs somebody to talk to about her day. The baby is still up . . . she should have been in bed two hours ago and that upsets me. The oldest comes right up to the door and complains about anything her father said or did during the evening. She talks about her job. My husband is in the other room hollering to my daughter, "Tracy, I don't ever get no time to talk to your mother because you're always monopolizing her time first before I even get a chance!" They all come at me at once.

The unarbitrated quarrels, the dirty dishes, and the urgency of other people's demands she finds at home contrast with her account of going to work:

> I usually come to work early just to get away from the house. I got to be there at a quarter after the hour, and people are there waiting. We sit. We talk. We joke. I let them know what is going on, who has to be where, what changes I have made for the shift that day. We sit there and chit-chat for five or ten minutes. There is laughing. There is joking. There is fun. They aren't putting me down for any reason. Everything is done in humor and fun from beginning to end. It can get stressful, though, when a machine malfunctions and you can't get the production out.

Another thirty-eight-year-old working mother of two, also a factory worker, had this to say:

> My husband is a great help [with caring for their son]. But as far as doing housework, or even taking the baby when I'm at home, no. When I'm home, our son becomes my job. He figures he works five days a week, he's not going to come home and clean. But he doesn't stop to think that I work seven days a week. . . . Why should I have to come home and do the housework without help from anybody else? My husband and I have been through this over and over again. Even if he would pack up the kitchen table and stack the dishes for me when I'm at work, that would make a big difference. He does nothing. On his weekends off, I have to provide a sitter for the baby so he can go fishing. When I have my day off, I have the baby all day long. He'll help out if I'm not here . . . the minute I'm here he lets me do the work.

To this working mother, her family was not a haven, a zone of relief and relaxation. It was a workplace. More than that, she could get relief from this domestic workplace only by going to the factory. As she continued: "I take a lot of overtime. The more I get out of the house, the better I am. It's a terrible thing to say, but that's the way I feel!"

I assumed that work would feel to workers like a place in which one could be fired at the whim of a profit-hungry employer, while in the family, for all its hassles, one was safe. Based as it is on the impersonal mechanism of supply and demand, profit and loss, work would feel insecure, like being in a jungle. In fact, a good number of workers I interviewed had worked for the company for twenty years or more, whereas they were on their second or third marriages. To these employed, *work* was their rock, their major source of security. They were getting their pink slips at home.

To be sure, almost all the workers I spoke to *wanted* to base their sense of stability at home, and many did. But I was also struck by the loyalty many felt toward the company and a loyalty *they felt* coming *from* it despite what might seem like evidence to the contrary—the speed-up, the restructuring, the layoffs at other companies. Even at Amerco in the early 1990s, if one division of the company was doing poorly, the company might "de-hire" workers within that division and rehire them in a more prosperous division. This happened to one female engineer, very much upsetting her, but her response to it was telling:

> I have done very well in the company for twelve years, and I thought my boss thought very highly of me. He'd said as much. So when our division went down and several of us were de-hired, we were told to look for another position within the company *or* outside. I thought, "Oh my God, *outside!*" I was stunned! Later, in the new division it was like a remarriage . . . I wondered if I could love again.

Work was not always "there for you," but increasingly home, as they had known it, wasn't either. As one woman recounted, "One day my husband came home and told me, 'I've fallen in love with a woman at work . . . I want a divorce.'"

Finally, the model of family-as-haven led me to assume that the individual would feel most known and appreciated at home and least so at work. Work might be where they felt unappreciated, "a cog in the machine"—an image brought to mind by the classic Charlie Chaplin film on factory life, *Modern Times.* But the factory is no longer the archetypical workplace and, sadly, many workers felt more appreciated for what they were doing at work than for what they were doing at home. For example, when I asked one forty-year-old technician whether he felt more appreciated at home or at work, he put it this way:

> I love my family. I put my family first . . . but I'm not sure I feel more appreciated by them [laughs]. My fourteen-year-old son doesn't talk too much to anyone when he gets home from school. He's a brooder. I don't know how good I've been as a father . . . we fix cars together on Saturday. My wife works opposite shifts to what I work, so we don't see each other except on weekends. We need more time together—need to get out to the lake more. I don't know . . .

This worker seemed to feel better about his skill repairing machines in the factory than his way of relating to his son. This is not as unusual as it might seem. In a large-scale study, Arthur Emlen found that 59 percent of employees rated their family performance "good or unusually good" while 86 percent gave a similar rating to their performance on the job.[18]

This overall cultural shift may be part of the reason many workers are going along with the work-family speed-up and not resisting it. A nationally representative study of 3,400 workers conducted in 1993 by the Families and Work Institute reflects two quite contradictory findings. On one hand, the study reports that 80 percent of workers felt their jobs required "working very hard" and 42 percent "often [felt] used up by the end of the work day." On the other hand, when workers were asked to compare how much time and energy they *actually* devoted to their family, their job or career, and themselves, with how much time they would have *liked* to devote to each, there was little difference. Workers estimated that they actually spent 43 percent of their time and energy on family and friends, 37 percent on job or career, and 20 percent on themselves. But they *wanted* to spend just about what they *were* spending—47 percent on family and friends, 30 percent on the job, and 23 percent on themselves.[19] Of the workers I talked to, about a fifth fit the pattern of reversed worlds, while for a substantial number of the rest it was a mild theme, and it may be a theme in the lives of other workers as well.

Three sets of factors seem to exacerbate this reversal of family and work cultures: trends in the family, trends at work, and a growing consumerism that reinforces trends in both. First, half of marriages in America end in divorce—the highest rate in the world. The high divorce rate may be due, in part, to the absence of policies that could buffer marriage against the rough edges of capitalism (job retraining in the face of an erratic demand for labor, for example). Partly it may be due to cultural shifts that lessen people's need for marriage and reduce restraints against divorce.

New in scope, too, are the numbers of working wives who work "two shifts," one at home and one at work, and face their husband's resistance to helping fully with the load at home—a strain that often leaves both spouses feeling unappreciated.[20] This, too, is a strain behind many divorces. Those in strained marriages often find a large pool of divorced people eligible for remarriage—itself a result of a high divorce rate. And after remarriage, associations with ex-spouses and new stepchildren raise special challenges for which not all parents are prepared, a likely factor behind the high divorce rate among those who remarry.

Meanwhile, another set of factors is affecting life at work. Many corporations have engineered, for top and upper-middle managers, and to a lesser extent staff, a world of friendly ritual and positive reinforcement. The company I studied, Amerco, had adopted a program called Total Quality. At the cost of several million dollars, it put all its employees, top to bottom, through a two-day Total Quality training program. In various divisions, workers were divided into teams that met regularly to discuss ways of improving productivity and creating strong team spirit. Indeed, the regular meetings of high-production teams became a widespread company rite, creating a Durkheimian solidarity at work that was sometimes missing at home. Meanwhile, the CEO issued a series of edicts such as "Amerco Values the Internal Customer," which, in everyday parlance, means that all employees should treat other employees as nicely as they try to treat customers. These edicts were designed to improve social relations in the company and were bandied about and discussed with public solemnity. Human relations employees gave seminars on human problems at work. High-production teams, based on cooperation between relative equals who manage themselves, tended to foster intense relations at work. The company frequently held ceremonies to give out awards for outstanding work. Halls were hung with new plaques praising one or another worker on recent accomplishments. Recognition luncheons, department gatherings, and informal birthday remembrances were common. Career planning sessions with one's supervisor and team meetings to talk over "modeling, work relations, and mentoring" with co-workers verged on, even as they borrowed from, psychotherapy. Sometimes Amerco workers attended more employee-of-the-month gatherings at work than birthday or other parties at home. Some married workers who eschewed wearing a wedding ring proudly sported a company pin on their lapels. For all its aggravation and tensions, the workplace was where quite a few workers felt appreciated and honored, and where they had real friends. By contrast, at home there were fewer "award ceremonies" and often a dearth of helpful feedback about mistakes.

In addition, courtship and mate selection, earlier more or less confined to the home-based community, may be moving into the sphere of work. The later age for marriage, the higher proportion of unmarried people, and the high divorce rate all create an ever-replenishing courtship pool at work. The gender desegregation of the workplace and the lengthened working day also provide opportunity for people to meet and develop romantic or quasi-romantic ties. At the factory, romance may develop in the lunchroom, pub, or parking lot; and for upper-management levels, at conferences, in "fantasy settings" in upscale hotels and dimly lit restaurants.[21]

So what felt like home and what felt like work? When I asked Amerco employees where they felt they were the most competent, at work or at home, they frequently answered, "At work." When I asked them where they felt the most relaxed, at work or at home, they often replied, "At work." When I asked them where they felt they could express who they really were, answers were mixed, but a good number said, "At work." When I asked them where they felt secure, most replied, "Home," although for some their multiple marriages told a different story. All in all, about a fifth of the Amerco employees described work as the "haven" and home as—if not a heartless world—a lesser haven.

Capitalism is the most important economic force in the world today, and it affects whatever it touches. But in all its social engineering, modern American capitalism is revealing itself to be not simply an economic but a *cultural* system as well. In almost all its incarnations, capitalism presents a challenge to local cultures, including the local culture of families. Like tribal cultures trampled by globalization, family cultures within the First World can find it hard to compete with the centrifugal force of the work cultures capitalism sets up. What Wal-Mart does to mom-and-pop stores, companies like Amerco do to the family lives of workers.

There is a gender pattern here: in a previous era, an undetermined number of men escaped the house for the pub, the fishing hole, and often the office. One might see—to quote from the title of an article by Jean Duncombe and Dennis Marsden—"workaholic men" and "whining women."[22] Now that women compose nearly half of the American labor force, some families are composed of workaholic parents and whining children.

Forces pulling workers out of family life and into the workplace are set into perpetual motion by consumerism. Consumerism acts to *maintain* the emotional reversal of work and family. Exposed to a continual bombardment of advertisements through a daily average of three hours of television (half of all their leisure time), workers are persuaded to "need" more things. To buy what they now need, they need money. To earn money, they work longer hours. Being away from home so many hours, they make up for their absence at home with gifts that cost money. They materialize love. And so the cycle continues.[23]

Once work begins to become a more compelling arena of appreciation than home, a self-fulfilling prophecy takes hold. For, if workers flee into work from the tensions at home, tensions at home can grow worse. The worse the tensions at home, the firmer the grip the workplace has on what workers have come to need.

So, for some people work had come to feel like family, and family more like work. But this is one of five models of work and family realized in various parts of the economic landscape. At the top of the class ladder we're likely to find a traditional model in which home and work each exhibit gender-specific pulls—work for men, home for women. This old-style model seems to be giving way increasingly to a modified traditional pattern in which women do part-time work and men full-time work. Lower down, we find the haven model, in which work is a heartless world and the family still a haven—many factory hands and other blue-collar workers fit this model, and the growth of low-wage minimum-security jobs may lead to more families of this type. Among dual-career couples in professional and managerial jobs, we find strong traces of the work-as-home and home-as-work model. At the bottom of the social ladder, we find the "double-negative" model, according to which neither a kin network nor work associates provide emotional anchors for the individual but rather a gang, fellow drinkers on the corner, or other groups of this sort. Throughout—perhaps as much due to luck as to planning and circumstance—we find that miraculous model, the dual-income couple with the yearned-for balance between home and work.

Which model of family and work comes to prevail depends in part on the power of external pressures bearing on both family and economy. One trend in the American economy today is toward cultural consolidation of life around work, to make the workplace into a little town and meet all needs there. Covertly it presses people into the model of reversed worlds.

Corporate cultural engineers have thus elaborated on the Amerco model by adding to their companies many goods and services of the mall and the lively civic culture of small-town America. Such "new company towns," as Jerry Useem calls them, provide a "one-stop" life.[24] A person can get almost everything he or she needs at the workplace. Companies in this way recruit and retain highly skilled workers in a period of low unemployment. They elaborate the pattern of work-as-home but perhaps reduce the feeling that home is work by outsourcing many tasks formerly done at home. By the same token such companies seem both to absorb home life into work and to reduce the extent to which home is a separate sphere of life.

In an article in *Fortune* magazine, Useem describes companies that offer an on-site bank, store, dry cleaner, hairdresser, and nail salon. Forty-six of *Fortune*'s "100 Best Companies to Work For," he notes, offer take-home meals. Twenty-six offer personal concierge services through which workers can hire someone to arrange delivery of that special bouquet, chose birthday gifts, or plan a child's bar mitzvah. A number of companies have dating services, and indeed a 1999 study by Roper Starch Worldwide found that 38 percent of employees surveyed reported having dated a co-worker.[25]

Companies are adding the kind of civic community that Robert Putnam claims in his book *Bowling Alone* has faded from American society.[26] Lands' End, a mail-order clothing company, and Amgen, a biotech firm, have developed employee clubs for "chess, genealogy, gardening, model airplanes, public speaking, tennis, karate, scuba diving and charity"—many activities we normally imagine belong with community or family life. SAS Institute, a software company in Cary, North Carolina, has a breast cancer support group, a single parents group, an international club that monthly prepares foods from its members' native lands, and a singles group called Mingle. In about a thousand companies nationwide, the Fellowship of Companies for Christ International offers on-site Bible study groups.

Such companies are not yet typical of American workplaces, but they point to an important corporate strategy for accomplishing two goals— retaining valued workers when valued workers are hard to get, and keeping them at work for long hours. How do you keep your talented workers happy? Solve one of their biggest problems—work-family balance. The Faustian bargain between company and worker seems to be this: "We'll bring civic life to you at work. You work long hours." As for balance, Useem notes, the chief of human resources at BMC, a software company in Houston, says, "I know this is hard to believe, but you feel like you can get away while you're here. [The office] gives you a balanced life without having to leave."[27] But this idea of balance leaves out Junior and Grandma, not to mention all the civic activities for which Alexis de Tocqueville once praised America. And the basis for BMC "balance" is only as firm as last quarter's profit margin.

The "new company towns" also carry the model of work as home and home as work in the unlikely direction of old-time socialism. In such companies as BMC, Lands' End, or SAS Institute, one authority sets out to meet all the needs of the people under its governance. Such company towns would seem to subtract much of the tough entrepreneurial struggle from daily life. There would even appear to be some gesture in the direction of living a well-balanced and unalienated life as Marx envisioned it under socialism. A person could be a fisher in the morning, a farmer in the afternoon, and a philosopher in the evening. Only, at BMC, the fish and produce would need to benefit the company.

Yet if such companies offer the old *socialist utopia* to an *elite* of knowledge workers in the top tier of an increasingly divided labor market, other companies may increasingly be offering the *worst of early capitalism* to *semiskilled* and *unskilled workers*. With the development of the two-tiered economy over the last twenty years, the bottom tier endures lower wages, less job security, and certainly less in the way of "home" at work. So jobs in garment industries or fast food or retail work would seem to reflect the aspect of capitalism of which Marx was most critical—take the work, ignore the worker.

Perhaps we are seeing signs of a pattern that will gradually become clear in the years ahead—socialism for the rich and capitalism for the poor.[28] Only there is a further paradox. The socialism of these new company towns is confined to "gated" workplaces—parallel to the gated communities in which many elite employees live. In the workplaces of the poor, the capitalist ethos of competitive individualism prevails, open to everyone, come one, come all. At the top, the company invests a lot in keeping the worker happy; at the bottom, the company invests very little. At the top, the worker may need to go to work to find entertainment, a sense of civic participation, even affection (those hugging seminars). At the bottom, many workers miss out on all those things. For if, as Robert Putnam argues in *Bowling Alone*, civic life in America has experienced a serious decline, workers without access to new company towns will be lacking civic participation as well.[29]

But for workers at the top and bottom alike, people will increasingly be required to work in order to be citizens. Neither the government (after the 1996 welfare reform) nor the family (with little paid parental leave, few good part-time jobs or job-shares, and most moms at work) will support people who "just" provide care.

In the end, work is a great part of human life. Thorstein Veblen once wrote lyrically about an "instinct" for workmanship, a love of craft that enhances our experience of being alive. Veblen was right. But writing a hundred years ago, it was hard for him to foresee a modern workplace that borrows a cultural sense of family and community from "real" families and communities so as to keep workers at the office. So he didn't explore what can happen when workers themselves come to want to do what companies want them to do—and when that may mean ten hours a day at the office. We need to add to Veblen's celebration of work a notion of work-life balance and to consider the balance not just between this and that part of a person's day, but a balance between this and that social world. Each pattern of work and family life is to be seen somewhere in the flight plan of late capitalism. For capitalist competition is not simply a matter of market expansion around the globe, but of local geographies of emotion at home. The challenge, as I see it, is to understand the close links between economic trends, emotional geographies, and pockets of cultural resistance. For it is in those pockets that we can look for "warm modern" answers.

16 THE CULTURE OF POLITICS

Traditional, Postmodern, Cold Modern,
and Warm Modern Ideals of Care

Among the visual images of care in the modern Western world, a classic view portrays a mother holding a child. Frequently, the mother is seated in a chair at home or in a dreamlike setting, such as her garden. Often found on old-fashioned birthday cards and in ads for yarn in women's magazines, the image is a secular, middle-class version of Madonna and Child. The caregiver in these images is a woman, not a man. She is at home, not in a public place. Moreover, the caregiving seems natural, effortless. She is sitting, quiescent, not standing or moving—stances associated with "working." She seems to enjoy caring for the child, and as the child's face often suggests, she is good at caring. Thus, the image of care is linked with things feminine, private, natural, and well functioning, and evokes an ideal of care.

Drawn from nineteenth-century upper-middle-class parlor life, this image has been put to extensive commercial use. Corporate advertisers often juxtapose the mother-and-child image with such products as health insurance, telephone service, Band-Aids, diapers, talcum powder, and a wide variety of foods.[1] Our constant exposure to the commercial image of mother puts us at one remove from it. In a parallel way, the very term "care" in America suffers from commercial overuse, associated as it is with orange juice, milk, frozen pizza, and microwave ovens. Thus, both the image and word for care have come to seem not only feminine, private, and natural but emotionally void, bland, dull, even sappy.

In the small but growing feminist literature on care, scholars have begun to challenge the silence on the issue in much conventional social theory. Such writers as Trudy Knijn, Clare Ungerson, Kari Waerness, and Joan Tronto note that care is more central in the lives of women than men, since it is more often women who care for children, the sick, and the elderly. While early feminist scholarship focused on the exploitative nature of women's traditional roles, recent feminist writers, as Kari Waerness puts it, "have struggled to redefine the possible grounds of feminist theory." The quest for new "cultural grounds" coincides with a dilemma that many modern women face. Waerness notes, "Women . . . are faced both with the task of caring for children, the ill, the disabled, and the elderly in the private sphere, while at the same time trying to achieve more command over their own lives and a greater measure of economic independence."[2]

But this is far from just a woman's problem. Recent trends in the United States have expanded the *need* for care while contracting the *supply* of it, creating a "care deficit" in both private and public life. In public life, the care deficit can be seen in federal and sometimes state cuts in funds for poor mothers, the disabled, the mentally ill, and the elderly. In reducing the financial deficit, legislators add to the "care deficit."

The care deficit lies latent behind a great deal of political debate. Those engaged in this debate in turn think in images reflecting four models of care.[3] These cultural models set down the basic terms of political debate about care and so deserve a closer look. The first is the *traditional* model, represented by the image of the homemaker mother. The second is the *postmodern* model, represented by the working mother who "does it all" with no additional help from any quarter and no adaptation in her work schedule. This image often goes along with a tacit lowering of standards of care, as well as making those lower standards seem normal. The third is the *cold modern* model represented by impersonal institutional care in year-round ten-hour daycare and old-age homes. The fourth is the *warm modern* model in which institutions provide some care of the young and elderly, while women and men join equally in providing private care as well. Each model implies a definition of care, as well as ideas about who gives it and how much of what kind of care is "good enough."

TWO SIDES OF A CARE DEFICIT

First, by the term "care" I refer to an emotional bond, usually mutual, between the caregiver and cared-for, a bond in which the caregiver feels responsible for others' well-being and does mental, emotional, and physical work in the course of fulfilling that responsibility. Thus, care *of* a person implies care *about* him or her. I'll focus here on care of the very young and old—care we still think of as "family care."[4]

Most care requires work so personal, so involved with feeling, that we rarely imagine it to be work. But it would be naïve to assume that giving care is completely "natural" or effortless. Care is a result of many small subtle acts, conscious or not.[5] Consider a case of an elderly woman who becomes sick and despondent. A middle-aged daughter visits. She helps her mother acknowledge her illness ("It's worth seeing a doctor") and drives her to the doctor. She lifts her mother's spirits through humor and conversation: she cheers her up. She hugs her mother, makes her chicken soup, deciphers the intricate insurance forms, pays the doctor, has extra talks with the doctor, and offers long-term care at home. These are some of the many ways to care. All the moments during the course of performing these acts when we are also trying to get into the task in the right spirit, with the appropriate feelings, can be considered the emotional work of care.[6] Thus, we put more than nature into caring; we put time, feeling, acting, and thought into it.

As the worldwide income gap has widened over the last forty years between the developed and the underdeveloped countries (the oil-rich and the Pacific Rim countries aside), the need for care has expanded in much of the developing world, especially Africa and parts of South America. In this essay I focus on the United States, a country that has grown relatively richer during this period. Even so, *within* this "core" of capitalism, the class gap has widened, and the care of many dependents seems to have eroded, too. Further research may uncover rough parallels between the American case and that of the countries of Western Europe, Canada, Australia, New Zealand, and Japan.[7] Perhaps these models can sensitize us to the often hidden cultural lining beneath the politics of care in the United States as well as elsewhere in the developed world. With the exception of Japan, similar conditions seem to prevail in these other developed countries: a flight of capital to cheap labor pools in the developing world, the disappearance of well-paid industrial jobs and the rise of poorly paid service jobs, the weakening of labor unions, and the influx of migrant workers, all of which put a squeeze on average blue-collar workers. In addition, the economic recession of the 1980s and cost cutting due to global competition in the 1990s have led to stagnation in the middle class and decline among the poor.

As a social-class divide has deepened, change has occurred in the structure of family and work. Over the past forty years, birth rates have fallen, reducing the demand for childcare. In the United States, Canada, Japan, and the Netherlands, the average number of children born to women was slightly above 3.0 in 1951 and below 1.9 in 1988.[8] At the same time, the proportion of elderly people rose, increasing the need for elder care.[9] From 1950 to 1990 the proportion of older people (sixty-five and over) in the U.S. population rose from 8 to 12 percent.

In most of the advanced industrial world, the divorce rate has also risen and, with it, the importance of the single-parent family. Half of American marriages end in divorce.[10] While we often imagine the single parent to be in a temporary phase before remarriage, a third of single mothers never remarry, and of the two-thirds who do remarry, over half divorce again. The divorce rate has thus increased the number of single-parent families, so that in 2000, 18 percent of children under age eighteen were living with single mothers and 4 percent with single fathers.[11] Since the remarriage rate for women is lower than that for men (because men tend to remarry younger women), and since divorced women are far more likely to gain custody of children, most single parents are women. Divorced men provide much less care for their children than married men, and divorced women much more. But since those divorced women also do paid work, the rising divorce rate creates the need for new care arrangements for their children.

Further, throughout the developed world with the exception of Japan, the proportion of all births that occur to unmarried women has risen. In the United States the rate rose from 5 percent in 1960 to 23 percent in 1986 and 33 percent in 2000.[12] Most unwed mothers cohabit with the fathers of their children, but the rate of breakup among cohabiting couples is higher than among married couples.[13] So, the single-parent home is the major source of care for many children.

The growing fragility of bonds between women and men has also weakened bonds between men and their children. After divorce, not only are fathers physically absent, but they reduce contact with their children and, over time, give them less money.[14] A national study found that, three years after divorce, half of American divorced fathers had not visited their children during the entire previous year and thus did not perform the most basic form of care.[15] After one year, half of divorced fathers were providing no child support at all, and most of the other half paid irregularly or less than the court-designated amounts.[16] Wealthy divorced fathers were just as likely to be negligent as poor ones. So, taken together, recent trends in the class structure, certain demographic shifts, and family decline have shifted the population in need of care, radically reduced social supports on the home front, and moved a good deal of the burden of care from men to women.

THE SUPPLY SIDE OF THE CARE DEFICIT

Meanwhile, as the need for public services has increased, American voters have come to favor *reducing* the supply of care that government provides, and many favor turning to the beleaguered family as a main source of care. They fall back on the image of Madonna and Child. Despite signs of distress and lower well-being among the growing number of poor children (declining academic performance and high rates of substance abuse, depression, and even teen suicide), much of the American middle class responds with "sympathy fatigue," for some of their children are in trouble too.

While the number of homeless and destitute people rose under the presidencies of Ronald Reagan and George H. W. Bush, government services began to fall. Both presidents tried to resolve the gap between demand and supply of care by a cultural move—privatizing our *idea* of care. President Bush cut the national budget for school lunches and Aid to Families with Dependent Children (AFDC), calling instead for volunteers who might model themselves on his nonworking wife, Barbara. In this way, Bush projected a collective, yet private, version of mother and child as a supposed solution for a growing array of social ills.

Under the Democratic administration of President Bill Clinton, the middle-class "sympathy fatigue" persisted and grew. For example, the Personal Responsibility Act, introduced in January 1995 and passed in 1996, called for permanent cuts in welfare to unwed mothers under age eighteen, to anyone who has received aid for sixty months, or to anyone who bears a child while on welfare. In 2002, under George W. Bush, the law requires that single parents receiving aid must be engaged in "constructive activities" for forty hours a week, and the care of their own children or elderly relations doesn't count as such. The beat goes on: Force carers into paid work. Reduce public care.

If the state refuses to provide a *public* solution to the care gap by funding service programs, can the *private* realm do the job? Like women in most of the developed world, American women have gone into paid work in extraordinary numbers. In 1960, 28 percent of married women with children under eighteen were in the labor force; by 1996, 68 percent of those mothers were working. More mothers than nonmothers now work. In 1948, 11 percent of married women with children aged six and younger worked outside the home. In 1991, 60 percent did. Today over half of all mothers of children one year and younger are in the labor force.

Working mothers are also working longer hours than they were twenty years ago. In *The Overworked American,* Juliet Schor argues that Americans are working "an extra month" each year compared to twenty years ago. They take shorter vacations, have fewer paid or even unpaid days off, and work longer hours. According to a 1992 national survey, the average worker spends 45 hours a week on the job, including overtime and commuting time.[17]

In truth, the private realm to which conservatives turn for a *solution* to the care deficit itself has many *problems* that call for care. Many in need of care are caught between the hardened sensibility of a taxable middle class coping with a recession and government cuts, on the one hand, and fewer helping hands because of overstretched kin networks, on the other.

"WHO WILL DO WHAT MOTHER DID?"

Working mothers face the daunting task of balancing work and family life, often in the absence of two things—partners who share work at home and a workplace that offers both parents flexible hours. Such women are caught in what I have called a "stalled gender revolution." It is a revolution because in two decades women have gone from being mainly at home to being mainly at work. It is "stalled" because women have undergone this change in a culture that has neither rewired its notion of manhood to facilitate male work-sharing at home, nor restructured the workplace so as to allow more control over and flexibility at work.

Caught in this stall, women have little time to care for their children and elderly parents, much less a sick neighbor, a depressed friend, a divorcing co-worker. Few can find time to volunteer at a homeless shelter. The private "supply" with which conservatives would answer the growing needs for care is largely made up of women caught in this stalled revolution.

Couples I describe in *The Second Shift* were struggling over who did how much of the "caring" for the home and children.[18] Care for the home was a tension point in their marriage. Frequently the couple disagreed about how much care each should provide, did provide, and in what spirit. Often they disagreed over how much really *needed to be done.* Men who fully shared the "second shift" often wished their wives were more *grateful* to them for being such unusually helpful husbands, especially when they got no praise from the outside world for doing housework. Wives who cut back their work hours to contribute more at home wanted their husbands to appreciate the sacrifices they were making at work. On both sides, hurt feelings over insufficient gratitude were rooted, I argue, in the low value placed on the caregiving work "mother used to do."

Of the husbands I interviewed, one out of five fully shared the care of children and home with his working wife. Of the 80 percent of husbands who did not share—but offered "help" with chores and childcare—over half had felt pressure from their wives to do more, but most resisted. Some working-class mothers pressed their husbands by indirect means. They got sick or played helpless at paying bills, shopping, and even cooking and sewing, because, as a one wife stated with a wink, "My husband does it so much better."

Other working mothers used direct means—dramatic confrontations or serious discussions. Met with intransigence, some wives staged "sharing showdowns." They went on "strike." They refused to cook. They let the laundry pile up. One mother even left a child waiting to be picked up at school when she knew her husband had forgotten. Another started charging her husband by the hour for work at home beyond her rightful half. In these ways, wives tried to force their husbands to do more but often failed to do so. Neither partner could afford the emotional "luxury" of a marriage free of a struggle about care. In the absence of wider changes in the culture of manhood and the workplace, two-job couples were suffering a microversion of the care deficit.

The present challenge, it seems to me, is to increase the supply of care while retaining women's hard-won gains at work. But, to pursue this goal, we must sensitize ourselves to competing cultural *images* of care, for it is in the persuasive power of these images that the struggle will be won. The couples I studied seemed to reflect four different images of care, which I present here as "pure types," though the views of any one person are usually a blend of several. These models also appear in public discourse on social policy and so provide a tool for decoding that discourse. Each model—traditional, postmodern, cold modern, and warm modern—is a response to the care deficit. Each raises different questions and places a different value on care. Each also competes with the others for cultural space in both private and public discourse.

The traditional solution is to retire women to the home where they provide unpaid care. Traditional discourse centers on the topic of where a woman should and shouldn't be—and caretaking is often incidental to the question of her proper role. Indeed, this "solution" basically calls for the wholesale reversal of industrialization and the de-liberation of women. Because men are removed from the realm of care, and care is retired to the devalued, premonetized realm, homemakers become a "colony" within an ever more male modern state—which has the power to impose its cultural hegemony.[19]

The advantage of this model to men is that women would do the caring work and the care itself would be "personal." The disadvantage is that powerful long-term trends are moving in the opposite direction and the vast majority of women would probably resist. As the economy has grown and families have shrunk, more women want to work outside the home; need the money; desire the security, challenge, and community; and aspire to the identity provided by a job. For women, the question is, "Do I really want to be a housewife?" And even if they do, in an era in which half of marriages end in divorce, the next question is, "Do I dare plan to do this all my life?"

In contrast to the traditional, the postmodern solution is to rid ourselves of the mother-and-child image, replace it with nothing, and claim that everyone is happy anyway. In this scenario, we leave matters much as they are—with women in the labor force and men doing little at home. We *legitimate* the care deficit by reducing the range of ideas about what a child, wife, husband, aged parent, or home "really needs" to thrive. Indeed, the words "thrive" and "happy" go out of fashion, replaced by thinner, more restrictive notions of human well-being implied by the terms "succeed," "cope," and "survive." Popular psychology and advice books often glamorize a life for women that is relatively free of the burden of this care.

The culture has produced new images for childhood and old age that correspond to this picture. An Orwellian "superkid" language has emerged to normalize what commentators in the recent past labeled neglect. In a 1985 *New York Times* article on new programs for latchkey children, a child-care professional is quoted making the case for the phrase "children in self-care" rather than "latchkey children," a term coined during World War II when many children whose mothers worked in defense industries went home alone wearing a key to the house around their necks. "Children in self-care" suggests that children are being cared for—but by themselves, independently.[20] The popular film *Home Alone* portrays a boy around eight who is accidentally left behind as his parents set off on a vacation in France. The child breaks open his brother's piggy bank to buy himself frozen pizza and fends off robbers—triumphing happily, independently, without any-one's help.

The advice book *Teaching Your Child to Be Home Alone*, by the psychother-apists Earl A. Grollman and Gerri L. Sweder, tells children, "The end of the workday can be a difficult time for adults. It is natural for them to sometimes be tired and irritable. . . . Before your parents arrive at the Center, begin to get ready, and be prepared to say good-bye to your friends so that pick-up time is easier for everybody."[21] Moreover, the psychotherapists severely advise children, "Don't go to school early just because you don't like staying home alone. Teachers are busy preparing for the day, and they are not expected to care for youngsters until school officially begins."[22] In another brochure designed for parents who leave their children in "self-care," Work and Family Directions, a nonprofit agency, presents a model "contract"— like a legal document but framed in a lace design—to be signed by parent and child concerning the terms of self-care.

The elderly, too, are increasingly portrayed as "content on their own." An American television advertisement showed how the elderly can "happily" live alone now in the company of a portable electronic device that they can push to signal an ambulance service in case they suffer a heart attack or fall. Like the term "children in self-care," the image of the "happy" older person home alone can become a disguise for postmodern stoicism.

Pressed for time, many of the two-job couples I studied questioned the need for various kinds of care. One husband said, "We don't really need a hot meal at night because we eat well at lunch." A mother questioned the meaning of cooking green vegetables when her son disliked them. Yet another challenged the need for her children's daily baths or clean clothes: "He loves his brown pants; why shouldn't he just wear them for the week?" Along with understandable revisions of old-fashioned ideas of "proper care," this line of thinking can lead to minimizing children's emotional needs as well. The father of a three-month-old child in nine-hour daycare said, "I want him to be independent." In the postmodern model, these reductions raise no eyebrows.

In the public sector, too, some new practices fit the postmodern model. The current practice in many hospitals of sending new mothers home the day after they give birth or sending patients home soon after serious surgery is postmodern. Eager to reduce costs, many insurance companies support ten-session psychotherapy instead of the longer time such therapy would need to be truly helpful. Above all, the failure of the American government to create a family policy that protects children and supports women is the ultimate expression of the postmodern model.

Fearful that traditionalists will exploit people's distress in order to return women to the home, some authors argue in part, "Stop feeling a loss. Don't feel nostalgic for the intact homes of the 1950s. You'll never get them back, and they weren't better anyway."[23] This critique of nostalgia is needlessly confused, I think, with the implicit postmodern message "Care, we don't need that much of it."

The advantage of a postmodern solution is that it is all too easy to implement. We only have to continue life as it often is, to make a virtue of current necessity, and say, "I'm fine. I don't need care," or "They are fine. They don't need care." The crucial disadvantage, of course, is that despite the wondrous variety of cultural ideas about "needs," we still do need care, and it takes a vigorous emotional effort to repress the wish to care or to be cared for.

The postmodern model places the least value on care because living within this model we learn to repress the very need for care and the problem of making that need visible is itself erased. Those who have to take care of unsuppressible needs anyway come to feel angry and resentful at the invisibility of their task. The *social* context—the care deficit—is culturally transformed into a *psychological* issue: *"Can I manage my emotional needs to match the minimalist norms of care?"*

The cold modern solution is to institutionalize all forms of human care. How much of a child's day or older person's life is to be spent in institutional care is a matter of degree, but the cold modern position presses for maximum hours and institutional control. Its premise is that what need for care we have can mostly be met outside the family. Don't rig it so that families can do more. Rig it so families can do less. An example is the Soviet model of 7:00 A.M. to 7:00 P.M. daycare, with alternative weeklong sleepover childcare available as well. The public debate reflecting this position often centers on what means of care is the most "practical, efficient, and rational," given the unquestioned realities of modern life.

Advocates of the cold modern ideal can be found among corporations that want to minimize the familial demands upon their workers so as to maximize the workers' devotion to the job. Some American companies have expanded daycare hours for "weekend workers" and have summer programs that keep children in daycare year-round. While such long hours are still uncommon for very young children, some workers—especially harried professionals and managers, now "working scared" under the threat of layoffs—are tempted to turn to cold modern solutions.

According to the cold modern scenario, an increasing amount of life for both women and men goes on within the cash economy, with daycare and nursing homes, sick care, and meals-on-wheels programs for invalids. Such programs are taking on more formerly private care. In contrast to the postmodern solution, here we are invited to believe that human beings need care. But in contrast to the traditional solution, nonfamilial institutions provide that care. There is no "colony of care" entrapping women at home. Men and women don't struggle over who takes care of the kids or do much care work at all. The tension point in this solution is between would-be and actual providers of care. The basic question for parents who put their children in daycare and middle-aged people who put elderly parents in senior citizens homes is: "How genuine or personal is institutional care?"

There is a fourth, warm modern ideal of care. It is modern because public institutions have a part in the solution and it's warm because we do not relinquish all care to them. It's also egalitarian because men and women share in what we do not relinquish. In contrast to the postmodern model, notions of need are not reduced or denied, so caring is recognized as important work. In contrast to the cold modern solution, it calls for fulfilling these needs, in part, personally.

Of the four models, the traditional turns to the past, the two "moderns" turn toward the future, and the postmodern makes a virtue of "grinning and bearing it" in the painful transition between the two. Of the four, only the warm modern ideal combines characteristics of society that are *both* warm *and* modern. It does so by calling for basic changes in both men and the structure of work. The warm modern model thus implies three arenas of struggle—male participation at home, time schedules in the workplace, and the value placed on care. While feminists are no less confused than anyone else in their thinking about care, probably most of us advocate a warm modern ideal, however hard it is to achieve in reality.

Nations, as well as individuals, adopt cultural models of care. Faced with a similar care deficit, developed nations have responded very differently. Switzerland and Portugal have tended toward the traditional model. The United States is moving steadily toward a synthesis of the postmodern and cold modern models, while Norway, Sweden, and Denmark still lead the world in establishing a warm modern model.[24]

What predisposes a society toward a warm modern model of care? Three factors are key. For one thing, an economy that depends on female labor: economic strength in male-dominated industries and alternative sources of cheap labor in female-dominated industries incline a society to retire affluent women to the home and establish the social desirability of this "alternative" for women. For another thing, one needs a public culture of care: a culture of extreme individualism, such as that in the United States, may legitimate individual rights, including the right to care, but discourages collective efforts to help provide it. Also, the stronger and more coordinated the warm modern model's "interest groups," the better its chances of winning.

The interest groups here include both paid and unpaid providers of care. For both the cold and warm modern models, the transfer of caring work out of the home to the public realm is viewed as positive (they differ in how much to transfer). But *both* modern models call for upgrading the status of public caregivers. If daycare workers or nursing home attendants are to upgrade the value of their work, they have to further "professionalize."[25] To do this, they need well-organized occupational groups to establish control over accreditation, monitor the entrances and exits of people from the field, and lobby for other measures to increase the public's appreciation for their emotional labor.

For advocates of the warm modern model, there is another task—upgrading the value of care in the *private* realm.[26] As the kin system weakens, informal support for carers may be waning. From whom does a single mother get thanks for her work at home? Who supports an unmarried or remarried father for keeping in touch with his children? Does a stepparent get recognized for taking good care of stepchildren or former stepchildren? For the warm modern model, these questions matter hugely.

In the end, each ideal of care implies a different view of the caregiver and so implies a different "trickle-down effect" to the cared-for. The more helpless a child or the more frail an older parent, the more keenly they sense the extent to which they are a "burden." The cultural politics of care touch the cared-for most of all. This is a politics, then, on behalf of those most in need. Also at stake, of course, is the value placed on gender equity. In a warm modern society, a government would not unload a host of social problems at the doorstep of housewives because that's not fair. At the same time, men would share the care of the young and the old not simply because it's fair but because it's important.

Part Five

SPEAKING PERSONALLY

17 INSIDE THE CLOCKWORK OF MALE CAREERS

An offhand remark made to me years ago has haunted me more and more ever since. I was talking at lunch with an acquaintance, and the talk turned, as it often does among women academicians just before it's time to part, to "how you manage" a full teaching schedule and family and how you feel about being a woman in a world of men. My acquaintance held a marginal position as one of two women in a department of fifty-five, a situation so common in 1973 that I don't fear for her anonymity here. She said in passing, "My husband took our son to the university swimming pool the other day. He got so *embarrassed* being the only man with all those faculty wives and their kids." When the talk turned to her work, she said, "I was in a department meeting yesterday, and, you know, I always feel self-conscious. It's not that people aren't friendly . . . it's just that I feel I don't fit in." She felt *uneasy* in a world of men, he embarrassed in a world of women. It is not only the double world of swimming pools and department meetings that has haunted me, but his embarrassment, her unease.

This conversation recurred to me when I met with the Committee on the Status of Women, a senate committee that formed on the Berkeley campus in 1972. We met in the Men's Faculty Club, a row of male scholars framed on the dark walls, the waitresses bringing in coffee and taking out dishes. The talk was about discrimination and about the affirmative action plan, a reluctant, ambiguous document that, to quote from its own elephant-footed language, "recognizes the desirability of removing obstacles to the flow of ability into appropriate occupational roles."

The well-meaning biologist on the committee was apologizing for his department, the engineer reminding us that they were "looking very hard" for a woman and an African American, and another reminding us that things were getting better all the time. But I remember feeling what many of us probably sensed but didn't say: that an enormously complex problem, an overwhelming reality—one world of swimming pools, children, and women, and another of men in departments and committee meetings; his embarrassment, her unease—was being delicately sliced into the tiny tidbits a giant bureaucracy could digest. I wondered if anything in that affirmative action plan, and others like it across the country, would begin to merge these double worlds. What such plans ignore is the fact that the existing academic career subcontracts work to the family—work that women perform. Without changing the structure of this career and its imperial relation to the family, it will be impossible for mothers to move far up in careers and for fathers to share at home.

I would like to start by asking a simple and familiar question: Why, at a public university like the University of California at Berkeley in 1972, did women compose 41 percent of the entering freshmen, 37 percent of the graduating seniors, 31 percent of the applicants for admission to graduate school, 28 percent of the graduate admissions, 24 percent of the doctoral students, 21 percent of advanced doctoral students, 12 percent of Ph.D.s, 38 percent of instructors, 9 percent of assistant professors, 6 percent of associate professors, and 3 percent of full professors?[1] This classic pattern was typical for women at all major universities in the early 1970s, and the situation in nearly all of them was, as in UC Berkeley, worse than it had been in 1930.[2]

I have heard two standard explanations for this classic pattern, but I doubt that either gets to the bottom of the matter. One explanation is that the university discriminates against women. If only tomorrow it could halt discrimination and become an impartial meritocracy, there would be many more academic women. The second explanation is that women are trained early to avoid success and authority and, lacking good role models as well, they "cool themselves out."

Since some excellent objective studies already address this question,[3] in this essay I explore my own experience, comparing it occasionally to findings in other studies, in order to explain why a third explanation rings more true to me: namely, that the classic profile of the academic career is cut to the image of the traditional man with his traditional wife. To ask why more women are not full professors, or "full" anything else in the upper reaches of the economy, we have to ask first what it means to be a male full professor—socially, morally, and humanly—and what kind of system makes them into what they become.

The academic career is founded on some peculiar assumptions about the relation between doing work and competing with others, competing with others and getting credit for work, getting credit and building a reputation, building a reputation and doing it while you're young, doing it while you're young and hoarding scarce time, hoarding scarce time and minimizing family life, minimizing family life and leaving it to your wife—the chain of experiences that seems to anchor the traditional academic career. Even if the meritocracy worked perfectly, even if women did not cool themselves out, I suspect there would remain in a system that defines careers this way only a handful of women at the top.

If Machiavelli had turned his pen, as so many modern satirists have, to how a provincial might come to the university and become a full professor, he might have given the following advice: Enter graduate school with the same mentality with which you think you will emerge from graduate school. Be confident, ambitious, and directed. Don't waste time. Get a good research topic early and find an important but kindly and nonprejudicial benefactor from whom you actually learn something. Most important, put your all into those crucial years after you get your doctorate—in your twenties and thirties—putting nothing else first then. Take your best job offer and go there, no matter what your family or social situation. Publish your first book with a well-known publisher, and cross the land to a slightly better position, if it comes up. Extend your now-ambitious self broadly and deeply into research, committee work, and editorships to make your name in your late twenties and at the latest early thirties. If somewhere along the way teaching becomes the psychic equivalent of volunteer work, don't let it bother you. You are now a full professor and can guide other fledglings along that course.

Perhaps I am caricaturing, but bear in mind that I am talking about why in the early 1970s only 3 to 4 percent of the full professors were women at universities like Berkeley, where I think it is fair to say this describes the cardboard outline of the "ideal" career. Ideals are the measuring rods of experience. Even if, as a moral dropout, a student rejects this ideal, the student finds himself or herself nonetheless in competition with others who rise to the top to exemplify and uphold the ideal.

But there is something hidden in the description of this academic career: the family. And men and women have had (and still have) different ties to the family. I think this is not accidental, for the university seeks to immunize itself against the vicissitudes of human existence out of its control. Some of these vicissitudes are expressed and absorbed in the family: birth at one end of the life cycle and death at the other. Lower ages at retirement handle the "problem" of death, and the exclusion of women the "problem" of birth. (If it could, the university would also guard against other human traumas, sickness, insanity, postdivorce depression, now removed from it by sabbaticals and leaves of absence.)

The family is in some sense a preindustrial institution and lives in a private, more flexible time, remote from the immortal industrial clock. The family absorbs vicissitudes that the workplace discards. It is the university's welfare agency, and women are its social workers. That is to say, the family serves a function for the university, and women have more to do with the family than men. As a result, Machiavelli's advice suits them less well. In the 1970s women Ph.D.s in the United States spent about 28 hours per week on household tasks.[4] More important, the twenties and sometimes the thirties are normally a time to bear and raise children. But it is precisely at this stage that one begins to hear talk about "serious contributions to the field" and "reputation," which are always more or less promising than those of others one's age. The result is apparent from a glance at a few crucial details in her curriculum vitae: How long did she take for the degree? Full-time, continuous work? Previous jobs, the best she could get? But the result shows too in how she sees herself in a career. For many academic women have been socialized at least twice, once to be women (as housewives and mothers) and once again to be like men (in traditional careers). The second socialization raises the issue of *assimilation* to the male culture associated with academic life; the first socialization raises the issue of what women abandon in the process. The question we must unbury lies between the first socialization and the second: How much do women want careers to change them and how much do women want to change careers?

DISCRIMINATION

When I entered Berkeley as a graduate student in 1962, I sat with some fifty other incoming students that first week in a methodology course. One of the two sociology professors on the podium before us said, "We say this to every incoming class and we'll say it to you. Look to your left and look to your right. Two out of three of you will drop out before you are through, probably in the first two years." We looked blankly to right and left, and quick nervous laughter jumped out and back from the class. I wonder now, years later, what each of us was thinking at that moment. I remember only that I didn't hear a word during the rest of the hour, for wondering whether it would be the fellow on my left, or the one on my right, or me. A fifth of my incoming class was female, and in the three years that followed, indeed, three-quarters of the women (and half of the men) did drop out.[5] But a good many neither dropped out nor moved on but stayed trapped between the M.A. and the orals, or the orals and the dissertation, fighting the private devil of a writing block, or even relaxing within that ambiguous passage, like those permanent "temporary buildings" that were still standing on the Berkeley campus decades after World War II. Some even developed a humor to counter the painful jokes about them, "What do you have in your briefcase there, samples?"

This happens to men, too, but why does it happen so much more to women? According to some analysts, women leave academe because of discrimination in such matters as getting fellowships, job offers, or promotions. Helen Astin, for example, concludes that this is a major reason, citing the fact that a full third of the women Ph.D.s she studied in the 1960s reported discrimination.[6] Others, such as Jessie Bernard, suggest that "it is only when *other* grounds for rejection are missing that prejudiced discrimination *per se* is brought into play."[7] I suspect that Bernard is more on the mark. While a third of academic women reporting discrimination is a great number, it is also remarkable that two-thirds did not report it.

Much of the discrimination argument rests on how broadly we define discrimination and how trained our eyes are for seeing it. Women have acclimatized themselves to discrimination, expect it, get it, and try to move around it. It is hard to say, since I continually re-remember those early years through different prisms, whether I experienced any discrimination myself. I don't think so, unless one counts the time I entered a professor's office to discuss my paper topic for his course. We had been assigned a reading that involved the link between mental illness and social class. Social class was measured, I had learned, by the Hollingshead and Redlich index of social class. Somewhere along in the interview, in the course of explaining the paper I was hoping to write, I was pretentious enough to mention the Hollingshead and Redlich index, which involves education, occupational prestige, and residence. The professor stopped me dead with a stony gaze. "Are you a *graduate* student?" (not an *under*graduate). It was like a punch in the stomach, and it took me a few seconds to recover.[8] The interview traveled on as if this exchange had never occurred and I left the office, with a lump in my throat, went to the women's bathroom, and cried. I blush now at my anxiety to please. But of course the problem was not that I was too pretentious, but that I did it badly. In the many imaginary rehearsals of second encounters (I never went back), the conversation went like this: "Hollingshead and Redlich index, mmmmmmm, it's better than the old Warner index, of course, but then it misses some of the more sophisticated indicators of the Chapin scale, dated as it is." By the time it occurred to me that the *man*'s occupation and education were taken as predictors of the social class of his wife and children, I stopped imagining conversations with this particular professor.

In a 1970s Carnegie survey of 32,000 graduate students and faculty, 22 percent of the men and 50 percent of the women graduate students in sociology agreed that the faculty does not "take female graduate students seriously," and in fact a quarter of the male faculty agreed that "female graduate students are not as dedicated to the field as males."[9]When the graduate students were asked the same question, a quarter—men and women alike—agreed that "women are not as dedicated." Only the female *faculty* refused to be recorded this way, perhaps feeling as I did when I filled out the questionnaire that there was no place to say, between the yes and the no, that dedication has to be measured against the visible or felt incentives to go on, and that lack of dedication may be a defensive anticipation of being ignored.

For women in particular the line between dropping out, staying on, and moving out has been a thin and fluctuating one. The Carnegie Commission study asked graduate students, "Have you ever considered in the past year quitting graduate school for good?" Only 43 percent of the women and 53 percent of the men had *not* considered it.[10] I considered it to the extent of interviewing at the end of my first miserable year for several jobs in New York that did not pan out. Beyond that, my uncertainty expressed itself in virtually every paper I wrote for the first two years. I can hardly read the papers now since it appears that for about a year and a half I never changed the typewriter ribbon. As one professor wrote on a paper, "Fortunately the writer's exposition and analysis are a pleasant contrast to a manuscript which in physical appearance promises the worst. A nice job of comparing Condorcet and Rousseau. . . . The writer would possibly have profited by . . . more systematically *resolving* at least tentatively the problem raised—for purposes of relieving her own apparent ambivalence on the issue." I am less sure now that it was Condorcet and Rousseau I was ambivalent about. That ambivalence centered, I imagine, on a number of issues, but one of them was probably the relation between the career I might get into and the family I might have. I say "probably" because I didn't see it clearly that way, for I saw nothing clearly then.

Powerful people often justify the categorical judgments that they apply to particular women on the grounds that family comes first. Now we call these judgments "discrimination." One department chairman caught in print before 1967 said what many chairmen probably still thought but no longer said:

> My own practice is to appoint women to about 50 percent of our graduate assistantships and to about 30 percent of our instructorships. My fear that this is too large of proportion of women appointees arises from the considerations: (1) that women are less likely to complete the degree programs upon which they embark; (2) that even if they do, marriage is very likely to intervene and to prevent or considerably delay their entry into the teaching profession; (3) that even when they do become full time teachers . . . their primary sense of responsibility is to their homes, so that they become professionally recognized only to a limited degree; (4) that they are far less likely than men to achieve positions of leadership in their profession.[11]

Such official judgments are not completely absurd. They rest on empirical evidence of *categorical* differences between men and women, regardless of special exceptions. To ignore this fact does not make it go away. In ignoring it, we seem tacitly to agree with university officials that the family is, after all, a private matter out of official hands. It prevents us from asking whether there isn't something about the academic system itself that perpetuates this "private" inequality.

WOMEN COOLING THEMSELVES OUT

The second explanation for the attrition of women in academe touches private inequality more directly: women sooner or later cool themselves out by a form of "auto-discrimination." Here, inequality is conceived not as the mark of a chairperson's pen, but as the consequence of a whole constellation of disadvantages that alter what a woman wants to do.

It is admittedly hard to distinguish between women who remove themselves from the university and women who are removed or who are moved *to* remove themselves. For me, there were innumerable aspects of graduate school that were not quite discriminatory and not quite not discriminatory either. Some things were simply *discouraging*: the invisibility of women among the teachers and writers of the books one read or among the faces framed on the walls of the faculty club; the paucity of women at the informal gathering over beer after the seminar. Then there were the prelecture jokes (to break the ice) that referred in some way to pretty girls as a distraction or to getting into "virginal" fields.[12] There was also the continual, semiconscious work of sensing and avoiding professors who were known to dislike or discredit women or particular types of women. One professor in my department seriously suggested adding more mathematics to the methodology requirement in order to reduce the number of women undergraduate majors. In addition, there was the low standing of the "female" specialties—like sociology of the family and education—which some early feminists like me scrupulously avoided for that stupid reason. The real thing to study, of course, was political sociology and general theory: those were virtually all-male classes, from which one could emerge with a "command" of the important literature.

Women can be discouraged by competition and by the need to be, despite their training, unambivalent about ambition. Ambition is no static or given thing, like having blue eyes. It is more like sexuality—variable, subject to influence, and attached to past loves, deprivations, rivalries, and the many events long erased from memory. Some people would be ambitious anywhere, but competitive situations tend to drive ambition underground in women. Despite supportive mentors, for many women there remains something intangibly frightening about a competitive environment, about competitive seminar talk, even about argumentative writing. While feminists have challenged the fear of competition—both by competing successfully and by refusing to compete—and while some male dropouts crossing over the other way advise against competing, the issue is hardly settled for most of us. For those who cannot imagine themselves inside a competitive environment, the question becomes: How much is something wrong with me and how much is something wrong with my situation?

MODELS OF PEOPLE AND PLACES

It is often said that a good female "role model" can make up for the pervasive discouragement women find in academe. By role model I mean simply a person whom a student feels she wants to be like or could become. It is someone she may magically incorporate into herself, someone who, intentionally or not, throws her a psychic lifeline. A role model is thus highly personal and idiosyncratic, although she may nonetheless fit a social pattern. I am aware of being part of an invisible parade of models. Even as I seek a model myself, I partly am one to students who are, in turn, models to still others. Various parades of role models crisscross each other in the university, and each goes back in psychological time.

For example, I distinctly remember my mother directing me at the age of sixteen toward a model of a professional woman who followed her husband from place to place outside the United States. My mother worked hard in support of my father's work in the foreign service, and while her own situation did not permit her a career, it was something she had always admired. At one cocktail party, crowded and noisy, she whispered in my ear, "Mrs. Cohen. Go talk to Mrs. Cohen. She's a *doctor,* you know." I hesitated, not knowing what I could say or ask. My mother made eye signs and I ventured over to Dr. (Mrs.) Cohen. As it turned out, she was the hostess of the party. One of her three small children was complaining that he couldn't unlock his bicycle. A tray of hors d'oeuvres had spilled and Mrs. Cohen was hysterical. She was ignoring her son and the spilled hors d'oeuvres for the moment and concentrating on stuffing some eggs, every fifth one of which she ate. As I began preparing the eggs with her, she explained how practicing psychiatry outside the country was impossible, that moving every two years messed up the relations she might have had with her patients, had she any patients. She popped yet another egg into her mouth and disappeared into the crowd. Yes, Mrs. Cohen was a model of something, the best model my mother could find for me, and only much later did I begin to really understand her situation and my mother's.

Actually it was not so much Dr. Cohen herself as it was her whole life, as part of what Hanna Papanek calls the "two person career,"[13] that became, for me, the negative model. From the perspective of the 1970s, I imagine that in twenty years young women will, in the same way, scan individual models to sense the underlying situation, the little imperialisms of a man's career on his wife's life. Dr. Cohen's husband had one role, and his role created two for her. Male careers in other fields, including academe, differ from this only in degree.

This is the second sense in which we can talk of models—models of *situations* that allow a woman to be who she gradually gets to want to be. Models of people and of situations, some appealing and some distressing, march silently across the university grounds. Among the inspiring leaders of this parade are also some frightening examples of women who lack the outer symbolic or material rewards of accomplishment: the degrees, the higher-level jobs, the promotions, the grants that their male counterparts have. In some cases, too, these women show the inner signs: a creativity that may have cramped itself into modest addenda, replications of old research, or reformations of some man's theory—research, in sum, that will not "hurt anyone's feelings." What is painful is not simply that a particular woman may have been denied a job, but rather that she may face the daily experience of being labeled a dull or unpromising dutiful daughter in research. The human pinch for such a woman is not simply having to choose between a full-time commitment to her profession or a family, but what it means to remain single among couples, to have her sexual life an item of amused curiosity. For others it isn't simply the harried life of trying to work and raise a family at the same time; it's the premature aging around the eyes, the third drink at night, the tired resignation when she opens the door to a sparkling freshman who wants to know "all about how social science can cure the world of war and poverty."[14] There are other kinds of models, too. By the early 1970s women had earned degrees and good jobs and, with it all, some had established egalitarian arrangements at home. But I think they are likely to remain a minority because of a tight job market and the career system itself and because women inside academe are often constrained from lobbying for more women. It's not *professional*. Speaking only for myself, I have found it extremely hard to lobby for change while sitting in a department meeting with dozens of senior male professors, among them my mentors. I have felt like a totem or representative more than an agent of social change, discredited for being that by some professors and for not being more than that by some feminists. Of course when I do speak up, it is with all too much feeling. It is immeasurably easier, a joyous release, to go to the private turf of my classroom, where I become intellectually and morally bold. If I had to locate what has been my own struggle, it would be right there in that committee room.

Women respond not simply to a psychological lifeline in the parade, but to the social ecology of survival. If we are to talk about good models we must talk about the context that produces them. To ignore this is to risk running into the problems I did when I accepted my first appointment as the first woman sociologist in a small department at the University of California at Santa Cruz. Some very strange things happened to me, but I am not so sure that anything happened to the department or university. Sprinkled thinly as women were across departments there, we created a new minority status where none had existed before, models of token women.

The first week there, I began receiving Xeroxed newspaper clippings and magazine articles praising the women's movement or detailing how bad the "woman situation" was in medicine or describing Danish women dentists. These clippings that began to swell my files were invariably attached to a friendly forwarding note: "Thought you'd be interested" or "Just saw this and thought of you." I stopped an older colleague in the hall to thank him for an article he had given me and inquired what he had thought of it. He hadn't read it himself. I began to realize that I was becoming my colleagues' friendly totem, a representation of feminism. "I'm all with you people" began to seem more like "You be it for us." And sure enough. For every paper I read on the philosophy of Charlotte Gilman, the history of the garment union, the dual-career family, or women and art, I wondered if I shouldn't poke a copy into the mailboxes of my clipping-sending friends. I had wound myself into a feminist cocoon and left the tree standing serenely as it was. No, it takes more than this kind of "model."

THE CLOCKWORK OF THE CAREER SYSTEM

It is not easy to clip and press what I am talking about inside the square boundaries of an "administrative problem." The context has to do with the very clockwork of a career system that seems to eliminate women not so much through malevolent disobedience to good rules as through making up rules to suit half the population in the first place.[15] For all the turmoil of the 1960s, those rules had not changed a bit by the early 1970s. The year 1962 was an interesting one to come to Berkeley, and 1972 a depressing one. The free speech movement in 1964 and the black power and women's liberation movements following it seem framed now by the fifties and Eisenhower on one side and the seventies, Nixon, and Ford on the other. The questions that lay flat under the book in the lecture hall in 1963 stood up to declare themselves in that stubborn public square that refused to be incorporated by the city-state around it. It was like slicing the *Queen Mary* in half: from boiler room to top deck, the chains of command within, the ties to industry and the military without, in what had announced itself as an otherworldly search for Truth—all were exposed for a moment in history. And then recovered, the boat made whole again and set afloat. It was what did *not* change that was most impressive. Now the free speech movement, black power, and women's liberation appeared as dissertation topics: "FSM, a Study of Information Dissemination," "Black Power as Status Mobility," "The Changing Image of Career Women," amid yet newer ones such as "In the Service of Light; a Sociological Essay on the Knowledge of Guru Maharaj Ji and the Experience of His Devotees." Each movement left a theater of its own, and frosted dinner-table conversations that at the end of the evening divided again by gender.

What did not change was the career system, brilliantly described by Clark Kerr in *The Uses of the University*.[16] But there are some things about competition uncritically implied in that book that I must focus on here. The first is the understanding, taken for granted, that work is shaped into a "career" and that a "career" comprises a series of positions and accomplishments, each tightly and competitively measured against other careers, so that even minor differences in achievement count. Universities and departments compete to get the "big names," and individuals compete to become the people who are competed for. There is competition between Berkeley and Harvard, between Stony Brook and New York University, between sociology and history, between this assistant professor and that one, the competition trickling down from level to level. The people at each level carefully inspect the relatively minor differences among a surprisingly narrow band of potential rivals for scarce but coveted rewards. This is perhaps more apparent in the almost-famous than the famous universities, and in the hard sciences, whose scientists have more to sell (and sell out), than in the soft. It is more apparent at professional conventions than in the classroom, more in graduate student talk than in undergraduate, more among males than females. The career itself is based on a series of contests, which in turn are based not so much on doing good work as on getting *credit* for doing good work.

A colleague explained this to me in a letter. (I had written him asking why employers are not more enthusiastic about part-time work for men and women.) Speaking about scientific and artistic creativity, he noted:

> Being the first to solve some problems helps you be the first to solve a problem which depends on the solution of the first [intellectual problem], *provided* that you get to work on the second problem before everybody learns how you solved the first. I think clienteles work pretty much the same way, that if you start being known as a good doctor in a certain social circle, or a good divorce lawyer, then if two of the person's friends recommend you as a good professional you are much more likely to get his business than if only one does. Where clienteles come in off the street or in response to advertisements, as in real estate, then it doesn't matter so much whether you work full time or not.

"Being the first" to solve the problem is not, under the career system, the same as getting the problem solved; "getting his business" away from someone else is not the same as meeting the client's needs. In the university, this means "being the first" in research and, to a much lesser extent, "getting the business" in teaching. To borrow from movement language, one can manage in this way to get a reputation in the "star system." Wanting to become a "star" or knowing you have to want to become one or becoming even a minor one is what women learn in man-made careers.

A reputation is measured against time—that is, against the year one is born. A number of studies have shown that, in modern times, intellectual achievements tend to come surprisingly early in life. In Harvey Lehman's massive study of eminent men in science, the arts, letters, politics, the military, and the judiciary, the average age of peak performance is early: for chemists and physicists the early thirties, in music and sculpture the late thirties, even in philosophy the late thirties and early forties. The link between age and achievement for many specialties housed in the university resembles that of athletes more than that of popes or judges. Interestingly, achievement came later in life for men before 1775—before the massive bureaucratization of work into the career system.[17] A reputation is an imaginary promise to the world that if one is productive young in life, one will be so later also. And the university, having little else to go on, rewards the promise of the young or fairly young.

Age discrimination is not some separate extra unfairness thoughtlessly tacked on to universities; it follows inevitably from the bottommost assumptions about university careers. If jobs are scarce and promising reputations important, who wants a fifty-year-old mother of three with a dissertation almost completed? Since age is the measure of achievement, competition often takes the form of working long hours[18] and working harder than the next person. This definition of work does not refer to teaching, committee work, office hours, phone conversations with students, or editing students' work, but refers more narrowly to one's *own* work. Time becomes a scarce resource that one hoards greedily, and time becomes the thing one talks about when one is wasting it. If "doing one's work" is a labor of love, love itself comes to have an economic and honorific base.

This conception of time becomes in turn an indelible part of the career-*self*.[19] Male-styled careers introduce women to a new form of time consciousness: it is not age measured against beauty, as in our "first" training, but age measured against achievement. That measure of age, as I have noted, is related to what else a person does, for example, in the family.

The career-self experiences time as linear and the career itself as a measured line, other parts of the self following along. Time is objectified in the academic vita, which grows longer with each article and book, and not with each vegetable garden, camping trip, political meeting, or child. One's multifold potential is treated much like a capital investment in an initially marginal enterprise. What is won for the garden is lost to the vita. For the career-self, casual comparisons to colleagues working on the same problem are magnified into contests: He got his article published first. His good news is my bad news. These comparisons become mental giants, while the rest of the world and self are experientially dwarfed.

If work, conceptualized as a career, becomes a measured line, the line often appears to be a rising one. Very often the rising career line is also, despite a residual cynicism about power, associated with a pleasant belief in the progress of the world. Even those who have refused to fit this profile know very well that they are measured against it by others who rise to the top and, from this top-of-the-career worldview, set the prevailing standards.

THE SOCIAL PSYCHOLOGY OF CAREER TALK

The academic career creates a culture of its own and a special sense of self. This is especially true for the elite and aspirants to it, but it holds for the stragglers and misfits as well. The marketplace is somewhere "out there" in the great beyond of supply and demand; it insinuates itself into the very fiber of human communication about things that matter.

Apart from writing, the main thing academics do is talk, and talk is perhaps the best illustration of the effects of this culture. Talk anywhere is influenced by the context in which it goes on. If a Cuban or a Wintu Indian happened to walk down the fourth floor of Barrows Hall at Berkeley, she or he might get the impression of a bare mustard yellow tunnel, long and dimly lit from above, casting ghostly shadows on the under-eyes of its "trespassers." Closed doors to left and right offer a few typed notices of class meeting schedules, envelopes containing graded examinations, and one wry sign, posted several months earlier by a man who had just won tenure: THIS MACHINE IS NOT IN ORDER. It might be experienced as a place where no one lives. It's the one place professors are supposed to be available to students, but since students unwittingly block the extension of one's vita, it's the one place from which professors are curiously absent. Only instructors not yet in the tenure race and older professors on the other side of it might answer to a knock. The rest are seemingly lost between their several offices (the institute, the department, the home). Often they pick up their mail at dawn or dusk when the department office is closed. The French call them the "hurried class." On a day when the printed notice says a middle-rank professor will be in, a small society of students assembles on the floor against the wall. They have penciled their names on a posted sheet that marks time in fifteen-minute pieces, and they may be rehearsing their lines.

In the fall of 1971 a male graduate student signed up for an office visit. On my door, in large, bold letters, he wrote: THOMPSON. That the name was larger than the others led me to expect a large, imposing figure. In fact, Thompson was three inches shorter than I, and I suppose he felt less imposing as well. For after he had seated himself carefully, slowly crossed his legs, and hunched down in the "student" chair, he began, without prodding on my part, to give a long, slow description of his intellectual evolution from mathematical models at the University of Michigan to historical sociology to possibly, just possibly—and this was why he was in my office—the sociology of the family. It took about half an hour to say. The remarkable thing was how slowly and deliberately he spoke, as if he were dictating a manuscript, qualifying each statement, painfully footnoting his generalizations, and offering summaries at the appropriate places, rather like the chairman of our department. After the interview was concluded, with a fumble over who should open the door (Whose doorknob was it? Is he a student or a man? Am I a woman or a professor?), I could hear THOMPSON behind me, talking with a graduate student friend, in a brisk, conversational dialogue, laughing a bit, rambling. He was talking *normally*. He wasn't selling smartness to a professor.

THOMPSON thought he was being judged in that interview against other graduate students. And he was right. Every month or two I do receive a confidential form from my department, asking me to rank from mediocre to excellent a series of ten to twenty graduate students. Professors are the last people most students come to with an intellectual problem, and the first people they come to when they have it solved. To expose their vulnerability or confusion is to risk being marked "mediocre" on the confidential form.

The culture of the career system is not, alas, confined to the office interview. Despite the signs of otherworldliness, the Volvos and blue-jean patches and beards, the university is a market world, a world of conspicuous consumption. It is not gold brooches and Cadillacs that are conspicuously consumed; it is intellectual talk. I sometimes get the impression in the corridor outside my office, at dinner parties, and in countless meetings, that vita is talking to vita, that tenure is being won in a conversational tournament, that examinations have slipped out of their end-of-semester slots and entered the walls and ceiling and floor of talk. The intellectual dozens, Leonard Kriegel calls it in his book *Working Through*. It is academic street-corner talk at which one is informally tracked as excellent, good, fair, poor, or terrible. If you bring someone out (as women are taught to do) instead of crowding him out, you get bad marks. Not to learn to talk this way at this place is like living without a skin; it is a required language.

It is often said that women do not speak up in class as much as men do, and I have noticed it too, occasionally even in my graduate seminar on the sociology of sex roles. The reason, I suspect, is that they are aware that they have not yet perfected the proper style. (It is often older women, not yet aware of the stylistic requirements, who speak up.) Some say also that women are ignored in conversation because they are sex objects; I think they are more often seen as conversational cheerleaders to the verbal tournament.

The verbal tournament seems also to require a socially shared negativism toward other people's work. It is often considered an evening well spent, for example, to tear down Merton's theory of anomie, or to argue that Susan Sontag is overrated, that Erving Goffman is passé, that Noam Chomsky's latest article, like most other things one has read lately, says nothing really new. It is as if from these collective wreckings of intellectual edifices the participants will emerge, in some small way, larger. But the negative talk about the stupidity of academic conversations, the drivel in the *American Sociological Review*, which one proudly claims not to have read in two years, also establishes a floor of civility, a silent pact to be friends or associates, regardless of one's rise or fall in market value. In a sad way, it says, "Despite the gridded walls around us, you and I share *something* in common after all."

There is still another kind of talk, not in one's private office, or in the halls, and rarely at parties, but in the main office: faculty talk to secretaries. That talk generally is brief, smiley, and rich with campus gossip or news of the Xerox machine or good places to eat. It obeys the rules of civility and obscures the irritations or jealousies that might momentarily stop work. It also tends to foster the secretaries' identification with the professorial career. In the 1970s we happened in my department to have a "liberated" secretarial pool, who saw this kind of talk through a feminist prism as condescending and manipulative, a sort of oil and grease of the machinery that maintains a pay and status for them far below what an early estimate of potential would have predicted. Unable to change their essential condition, they jealously guarded their poster of a Vietnamese woman on the wall in the main office and gave up smiling at anyone who daily invaded their public space, they having no private space at all. Their new model of talk was that between a union negotiator and business representative. Here it was not vita talking to vita, but worker talking to boss, be it man or (assimilated) woman. The administration considered the secretarial pool a "problem," but their new style was more basically a challenge not only to their inferior status, but to what about talk holds it in place.

Women compromise with the career culture in various ways. It is as common among women as it is among men to consider market talk gauche—who got what job, was awarded what grant, or had an article accepted by which journal. On the other hand, a woman is "unserious" or fuzzy-headed if she appears to be out of it altogether. The compromise some women affect is to publicly endorse anticompetitive or noncompetitive values while privately practicing the competitive ones. One publicly discredits the "rat race" and then, at home on weekends, climbs quietly onto the revolving wheel.

Academic talk reflects academic life and academic life reflects a marketplace. Ideas become products that are "owned" or "borrowed" or "stolen" from their owners, products that through talk and in print rise and fall in market value, products that have become alienated from their producers. The marketplace pervades the life of conservatives and radicals alike; for both, ideas are "products." Even if, with the growth of giant monopolies, the country *as a whole* is no longer capitalist in the old-fashioned sense, in a peculiar way the university, especially for its junior members, is.

I suspect that a different system would produce a different talk. And women trained to this career unwittingly learn to admire in others and perfect in themselves the talk that goes with the system—for it is uncompetitive, undressed, nonproduct, supportive talk that is, in the last analysis, discriminated against.

Even writing about career talk in cynical language, I find that, bizarrely enough, I don't *feel* cynical; and I have tried to consider why. I think it is because I know, in a distant corner of my mind, that the very impersonality that competition creates provides the role of the "humanizer" that I so enjoy filling. I know that only in a hierarchy built on fear (it's mislabeled "respect") is there a role for those who reduce it. Only in a conservative student body is there a role for the "house radical." Only in a department with no women are you considered "really something" to be the first. A bad system ironically produces a market, on its underside, for the "good guys." I know this, but somehow it does not stop me from loving to teach. For it is from this soft spot, in the underbelly of the whale, that a counteroffensive can begin against women's second socialization to career talk and all that goes with it.

THE CAREER CULTURE AND THE FAMILY

The links between competition, career, reputation, and time consciousness extend to life that is at once outside the university but inside the career culture: that is, to the family and to the faculty wife. The university has no *formal* administrative policy toward the families of its members. I have never heard of the university equivalent to the "farming out system" in early industry or of families being brought into the university the way they were taken into nineteenth-century factories. Certainly we do not hear of a family winning a Ford Foundation grant, aunts and uncles doing the interviewing, husband and wife the analysis and writing, leaving footnotes to the children. While books have been typed, if not partly written, by wives, the family in the university has never been the productive *unit.*

Nonetheless, I think we have what amounts to a tacit policy toward the family. Let us consider the following: *if all else were equal,* who would be most likely to survive under the career system—a man married to a full-time housewife and mother; or a man whose wife has a nine-to-five job and the children in daycare; or a man who works part-time, as does his wife, while their children are small? I think the general principle that determines the answer is this: *To the extent that his family does not positively help him in his work or makes demands on his time and psychic energy that compete with those devoted to his job, they lower his chances for survival. This is true insofar as he is competing with other men whose wives either aid them or do not interfere with their work.* Other things being equal, the university rewards the married family-free man.

But intellectual productivity is sometimes discussed as if it were a gift from heaven to the chosen few, which has nothing to do with families or social environment at all. If we inspect the social context of male productivity, we often find nameless women and a few younger men feeding the "productive one" references, computer outputs, library books, and cooked dinners. Women, single or married, are in competition not simply with men, but with the *heads of small branch industries.*

A few book prefaces tell the familiar story. A book on racial oppression written in 1972:

Finally, I would like to thank my wife _____, who suffered the inconveniences that protracted writing brought about with as much graciousness as could be expected, and who instructed our children, _____ and _____, to respect the privacy of their father's work.

An earlier book, 1963:

In many ways my wife Suzanne should be co-author. She shared the problems of planning and carrying out the field work, and the life of a wife-mother-interviewer in another culture was more demanding than either of us might have imagined. Although she did not take part in the actual writing, she has been a patient sounding board, and her concern with individual cases provided a needed balance to my irrepressible desire to paint the broad picture.

Still one more, 1962:

_____, to whom I was then married, helped in the field work, and a number of the observations in the book are hers.

These are excellent books, and they have taught me a great deal, but then so have their prefaces.

If this puts liberated men at a competitive disadvantage, needless to say it does the same to liberated women. It is a familiar joke in women's circles to say, "What I really need is a wife." Young women in graduate school, according to the 1969 Carnegie survey, were much more likely (63 percent) to have husbands in academe than were men to have academic wives (14 percent). Typed page for typed page, proofread line for proofread line, soothing hour for soothing hour, I suspect that, all else being equal, a traditional male, minus a modern woman, is more likely than anyone else to end up a branch manager.

This total situation is often perceived as a "woman's problem," her role conflict, as if that conflict were detachable from the career system itself. It is her problem to choose between a few prepackaged options: being a housewife, or professor, or trying to piece together a collage of wife, mother, and *traditional* career. The option we do not hear about, one that would make it a man's problem or a university problem as well, is parenthood with a radically new sort of career. Affirmative action plans aren't talking about this.

Given the academic career as it is now, women can only improvise one or another practical solution for fitting their families to their careers. Many professional women of my generation either waited to have children until two years into their first "real" job or had them before beginning graduate school. One had her children in between and resolved the dual pressures by using her children as data for her books. Those who waited until they were in their late twenties or early thirties often did so precisely to avoid premature discrimination, only to discover that the real pressure point lay not behind but slightly ahead. Nearly half the women who remain in academic life solve the problem by not marrying or not rearing children at all. In a 1962 study of 21,650 men and 2,234 women scientists and engineers, women were six times more likely than men never to marry. Those women who married were less likely than their male colleagues to raise a family: 36 percent of women and 11 percent of men had no children. Those women who did have children had fewer: the families of women scientists and engineers were, compared with those of their male counterparts, one child smaller.[20] Among graduate students, the proportion who consider dropping out increases for women with each new child born, but remains the same for men.[21] Another study of people who received their doctorates between 1958 and 1963 in a number of fields found that only 50 percent of the women had married by 1967. Among the men, 95 percent had married.[22]

Half of the women and nearly all of the men married—it's a painful little statistic, and I say that without being derogatory to single women. It is one thing for a woman to freely *decide* against marriage or children as issues on their own merits. But it is quite another matter to be forced into the choice because the career system is shaped for and by the man with a family who is family-free.[23]

SITUATION AND CONSCIOUSNESS

It is for the minority of academic women with children that the contradictions exist in their full glory. My own solution may be uncommon, but not the general contours of my dilemma. When I first decided to have a child at the age of thirty-one, my thoughts turned to the practical arrangements whereby I could continue to teach, something that means a great deal to me. Several arrangements were possible, but my experiment was a preindustrial one—to introduce the family back into the university, to take the baby with me for office hours on the fourth floor of Barrows Hall. From two to eight months, David was, for the most part, the perfect guest. I made him a little cardboard box with blankets where he napped (which he did most of the time), and I brought along an infant seat from which he kept an eye on key chains, colored notebooks, earrings, and glasses. Sometimes waiting students took him out into the hall and passed him around. He became a conversation piece with shy students, and some returned to see him rather than me. I put up a fictitious name on the appointment list every four hours and fed him alone or while on the telephone.

The baby's presence proved to be a Rorschach test, for people reacted very differently. Older men, undergraduate women, and a few younger men seemed to like him and the idea of his being there. In the next office there was a distinguished professor of seventy-four; it was our joke that he would stop by when he heard the baby crying and say, shaking his head, "Beating the baby again, eh?" Publishers and book salesmen in trim suits and exquisite sideburns were generally shocked. Graduate student women would often inquire about him tentatively, and a few feminists were put off, perhaps because babies were out of fashion and because his presence seemed "unprofessional."

One incident brought into focus my identity and the university's bizarre power to maintain relationships in the face of change. It happened around 1971. A male graduate student, John, had come early for his appointment. The baby had slept longer than usual and got hungry later than I had scheduled by Barrows Hall time. I invited the student in. Since we had never met before, he introduced himself with extreme deference, and as I am often tempted to do, I responded to that deference by behaving more formally than I otherwise might. He began tentatively to elaborate his interests in sociology and to broach the subject of asking me to serve on his orals committee. He had the onerous task of explaining to me that he was a clever student, a trustworthy and obedient student, but that academic fields were not organized as he wanted to study them, and of asking me, without knowing what I thought, whether he could study Marx under the rubric of the sociology of work.

In the course of this lengthy explanation, the baby began to cry. I gave him a pacifier and continued to listen all the more intently. The student went on. The baby spat out the pacifier and began to wail. Finally, trying to be casual, I began to feed him. He wailed now the strongest, most rebellious wail I had ever heard from this small armful of person.

The student uncrossed one leg and crossed the other and held a polite smile, coughing a bit as he waited for this little crisis to pass. I excused myself and got up to walk back and forth with the baby to calm him down. "I've never done this before. It's just an experiment," I remember saying.

"I have two children of my own," he replied. "Only they're not in Berkeley. We're divorced and I miss them a lot." We exchanged a human glance of mutual support, talked of our families more, and soon the baby calmed down.

A month later, when John had signed up for a second appointment, he entered the office and sat down formally. "As we were discussing last time, Professor Hochschild. . . ." Nothing further was said about the prior occasion, but more astonishing to me, nothing had changed. I was still Professor Hochschild and he was still John. Something about power lived on regardless.

In retrospect, I felt a little like one of the characters in *Dr. Dolittle and the Pirates,* the pushmi-pullyu, a horse with two heads that see and say different things. The pushmi head was relieved that motherhood had not reduced me as a professional. But the pullyu wondered what the pervasive power differences were doing there in the first place. And why weren't children in offices occasionally part of the "normal" scene?

At the same time I felt envious of the smooth choicelessness of my male colleagues who did not bring their children to Barrows Hall. I sometimes feel this keenly when I meet a male colleague jogging on the track (it's a popular academic sport because it takes little time) and then meet his wife taking their child to the YMCA kinder-gym program. I feel it too when I see wives drive up to the building in the evening, in the station wagon, elbow on the window, two children in the back, waiting for a man briskly walking down the steps, briefcase in hand. It seems a particularly pleasant moment in the day for them. It reminds me of those Friday evenings, always a great treat, when my older brother and I would pack into the back of our old Hudson, and my mother with a picnic basket would drive up from the suburbs to Washington, D.C., at five o'clock to meet my father walking briskly down the steps of the State Department, briefcase in hand. We picnicked at the Tidal Basin near the Jefferson Memorial, my parents sharing their day, and in that end-of-the-week mood, we came home.

Whenever I see similar scenes, something inside rips in half, for I am neither and both the brisk-stepping carrier of a briefcase and the mother with a packed picnic lunch. The university is designed for such men, and their homes for such women. It looks easier for them, and part of me envies them for it. Beneath the envy lies a sense of my competitive disadvantage vis-à-vis the men to whom I am compared and to whom I compare myself. Also beneath it, I am aware of the bizarreness of my experiment with the infant box, and paradoxically aware too that I am envious of a life I would not really like to live.

The invisible half of this scene is, of course, the woman in the station wagon. She has "solved" the problem in one of the other possible ways. But if both her way and my way of solving this "problem" seem to lead to strains, it may be that the problem is not only ours. It may be the inevitable result of a public system arranged not for women with families but for family-free men.

THE WHOLE OF THE PROBLEM: THE PARTS OF A SOLUTION

The problem for American women of the 1970s was not so much going to work, since over 40 percent of women of working age were in the labor force already and nine out of ten women worked sometime in their lives. The problem is one of moving *up*, and that means moving into careers. More fundamentally, the problem for women in academic or other sorts of careers is to alter the link between family and career and, more generally, between private and public life. Several alternatives seem both possible and just.

First, women might adopt a relation to home and family indistinguishable from that of their male competitors. Women could marry househusbands if they can find them, or in their absence hire substitute wife-mothers. Academic women could thereby establish a two-roled life for another person (a husband) or divide such roles between husband and housekeeper. If the housekeeper were well paid and unionized, perhaps we could still talk about justice; otherwise I think not. But neither a housekeeper nor a child-care center would solve the problem completely, since tending the sick, caring for the old, writing Christmas cards, and just being there for people in their bad moments—what wives do—still need doing. In my view, even when we have eliminated the needless elaboration of a wife's role, a humanly satisfying life requires that someone do these things.

Second, academic men who want careers might give up marriage or children, just as many academic women have. If the first alternative makes women more like men, this one makes men more like academic women, in extending to them the familiar two-box choice of family or career. This would be more just, but it would be a sad justice and I doubt it would be popular among men.

One can understand women who opt for the first alternative, given the absence of other choices. Insofar as it involves a reverse family imperialism, however, I do not see why it is any better than the original male one. Because I value at least the option of family life, I cannot endorse the second solution either. Since neither appeals to me as a long-range solution, I am led to a third alternative: the possibility of an egalitarian marriage with a radically different career to go with it. This means creating a different system in which to work at this different career, a system that would make egalitarian marriage *normal*.

The university makes virtually no adjustments to the family, but the traditional family makes quite a few to the university. And it is not so much the brisk-stepping man with the briefcase as it is his wife with the picnic basket who makes the adjustments for "the family's sake" (somehow amorphously connected to his career). I think the reason for this is that it is easier to change families than universities. But the contradictions of changing families without changing careers leads to either migraine headaches or hearty, rebellious thoughts.

Any vision of changing something as apparently implacable as the career system may seem at first ludicrous or utopian. But as Karl Mannheim once pointed out, all movements for social change need a utopia, built of parts borrowed from different or theoretical societies.[24] This need not be a utopia for dreaming that remains separate from waking life, but a utopia that, like reading a good book, shows us where and how far we have to go, a vision that makes sense of frustration by analyzing its source. At a time when utopias already seem quaint, when public visions seem a large shadow over many small private aims, when jobs are scarce and competition magnified, now more than ever we need a guiding vision.

For a start, all departments of twenty full-time men could expand to departments of forty part-time men and women. This would offer a solution to our present dilemma of trying to meet the goals of affirmative action within a "steady state" (or declining) economy. It would mean more jobs for women and men. It would democratize and thus eliminate competitive disadvantages and offer an opportunity to some of those women in the station wagon. In many fields, research would leap ahead if two people rather than one worked on problems. Teaching would certainly not be hurt by the arrangement and might benefit from the additional energies.

While administrative arrangements would be manageable, I can imagine queries about efficiency. Is it economical to train forty Ph.D.s to work part-time when twenty could do the same amount of work? And what of those who simply do not want part-time work? One can point to the glut of Ph.D.s and argue that if those currently teaching in universities would divide and share their jobs, many more might gain the chance to work. The effect would not eliminate but reduce competition for university jobs.

Part-time work is very often more like three-fourths-time work, for one teaches students rather than classes. If a graduate student moves to Ecuador and sends me his paper, I read it. If a former student comes around to the house, I talk to her. If there is a meeting, I don't leave halfway through. Part-time often turns out to be a release in quantity to improve quality.

But that raises the financial issue. The sorry fact is that, for financial reasons, most men and some women can't afford half-time work. Maybe workers could pay into a fund while they are still childless and draw from it when they have children. Universities could subsidize housing. And much of what academics define as financial need is based on their experience with public support for the general *context* of their lives. If the public schools were really good, they wouldn't be so tempted to spend money on private schools. If low-cost housing were readily available in cities, they wouldn't have to struggle to make a down payment. If public transportation worked, they wouldn't need two cars.

Hearsay has it that a group of MIT male assistant professors, who had worked late evenings because they were in competition with each other for advancement while their wives took care of the children, made a pact to cut down their hours and spend more time with their young children. Maybe many private pacts could lead to a larger public one, but only when those who set the standards are part of it.

While one may debate the virtues or defects of competition, it is an aspect of university life that we need not take for granted, that can and should be modified. Some elements of my own utopia are borrowed from the Cuban experiment, since it bears on the issue of competition. The Cuban revolution has made many mistakes, and not all of its successes are applicable to a rich industrial country. But one lesson to be learned from Cuba is that competition can be modified not only by splitting jobs (which it did not try to do), but by creating jobs to fit social needs. This may seem a bit far afield in an essay on universities, but my analysis brings me to it. For in my view, we cannot change the role of women in universities without changing the career system based on competition, and we can't change that competitive structure without also altering the economy, the larger fit of supply and demand of workers. We need thus to explore experiments in altering that.

I visited the University of Havana in the summer of 1967 and joined some students and faculty who were working together doing "productive labor" (they don't think this phrase is redundant), planting coffee plants in the belt surrounding Havana. As we moved along the rows, people talked about the university before the revolution. It sounded in some ways like a more intense version of Berkeley in both the 1960s and 1970s. The competition was so fierce for the few professional jobs in the cities that rich students bought grades. (That is only one step removed from the profitable cynicism of the term paper industries, like "Quality Bullshit" in Berkeley, where students could buy a custom-written paper from some unemployed graduate students.)

At the same time, Cuban students hung around the university cafés dropping out and back in again, wondering who they were. Before 1958 there were some 3,000 students at the University of Havana trying to enter the diplomatic service, while there was only a handful of electrical engineers in the whole country. The revolution put the university in touch with economic realities, and it changed those economic realities by inventing jobs where there was a social need for them. Since the revolution, the task has not been to restrict admission, but to supply the tremendous need for doctors, dentists, teachers, and architects as providers for the poor, paid by the government. The revolution simply recognized and legitimated a need that had always been there.

Corresponding to the supply of graduates American universities turn out each year, there is, I believe, a "social need." There is, for example, a great need for teachers in crowded classrooms, and yet we speak of the teacher "surplus." Despite the American Medical Association and the fierce competition to enter medical school, we need doctors in our inner cities. We need quality daycare, community organizers, traveling artists. Yet there are, we say, "too many people" and "not enough jobs." If social need coincided with social demand for skills, if market value were coextensive with real value, we could at least in some fields eliminate *needless* competition generated outside the university, which affects what goes on inside as well. I personally do not think "education for leisure" is the answer, for it ignores all the social ills that persist in the rich United States, not to mention many more outside it. If we redefine what a social need is, and design jobs to meet social needs, we also reduce the exaggerated competition we see in universities, a competition that inevitably moves women out. If the division of jobs alleviates competition among academics, the creation of jobs can alleviate competition among would-be workers, including, of course, professors.[25]

There is another lesson to be learned from Cuba. Insofar as American career women become like career men, they become oriented toward success and competition. Just as manhood has traditionally been measured by success, so now academic womanhood is defined that way. But manhood for the middle-class American academic man is based *more* on "doing well" than on "doing good." Manhood in professional circles is linked to "success," which is kept scarce and made to seem valuable. Men are socialized to competition because they are socialized to scarcity. It is as if sexual identity, at least in the middle class, were not freely given by nature, but conserved only for those who earn it. Manhood at birth seems to be taken from men, only for them to re-win it. The bookish boy is defined as girlish and then, with a turnabout, earns his manhood as a creative scholar in the university. To fail to do well at this is to be robbed in degrees of manhood.

I think there is a human propensity to achieve competence, what Thorstein Veblen called simply an "instinct for workmanship," but it comes to have secondary meaning for *manhood*. Competition that takes the form of secrecy attached to new ideas before they are in final draft for the publisher, the vita talk, the 60-hour work weeks, the station wagon wife, all are related to this secondary meaning of work, this second layer of value associated with success and manhood. It is this second meaning that women feel they must analogously adopt and compete with.

Yet the reputation so won is often totally detached from social usefulness or moral purpose. For such men, *morality* has become a *luxury*. Women who learn to aspire to this deficiency lose what was valuable from our first training—a training not only to be invisible, but in a larger sense, to "do good" rather than simply "do well." Insofar as women, like other marginal groups, *overconform* in the attempt to gain acceptance, we find ourselves even more oriented toward success, and less toward morality, than some men.

The Cuban revolution seems to me to have solved at least this dilemma, simply by trying structurally to equate "doing well" with "doing good," achievement with moral purpose. The assimilation of Cuban women entering a male-dominated economy does not seem to mean the eclipse of morality. Cuban women have not escaped the doll's house to enter a career based on "bourgeois individualism." Despite many other problems, they escaped that as well.

A year after I returned from Havana, still a graduate student, I began the Women's Caucus of the Sociology Department at Berkeley. Similar groups were springing up in English, history, anthropology, and other departments here and there across the country. It was the time of the women's movement, and women graduate students—facing the scene I've described, with few women faculty to guide the way—were dropping out left and right. Apart from one woman—who had long been a lecturer, not a professor, and who was wrongly seen as an adjunct to her husband, a bigwig in the department—all the professors in our department were men. Yet a fifth of the graduate students were women, hoping one day to become professors. How was this to happen?

A series of women had come into my office in the fall of that year, each talking casually about dropping out of graduate school. When one highly able student, Alice Abarbinel, said she planned to drop out, something in me snapped. "Why would *Alice* drop out?" I knew why X or Y might drop out, but Alice? She was doing so *well*. She seemed so at ease. It was one of those parts that made me question the whole. A week later, after talking with friends, I invited women graduate students to my apartment, where something odd occurred.

We sat cross-legged in a circle on the living room floor, drank coffee and beer, ate potato chips, and felt that something new might be happening. But when I asked whether there was some problem we shared *as women* that might be causing us to become discouraged, one by one people answered, "No." "No." "No." One woman said, "No, I have an incomplete, but I had a hard time defining my topic." Another said, "I have been blocked too, but I have a difficult professor, nothing to do with his being a man." Someone else said, "I'm just not sure I'm in the right discipline." No one hinted that there might be a link between all these hesitations and being a woman. I remember turning to a friend and confiding, "Never mind, we've tried." But after the meeting was adjourned, a curious thing happened. No one left. Two hours later, graduate students were huddled in animated groups, buzzing about professors, courses, housing, loved ones. An invisible barrier had dropped. After that first meeting we met periodically for several years. We were at our best questioning the basic concepts in sociology, and in trying to picture what sociology would look like if women's experiences counted as much as men's. What *is* social status? Social mobility? These are concepts so central to sociology but how do you measure a woman's status—by her husband's occupation (as it was done in the early part of the twentieth century) or by her own occupation? And if she's a homemaker, what then? And does her job affect her spouse's social status? Do we measure her occupational mobility by comparing her occupation with her father's? Or her mother's? How do relations between the genders differ for the rich and the poor?

While we talked much of changing the society within which we sought equality, not much changed about the clockwork of male careers. In those years there was some talk about race, ethnicity, and sexual choice, but these were topics whose centrality was yet to be fully understood.

To talk as I have about the evils of the system as they affect a handful of academic women is a little like talking about the problems of the suburb while there are people trapped in the inner city. But there are problems both with trying to find a meaningful career and with having one on the system's terms. Both finding an academic job and remaining humane once you have had one for a while are problems that lead ultimately to assumptions about the families that lie behind careers. From the vantage point of the early 1970s, women are either slowly eliminated from academic life or forced imperceptibly to acquire the moral and psychic disabilities from which male academics have had to suffer.

If we are to bring more women into the university at every level, we shall have to do something more extreme than most affirmative action plans have imagined: change the entente between the university and its service agency, the family. If we change this, we also introduce into academe some of the values formerly the separate specialty of women. We leaven the ethos of "making it" with another ethos of caretaking and cooperation, leaven the gesellschaft with the *values* of gemeinschaft. It is, after all, not simply women but some feminine values that have been discriminated against. It is not simply that we lack role models who happen to be women, but that we lack exemplars of this alternative ethos.

What I am trying to say is that social justice, giving women a fair break, is a goal that speaks for itself, and a goal that calls for men doing their fair share in private life and for women getting their fair chance in public life. But there are two ways of creating this social justice. One involves fitting into the meritocracy as it is; the other aims to change it. Insofar as we merely extend "bourgeois individualism" to women, ask for "a room of one's own," a reputation, sparring with the others, we fit in nicely with the normal distortion of the importance of success versus moral purpose, the experience of time, or quality of talk that middle-class men have experienced.

The very first step is to reconsider what parts in the cultural recipe of our first socialization to nurturance and caring are worth salvaging in ourselves, and the second step is to consider how to extend and institutionalize them in our place of work. The second way of creating social justice less often speaks for itself: it is to democratize and reward that cooperative, caretaking, morally concerned, not-always-lived-up-to womanly virtue of the past. We need *that* in careers, that among our full professors of either sex. My utopian university is not a Tolstoyan peasant family, but it is also not vita talking to vita. It requires a move in the balance between competition and cooperation, doing well and doing good, taking time to teach a child to swim and taking time to vote in a department meeting. When we have made *that* change, surely it will show in book prefaces and office talk.

THE VIEW FROM 2000 AND BEYOND

As I reflect now on this essay written in 1973, I'm struck by what has changed—the increasing numbers of women in sociology and their impact—but also by what has not—the clockwork of male careers. When I was an assistant professor in 1971, at UC Berkeley, 12 percent of all Berkeley Ph.D.s were women, 9 percent of all assistant professors, 6 percent of associate professors, and 3 percent of all full professors. At Yale the first female faculty member was hired in 1959; at Harvard the first female was appointed to a full professorship in 1947; and, as of 1961, Princeton had no women full professors. As late as 1970 there were only two tenured women in Harvard's Faculty of Arts and Sciences. At Berkeley and other top-ranked research universities there were proportionately fewer women than at U.S. universities and colleges as a whole. Both at Berkeley and in the United States, things have changed enormously. In 2000 at UC Berkeley women made up 33 percent of assistant professors, 39 percent of associate professors, and 17 percent of full professors. And among faculty at four-year colleges and universities in the United States as a whole, in 2002 a greater number of women appear at every level of academic life. Here are the changes:

WOMEN AT FOUR-YEAR COLLEGES/UNIVERSITIES	1970–71	2002
Percentage entering freshmen	43	57
Percentage earning Ph.D.s	13	44
Percentage assistant professors	21	45
Percentage associate professors	15	35
Percentage full professors	9	21 [26]

Also on the bright side, the social sciences have begun to reflect the shift. In 1962 little had been written that was explicitly about women. Between 1873 and 1960 fewer than 1 percent of all books in the *Subject Guide to Books in Print* were expressly on the subject of women. During that time only sixteen history doctoral theses concerned women, one of them, "Recent Popes on Women's Position in Society," written by a man. Today we have an academic industry. The task is to pick the pearls from the hundreds of articles that appear each year. Now, there is first-rate scholarship on women of color, on men from a feminist perspective, and on the lesbian and gay experience.

But the other side of the story is telling too. Over the last twenty-five years, many more women have been juggling work and home alone—a situation that is even harder to fit into the clockwork of male careers. Meanwhile, it remains true that academic women today are still less likely to marry or to have children. And if they do have children, they have fewer than their male counterparts. A forthcoming study of women at UC Berkeley shows just how hard it still is to combine a career with having children. Among tenured faculty in their forties who teach in the hard sciences at UC Berkeley, 70 percent of men and 50 percent of women have children.

Among tenured faculty in their forties who teach in the humanities and social sciences, 60 percent of males and only 38 percent of females have children.[27]

Students raising families can go more slowly in earning their degree, but then they are seen as delinquent according to a new measure Berkeley has devised called "normative time." You get financial privileges if you move rapidly through a degree program but not if you don't. Among ladder-rank faculty, I know of a tiny handful on the entire campus who work less than full-time. There are some part-time lecturers, but they form part of a secondary labor force of instructors hired year to year at lower pay. That's hardly the answer. The clockwork of male careers has proved easier to join than to change. More women, including women of color, have careers, but the clockwork of careers goes on and on.

Looking back at the culture at large, over the last quarter century, we see that certain aspects of the women's movement have entered the mainstream of American life through a process Herbert Marcuse described as "resistance through incorporation." American culture incorporated what of feminism fit with capitalism and individualism, but it resisted the rest. It incorporated the idea of equal pay for equal work and diversity but dispensed with any challenge to the priorities of the system women wanted in on. So it looks to me as if the good fight is still ahead.

NOTES

INTRODUCTION: TWO SIDES OF AN IDEA

1. United States Department of Labor Statistics 2000, tables 4–6.

2. Yet another part of the picture is our growing commodity culture. In a sense the care gap creates a social vacuum. Over the last thirty years people have come to talk less, visit less, and have friends over less at home, even as they watch TV and shop more (Putnam 2000). The care gap makes way for a commodity culture, and the commodity culture offers material substitutes for care. Or, even more insidiously, it "materializes" care so that we increasingly give and receive love only through the things we buy (see Putnam 2000 and Schor 1998).

3. Merleau-Ponty 1964.

4. Weber 1963, p. 416.

5. Pierre Bourdieu's term for this is "misconnaissance."

6. See Putnam 2000, p. 95.

CHAPTER 1. THE COMMERCIAL SPIRIT OF INTIMATE LIFE AND THE ABDUCTION OF FEMINISM

This essay is a slightly revised version of "The Commercial Spirit of Intimate Life and the Abduction of Feminism: Signs from Women's Advice Books," published in *Theory, Culture & Society* 112, no. 2 (1994): 1–24, and reprinted by permission of Sage Publications Ltd. It grew out of a paper delivered at a plenary session on "Postmodernism," German Sociological Association, October 10, 1990. For clarifying discussions, my thanks to Paul Russell. For other stimulating discussions, many thanks to the students in Gender, Culture and Society at Swarthmore College, Swarthmore, Pennsylvania, 1992. For helpful readings my thanks also go to Adam Hochschild, Ruth Russell, and Cas Wouters. Thanks also to Carroll Smith Rosenberg and Michelle Fine, discussants at the Penn-Mid Atlantic Feminist Scholars Group, at the University of Pennsylvania in fall 1992.

1. Weber 1958, p. 181; see also Fromm 1956. I use the term "commercial spirit of intimate life" to refer not to the exchange of things for money, but to the *culture* governing personal relationships that accompanies advanced capitalism. (Thanks to Cas Wouters on this point.)

Weber's thesis has attracted various criticisms. Some have argued that capitalism existed in some places before the rise of Protestantism and in the absence of it (i.e., there were Catholic capitalists). But these criticisms don't bear on the association I seek to focus on here—which is between Protestantism and the spirit of capitalism and not between either of these and capitalism itself.

2. A recent Gallup poll showed that one out of three Americans has bought a "self-help book" (Wood 1988). According to Steven Starker's telephone survey of 1,000 residents of Portland, Oregon, the average respondent read 2.82 self-help books a year. Women were more likely to buy and read a self-help book, and bought more books on love and relationships, stress and anxiety, and weight loss while men bought more on self-improvement and motivation. *Working* women were nearly *twice as likely* as nonworking women to buy books on self-improvement, motivation, and love and relationships. Both working and nonworking women were equally prone to buy books on stress and anxiety (see Starker 1989, Radway 1984, and Long 1986). Simonds interviewed 30 readers, mostly white, employed, middle class in income and education, two-thirds single or divorced (1992, chap. 1). All the best-sellers focused on heterosexual love; we lack data on the sexual orientation of readers and lack research on gay and lesbian advice books. On reading the cultural tea leaves of advice books, see Elias 1978, Giddens 1991, and Simonds 1992.

3. In his classic book *Distinction* (1984), Pierre Bourdieu spoke of "cultural agents," or intermediaries, who actively shape, rather than passively transmit, culture. Writers of advice books are "cultural intermediaries." (Most authors of the books I studied were women, and the most common professions were psychologist, counselor, and writer.) Bourdieu applies an economizing metaphor to culture—"cultural capital"—which implies that culture is something we have or don't have, like table manners, a talent for conversation, and self-confidence (1984, p. 4). I use the term "culture" to refer to a set of practices and beliefs that we hold, do, and partly are.

4. For this study I selected books from a list of hardback or paperback (trade and mass-market) books found on the best-seller lists of *Publishers Weekly*. The criteria used by *Publishers Weekly* to determine a best-seller changed through the years, and I have followed its changes. I selected books that were addressed to women or centrally concerned women's personal or work lives. I excluded diet books, and inspirational or self-development books that did not address or directly bear on women. Books excluded from the list on which I base rough numerical calculations—i.e., books I read but didn't study—include non-best-selling advice books for women and advice books for men.

The original list includes a "core" of pure advice books modeled on psychotherapy or on a social science study based on interviews. Examples of this type are Susan Forward and Joan Torres's *Men Who Hate Women and the Women Who Love Them* (1987). Adopting the metaphors of "sickness" and "healing," which psychiatry itself adopted from medicine, these advice books tell stories of patients' emotional symptoms and cures. Other books quote and interpret hundreds of interviews and report the "findings."

The list also includes a second type of book, which focuses on social practices—dress, manner—with little discussion of the animating ideas or motives behind them. An example of this type would be Judith Martin's *Miss Manners' Guide to Rearing Perfect Children* (1984) or Abigail Van Buren's *The Best of Dear Abby* (1981). A more diverse third group of books includes autobiography, humor, and commentary. Examples are Bill Cosby's *Love and Marriage* (1989), Erma Bombeck's *The Grass*

Is Always Greener over the Septic Tank (1976), and the Boston Women's Health Book Collective, *Ourselves and Our Children* (1978). (For cross-cultural comparisons, see Brinkgreve 1962, Brinkgreve and Korzec 1979, Elias 1978, and Wouters 1987.)

Although I focus on books published between 1970 and 1990, a look back to the turn of the century reveals three types of books, of which the 1970–90 collection reflects two. The three types are traditionals, tradition-for-moderns, and moderns. By tradition-for-moderns, I refer to advice books that curiously mix a belief in male dominance with an appeal to modern goals ("increased female power") and/or an evocation of modern dilemmas. Modern advice books, as I define the term here, advocate equality between the sexes. For a study of nineteenth-century advice books, see Ehrenreich and English (1978). An example of a "plain" traditional advice book is Grace Dodge's (1892) *Thoughts of Busy Girls*, which explains the value of modesty, purity, altruism, dedication, and capacity for moral reform, without appeals to empowerment, freedom, or equality, and without reference to the fear, once married, of being left.

5. See Lasch 1977, Swidler 1980, Cancian 1987, Evans 2002.
6. Harrington and Bielby 1991.
7. See Kaminer 1992, Simonds 1992, Tavris 1993.
8. Morgan 1973, pp. 114–15.
9. Ibid., p. 123.
10. Ibid., p. 89.
11. Ibid., pp. 11–12.
12. Ibid., p. 73.
13. Dowling 1981, p. 237.
14. Chodorow 1978.
15. Dowling 1981, pp. 233–34.
16. Ibid., p. 1.
17. Ibid., p. 21.
18. Ibid., p. 32.
19. Weber 1958, p. 182.
20. Ibid., p. 89.
21. Norwood 1985, p. 292.
22. Ibid., pp. 139, 181.
23. Ibid., p. xiii.
24. Ibid., p. 274.
25. Brown 1982.
26. Gray 1992.
27. Williamson 1993, p. 11.
28. Ibid., p. 46.
29. Vedral 1993, Rabin 1993.
30. Hochschild 1989.

CHAPTER 2. THE COMMODITY FRONTIER

This essay was written for a Festschrift volume in honor of Neil Smelser, *Self, Social Structure, and Beliefs: Essays in Sociology*, edited by Jeff Alexander, Gary Marx, and Christine Williams (Berkeley: University of California Press, forthcoming).

1. Ad found on the Internet, 2001, courtesy of Bonnie Kwan.

2. On the topic of the meaning of money and purchasing, see the foundational work of Viviana Zelizer (1994, 1996, 2000). In "Payments and Social Ties" she makes a persuasive case that the exchange of money and the market realm generally can be assigned any number of meanings. Our job, she argues, is to study, not prejudge them. This is what I attempt here. On discerning the "edge," please see Eviatar Zerubavel's *The Fine Line* (1991).

3. While many modern thinkers wouldn't question this ad or the "wife and mother industry," a good number see it as problematic and do so on very different, though equally challenging, grounds. In *The Minimal Family* Jan Dizard and Howard Gadlin argue that the commodification of former family activities takes the familism—and a family sense of give-and-take—out of families. In *The Overspent American* Juliet Schor critiques American overconsumption of natural resources as a troubling model to be emulated by the rest of the world. In *Everything for Sale* Robert Kuttner cautions us about the retreat from government protection of the public good. Meanwhile Barbara Ehrenreich updates Thorstein Veblen's critique of overconsumption of goods and services as a form of status seeking. (See Dizard and Gadlin 1990, Schor 1998, Kuttner 1997, and Ehrenreich 2001.)

4. One person argued that the man tried to make this proposition "sound" like a normal transaction. But he wondered how the man could explain his hireling's role "in his life to his business partners." One suspicious student remarked, "This is a crazy man who wants a sex slave. Why else would he say 'no sex' while also stipulating that the woman has to be beautiful and unattached?" Another noted, "You don't know what's behind the screen." While a number were suspicious of the man's *motives*, very few suspected the veracity of the *ad* itself. I myself believe the ad is real. Even if it was a hoax, the ad is so close to reality that virtually all the students took it as real, and it might as well have been.

5. See Simmel 1990. Also, in "Depth Psychology and the Social Order" (in Smelser 1998), Smelser distinguishes between four categories of ego defense, each with its corresponding relevant affect and object. At one time or another, people doubtless appeal to all these types of defenses in the course of confronting the threat of commodification and the cultural incongruities it introduces. But one ego defense stands out—depersonalization.

6. Sharpe 2000, pp. 108–10. The president of a Massachusetts-based agency, Parents in a Pinch, Inc., reported that rather than grandparents themselves helping working parents, she found that frequently grandparents bought the service for a busy working daughter as a gift. Presumably many of them were themselves also working and too busy to help out.

7. The last is an announcement heard on commercial radio in southern Maine, July 2000.

8. Sharpe 2000, p. 110.

9. Internet notice, found under craigslist.org "Part Time Personal /Assistant Available"

10. Sharpe 2000, p. 110.

11. Saskia Sassan (2003) argues that globalization is currently creating new social-class patterns. The professional class in rich countries now draws more exclu-

sively on female immigrant labor, the growing supply of which is itself a product of economic dislocations that stem from globalization.

12. Mintz and Kellogg 1988.

13. It is not that the "old" commodification does not occur today. In *Disposable People* (1999), Kevin Bales shows how globalization is giving rise to a new slavery every bit as serious as the old one. But slavery in the modern era is different from slavery in the past, for it now strikes the modern Western mind as deeply immoral.

14. See Smelser 1959. Dividing up the wife-mother role as implied in the ad is "structural" in the sense that a person in a given role (a paid hostess/masseuse outside the family) carries out a function that a wife might be expected to perform inside the family. But it is also psychological and cultural, for this role is also the focus of strongly felt beliefs. And these in turn are strongly related to the gemeinschaft side of the Parsonian pattern variables—affectivity, diffuseness, ascription, particularism.

15. Doohan 1999. A *New York Times* report of September 1, 2001 (Steven Greenhouse, "Americans' International Lead in Hours Worked Grew in the 90's Report Shows"), suggests that Americans added a full week to their work year during the 1990s, climbing to 1,979 hours on average last year, up 36 hours from 1990.

16. McLanahan and Sandefur 1994.

17. Gillis (1996b) points out very different assumptions about the public/private divide and the degree to which the private was thought to need protection from the public. We can also distinguish between different "bandwidths" of commodification—commodities that are chipped off from family life, vs. commodities chipped off from nature, etc. See also Hays 1996.

18. Certainly, American life before the advent of industrial capitalism was unstable, and there are some ways in which industrial capitalism has, through the creation of a middle class, removed many people from the hardships of poverty and, in so doing, stabilized family life (see Mintz and Kellogg 1988). At the same time, the dynamism of capitalism coupled with a state that—by European standards—does little to protect workers from market fluctuations or changing economic demands and offers few provisions to aid in family care, makes America a somewhat harsher, if freer, society in which to live.

19. See Lasch 1977 and Putnam 2001. As Claude Fischer has pointed out (in a talk at the Center for Working Families, UC Berkeley, April 2001), geographic mobility itself is not new to Americans. While rates of long-distance mobility have remained relatively constant since the mid-nineteenth century, mobility within local areas has actually decreased.

20. Wellman et al. 1997, Wellman 1999.

21. In "Collective Myths and Fantasies: The Myth of the Good Life in California," Smelser notes that a myth is a "psychodynamic blending of fiction and fact to complete the inevitable logic of ambivalence in myth . . . there is no happy myth without its unhappy side" (see Smelser 1998, pp. 111–24). So, too, with the myth of infinite commodification, there is the bright side (the fantasy of the perfect "wife-like employee") and the dark side (the fear of estrangement and existential aloneness).

22. Greven 1972.

23. Clemens (Mark Twain) 1962, p. 226. See also Erikson 1950.

24. Dating services and mail-order bride services commodify the *finding* of wives, of course, though not the wives themselves (*New Yorker*, June 18, 25, 2001, p. 149).

25. The chain accepts children six weeks to twelve years and provides a number to call for the center nearest you. See Hochschild 1997a, p. 231.

26. Heard on Maine Public Radio, October 14, 2001.

27. For a discussion of the "potential self," see Hochschild 1997a, p. 235.

28. Thanks to Allison Pugh (Sociology Department, University of California, Berkeley) for this example.

CHAPTER 3. GENDER CODES AND THE PLAY OF IRONY

This essay was prepared for the Second Indo-Canadian Symposium on "Institution, Communication and Social Interaction: The Legacy of Erving Goffman," Mysore, India, December 29, 1987–January 1, 1988, and published in *Beyond Goffman: Studies on Communication, Institution, and Social Interaction*, edited by Stephen Harold Riggins (Paris: Mouton, 1990), pp. 277–94; it is reprinted here with permission of the publisher, Mouton de Gruyter. (For the relevant discussions of gender, see Goffman 1976, 1977, and 1967a.) There is a rich literature on the history of advice books for men as well as women. See, for example, Norbert Elias's classic *The History of Manners* (1978).

1. Goffman 1959, p. 5.

2. See West and Zimmerman 1987.

3. See Hochschild 1983, pp. 201–22.

4. Swidler 1986; Goffman 1959, 1974, 1977.

5. Morgan 1973, p. 117.

6. Brown 1982, p. 40. She assumes that rationality is "male" (in a male or female) and emotionality is "female" (again, in a male or female). But, like many people, she assumes rationality and emotionality don't mix.

7. Morgan 1973, pp. 71, 184.

8. Ibid., p. 73.

9. Ibid.

10. Brown 1982, p. 264.

11. Ibid., pp. 209, 262.

12. Ibid., p. 210.

13. Ibid., p. 209.

14. Friedman 1985, p. 173.

15. Steinem 1986, p. 205.

16. Brown 1982, p. 271.

17. Morgan 1973, p. 82.

18. Ibid., p. 63.

19. Ibid., p. 283.

20. Friedman 1985, p. 36.

21. Adams 1985.

22. Friedman 1985, pp. 109, 110.

23. Ibid., p. 109.

24. Hite 1987, Hochschild 1987.

CHAPTER 4. LIGHT AND HEAVY

Kazuko Tanaka teaches sociology at Kokugakuin University in Tokyo. Our essay, originally titled "Ways to See Working Mothers: American and Japanese Advice Books for Women 1970–1990," was first published in *Unresolved Dilemmas: Women, Work and the Family in the United States, Europe and the Former Soviet Union,* edited by Kaisa Kauppinen and Tuula Gordon (Aldershot, England: Ashgate Publishing, 1997), pp. 196–214, and is reprinted here by permission of the publisher. Throughout this essay we have used Western name order for the Japanese authors we discuss.

1. Bourdieu 1977, Goffman 1974, Collins 1975. As Pierre Bourdieu has argued, culture is a response to the practical questions of living. When people face novel situations, when uncertain outcomes are potentially consequential, and when people are thus anxious about what to do, they seek guidance. They seek it from what Bourdieu calls "cultural intermediaries"—radio commentators, TV personalities, film stars, and writers of advice books. Writers of advice books, in particular, tend to tell long stories, which implicitly clear an emotional pathway to a line of action that seems problematic—like not rising to make breakfast in the morning.

2. Hamao 1972, p. 20.
3. Suzuki 1984.
4. Molloy 1977, p. 18.
5. Sen 1980, p. 32.
6. Hamao 1972, p. 62.
7. Suzuki 1983b, pp. 17–18.
8. Hirose 1985, pp. 140–44.
9. Ibid., pp. 140–41, 241.
10. Ward 1989, p. 16.
11. Dobson 1987, p. 129.
12. Bombeck 1972, pp. 113, 55.
13. Cosby 1989, p. 247.
14. Mizuno 1978, p. 105.
15. Hamao 1972, p. 62.
16. Ibid., p. 5.
17. Shiotsuki 1970, p. 3.
18. Saimon 1990, pp. 227–28.
19. Cowan and Kinder 1985, pp. xvi, xiii.

CHAPTER 5. THE CAPACITY TO FEEL

Originally titled "The Sociology of Feeling and Emotion: Selected Possibilities," this essay was first published in *Another Voice: Feminist Perspectives on Social Life and Social Science,* edited by Marcia Millman and Rosabeth Moss Kanter (Garden City, N.Y.: Anchor Press/Doubleday, 1975 [© *Sociological Inquiry*]), pp. 280–307, and is reprinted with permission of Blackwell Publishing, Oxford.

I wrote this essay in 1974 (it appeared in 1975), and since that time a new subfield of sociology, the sociology of emotions, has come into being as well as the International Society for Research on Emotions, both founded in the 1980s. For a bibliography of works in the field, please see *The Managed Heart* (Hochschild 1983; reprinted with new afterword, 2003).

1. To be sure, the great sociologists, especially Durkheim, Marx, and, of course, Freud, *have* touched on the subject of emotion.

2. Goffman 1959, p. 4.

3. For example, Slater (1968) suggests the Greek captive-slave mother takes out unconscious aggression on her son, creating homosexuality in him. See also Slater 1964, 1966; Seeley 1967; and Marcuse 1955.

4. Allport and Odbert 1936, p. 3.

5. Kephart 1967.

6. Weber 1966.

7. Some writers find roots in phenomenology (Davitz 1969, Block 1957, Sartre 1948), Freud (Seeley 1967, Slater 1964), or Simmel (Klatsky and Teitler 1973), while others bypass social science altogether and go back to Descartes (Davis 1936)—a sign surely of an intellectual infancy with a quiet disagreement about parentage.

8. Moreover, each approach uses "emotion" differently. In the first approach, the term refers to a concept actors use to make sense of their experience. In the second, "emotion" refers to a concept the social scientist uses to make sense of the actor's experience by referring to the actor's unconscious. In the third, it also refers to a concept the social scientist uses, but here it is defined as the association between bodily or psychic experience and the cultural meaning and label assigned to it. My preference is to start with the third conceptualization and extend it to incorporate insights drawn from the other two approaches.

9. Jones et al. 1972.

10. Levy 1973.

11. Blum and McHugh 1971.

12. Dollard et al. 1939, Seeley 1967, Slater 1964, Gorer 1964, Mead 1949, Erikson 1950, Malinowski 1927.

13. Dollard et al. 1939, p. 7.

14. Stanley Schachter exemplifies the first, Joel Davitz the second, and Robert Levy the third approach. For Schachter, emotion is basically physiological arousal with a label attached (Schachter and Wheeler 1962, Schachter 1964, Walster 1976). In one experiment, he gave injections of epinephrine to some subjects and placebos to others. Some subjects were informed, others misinformed, and others told nothing about what physiological experience to expect. Then all subjects were placed in either an anger-inducing situation (in a room with an angry person) or a euphoria-inducing situation (in a room with a man shooting paper planes, etc.). Those who were physiologically aroused by the drug, had no explanation provided, and were exposed to angry or euphoric company tended to label their own state as like that of their partner. Thus, subjects labeled differently "the same" physiological experience depending on their explanation for it and on the social milieu. Davitz (1969) does the opposite of Schachter. He holds the labels constant and examines variations in the reported experience attached to them. He had respondents complete a list of items for fifty emotions, reporting physical sensations, perceptions of situation, and expressive behavior. For his limited college sample, he found considerable consensus about the link between emotion label and experience, although more so for some emotions.

15. Kephart 1967, p. 472.

16. Some deal with jealousy (Davis 1936), envy (Foster 1972, Schoeck 1966), embarrassment (Modigliani 1968, Gross and Stone, 1964), trust (Deutsch 1958, Klatsky and Teitler 1973), aggression and hostility (Berkowitz 1962, Gurr and Ruttenberg 1967, Walters 1966), grief (Averill 1968), and love (Goode 1974, Huizinga 1970, Lewis 1959, Moller 1958, Rubin 1973).

17. See Moller 1958, Lewis 1959, Gross and Stone 1964.

18. Foster 1972.

19. Davis 1936.

20. Jealousy is what we feel when we fear someone will take away what we already have.

21. Chodorow 1999.

22. Foster 1972.

23. Talcott Parsons applied the idea of currency to power (1968).

24. "False" has at least two meanings: the discrepancy between perceived display and inferred feeling ("artificiality") and the discrepancy between the true or original nature of something and its presenting version ("inauthenticity"). I use the term in its first sense.

25. Expression contexts also vary over time, with changes of style in emotional expression. Perhaps we can get at this by examining the film industry, especially "bad" films and what is popular at different times. Hollywood is to emotional life what the State Department is to foreign relations. Hollywood exercises a certain cultural hegemony over the world of emotion, teaching us how kissing and fighting "are done," how feelings are to be expressed and managed.

26. Bugental, Love, and Gianetto 1971.

27. Paul Eckman, personal communication.

28. Some treat emotion as the great equalizer, assuming that the powerful do not necessarily enjoy more good feelings than the powerless. I am skeptical, for I doubt that power and emotion are unconnected.

29. Coser 1960, p. 95.

30. See Dollard et al. 1939, pp. 40–44, and Levy 1973, p. 286. In the case of positive emotions going up, there are often latent secondary gains. When a lower-status person positively identifies with a higher-status one, there may be a "magical transfer" of goods ("I have by identification with my boss what I may not have otherwise—her/his power and prestige"). See Hochschild 1973, chap. 5.

31. Four main factors seem to account for a change in aim: a change in the strength of the incentives for aiming in a given direction, a change in the strength of the controls constraining the aim, a change in the conditions that serve as "outlets" or safety valves, and a change in extent of contact and affective integration of the people involved.

CHAPTER 6. WORKING ON FEELING

This essay was originally published under the title "Emotion Work, Feeling Rules, and Social Structure" in *American Journal of Sociology* 85, no. 3 (1979): 551–75 (copyright © 1979 by The University of Chicago. All rights reserved.). It summarizes part of the argument presented in *The Managed Heart* and "The Capacity to Feel" (chapter 5 in this book). This study has been generously supported by a Guggenheim Fellowship. Although gratitude in footnotes like this is (as this essay demonstrates) conventionalized, and although convention makes authenticity hard to decipher, I want anyway to express appreciation to Harvey Faberman, Todd Gitlin, Adam Hochschild, Robert Jackson, Jerzy Michaelowicz, Caroline Persell, Mike Rogin, Paul Russell, Thomas Scheff, Ann Swidler, Joel Telles, and the anonymous reviewers for the *AJS*.

1. Styron 1951, p. 291.

2. Goffman 1961, p. 23.

3. W. McDougall (1948) and, to some extent, S. S. Tomkins (1962) both focus on the relation of emotion to drive or instinct (Tomkins elaborates a relation between emotion and "drive signals" whereby emotion is said to amplify drive signals). The central issues on which the two theoretical camps divide are fixity, reflexivity, and origin. The organismic theorists, unlike their interactive counterparts, assume a basic fixity of emotion, based in biological givens. They assume that basically social interaction does not affect emotion itself; the social surface remains what is implied by the term "surface." In the interactive account, not so. Labeling, management, and expression of feeling (more clearly differentiated by the interactionists) are processes that can reflexively "act back" on emotion, and indeed come to constitute what we mean by the term "emotion." Again, the organismic theorists are more concerned with tracing emotion back to its origins. For Freud and James the origins were energic or somatic, and for Darwin, phylogenetic. The interactive theorists are less concerned with origin than with the interface of a situation and an experience. The focus on origin leads the organismic theorists to focus on commonalities between different peoples, and between people and animals. The focus on social interface leads the interactionists to focus on differences. For recent innovations in the interactive tradition, see Kemper 1978b and Averill 1976.

4. See Freud 1911, 1915a, 1915b; Lofgren 1968; Darwin 1872, 1955; James and Lange 1922.

5. Ekman 1972, 1973.

6. Collins 1975, p. 59.

7. Gerth and Mills 1964; Goffman, 1956, 1959, 1961, 1967, 1974; Lazarus 1966; Lazarus and Averill 1972; Schachter and Singer 1962; Schachter 1964; Kemper 1978b; Katz 1977; Averill 1976. Schachter and Gerth and Mills, whom I see as members of the interactive camp, lay no particular stress on volition. Goffman stresses phenomena that tacitly call for will and points to the patterned results of it. But he provides no theoretical account of will itself. He posits no actor qua emotion manager who might accomplish the acts that, by inference, must get accomplished to pull off the encounters he describes so well. In my view we must reinstitute a self capable of experiencing emotion and of working on it in socially patterned ways. (On the issue of will, see Piaget in Campbell 1976 and Solomon 1973.)

8. Schafer 1976.

9. See Mead 1934, Blumer 1969, Shott 1979.

10. Goffman 1974.

11. Goffman 1961, p. 23.

12. See Benedict 1946; Fromm 1942; Horney 1937; Erikson 1950; Riesman 1952, 1960; Swanson and Miller 1966; Gerth and Mills 1964.

13. Goffman, 1976, p. 77. Thanks to Harvey Farberman for discussion on this point.

14. To link the momentary act of emotion work with the concept of personality, we must alter our perspective on time. An emotive episode and the attempt to shape it take, after all, a brief strip of time. The situations Goffman studies are often momentary. He focuses on the act, and the act ends, so to speak, when the theater closes and starts again when it reopens. If we extend Goffman's analysis, by speaking now of "deep" acting, we, like him, are focusing on short episodes, on "stills" from which long movies are composed. The notion of personality implies a fairly durable, trans-situational pattern. The Casper Milquetoast personality may lead an anxiety-avoidant life of seventy-three years. Not momentary stills, but decades and lifetimes are at issue. Again, we must shift our situationist focus at the structural end when we come to speak of institutions, which often outlive people.

15. Goffman 1961, p. 23.

16. Shapiro 1965, p. 192 (emphases mine).

17. Ibid., p. 164.

18. The illustrations of emotion work come from a content analysis of 261 protocols given to students in two classes at the University of California, Berkeley, in 1974. Many of the illustrations come from answers to the question "Describe as fully and concretely as possible a real situation, important to you, in which you experienced either changing a real situation to fit your feelings or changing your feelings to fit a situation. What did it mean to you?" Three coders coded the protocols. Thirteen percent of the men but 32 percent of the women were coded as "changing feeling" instead of changing situation, and of those who changed feelings, far more women reported doing so agentially rather than passively. In all cases, emphasis in these illustrations is mine.

19. There may be various types of cognitive emotion work. All can be described as attempts to shift our way of classifying experience. We intuitively ask: Is this a blame-in situation? A blame-out situation? A credit-in or a credit-out situation? What category in my classification schema of emotions fits the emotion I'm feeling right now? (Is it anger, general anxiety, disappointment?) To translate this idea into Richard Lazarus's framework, we might speak of the individual trying consciously to alter his or her appraisal of a situation so as to change the coping process (Lazarus 1966).

20. That we can single out such a thing as "feeling rules" is itself a commentary on the ironic stance we nowadays take to the events of daily life. Modern urban cultures foster much more distance (the stance of the observing ego) from feeling than do traditional cultures. Jerzy Michaelowicz, a graduate student at the University of California, San Diego, observed that traditional and tight-knit subcultures put people directly inside the framework of feeling rules and remove ironic distance and a sense of choice about them. He reported on some research in which one Hassidic rabbi was asked, "Did you feel happy at the Passover ceremony?" "Of course!" came the incredulous reply.

21. Lyman and Scott 1970.

22. But this, too, seems to be culturally variable. Erving Goffman points out that hangings in the sixteenth century were a social event that the participant was "supposed to enjoy," a rule that has since disappeared from civilian society.

23. In *The Elementary Forms of Religious Life,* Durkheim conveys just this understanding of the relation of world view to feeling rules: "When the Christian, during

the ceremonies commemorating the Passion, and the Jew, on the anniversary of the fall of Jerusalem, fast and mortify themselves, it is not in giving way to a sadness which they feel spontaneously. Under these circumstances, the internal state of the believer is out of all proportion to the severe abstinences to which they submit themselves. If he is sad, it is primarily *because he consents to being sad. And he consents to it in order to affirm his faith*" (1961, p. 274; emphasis mine). Again, "An individual . . . if he is strongly attached to the society of which he is a member, *feels that he is morally held to participating in its sorrows and joys;* not to be interested in them would be equivalent to breaking the bonds uniting him to the group: it would be renouncing all desire for it and contradicting himself" (1961, p. 446; emphasis mine). Also see Geertz 1964 and Goffman 1974.

24. Collins suggests that elite groups contend not only for access to the means of economic production or the means of violence but also for access to the means of "emotion production" (1975, p. 59). Rituals are seen as useful tools for forging emotional solidarity (that can be used against others) and for setting up status hierarchies (that can dominate those who find that the new ideals have denigrating effects on themselves).

25. The seemingly static links among ideology, feeling rules, and emotion management come alive in the process of social exchange. Students of social interaction have meant two things by the term "social exchange." Some refer to the exchange of goods and services between people (Blau 1964, Simpson 1972, Singelmann 1972). Others (George Herbert Mead) refer to an exchange of gestures, without the cost-benefit accounting embedded in the first usage. Yet acts of display, too, are exchanged in the limited sense that the individual often feels he or she owes or is owed a gesture of feeling. I refer, then, to exchange of acts of display based on a prior, shared understanding of entitlement.

26. Hochschild 1983, p. 82.

CHAPTER 7. THE ECONOMY OF GRATITUDE

This essay was originally published in *The Sociology of Emotions: Original Essays and Research Papers,* edited by David Franks and Doyle McCarthy (Greenwich, Conn.: JAI Press, 1989), pp. 95–113, and is reprinted by permission of Elsevier Science. Special thanks to Adam Hochschild, Ann Swidler, Peggy Thoits, Steve Gordon, and David Franks for insightful criticism.

1. Among the few social analyses of gratitude are those of Georg Simmel (1950, pp. 379–95) and Marcel Mauss (1967). In a very different tradition, largely based on experimental research, equity theory (though it does not treat gratitude per se) explores the circumstances that lead couples to feel that a social bond is satisfying or fair (see Walster 1976).

2. See Carrington 1999.

3. See Davitz 1969, p. 60.

4. See Ogburn 1932, pp. 200–213. Ogburn argues that the material culture changed at a faster rate than the nonmaterial culture—e.g., the folkways, social institutions—including the family. Ogburn's use of the term "culture" obscures the role of power and interest; culture simply "lagged behind" the economy, without serving

the interests of any particular social group. In my analysis here, the lag serves the interests of men who feel they have less to gain from the social changes that economic opportunity and need have now opened up to women.

5. In the nineteenth century, economic trends most directly affected men, because industrialization drew them more than women into wage labor. This caused men to change their basic life ways more, and women to "culturally lag."

6. Lasch 1977. Thanks to Eqbal Ahmad for the term "shock absorber."

7. Hochschild 1989. Both husbands and wives worked 35 hours or more and cared for at least one child six years or under. Although a fifth of husbands fully shared housework and parenting, a fifth did very little; the rest helped a moderate amount.

8. These and other personal names in this essay are fictitious.

9. The two couples differ in social class, ethnicity, and religion. Other research suggests a greater traditionalism among the working class, among the politically conservative, and among couples in which the wife and the husband's mother are homemakers. Differences in religious culture appear to have little effect: Jews are slightly more egalitarian, Catholics slightly less—but religious differences may also reflect class ones. (See Baruch and Barnett 1988, Pleck 1982, Kimball 1983, Hood 1983.)

10. When a man endorsed the new gender rules (of status transfer), he could receive his wife's salary as a gift. Such a wife did not have to "make up for" transgressing a rejected rule by a return of "extra" favors. One wife, a word processor, explained the response of her husband (a night watchman) to a recent promotion: "I really don't think it affects anything, because we look at it this way: If I make more than Will, or he makes more than me, we are both reaping the benefits of that." The gift is offered and—culturally as well as materially—received.

Just as many men could not accept their wives' salaries if they were higher than their own, so many men could not accept their rises, after a point, in professional status. Men often reacted to a wife's period of occupational training differently from the way women reacted to that of their husbands. When men were in training for a career, a working wife treated the training as a promissory note for a future gift. She often therefore took over housework and childcare to let him study. But men did not similarly take their wives' occupational training in the same spirit. In one extreme example, a husband commented on his wife's writing of a Ph.D. thesis in political science: "I hate it. I can't tell you how I hate it. I feel I'm getting nothing out of it. It isn't a job. It isn't a cooked meal. It's nothing. I just hate it." At the time of the interview there was a glut on the academic market, but no man writing a dissertation who participated in the study was greeted with such a response.

11. Seth was a mixed traditional—or "pseudo-egalitarian"—in the sense that his rhetoric was more liberal than his economy of gratitude. This slippage between the surface and depth of an attitude is a common adaptation to the pressure to change—which in this case came from his wife.

12. There is considerable research evidence that women attribute more personal events (e.g., winning a game, doing well on an exam) to "luck" than men do. This finding has often been attributed to women's lower "locus of control." My field observations correspond to the laboratory evidence, and simply add an explanation both for the lower locus of control and for their social management of it.

CHAPTER 8. TWO WAYS TO SEE LOVE

This essay is adapted from a talk given to the German Psychoanalytic Association in Saarbrucken, Germany, October 1, 1995. Originally titled "The Sociology of Emotion as a Way of Seeing," it was published in *Emotions in Social Life: Critical Theories and Contemporary Issues*, edited by Gillian Bendelow and Simon J. Williams (London: Routledge, 1998), pp. 3–15, and is reprinted by permission of the publisher.

1. See Collins 1990. Within American sociology, the sociology of emotions is now one of over twenty subfields. It was established in the mid-1980s and publishes a quarterly newsletter with notes about new articles and books in the field. The British Sociological Association has a "study group" as does the International Sociological Association. Also in the mid-1980s, the International Association for Research on Emotion was established to bring together social scientists interested in the study of emotion.

2. Hochschild 1983, p. 59. The wording is slightly modified for the sake of coherence.

3. Dr. Christa Rohde-Dachser holds the Sigmund Freud Chair in Psychology at the University of Frankfurt and is affiliated with the Institut für Psychoanalyse at the University of Frankfurt.

4. If culture is a medium, most sociologists would say it is not a *passive* medium but an active one. Culture might be said to function like D. W. Winnicott's (1965) notion of a "facilitating environment."

5. As the historian John Gillis (1994) argues, the value placed on family life has never been greater than it is today. Indeed, family values are more and more our only values. The sense of sacredness that the Judeo-Christian tradition once attached to the Family of God, the church, expressed through and to the wide community, has become increasingly secular and private. As Gillis notes, "The Victorians were the first to make room for a spiritualized home, and create within their homes a series of special family times and places where an ideal family could experience itself free from the distractions of everyday life. Families have become fetishized."

6. Derne 1994, 1995.

7. One can trace over time the transmutation of this ideal of love—its growing association with sexual expression, with marriage, with procreation, and indeed, with the institution of the bourgeois family. In the United States this new cultural synthesis of romantic love, with marriage and procreation, came to fullest development in the 1950s, when a full 95 percent of the population married at some point in their lives.

8. The divorce rate has greatly affected the relations between fathers and children; one study found that half of American children ages eleven to sixteen living with their divorced mothers had not seen their fathers during the entire previous year. An in-depth study of divorcing families in California found that half the men and two-thirds of the women felt more content with the quality of their lives after divorce, though only one in ten children did. Half of the women and a third of the men were still intensely angry at their ex-spouses ten years after the divorce. See Wallerstein and Blakeslee 1989 and Hochschild 1991, pp. 106–15. Also see Hetherington 2002.

9. In *Love as Passion* (1986) Niklas Luhmann suggests that sexuality has become

a "communicative code," a language rather than an experience, integrated with a full range of implied social ties and controls. Also see Alberoni 1983.

10. Hackstaff 1994.

11. Ann Swidler (2001) and Francesca Cancian (1987) argue that commitment has become a diminishing part in people's idea of love, while the idea of growth and communication has become a more important part. Data from national opinion polls document a twenty-year decline in commitment to long-term love, suggesting some evidence for this assertion.

12. See DaCosta 1998. The idea that people have become more guarded in the wake of greater freedoms runs counter to popular notions of the 1970s and 1980s as a period of the "culture of narcissism," as the historian Christopher Lasch (1979) called it.

13. See Schaffner 1994.

14. The very act of managing emotion can be seen as part of what the emotion becomes. But this idea gets lost if we assume, as the organismic theorists do, that how we manage or express feeling is extrinsic to emotion. The organismic theorists want to explain how emotion is "motored by instinct," and so bypass the question of how we come to assess, label, and manage emotion. The interactional theorists assume, as I do, that culture can impinge on emotion in ways that affect what we point to when we say "emotion" (Hochschild 1983, pp. 18, 28; also appendixes A and B).

CHAPTER 9. PATHWAYS OF FEELING

Adapted from "Ideologies, Strategies and Emotional Pathways" in *Research Agendas in the Sociology of Emotions,* edited by Theodore D. Kemper, by permission of the State University of New York Press. © 1990 State University of New York. All rights reserved.

1. See Thoits 1989. Also Swidler 1986 and Goffman 1969.

2. Warner, Wellman, and Weitzman 1977.

3. If we move from the individual to the organization as the unit of analysis, we see that organizations provide contexts in which strategies unfold. In the Delta Airlines training program I studied for *The Managed Heart,* flight attendants were told not only how to seem but how to see and feel about lost, grumpy, or unruly customers, bossy pilots, or complaining co-workers. Airlines may carry explicit training in feeling rules further than other organizations, but I believe the principle is the same in other organizations that serve the public. Churches, schools, and companies promote a sense of the dos and don'ts of feeling. What are these sets of feeling rules? Who are the "lieutenants" who enforce them, and who rebels against them? By what social rituals, formal and informal procedures, do organizations get people to feel the "right" way?

In the *Managed Heart* I suggested that one-third of all American jobs call for emotional labor: a quarter of those men hold and a half of those women do. Others, too, have studied the emotional labor of service workers; for example, Smith (1988a, 1988b) has studied emotional labor among nurses, and Tolich (1988) has studied it among supermarket checkers. But questions remain: Precisely how does the emotional labor of an executive differ from that of a secretary? How does the emotional labor of a doctor differ from that of a nurse, or that of a male doctor from that of a female one? In addition, how do occupational cultures set the margins for hostility, jealousy, fellow-feeling in different ways? Do offices with all-male employees have different emotional cultures from offices with all-female workers? How does gender influence emotional labor? Jennifer Pierce (1988) has compared the nature of the emotional labor of men and women in three occupations: litigation attorneys (a stereotypically male profession), paralegals (in between), and legal secretaries (a stereotypically female job). See also Ortiz 1988 and Dressler 1987.

4. Hochschild 1983 and Clark 1987.

CHAPTER 10. FROM THE FRYING PAN INTO THE FIRE

This essay, which has been substantially revised, takes as its starting point "Globalization, Time, and the Family," first published in German by the Institut für die Wissenschaften von Menchen, Vienna, 1998, and included in *Am Ende des Millenniums*, edited by Krzysztof Michalski (Stuttgart: Klett-Cotta, 2000), pp. 180–203.

1. See Hochschild 1997a.

2. Cell phones, home fax machines, car dictating machines, and similar gadgets are marketed, purchased, and used on the premise that these machines, like the cereal, will "save time"—so that the consumer can then enjoy more leisure. In practice, though, such technology often becomes a delivery system for pressure to do more paid work. Along with new technology come new norms. Electronic mail, for example, once hailed as a way of "saving time" has escalated expectations shortening the period of time one has before one is considered rude or inattentive not to reply.

3. Among affluent Americans, time-saving goods and services also force parents to define parenthood less in terms of production and more in terms of consumption. For example, a "good mother" in the American middle class is often seen as one who prepares her child's birthday, bakes the cake, blows up the balloons, invites her child's friends to a party. Increasingly, the busy working mother is tempted to buy the cake; in addition, new birthday services are available in American cities to help organize the party, send out the invitations, buy the gifts, blow up the balloons, and set up the food. The definition of a "good mother" moves from production to consumption. The "good mother" is now one who enjoys the party with the child. The gift is one of derationalized time.

4. See Gillis 1994; also Popenoe 1989 and Putnam 2000.

5. Schor 1998, pp. 16–17.

6. Cox 2001, p. 124.

7. Some commentators blame women's movement into paid work for the strains experienced at home—including the high divorce rate. But I would argue that it is not women's paid work per se, but work in the absence of the necessary social adjustments in the structure of care—male sharing of care at home, family-friendly workplace policies, and social honor associated with care—that make the difference.

8. Doohan 1999. The 600-page ILO report compared hours of work in 240 countries. Useem (2000) cites 751 time-management titles listed on Amazon.com, including *Eating on the Run* and *Please Hold: 102 Things to Do While You Wait on the Phone.*

9. Galinsky, Bond, and Friedman 1993, p. 9.

10. "Families and the Labor Market, 1969–1999: Analyzing the Time Crunch," May 1999, Report by the Council of Economic Advisors, Washington, D.C. Also a 2000 report found that 46 percent of workers work 41 hours or longer, 18 percent of them 51 hours or longer (see Center for Survey Research and Analysis, University of Connecticut, "2000 Report on U.S. Working Time"). Another recent study found that elementary school teachers—those in what is often thought to be a "woman's" job—reported working ten-hour days (see Drago et al. 1999). Less time away from work means less time for children. Nationwide, half of children wish they could see their fathers more, and a third wish they could see their mothers more (Coolsen, Seligson, and Garbino 1985; Hewlett 1991, p. 105). A growing number of commentators draw links, often carelessly, between this decline in family time and a host of problems, including school failure and alcohol and drug abuse (Hewlett 1991).

CHAPTER 11. THE COLONIZED COLONIZER

This essay is the Afterword to *Breaking the Silence*, edited by Leela Gulati (New Delhi: Sage Publications, forthcoming) and is used here with permission of the publisher.

1. I was based at the Centre for Development Studies in Trivandrum, Kerala, from November 1997 to April 1998. The conference papers were later gathered in the *Indian Journal of Gender Studies* 6, no. 2 (July–December 1999), though some of the original papers presented were not included and others were added. The essays by Nabaneeta Sen, Leela Gulati, Prita Desai, and Vina Majumdar that I discuss below are all included in it. The lives described in the volume fit well-known patterns described in Leela Dube's classic *Women and Kinship* (1997), Jasodhara Bagchik Jaba Gurha and Piyali Sengupta, *Loved and Unloved, the Girl Child in the Family* (1999), and A. M. Shah, *The Family in India: Critical Essays* (1999).

2. Sen 1999, p. 226. In the realm of class as well as race and gender, the already-loaded relations within the family become more loaded still with the hopes, resentments, love, and envy parents project onto children, and children project back. In *The Hidden Injuries of Class* (1993), Richard Sennett explores the Narayanis and Radharanis (in a son's story) of the American working class. Working-class fathers who believe in the Horatio Alger ethic but fail, in their own eyes, to live up to its promise both worship and resent the social rise of their sons. It is often noted that disparaged groups of all sorts—women, Jews, Arabs, African Americans, the poor, the colonized—can be prejudiced against others of their category and against themselves. Some Jews disparage other Jews or themselves for ways in which they look or seem Jewish. African Americans speak of other blacks, even themselves, as "too dark" and so on. Less appreciated is the syndrome of *subcontracted* oppression—the colonized colonizer—as it applies to each of these groups. And still less understood are the many subtle ways in which the subcontracted job of administering unkind customs infuses the parent-child bond, the topic of this essay.

3. Sen 1999, p. 228.

4. Harris 1977.

5. See Gulati 1999, p. 193. In a different way, this culture of silence made itself felt in the social sciences and arts. Nabaneeta Sen describes how Radharani much

later in life wrote lively poems echoing the voices of the kitchen, the bedroom, the girls' hostel, the young bride, the widowed aunt. For twelve years no one linked these poems with Radharani because she published them under a pseudonym, Aparajita Devi. Meanwhile under her own name, she published a series of tepid, unisex poems, which kept mum about women's real experiences. When at last Radhirani admitted that she herself wrote the lively "Aparajita poems," she disparaged them, saying she'd written them simply to illustrate how "men think women write." Writing them and then disparaging them were surely acts of profound ambivalence. In fact, the very writing of these poems broke a powerful taboo against voicing not only complaints, but a feminine viewpoint on experience. And that was a risk. So Radhirani had Aparajita, her pseudonym, do it "for her." But authenticity had the last word. Aparajita's lively poems were wildly popular and far outlasted the abstract, insipid poems to which Radharani freely linked her name.

6. Sen 1999, p. 223.

7. Ibid., p. 229.

8. Ibid., p. 231.

9. Anna Freud describes a compensatory form of identification—a living through others as "altruistic surrender" (see Hochschild 1973). As she notes, "Impulses that appeared impossible to fulfill are not repressed. Rather through identification and projections, the individual finds a proxy in the outside world to serve as a repository for them" (1984 [1936]).

10. Sen 1999, p. 232.

11. Majumdar 1999, p. 234.

12. Desai 1999, pp. 243, 248, 256, 258.

13. Desai 1999, p. 258.

14. We too often imagine that parental love is a matter so basic to human life that tyranny forms a thin patina upon it. But as the anthropologist Nancy Scheper-Hughes noted in *Death without Weeping* (1993), the poor mothers she interviewed in a Brazilian shantytown who had lost one or two of their many babies "gave them up to Jesus" without grief. The laws of evolution have doubtless rigged mothers to love their babies. But social circumstances have more power to shape that love than we might think.

15. Papenek 1974.

16. This is consistent with the observation of Ann Swidler (2001).

CHAPTER 12. THE FRACTURED FAMILY

This essay was first published in *The American Prospect* 2, no. 6 (June 23, 1991): 106–15. It is reprinted with permission of The American Prospect, 5 Broad Street, Boston, MA 02109. All rights reserved.

1. Wallerstein and Blakeslee 1989.

2. Lamb 1986, pp. 8, 11.

3. Furstenberg et al. 1983.

4. Wallerstein and Blakeslee 1989.

5. Peterson and Zill 1986.

6. Dugger 1992.

7. Furstenberg 1991, Furstenberg et al. 1983, Furstenberg and Cherlin 1991.

CHAPTER 13. CHILDREN AS EAVESDROPPERS

This essay was first published in *Working Families: The Transformation of the American Home,* edited by Rosanna Hertz and Nancy L. Marshall (Berkeley: University of California Press, 2001), pp. 340–53, and is reprinted with permission of the publisher. Many thanks to Rosanna Hertz, Nancy Marshall, and especially to Allison Pugh for very astute editorial guidance and for suggesting that children's ears are like "tuning forks." Thanks, too, to Christopher Davidson for excellent research assistance and to Bonnie Kwan for typing and for the benefit of her unusual organizational skills.

1. Agee 1968 [1957], p. 277.
2. Campbell 1991.
3. Hochschild 1997a.
4. Laing 1969 and Winnicott 1986.
5. See Thorne 1987, 1993, 1998; Briggs 1992; Fine and Sandstrom 1988; Mayall 1994; Corsaro and Miller 1992; Scheper-Hughes and Sargent 1988; Van Manen and Levering 1996.
6. Uttal 1993, 1996, 1998; Macdonald 1998; Wrigley 1995.
7. Hochschild 1997a, p. 81.
8. Winnicott 1986.
9. Lareau 1998a, 1998b; Lareau and Horvat 1999.
10. Rubin 1976.
11. Whyte 1956 and Gans 1962.
12. Goffman 1959.
13. Bluebond-Langer 1980.
14. Stack and Burton 1994.
15. At this writing, I don't know of research that compares parents' relative *satisfaction* with market care versus care offered by kin or friends. Despite the current tendency to romanticize family and community, many middle-class working parents of a four-year-old would prefer an exciting Montessori preschool experience (if only they could afford it) to the care of a crotchety and unimaginative Aunt Matilda. Still, relatives are relatives, and the move to market care is likely to remain a source of some anxiety.
16. As the research of Lynet Uttal has shown, parents and babysitters negotiate many different kinds of deals—some based on the idea that mothers are giving over part of their responsibility to the childcare provider, and some based on the idea that she's sharing it. Many parents, Uttal notes, are changing their definition of childrearing from being a private activity to that of a social activity (1998, p. 575). Uttal is onto something important here. She raises the question: Just how does a parent divide responsibility with a care provider? And quite apart from that, what is the nature of the *bond* between them?
17. See Uttal 1998 and Stack and Burton 1994.

CHAPTER 14. LOVE AND GOLD

This essay also appears in *Global Woman: Nannies, Maids, and Sex Workers in the New Economy,* edited by Barbara Ehrenreich and Arlie Russell Hochschild (New York: Metropolitan Books, 2003), and is used here by permission of the publisher.

1. Information about Rowena Bautista is drawn from Robert Frank, "High-Paying Nanny Positions Puncture Fabric of Family Life in Developing Nations," *Wall Street Journal,* December 18, 2001. All interviews not otherwise attributed were conducted by the author. Also see Hochschild 2000, pp. 32–36. Rhacel Parreñas's discussion of the "globalization of mothering" in her 1999 dissertation first got me thinking about this subject; see also her *Global Servants* (2001). Also see the film *When Mother Comes Home for Christmas,* directed by Nilita Vachani. On the whole, until very recently there has been little focus on a "care drain," even among academics whose work centers on gender. Much writing on globalization focuses on money, markets, and male labor. Much research on women and development, on the other hand, emphasizes the impact of structural adjustments policies (linked to World Bank loans) on the daily lives of women and children. Meanwhile, most research on working women in the United States and Europe concentrates on the picture of a detached, two-person balancing act or the lone "supermom," omitting childcare workers from the picture. Fortunately, in recent years, scholars Evelyn Nakano Glenn, Janet Henshall Momsen, Mary Romero, Grace Chang, and others have produced important research on migrant domestic workers.

2. *New York Times,* September 1, 2001, A8.

3. Greider 1998, p. 21.

4. Castles and Miller 1998, p. 8. See also Zlotnik 1999.

5. Castles and Miller 1998, p. 5.

6. Ibid., p. 9. Also see the Technical Symposium on International Migration and Development, the United Nations General Assembly, Special Session on the International Conference on Population and Development, The Hague, Netherlands, June 29–July 2, 1998, Executive Summary, p. 2. See also *Migrant News,* no. 2 (November 1998): 2.

7. Castles and Miller 1998, p. xi.

8. Hochschild 1997a, pp. xxi, 268.

9. Folbre 2001, p. 55.

10. Parreñas 1999, p. 60.

11. Ibid., pp. 123, 154.

12. Ibid., p. 123.

13. Frank, "High-Paying Nanny Positions."

14. Sau-Ling Wong 1994.

15. Ariès 1962; Hays 1996.

16. Massey 1998, 1999.

CHAPTER 15. EMOTIONAL GEOGRAPHY AND THE FLIGHT PLAN OF CAPITALISM

Originally titled "Emotional Geography versus Social Policy: The Case of Family-Friendly Reforms in the Workplace," this essay was first published in *Gender Relations in Public and Private: New Research Perspectives,* edited by Lydia Morris and E. Stina Lyon (Houdmills, Basingstoke: Macmillan Press, 1996), pp. 13–36, and is reprinted by permission of the publisher.

1. Doohan 1999.

2. See Schwartz 1989.

3. In the nineteenth century, Tamara Hareven (1975, 1982) argues, events were

measured in "family time," according to a family timetable (births, marriages, deaths) and by family units (generations) and oriented to family needs (the need to tend newborns, the dying). Formerly resistant to rationalization, in the last thirty years family life has become increasingly planned and geared to the industrial clock. "Quality time" is demarcated from "quantity time," just as time at the office "working" is designated as separate from time "goofing off around the water cooler." One shouldn't, one feels, be chatting aimlessly in a "quantity" sort of way when one is having "quality" time with a child. Even life-cycle events such as marriages and births are now sometimes planned according to the needs of the office (Martin 1992).

4. Galinsky, Friedman, and Hernandez 1991.

5. Friedman 1991, p. 50.

6. Galinsky, Friedman, and Hernandez 1991, p. 123.

7. Friedman 1991; Galinsky, Friedman, and Hernandez 1991.

8. On the declinist view, see Lasch 1977 and Popenoe 1989; on adaptationist, see Skolnick 1991.

9. Kanter 1977, Zedek et al. 1992.

10. Hofstede 1980, Kanter 1983, Alvesson and Berg 1992, Martin 1992, Trice and Beyer 1993.

11. For exceptions see Van Maanen and Kunda 1989, Bowen and Orthner 1991, Negrey 1993.

12. Giddens 1976.

13. Ibid., pp. 121, 157.

14. But this does not include churchgoing, which does not appear to decline as parents' hours of work increase. See Fischer, Hout, and Latham 2000.

15. Useem 2000, pp. 62–70.

16. Blyton 1985 and Fuchs 1991.

17. Kanter 1977, Lasch 1977.

18. Emlen, Koren, and Grobs 1987; Friedman 1991, p. 16.

19. Galinsky, Bond, and Friedman 1993, pp. 1, 98.

20. Hochschild 1989.

21. Kanter 1989, p. 281.

22. Duncombe and Marsden 1993.

23. Schor 1992.

24. Useem 2000.

25. Ibid. Also see the Introduction to revised edition (2000) of *The Time Bind* (Hochschild 1997a).

26. Putnam 2000.

27. Useem 2000, pp. 63–64.

28. Thanks to Jim Stockinger for a conversation on this point.

29. Putnam 2000.

CHAPTER 16. THE CULTURE OF POLITICS

This chapter was first published in *Social Politics: International Studies in Gender, State, and Society* 2, no. 3 (fall 1995): 331–46, and is reprinted by permission of Oxford University Press. Many thanks to Adam Hochschild, Ann Swidler, and Sonya

Michel for helpful comments and to Laurie Schaffner for excellent research assistance. In addition, the idea of an increasing need and declining supply of care developed from a conversation with Trudie Knijn.

1. Sometimes this is done by directly applying the same image to a new context and sometimes by posing its negative opposite. Government agencies and voluntary organizations, for example, often exhort citizens to give to the needy by picturing a forlorn child alone in a public place, away from a cozy lap.

2. Waerness 1987, pp. 229, 208. See also Holter 1984, Waerness 1984, Sassoon 1987, Ungerson 1990, Knijn 1994, and Tronto 1993.

3. The four models I describe came out in bits and pieces in the interviews with couples described in *The Second Shift* (1989). In that work, I focus on family dynamics, while in this essay I focus on the public fate of these four ideals of care.

4. Abel and Nelson 1990.

5. Ruddick 1989.

6. Hochschild 1983, Smith 1988a.

7. In the developing world, the debt crisis since the 1970s and the rising cost of imports and declining value of exports, in addition to the abiding problems of underdevelopment, have hurt whole populations, but most of the harm passes down to the most vulnerable segments: migrants, refugees, and particularly women and children, among whom rates of sickness and death have risen (Vickers 1991).

8. In Germany, the change in that period was smaller (from 2.1 to 1.4 percent), as was true in France, England, Italy, and Denmark.

9. The proportion of older people has risen in most of Europe. In Sweden, 10 percent of the population was over sixty-five in 1950 and 18 percent in 1990. In Canada and the United States, the gain was smaller (from 8 to about 12 percent). Most other countries had rates of rise in between those two. To some extent, the declining number of children needing care was replaced by a rising number of older people.

10. In Western Europe, the corresponding ratio is about one divorce for every three or four marriages. Japan has had historically low divorce rates, but since 1960 divorce has been rising there too. Divorce statistics also understate the social reality of dissolution, since separations and breakups among cohabiting couples are not counted.

11. Center of Budget and Policy Priorities fact sheet, June 15, 2001 (http://www.cbpp.org/6-15-01wel2.htm).

12. Sorrentino 1990, p. 44. In this period, the Swedish rate rose from 11 to 48 percent. In the Netherlands, the increase was only from 1 to 9 percent, with Italy and Germany in this more modest range. The rate is now highest in the United States, Denmark, Sweden, France, and the United Kingdom.

13. In Sweden, 28 percent of children living with their divorced mothers had no contact with their fathers after the divorce.

14. Arendell 1986, Weitzman 1985.

15. Furstenburg and Cherlin 1991, Wallerstein and Blakeslee 1989.

16. Arendell 1986.

17. Schor 1992; Galinsky, Bond, and Friedman 1993.

18. Hochschild 1989. The study reported in *The Second Shift* was based on in-depth interviews of fifty two-job couples (who have children six years or younger)

and their care providers in the San Francisco Bay Area. I also observed a dozen families in their homes, following workers from home to workplace and back.

19. In European countries such as the Netherlands, immigrant labor may inhibit European women's full participation in the economy, partly predisposing the society to a traditional or quasi-traditional solution (Knijn 1994).

20. Hochschild 1989, p. 231.

21. Grollman and Sweder 1989, p. 14.

22. Ibid., p. 4.

23. Coontz 1992, Stacey 1990.

24. Moen 1989.

25. Wilensky 1964.

26. Abel and Nelson 1990, Sidel 1990.

CHAPTER 17. INSIDE THE CLOCKWORK OF MALE CAREERS

This essay appeared in my typewriter in an atmosphere of great secrecy. It was published in 1975, but I kept mum about it around my department. Sadly, I believe the story it tells is as relevant today as when I wrote it.

This essay was first published in *Women and the Power to Change*, edited by Florence Howe (New York: McGraw-Hill, 1975), and an updated version appeared in *Gender and the Academic Experience: Berkeley Women Sociologists*, edited by Kathryn Meadow Orlans and Ruth Wallace (Lincoln: University of Nebraska Press, 1994), pp. 125–39, from which it is reprinted by permission of the publisher.

1. Ervin-Tripp 1973.

2. Graham 1971.

3. See Rossi and Calderwood 1973, Mitchell 1968, and a publication based on the recent massive survey sponsored by the Carnegie Commission: Feldman 1974. See also Carnegie Commission on Higher Education 1973.

4. Graham 1971.

5. Where did these women go? Several I knew stopped their degrees—trying to find a way to continue—to follow their men where military service, schooling, or work took them, or to have children, or to work while their husbands continued their studies. One woman dropped out of a later class more flamboyantly, writing a notice that stayed for a long time on the blackboard of the graduate student lounge, a reminder to buy her avocado and bean-sprout sandwiches at a small stall on Sproul Hall plaza.

A Decennial Report from the Harvard and Radcliffe College Class of 1963 contained essays about what happened to people since their graduation, many like the following: "We have moved from NYC to the mountains above Boulder . . . a very happy change. Dan is teaching math at Colorado University and I continue slow progress on my dissertation while waiting for another baby in May, and caring for Ben, already very much with us."

6. Astin 1969.

7. Bernard 1966, p. 49.

8. Feldman's data suggest that in those fields where 30 to 50 percent of the students are female—and sociology is among these—40 percent of the males and 50 percent of the females said the professor closest to them viewed them "as a student"

278   NOTES TO PAGES 231-244

or else had no contact with them outside the classroom. Sixty percent of the males and 49 percent of the females said their closest professor viewed them "as a colleague" or "as an apprentice" (recomputed from Feldman 1974, table 33, pp. 92–93).

9. Ibid., p. 71.

10. Sells 1969. There were more (39 percent) single women than men (29 percent), and 43 percent of the single women and 61 percent of single men did not consider dropping out in the last year.

11. Bernard 1966, p. 43.

12. It is often said that feminists lack a sense of humor. Actually it's that, after discovering the joke is on us, we've developed a different one.

13. Papanek 1973.

14. I do not define those women as oppressed who *think* they are or have been. Some are declaratively self-conscious and others not, and they may be variously analytical and insightful about the effects of personal and institutional sexism. On the whole, among older women academics in the 1970s, I think a "Protestant" cultural style of dealing with oppression prevailed, according to which it is unseemly to be long-suffering or indeed to have any problems at all that show. The "Catholic" or "Jewish" cultural styles, according to which it is more legitimate to openly acknowledge pain, were at least at the time more appropriate.

15. In what follows, I focus on the problems for women of the career system, assuming that the virtues of academe make it worth criticizing. Perhaps I need not say that few people love their work as much as professors do, and I, too, can genuinely not imagine a more engrossing and worthwhile life than one devoted to discovering how the world works and inspiring an appreciation for culture and inquiry. But this essay is not about why women should be in the university; it is about why they are not.

16. Kerr 1963.

17. Lehman 1952, 1962, 1965.

18. Not all competition can be explained in these terms, but competition may partly account for why some occupational groups work longer hours than others. For example, among managers, officials, and proprietors, that 27 percent of males in 1970 worked 60 hours or more per week, while only 2 percent of clerical workers worked that hard. Self-employed workers, such as farm managers, worked harder than employees. In large bureaucracies, it tended to be those at or near the top who worked the longest hours—the careerists.

19. Some of the ideas presented here come from reading Dorothy Lee's *Freedom and Culture* (1965), a study of American Indians and a book that forces one to rethink the concept of the individual *versus* society, a favored antagonism of Western sociologists. The Wintu Indians, whom she describes, do not conceptualize a "self" upon which to base a career; the very concept of self does not have a meaning in their tribal configuration, and there is no word in the language corresponding to it.

20. David 1973.

21. According to Carnegie data, 57 percent of men with no children, 58 percent with one, 58 percent with two, and 59 percent with three considered quitting for good in the last year. For women, it was 42 percent with no children, 48 percent with one, 42 percent with two, and 57 percent with three. Three seems to be a crucial

number. Among graduate students nationally between 1958 and 1963, 44 percent of men and 55 percent of women actually did drop out, but 49 percent of men with children and 74 percent of women with children did so (Sells 1969).

Simon, Clark, and Galway (1967) found that married women without children were slightly less likely to have published a book than were women with children. Age was not considered, and of course it might account for this otherwise unexpected finding. Forty percent of unmarried, 47 percent of married/childless, and 37 percent of married mothers were assistant professors; 28 percent, 16 percent, 15 percent were associates; and 18 percent, 8 percent, and 8 percent were full professors (ibid.). Fifty-eight percent of unmarried women, 33 percent of married/childless, and 28 percent of those married with children (among those earning their degrees in 1958–59) had tenure. Another study comparing men and women showed that twenty years after getting their degrees, 90 percent of the men, 53 percent of the single women, and 41 percent of the married women had reached a full professorship (Rossi 1970).

22. Simon, Clark, and Galway 1967.

23. A woman's college that has administered questionnaires each year between 1964 and 1971 to entering freshmen found that 65 percent of the class of 1964 wanted to be housewives with one or more children. In the following years the percentage dropped steadily: 65, 61, 60, 53, 52, 46, and 31. The proportion who wanted career and marriage with children doubled, from 20 to 40 percent between 1964 and 1971 (see Carnegie Commission 1973).

24. Mannheim 1936.

25. How a nation or university "legislates" that supply meets demand for jobs without becoming authoritarian raises not simply an administrative but a serious political issue to which I have no easy answer. Here I only mean to show that dividing up old jobs and creating new ones is a possible way of alleviating competition that underlies the career system.

26. The 1970–71 figures come from the Carnegie Commission on Higher Education 1973, p. 11. Many thanks to Jerry Karabel for the material on Yale, Harvard, and Princeton. The 2002 figures come from the U.S. Department of Education's National Center for Education Statistics website (http://nces.ed.gov).

27. Hal Cohen, "The Baby Bias," *New York Times* "Education Life," August 4, 2002, sec. 4A, p. 25.

BIBLIOGRAPHY

Abel, Emily, and Margery Nelson. 1990. *Circles of Care: Work and Identity in Women's Lives*. Albany: State University of New York Press.

Adams, Margaret. 1985. "The Compassion Trap." In Vivian Gornick and Barbara K. Morgan, eds., *Women in Sexist Society*. New York: Basic Books.

Afshar, Haleh, and Carolyne Dennis, eds. 1991. *Women and Adjustment Policies in the Third World*. London: Macmillan.

Agee, James. 1968 [1957]. *A Death in the Family*. New York: Avon.

Alberoni, Francesco. 1983. *Falling in Love*. New York: Random House.

Allport, Gordon, and H. S. Odbert. 1936. "Trait Names: A Psycho-lexical Study." *Psychological Monographs* 47: 1–171.

Alvesson, Mats, and Per Olof Berg. 1992. *Corporate Culture and Organizational Symbolism: An Overview*. Berlin: Walter de Gruyter.

Anderson, Elijah. 1990. *StreetWise: Race, Class and Change in an Urban Community*. Chicago: University of Chicago Press.

Apthorpe, Raymond J. 1972. "Comments" [on Foster 1972]. *Current Anthropology* 13: 203–4.

Arendell, Terry. 1968. *Mothers and Divorce*. Berkeley: University of California Press.

———. 1986. *Women and Divorce*. Berkeley: University of California Press.

———. 1992. "After Divorce: Investigations into Father Absence." *Gender and Society* 9, no. 4: 562–86.

Ariès, Philippe. 1962. *Centuries of Childhood*. New York: Vintage.

Armstrong, Paul. 1990. *Conflicting Readings: Variety and Validity in Interpretation*. Chapel Hill: University of North Carolina Press.

Arnold, Magda B. 1968. *The Nature of Emotion*. Baltimore: Penguin.

Astin, Helen. 1969. *The Woman Doctorate in America*. New York: Russell Sage Foundation.

Averill, James. 1968. "Grief." *Psychological Bulletin* 70: 721–48.

———. 1976. "Emotion and Anxiety: Sociocultural, Biological, and Psychological Determinants." In M. Zuckerman and C. D. Spielberger, eds., *Emotion and Anxiety: New Concepts, Methods, and Applications*. New York: Wiley, pp. 87–130.

Bailyn, Lotte. 1993. *Breaking the Mold: Women, Men, and Time in the New Corporate World*. New York: Free Press.

Bakan, Abigail, and Daiva Stasiulis, eds. 1997. *Not One of the Family: Foreign Domestic Workers in Canada*. Toronto: University of Toronto Press.

Bales, Kevin. 1999. *Disposable People: New Slavery in the Global Economy*. Berkeley: University of California Press.

Bane, Mary Jo. 1976. *Here to Stay: American Families in the Twentieth Century.* New York: Basic Books.

Baruch, Grace, and Rosalind Barnett. 1988. "Correlates of Fathers' Participation in Family Work: A Technical Report." In Phyllis Bronstein and Carolyn Pope Cowan, eds., *Fatherhood Today: Men's Changing Role in the Family.* New York: Wiley, pp. 66–78.

Bauman, Zygmunt. 1989. *Legislators and Interpreters.* Cambridge, England: Polity.

Beard, Henry. 1981. *Miss Piggy's Guide to Life.* New York: Muppet Press/Alfred A. Knopf.

Bell, Daniel. 1973. *The Coming of Post-Industrial Society.* New York: Basic Books.

Bellah, Robert. 1994. "Understanding Caring in Contemporary America." In Susan S. Phillips and Patricia Benner, eds., *The Crisis of Care: Affirming and Restoring Caring Practices in the Helping Professions.* Washington, D.C.: Georgetown University Press.

Bellah, Robert, Richard Madsen, William Sullivan, Ann Swidler, and Steven M. Tipton. 1985. *Habits of the Heart: Individualism and Commitment in American Life.* Berkeley: University of California Press.

Benedict, Ruth. 1946. *Patterns of Culture.* New York: Penguin.

Beneria, Lourdes, and M. J. Dudley, eds. 1996. *Economic Restructuring in the Americas.* Ithaca: Cornell University Press.

Berkowitz, Leonard. 1962. *Aggression.* New York: McGraw-Hill.

Bernard, Jessie. 1966. *Academic Women.* New York: World.

Bernstein, Basil. 1971. *Class, Codes, and Control.* New York: Schocken.

Billingsley, Andrew. 1993. *Climbing Jacob's Ladder: The Enduring Legacy of African American Families.* New York: Simon and Schuster.

Blau, Peter. 1964. *Exchange and Power in Social Life.* New York: Wiley.

Block, J. 1957. "Studies in the Phenomenology of Emotions." *Journal of Abnormal and Social Psychology* 54: 358–43.

Bluebond-Langer, Myra. 1980. *The Private Worlds of Dying Children.* Princeton: Princeton University Press.

Blum, Alan F., and Peter McHugh. 1971. "The Social Ascription of Motives." *American Sociological Review* 36: 98–109.

Blumer, Herbert. 1969. *Symbolic Interactionism: Perspective and Method.* Englewood Cliffs, N.J.: Prentice-Hall.

Blyton, Paul. 1985. *Changes in Working Time: An International Review.* New York: St Martin's Press.

Bombeck, Erma. 1976. *The Grass Is Always Greener over the Septic Tank.* New York: McGraw-Hill.

———. 1978. *If Life Is a Bowl of Cherries What Am I Doing in the Pits?* New York: Dell.

———. 1979. *Aunt Erma's Cope Book.* New York: Fawcett Crest.

———. 1983. *Motherhood: The Second Oldest Profession.* New York: Dell.

———. 1987. *Family: The Ties that Bind . . . And Gag.* New York: McGraw-Hill.

Boston Women's Health Book Collective. 1978. *Ourselves and Our Children.* New York: Random House.

Bourdieu, Pierre. 1977. *Outline of a Theory of Practice.* Cambridge: Cambridge University Press.

————. 1984. *Distinction: A Social Critique of the Judgment of Taste,* trans. R. Nice. Cambridge: Harvard University Press.

Bourdieu, Pierre, and Loic J. D. Wacquant. 1992. *An Invitation to Reflexive Sociology.* Chicago: University of Chicago Press.

Bowen, Gary L., and Dennis K. Orthner. 1991. "Effects of Organizational Culture on Fatherhood." In F. W. Bozett and S. M. H. Hanson, eds., *Fatherhood and Families in Cultural Context.* New York: Springer.

Bowlby, John. 1969. *Attachment and Loss.* New York: Basic Books.

Briggs, Jean. 1992. "Mazes of Meaning: How a Child and a Culture Create Each Other." In W. A. Corsaro and P. J. Miller, eds., *Interpretive Approaches to Children's Socialization: New Directions for Child Development.* Jossey-Bass Education series No. 58. San Francisco: Jossey-Bass, pp. 25–49.

————. 1998. *Inuit Morality Play: The Emotional Education of a Three-Year-Old.* Cambridge: Harvard University Press.

Brinkgreve, Christien. 1982. "On Modern Relationships: The Commandments of the New Freedom." *Netherlands Journal of Sociology* 18: 47–56.

Brinkgreve, Christien, and M. Korzec. 1979. "Feelings, Behavior, Morals in the Netherlands, 1938–1978: Analysis and Interpretation of an Advice Column." *Netherlands Journal of Sociology* 15: 123–40.

Brochmann, Grete. 1990. *The Middle East Avenue: Female Migration from Sri Lanka: Causes and Consequences.* Report 7, Institute for Social Research, Oslo, Norway.

Brown, Helen Gurley. 1982. *Having It All.* New York: Pocket Books.

Bugental, Daphne, Leonore Love, and Robert Gianetto. 1971. "Perfidious Feminine Faces." *Journal of Personality and Social Psychology* 17: 314–18.

Burke, James H., and Alice Payne Hackett. 1977. *Eighty Years of Best Sellers, 1895–1975.* New York: Bowker.

Campbell, Bebe Moore. 1990. *Sweet Summer: Growing Up with and without My Dad.* New York: HarperCollins.

Campbell, Sarah, ed. 1976. *The Piaget Sampler.* New York: Wiley.

Cancian, Francesca. 1987. *Love in America: Gender and Self-Development.* Cambridge: Cambridge University Press.

Carlson, Anton J., et al. 1959. *Feelings and Emotions: The Mooseheart Symposium.* New York: McGraw-Hill.

Carnegie Commission on Higher Education. 1973. *Opportunities for Women in Higher Education.* New York: McGraw-Hill.

Carrington, Christopher. 1999. *No Place Like Home: Relationships and Family Life among Lesbians and Gay Men.* Chicago: University of Chicago Press.

Castles, Stephen, and Mark Miller. 1998. *The Age of Migration: International Population Movements in the Modern World.* 2d ed. New York: Guilford Press.

Chang, Grace. 2000. *Disposable Domestics.* Cambridge, Mass.: South End Press.

Chant, Sylvia. 1996. *Women-Headed Households: Diversities and Dynamics in the Developing World.* London: Macmillan.

Chant, Sylvia, and Kathy McIlwaine. 1995. *Women of a Lesser Cost: Female Labour, Foreign Exchange, and Philippine Development.* London: Pluto Press.

Chodorow, Nancy. 1978. *The Reproduction of Mothering.* Berkeley: University of California Press.

————. 1990. "Individuality and Difference in How Women and Men Love." In *Feminism and Psychoanalytic Theory*. Berkeley: University of California Press.

————. 1999. *The Power of Feelings: Personal Meanings in Psychoanalysis, Gender, and Culture*. New Haven: Yale University Press.

Clanton, Gordon, and Lynn G. Smith. 1977. *Jealousy*. Englewood Cliffs, N.J.: Prentice-Hall.

Clark, Candace. 1987. "Gender, Status Shields, and Humiliation: The Case of the American Elderly." Paper presented at the Southern Sociological Society, Atlanta, Ga.

————. 1993. "Emotions and Social Bonds." *Social Psychology Quarterly* 56, no. 4: 300–304.

Clemens, Samuel Langhorne. 1962. *Adventures of Huckleberry Finn*. Norton Critical Editions. New York: Norton.

Collins, Randall. 1975. *Conflict Sociology*. New York: Academic Press.

————. 1990. "Stratification, Emotional Energy, and the Transient Emotions." In Theodore D. Kemper, ed., *Research Agendas in the Sociology of Emotions*. Albany: State University of New York Press.

Coolsen, Peter, Michelle Seligson, and James Garbino. 1985. *When School's Out and Nobody's Home*. Chicago: National Committee for the Prevention of Child Abuse.

Coontz, Stephanie. 1992. *The Way We Never Were*. New York: Basic Books.

Cornia, G., R. Jolly, and F. Stewart, eds. 1987. *Adjustment with a Human Face*. Oxford: Clarendon Press.

Corsaro, W. A., and P. J. Miller, eds. 1992. *Interpretive Approaches to Children's Socialization*. San Francisco: Jossey-Bass.

Cosby, Bill. 1987. *Fatherhood*. New York: Berkley Press.

————. 1989. *Love and Marriage*. New York: Bantam Books.

Coser, Rose. 1960. "Laughter among Colleagues." *Psychiatry* 23: 81–95.

Cowan, Connell, and Melvyn Kinder. 1985. *Smart Women, Foolish Choices*. New York: Signet Books.

Cox, Harvey. 2001. "Mammon and the Culture of the Market: A Socio-Theological Critique." In Richard Madsen, William M. Sullivan, Ann Swidler, and Steven M. Tipton, eds., *Meaning and Modernity: Religion, Polity, and Self*. Berkeley: University of California Press, pp. 124–35.

Cross, Gary. 1988. *Work Time and Industrialization: An International History*. Philadelphia: Temple University Press.

Cutright, P. 1986. "Child Support and Responsible Male Procreative Behavior." *Sociological Focus* 19, no. 1: 27–45.

DaCosta, Kim. 1998. "Rationalizing Love with Men, Essentializing Love of Children." M.A. thesis, Sociology Department, University of California, Berkeley.

Darwin, Charles. 1955 [1872]. *The Expression of the Emotions in Men and Animals*. New York: Philosophical Library.

David, Deborah. 1973. "Marriage and Fertility Patterns of Scientists and Engineers: A Comparison of Males and Females." Paper delivered at the American Sociological Association Convention, New York, September.

Davis, Kingsley. 1936. "Jealousy and Sexual Property." *Social Forces* 14: 395–410.

————. 1988. "Wives and Work: A Theory of the Sex Role Revolution and Its Consequences." In Sanford M. Dornbusch and Myra Strober, eds., *Feminism, Children and the New Families*. New York: Guilford Press.

Davitz, Joel. 1969. *The Language of Emotion*. New York: Academic Press.

De Angelis, Barbara. 1990. *Secrets about Men Every Woman Should Know*. New York: Dell.

Derne, Steve. 1994. "Violating the Hindu Norm of Husband-Wife Avoidance." *Journal of Comparative Family Studies* 25, no. 2: 247–67.

———. 1995. *Culture in Action: Family Life, Emotion, and Male Dominance in Banaras India*. Albany: State University of New York Press.

Desai, Prita. 1999. "The Times That Are A-changing." *Indian Journal of Gender Studies* 6, no. 2 (July–December).

Deutsch, M. 1958. "Trust and Suspicion." *Journal of Conflict Resolution* 2: 265–79.

Dizard, Jan, and Howard Gadlin. 1990. *The Minimal Family*. Amherst: University of Massachusetts Press.

Dobson, James C. 1987. *Parenting Isn't for Cowards*. Dallas: Word.

Dodge, Grace, ed. 1892. *Thoughts of Busy Girls*. New York: Cassell.

Dollard, J., et al. 1939. *Frustration and Aggression*. New Haven: Yale University Press.

Doohan, John. 1999. "Working Long, Working Better?" *World of Work: The Magazine of the International Labour Organization*, no 31, September/October.

Dowling, Colette. 1981. *The Cinderella Complex*. New York: Pocket Books.

Drago, Robert, et al. 1999 "New Estimates of Working Time for Teachers." *Monthly Labor Review* 122 (April): 31–41.

Dressler, Paula. 1987. "Patriarchy and Social Welfare Work." *Social Problems* 34, no. 3: 294–308.

Dugger, C. W. 1992. "Establishing Paternity Earlier to Gain Child Support Later." *New York Times*, January 3: A1–B6.

Duncombe, Jean, and Dennis Marsden. 1993., "Workaholics and Whining Women, Theorizing Intimacy and Emotion Work: The Last Frontier of Gender Inequality?" Unpublished paper, Department of Sociology, University of Essex, England.

Durkheim, Emile. 1961. *The Elementary Forms of Religious Life*. New York: Collier.

Ehrenreich, Barbara. 1983. *The Hearts of Men: American Dreams and the Flight from Commitment*. Garden City, N.Y.: Anchor Books.

———. 1986. "Strategies of Corporate Women." *New Republic*, January 27: 28–31.

———. 2001. *Nickel and Dimed: On (Not) Getting By in America*. New York: Metropolitan Books.

Ehrenreich, Barbara, and Deirdre English. 1978. *For Her Own Good: 150 Years of the Experts' Advice to Women*. Garden City, N.Y.: Anchor Press/Doubleday.

Ehrenreich, Barbara, and Arlie Russell Hochschild, eds. 2003. *Global Woman: Nannies, Maids, and Sex Workers in the New Economy*. New York: Metropolitan Books.

Ekman, Paul. 1972. "Universals and Cultural Differences in Facial Expressions of Emotion." In J. K. Cole, ed., *Nebraska Symposium on Motivation 1971*. Lincoln: University of Nebraska Press.

———, ed. 1973. *Darwin and Facial Expression*. New York: Academic Press.

Elias, Norbert. 1978. *The History of Manners*. Vol. 1 of *The Civilizing Process*. New York: Pantheon.

———. 1982. *Power and Civility*. Vol. 2 of *The Civilizing Process*. New York: Pantheon.

————. 1987. "On Human Beings and Their Emotions: A Process-sociological Essay." *Theory, Culture, and Society* 4, nos. 2–3: 339–61.

Elson, D. 1994. "Micro, Meso and Macro: Gender and Economic Analysis in the Context of Policy Reform." In I. Bakker, ed., *The Strategic Silence: Gender and Economic Policy*. London: Zed Books with North-South Institute.

Emlen, Arthur, Paul Koren, and Deana Grobe. 1987. "Dependent Care Survey: Sisters of Providence." Final report, Regional Research Institute for Human Services, Portland State University, Portland, Oregon.

Endo, Shusaku. 1973. *Lazy Man's Guide to Love*. Tokyo: Kodanska.

Engelstad, Fredrik. 1993. "Family Structure and Institutional Interplay." In Annlang Leira, ed., *Family Sociology—Developing the Field*. Oslo: Institut fur Samfunnsforskning.

Erikson, Erik. 1950. *Childhood and Society*. New York: Norton.

Ervin-Tripp, Susan M. 1973. "Report of the Committee on the Status of Women." University of California, Berkeley, May 21.

Evans, Mary. 2002. *Love: An Unromantic Discussion*. London: Polity.

Featherstone, Mike. 1988. "In Pursuit of the Postmodern: An Introduction." *Theory, Culture, & Society* 5: 195–215.

————. 1989. "Towards a Sociology of Postmodern Culture." In Hans Haferkamp, ed., *Social Structure and Culture*. Berlin: Walter de Gruyter. Reprinted 1991 in M. Featherstone, *Consumer Culture and Postmodernism*. London: Sage.

Feber, Marianne, and Julie Nelson, eds. 1993. *Beyond Economic Man: Feminist Theory and Economics*. Chicago: University of Chicago Press.

Feldman, Saul. 1974. *Escape from the Doll's House: Women in Graduate and Professional School Education*. New York: McGraw-Hill.

Finch, Janet, and Dulcie Groves, eds. 1983. *A Labour of Love: Women, Work, and Caring*. London: Routledge and Kegan Paul.

Fine, Gary, and K. L. Sandstrom. 1988. *Knowing Children: Participant Observation with Minors*. London: Sage.

Fineman, Steven, ed. 1993. *Emotion in Organizations*. London: Sage.

Fischer, Claude, Michael Hout, and Nancy Latham. 2000. "The Time Bind and God's Time." Working paper, Center for Working Families, University of California at Berkeley, July.

Folbre, Nancy. 2001. *The Invisible Heart: Economics and Family Values*. New York: New Press.

Forest, James J. 1988. "Self-Help Books." *American Psychologist* 43, no. 7: 599.

Forward, Susan, and Joan Torres. 1987. *Men Who Hate Women and the Women Who Love Them*. New York: Bantam Books.

Foster, George M. 1972. "The Anatomy of Envy: A Study in Symbolic Behavior." *Current Anthropology* 13: 165–202.

Franklin, Benjamin. 1938–40. "Necessary Hints to Those Who Would Be Rich." In Jared Sparks, ed., *The Works of Benjamin Franklin: Containing Several Political and Historical Tracts Not Included in Any Former Edition and Many Letters, Official and Private Not Hitherto Published*. Boston: Hillard Gray (orig. 1736).

Franks, David, and Doyle McCarthy, eds. 1989. *Original Papers in the Sociology of Emotions*. New York: JAI Press.

Freud, Anna. 1984 [1936]. *The Ego and the Mechanisms of Defense.* Madison, Conn.: International Universities Press.

Freud, Sigmund. 1911. "Formulations regarding the Two Principles in Mental Function." *Collected Papers,* vol. 4. New York: Basic Books.

———. 1915a. "Repression." *Standard Edition,* vol. 14. London: Hogarth Press.

———. 1915b. "The Unconscious." *Standard Edition,* vol. 14. London: Hogarth Press.

Friday, Nancy. 1977. *My Mother, My Self.* New York: Dell.

Friedman, Dana. 1991. "Linking Work-Family Issues to the Bottom Line." New York: Conference Board.

Friedman, Sonya. 1985. *Smart Cookies Don't Crumble: A Modern Woman's Guide to Living and Loving Her Own Life.* New York: Pocket Books.

Frijda, Nico. 1988. "The Laws of Emotion." *American Psychologist* 43, no. 5: 349–58.

Fromm, Erich. 1942. *Escape from Freedom.* New York: Farrar and Rinehart.

———. 1956. *The Art of Loving.* New York: Harper.

Fuchs, Victor R. 1991. "Are Americans Under-Investing in Their Children?" *Society* 28, no. 6: 14–25.

Furstenberg, F., Jr. 1991. "Daddies and Fathers: Men Who Do for Their Children and Men Who Don't." Unpublished paper, Sociology Department, University of Pennsylvania.

Furstenberg, F., Jr., et al. 1983. "The Life Course of Children of Divorce: Marital Disruption and Parental Contact." *American Sociological Review* 48: 656–68.

Furstenburg, Frank, and Andrew Cherlin. 1991. *Divided Families: What Happens to Children When Parents Part.* Cambridge: Harvard University Press.

Galinsky, Ellen, James Bond, and Dana Friedman. 1993. *The Changing Workforce: Highlights of the National Study.* New York: Families and Work Institute.

Galinsky, Ellen, Dana F. Friedman, and Carol A. Hernandez. 1991. *The Corporate Reference Guide to Work/Family Programs.* New York: Families and Work Institute.

Gans, Herbert. 1962. *The Urban Villagers: Group and Class in the Life of Italian Americans.* New York: Free Press.

Geertz, Clifford. 1964. "Ideology as a Cultural System." In Clifford Geertz, *The Interpretation of Cultures.* London: Hutchinson.

Geertz, H. 1959. "The Vocabulary of Emotion." *Psychiatry* 22: 225–37.

Gergen, Kenneth J. 1994. *Realities and Relationships: Soundings in Social Construction.* Cambridge: Harvard University Press.

Gerson, K. 1993. *No Man's Land: Men's Changing Commitments to Family.* New York: Basic Books.

Gerth, Hans, and C. Wright Mills. 1964. *Character and Social Structure: The Psychology of Social Institutions.* New York: Harcourt, Brace and World.

Gibson, J. J. 1975. "Events Are Perceivable but Time Is Not." In J. E. Fraser, N. Lawrence, and D. Park, eds., *The Study of Time II: Proceedings of the Second Conference of the International Society for the Study of Time.* Lake Yamanaka, Japan.

Giddens, Anthony. 1976., *New Rules of Sociological Method.* New York: Basic Books.

———. 1981. *A Contemporary Critique of Historical Materialism,* Vol. 1. Berkeley: University of California Press.

———. 1991. *Modernity and Self-Identity.* Stanford: Stanford University Press.

Gillis, John R. 1994 "What's behind the Debate on Family Values?" Plenary Session,

Section on Sociology of Family, American Sociological Association, Chicago, August.

————. 1996a. "Making Time for Family: The Invention of Family Time(s) and the Re-Invention of Family History." *Journal of Family History* 21, no. 1: 4–21.

————. 1996b. *A World of Their Own Making: Myth, Ritual, and the Quest for Family Values*. New York: Basic Books.

Gilman, Charlotte. 1899. *Women and Economics*. Boston: Small, Maynard.

Gitlin, Todd. 1989. "Postmodern Culture." *Dissent* (Winter): 100–108.

Gladwin, C. H., ed. 1991. *Structural Adjustment and African Women Farmers*. Gainesville: University of Florida Press.

Glenn, Evelyn Nakano. 1992. "From Servitude to Service Work: The Historical Continuities of Women's Paid and Unpaid Reproductive Labour." *Signs* 18, no. 1: 1–44.

Glenn, Evelyn Nakano, Grace Chang, and Linda Forcey, eds. 1994. *Mothering Ideology: Experience and Agency*. New York: Routledge.

Goffman, Erving. 1956. "Embarrassment and Social Organization." *American Journal of Sociology* 62 (November): 264–71.

————. 1959. *The Presentation of Self in Everyday Life*. New York: Doubleday Anchor.

————. 1961. "Fun in Games." In Goffman, *Encounters*. Indianapolis: Bobbs-Merrill.

————. 1967. *Interaction Ritual*. Garden City, N.Y.: Doubleday.

————. 1969. *Strategic Interaction*. Philadelphia: University of Pennsylvania Press.

————. 1974. *Frame Analysis: An Essay on the Organization of Experience*. New York: Harper and Row. Reprint, Boston: Northeastern University Press, 1997.

————. 1976. *Gender Advertisements*. Society for the Anthropology of Visual Communication 3, no. 2: 65–154. Reprint, Cambridge, Mass.: Harvard University Press, 1979.

————. 1977. "The Arrangement between the Sexes," *Theory and Society* 4: 301–31.

————. 1979. "Footing." *Semiotica* 25, nos. 1–2: 1–29.

Goldscheider, F. K., and L. J Waite. 1991. *New Families, No Families? The Transformation of the American Home*. Berkeley: University of California Press.

Goode, William. 1970 [1963]. *World Revolution and Family Patterns*. New York: Free Press.

————. 1974. "The Theoretical Importance of Love." In Rose Coser, ed., *The Family, Its Structure and Functions*. New York: St. Martin's, pp. 143–56.

Gordon, Steven. 1981. "The Sociology of Sentiments and Emotion." In Morris Rosenberg and Ralph Turner, eds., *Social Psychology, Social Perspectives*. New York: Basic Books.

————. 1985. "Micro-Sociological Theories of Emotions." *Micro-Social Theory Perspectives on Sociological Theory* 2: 113–47. London: Sage.

————. 1991. "The Socialization of Children's Emotions: Emotional Culture, Competence and Exposure." In Carolyn Saarni and Paul Harris, eds., *Children's Understanding of Emotions*. Cambridge Studies in Social and Emotional Development. New York: Cambridge University Press.

Gorer, G. 1964. *The American People*. New York: Norton.

Graham, Patricia A. 1971. "Women in Academe." In Athena Theodore, ed., *The Professional Woman*. Cambridge, Mass.: Schenkman.

Grant, Toni. 1988. *Being a Woman*. New York: Random House.

Gray, Francine du Plessix. 1990. *Soviet Women: Walking the Tightrope.* New York: Doubleday.

Gray, John. 1992. *Men Are from Mars, Women Are from Venus.* New York: HarperCollins.

Greer, Germaine. 1971. *The Female Eunuch.* New York: McGraw-Hill.

Greider, William. 1998. *One World Ready or Not.* New York: Simon and Schuster.

Greven, Philip. 1972. *Four Generations: Population, Land, and Family in Colonial Andover, Massachusetts.* Ithaca, N.Y.: Cornell University Press.

Griswold, Wendy. 1987. "A Methodological Framework for the Sociology of Culture." *Sociological Methodology* 17: 1–35.

Grollman, Earl A., and Gerry L. Sweder. 1989. *Teaching Your Child to Be Home Alone.* New York: Lexington Books.

Gross, F., and G. Stone. 1964. "Embarrassment and the Analysis of Role Requirements." *American Journal of Sociology* 80: 1–15.

Gulati, Leela. 1999. "The Tyranny of Tradition." *Indian Journal of Gender Studies* 6, no. 2 (July–December).

Gurr, T., and C. Ruttenberg. 1967. "The Conditions of Civil Violence." Princeton: Center of International Studies, Princeton University.

Haavio-Mannila, Elina. 1988. "Cross-Gender Relationships at Work and Home over the Family Life Cycle." In Suzanne K. Steinmetz, ed., *Family and Support Systems across the Life Span.* New York: Plenum Press.

———. 1998. "Emotional Relations at Work." *Finnish Work Research Bulletin* 2b: 12–15.

———. 1992. *Work, Family, and Well Being in Five North and East European Capitals.* Helsinki: Suomalainen Tiedeakatemia, Sraj B, 255.

Hacket, Alice Payne. 1966. *Seventy Years of Best-Sellers, 1895–1965.* New York: Bowker.

Hackstaff, Karla. 1994. "Divorce Culture: A Breach of Gender Relations." Diss., Sociology Department, University of California, Berkeley.

Hall, Stuart, Doreen Massey, and Michael Rustin, eds. 1999. "Emotional Labour." *Soundings: A Journal of Politics and Culture* 11.

Hamao, Minoru. 1972. *How to Discipline Girls: To Bring Them Up Docile and Feminine.* Tokyo: Koubunsha Kappa Homes. (In Japanese.)

Hareven, Tamara. 1975. "Family Time and Industrial Time: Family and Work in a Planned Corporation Town, 1900–1924." *Journal of Urban History* 1: 365–89.

———. 1982. *Family Time and Industrial Time: The Relationship between Family and Work in a New England Industrial Community.* New York: Cambridge University Press.

Harrington, C. Lee, and Denise D. Bielby. 1991. "The Mythology of Modern Love: Representations of Romance in the 1980's." *Journal of Popular Culture* 24, no. 4: 129–43.

Harris, Marvin. 1977. *Cannibals and Kings: The Origins of Culture.* New York: Random House.

Hays, Sharon. 1996. *The Cultural Contradictions of Motherhood.* New Haven: Yale University Press.

Henry, O. 1961. "The Gift of the Magi." In Eugene Current-Garcia and Walton R. Patrick, eds., *What Is the Short Story?* Glenview, Ill.: Scott, Foresman.

Hertz, R. 1986. *More Equal than Others: Women and Men in Dual Career Marriages.* Berkeley: University of California Press.

Hetherington, E. Mavis. 2002. *For Better or For Worse: Divorce Reconsidered.* New York: Norton.

Hewlett, Sylvia Ann. 1991. *When the Bough Breaks: The Cost of Neglecting Our Children.* New York: Basic Books.

Hillman, James. 1964. *Emotion: A Comprehensive Phenomenology of Theories and Their Meanings for Therapy.* Evanston: Northwestern University Press.

Hinrichs, Karl, William Roche, and Carmen Sirianni, eds. 1991. *Working Time in Transition: The Political Economy of Working Hours in Industrial Nations.* Philadelphia: Temple University Press.

Hirose, Kumiko. 1985. *Women's Capacity Depends on Language.* Tokyo: Lyonsha. (In Japanese.)

Hirschorn, Larry. 1987. "Organizing Feelings toward Authority: Two Case Studies of Work Groups." Wharton Center for Applied Research, Philadelphia.

Hite, Shere. 1987. *Women and Love: A Cultural Revolution in Progress.* New York: Knopf.

Hochschild, Arlie Russell. 1973. *The Unexpected Community.* Englewood Cliffs, N.J.: Prentice-Hall.

———. 1977. "Reply to Scheff." *Current Anthropology* 18, no. 3 (September): 494–95.

———. 1983. *The Managed Heart: Commercialization of Human Feeling.* Berkeley: University of California Press. Reprint, with new afterword, Berkeley: University of California Press, 2003.

———. 1986. "The Totalled Woman." *New York Times Book Review,* May 11.

———. 1987. "Why Can't a Man Love Like a Woman?" Review of Shere Hite's *Women and Love. New York Times Book Review,* November 15.

———. 1989. *The Second Shift: Working Parents and the Revolution at Home.* New York: Viking.

———. 1996. "Emotional Geography versus Social Policy: The Case of Family-Friendly Reforms in the Workplace." In Lydia Morris and E. Stina Lyon, eds., *Gender Relations in Public and Private: Changing Research Perspectives.* London: Palgrave/Macmillan.

———. 1997a. *The Time Bind: When Work Becomes Home and Home Becomes Work.* New York: Metropolitan Books. Revised edition, with new introduction, New York: Holt, 2000.

———. 1997b. "Why Can't a Man Be More Like a Woman?" *New York Times Book Review,* November 15.

———. 2000. "The Nanny Chain." *American Prospect,* January 3: 32–36.

———. 2002. "Why We Need Dreams." *Swarthmore Bulletin* (Fall): 80–81.

Hofstede, Geertz. 1980. *Culture's Consequences: International Differences in Work-Related Values.* London: Sage.

Holter, Harriet, ed. 1984. *Patriarchy in a Welfare Society.* Oslo: Norwegian University Press.

Hondagneu-Sotelo, Pierrette, and Ernestine Avila. 1997. "'I'm Here, but I'm There': The Meanings of Latina Transnational Motherhood." *Gender and Society* 11, no. 5 (October): 548–71.

Hood, Jane. 1983. *Becoming a Two-Job Family.* New York: Praeger.

Horney, Karen. 1937. *The Neurotic Personality of Our Time.* New York: Norton.

Huber, Joan, and Glenna Spitze. 1983. *Sex Stratification: Children, Housework, and Jobs.* New York: Academic Press.

Huizinga, J. 1970. *The Waning of the Middle Ages.* London: Arnold.

James, Henry. 1879. *What Maisie Knew.* Chicago: H. S. Stone.

James, William, and Carl B. Lange. 1922. *The Emotions.* Baltimore: Williams and Wilkins.

Johnson, Colleen Leahy. 1988. *Ex Familia: Grandparents, Parents, and Children Adjust to Divorce.* New Brunswick: Rutgers University Press.

Jones, L. E., et al. 1972. *Attribution.* Morristown, N.J.: General Learning Press.

Kaminer, Wendy. 1992. *I'm Dysfunctional You're Dysfunctional.* Reading, Mass.: Addison-Wesley.

Kanter, Rosabeth. 1977. *Work and Family in the United States: A Critical Review and Agenda for Research and Policy.* New York: Russell Sage Foundation.

———. 1983. *The Change Masters.* New York: Simon and Schuster.

———. 1993. *Men and Women of the Corporation.* New York: Basic Books.

Katz, Judith. 1977. "Discrepancy, Arousal, and Labelling: Towards a Psycho-Social Theory of Emotion." Mimeographed. Toronto, York University.

Kayama, Uzo. 1981. *This Love Forever: Yakadaisho's Diary of Childrearing.* Tokyo: Kobunsha. (In Japanese.)

Kemper, Theodore. 1978a. *A Social Interactional Theory of Emotions.* New York: Wiley.

———. 1978b. "Toward a Sociological Theory of Emotion: Some Problems and Some Solutions." *American Sociologist* 13 (February): 30–41.

———. 1981. "Social Constructionist and Positivist Approaches to the Sociology of Emotions." *American Journal of Sociology* 87: 337–62.

———, ed. 1989. *Recent Advances in the Sociology of Emotions.* Albany: State University of New York Press.

Kemper, Theodore, and Arnold Birnbaum. 1988. "Sine Ira Ac Studio? Emotional Nexi in Weber's Ideal-Typical Conception of Organizations." Paper delivered at the American Sociological Association Meetings, Atlanta, August.

Kephart, William. 1967. "Some Correlates of Romantic Love." *Journal of Marriage and the Family* 29: 470–74.

Kerr, Clark. 1963. *The Uses of the University.* Cambridge: Harvard University Press.

Kimball, Gayle. 1983. *The 50–50 Marriage.* Boston: Beacon Press.

Klatzky, Sheila, and Marcel Teitler. 1973. "On Trust." Working Paper 73–79, presented at the annual meeting of the American Sociological Association, Washington, D.C., August.

Knijn, Trudy. 1994. "Fish without Bikes: Revisions of the Dutch Welfare State and Its Consequences for the (In)dependence of Single Mothers." *Social Politics* 1: 83–105.

Kohn, Melvin. 1963. "Social Class and the Exercise of Parental Authority." In Neil Smelser and William Smelser, eds., *Personality and Social Systems.* New York: Wiley.

———. 1969. *Class and Conformity.* Homewood, Ill.: Dorsey.

Kohut, Heinz. 1971. *The Analysis of the Self.* New York: International Universities Press.

Kriegel, Leonard. 1972. *Working Through.* New York: Saturday Review Press.

Kuttner, Robert. 1997. *Everything for Sale: The Virtues and Limits of Markets.* New York: Alfred A. Knopf.

Laing, R. D. 1969. *The Politics of the Family*. Toronto: Canadian Broadcasting Corporation.

Lakoff, George. 1980. *Metaphors We Live By*. Chicago: University of Chicago Press.

Lamb, Michael E., ed. 1986. *The Father's Role: Applied Perspectives*. New York: John Wiley.

Lamphere, L., et al. 1993. *Sunbelt Working Mothers*. Ithaca: Cornell University Press.

Lareau, Annette. 1998a. "Class and Race Differences in Children's Worlds." Presented at the Eastern Sociological Society annual meetings, Philadelphia, March.

———. 1998b. "Embedding Capital in a Broader Context: The Case of Family-School Relationships." In Bruce Biddle and Peter Hall, eds., *Social Class, Poverty, and Education*. New York: Garland Press.

Lareau, Annette, and E. M. Horvat. 1999. "Moments of Social Inclusion: Race, Class, and Cultural Capital in Family-School Relationships." *Sociology of Education* 72: 37–53.

Lasch, Christopher. 1977. *Haven in a Heartless World*. New York: Basic Books.

———. 1979. *The Culture of Narcissism*. New York: Norton.

Lazarus, Richard S. 1966. *Psychological Stress and the Coping Process*. New York: McGraw-Hill.

Lazarus, Richard S., and James R. Averill. 1972. "Emotion and Cognition: With Special Reference to Anxiety." In D. C. Spielberger, ed., *Anxiety: Current Trends in Theory and Research*, vol 2. New York: Academic Press.

Lazarus, Richard S., Allen D. Kanner, and Susan Folkman. 1979. "Emotions: A Cognitive-phenomenological Analysis." In R. Plutchik and H. Kellerman, eds., *Theories of Emotion*. New York: Academic Press.

Lazarus, R. S., A. D. Kanner, and S. Folkman. 1980. "Emotions: A Cognitive Phenomenological Analysis." In R. Plutchik and H. Kellerman, eds., *Emotion: Theory, Research, and Experience*. New York: Academic Press.

Lear, Jonathan, 1990. *Love and Its Place in Nature: A Philosophical Interpretation of Freudian Psychoanalysis*. New York, Farrar, Straus and Giroux.

Lee, Dorothy. 1965. *Freedom and Culture*. Englewood Cliffs, N.J.: Prentice-Hall.

Lehman, H. 1952. *Age and Achievement*. Princeton: Princeton University Press.

———. 1962. "More about Age and Achievement." *The Gerontologist* 2, no. 3: 141–48.

———. 1965. "The Production of Masterworks Prior to Age Thirty." *The Gerontologist* 5, no. 1: 24–29

Lerner, Harriet Goldhor. 1985. *Dance of Anger*. New York: Harper and Row.

Levine, J. A., et al. 1993. *Getting Men Involved: Strategies for Early Childhood Programs*. New York: Scholastic Inc., Early Childhood Division.

Levinger, G. K., with O. C. Moles. 1979. *Divorce and Separation: Context, Causes, Consequences*. New York: Basic Books.

Levy, Robert I. 1973. *Tahitians, Mind, and Experience in the Society Islands*. Chicago: University of Chicago Press.

Lewis, C. S. 1959. *The Allegory of Love*. New York: Oxford University Press.

Loden, Marilyn. 1985. *Feminine Leadership, or How to Succeed without Being One of the Boys*. New York: Times Books.

Lofgren, L. Borge. 1968. "Psychoanalytic Theory of Affects." *Journal of the American Psychoanalytic Association* 16 (July): 638–50.

Lofting, Hugh. 1968. *Dr. Dolittle and the Pirates*. New York: Beginner Books, Random House.

Long, Elizabeth. 1986. "Women, Reading, and Cultural Authority: Some Implications of the Audience Perspective in Cultural Studies." *American Quarterly* (Fall): 591–611.

Luhmann, Niklas. 1986. *Love as Passion: The Codification of Intimacy*. Cambridge: Harvard University Press.

Lyman, Stanford, and Marvin Scott. 1970. *Sociology of the Absurd*. New York: Appleton-Century-Crofts.

MacCannell, Dean, and Juliet Flower MacCannell. 1987. "The Beauty System." In Nancy Armstrong and Leonard Tennenhouse, eds., *The Ideology of Conduct*. New York: Methuen, pp. 206–36.

Macdonald, Cameron Lynne. 1998. "Manufacturing Motherhood: The Shadow Work of Nannies and Au Pairs." *Qualitative Sociology* 21, no. 1: 25–53.

Mahler, Margaret S. 1968. *On Human Symbiosis and the Vicissitudes of Individuation*. New York: International Universities Press.

Majumdar, Vina. 1999. "Women in Three Generations." *Indian Journal of Gender Studies* 6, no. 2 (July–December).

Malinowski, B. 1927. *Sex and Repression in Savage Society*. New York: Harcourt, Brace.

———. 1930. "The Principle of Legitimacy." In V. F. Calverton and S. D. Schmalhausen, eds., *The New Generation*. New York: Macauley.

Mannheim, Karl. 1936. *Ideology and Utopia: An Introduction to the Sociology of Knowledge*, trans. L. Wirth and E. Shils. London: Harcourt, Brace.

Marcuse, H. 1955. *Eros and Civilization*. New York: Vintage.

Martin, Joanne. 1992. *Cultures in Organizations: Three Perspectives*. New York: Oxford University Press.

Martin, Judith. 1984. *Miss Manners' Guide to Rearing Perfect Children*. New York: Atheneum.

Massey, Douglas S. 1998. "March of Folly: US Immigration. Policy after NAFTA." *American Prospect* (March–April): 22–33.

———. 1999. "The Dynamics of Mass Migration." *Proceedings of the National Academy of Sciences of the United States* 66, no. 9: 5328–36.

Mauss, Marcel. 1967. *The Gift: Forms and Functions of Exchange in Archaic Societies*. New York: Norton.

Mayall, Barry, ed. 1994. *Children's Childhoods: Observed and Experienced*. London: Falmer.

McCarthy, Eugene, and William McGaughey. 1981. *Nonfinancial Economics: The Case for Shorter Hours of Work*. New York: Praeger.

McDougall, W. 1937. "Organization of the Affective Life: A Critical Survey." *Acta Psychologica* 2: 233–46.

———. 1948. *An Outline of Psychology*. 12th ed. London: Methuen.

McLanahan, Sara, and Gary Sandefur. 1994. *Growing Up with a Single Parent*. Cambridge: Harvard University Press.

Mead, George Herbert. 1934. *Mind, Self and Society*, ed. Charles Morris. Chicago: University of Chicago Press.

Mead, Margaret. 1949. *Male and Female*. New York: Morrow.

Memmi, Albert. 1991 [1965]. *The Colonizer and the Colonized*. Boston: Beacon.

Merleau-Ponty, Maurice. 1964. *The Primacy of Perception, and Other Essays on Phenomenological Psychology, the Philosophy of Art, History, and Politics,* ed. James M. Edie. Evanston, Ill.: Northwestern University Press.

Mies, Maria. 1982. *The Lacemakers of Narsapur: Indian Housewives Produce for the World Market.* Westport, Conn.: Lawrence Hill.

Miki, Tokuchika. 1973. *Art of Childrearing.* Tokyo: Kodansha. (In Japanese.)

————. 1974. *Woman's Expression.* Tokyo: Shodensha. (In Japanese.)

Mills, C. Wright. 1963. *Power, Politics and People.* London: Oxford University Press.

Mills, Trudy, and Sherryl Kleinman. 1988. "Emotions, Reflexivity and Action: An Interactionist Analysis." *Social Forces* 66: 1009–27.

Mintz, Steven, and Susan Kellogg. 1988. *Domestic Revolutions: A Social History of American Family Life.* New York: Free Press.

Mitchell, Charlene. 1985. *The Right Moves: Succeeding in a Man's World without a Harvard MBA.* New York: Macmillan.

Mitchell, Susan. 1968. *Woman and the Doctorate.* Washington, D.C.: U.S. Department of Health, Education, and Welfare, Office of Education, Bureau of Research.

Mizuno, Hajime. 1978. *How to Grow Old Together,* vols. 1 and 2. Tokyo: Kodansha. (In Japanese.)

Modigliani, A. 1968. "Embarrassment and Embarrassability." *Sociometry* 31: 313–26.

Moen, Phyllis. 1989. *Working Parents: Transformations in Gender Roles and Public Policies in Sweden.* Madison: University of Wisconsin Press.

Moller, Herbert. 1958. "The Social Causation of the Courtly Love Complex." *International Quarterly* 1: 137–63.

Molloy, John T. 1977. *The Woman's Dress for Success Book.* New York: Warner Books.

Morgan, Edmund. 1944. *The Puritan Family: Religious and Domestic Relations in 17th-Century New England.* New York: Harper and Row.

Morgan, Marabel. 1973. *The Total Woman.* Boston: G. K. Hall.

Morrison, Toni. 1994. *The Bluest Eye.* New York: Plume Books.

Negrey, Cynthia. 1993. *Gender, Time, and Reduced Work.* Albany, N.Y.: SUNY Press.

Norwood, Robin. 1985. *Women Who Love Too Much.* New York: Pocket Books.

Ogburn, William. 1932. *Social Change.* New York: Viking Press.

O'Neill, Nena, and George O'Neill. 1972. *Open Marriage.* New York: Avon Press.

Ortiz, Steven M. 1988a. "Game Face: Emotion and Display Work of the Male Athlete." Unpublished manuscript, Department of Sociology, University of California, Berkeley.

————. 1988b. "Emotional Life of the Athlete's Wife." Paper given at the Pacific Sociological Association, Las Vegas, Nevada, April 5–8.

Owen, John. 1989. *Reduced Working Hours: Cure for Unemployment or Economic Burden?* Baltimore: Johns Hopkins University Press.

Panda, Pradeep Kumar. 1997. "Gender and Structural Adjustment: Exploring the Connections." Unpublished paper, Center for Development Studies, Thiruvananthapuram, Kerala, India.

Papanek, Hanna. 1973. "Men, Women, and Work: Reflections on the Two-Person Career." In Joan Huber, ed., *Changing Women in a Changing Society.* Chicago: University of Chicago Press.

————. 1974. "Changes in the Status of Women and Their Significance in the Process of Social Change: Indonesian Case Studies." Paper presented to the Sixth

International Conference on Asian History, International Association of Historians of Asia, Yogyakarta.

Parreñas, Rhacel Salazar. 1998. "The Global Servants: (Im)Migrant Filipina Domestic Workers in Rome and Los Angeles." Diss., Department of Ethnic Studies, University of California, Berkeley.

—————.2001. *The Global Servants: Migrant Filipina Domestic Workers in Rome and Los Angeles.* Stanford: Stanford University Press.

Parsons, T. 1968. "On the Concept of Value-Commitments." *Sociological Inquiry* 38: 135–60.

Peterson, J., and N. Zill. 1986. "Marital Disruption, Parent-Child Relationships, and Behavior Problems in Children." *Journal of Marriage and the Family* 48: 295–307.

Pierce, Jennifer. 1988. "Gender and Emotional Labor: An Examination of Women and Men at Work in a Corporate Law Firm." Diss. prospectus, Sociology Department, University of California, Berkeley.

Pleck, Joseph. 1982. "Husbands' and Wives' Family Work: Paid Work and Adjustment." Working Paper 95. Wellesley, Mass.: Wellesley College Center for Research on Women.

—————. 1983. "Husbands' Paid Work and Family Roles: Current Research Issues." In H. Lopata and J. H. Pleck, eds., *Research in the Interweave of Social Roles,* vol. 3: *Families and Jobs.* Greenwich, Conn.: JAI Press.

—————. 1985. *Working Wives, Working Husbands.* Beverly Hills, Calif.: Sage.

Plutchik, Robert. 1962. *The Emotions: Facts, Theories, and a New Model.* New York: Random House.

Polatnick, Margaret. 1974. "Why Men Don't Rear Children: A Power Analysis." *Berkeley Journal of Sociology* 18: 45–86.

Popenoe, David. 1989. *Disturbing the Nest: Family Change and Decline in Modern Societies.* Aldine De Gruyter.

Potter, Patricia. 1988. "'I Killed 'Em:' Comedians' Emotional Labor." Paper presented at the American Sociological Association, Atlanta, August.

Putnam, Robert D. 2000. *Bowling Alone: The Collapse and Revival of American Community.* New York: Simon and Schuster.

Rabin, Susan. 1993. *How to Attract Anyone, Anytime, Anyplace.* New York: Plume.

Rabkin, Richard. 1968. "Affect as a Social Process." *American Journal of Psychiatry* 125 (December): 772–79.

Radway, Janice. 1984. *Reading the Romance: Women, Patriarchy, and Popular Literature.* Chapel Hill: University of North Carolina Press.

Rapaport, D. 1942. *Emotions and Memory.* Baltimore: Williams and Wilkins.

—————. 1953. "On the Psychoanalytic Theory of Affects." *International Journal of Psycho-Analysis* 34: 177–98.

Reymert, Martin, ed. 1950. *Feelings and Emotions: The Mooseheart Symposium.* New York: McGraw-Hill.

Riesman, David. 1952. *Faces in the Crowd: Individual Studies in Character and Politics.* New Haven: Yale University Press.

—————. 1960. *The Lonely Crowd: A Study of the Changing American Character.* New Haven: Yale University Press.

Rodin, N., and A. Russell. 1982. "Increased Father Participation and Child Development Outcomes." In M. E. Lamb, ed., *Nontraditional Families: Parenting and Child Development.* Hillsdale, N.J.: Erlbaum.

Rollins, Judith. 1985. *Between Women: Domestics and Their Employers.* Philadelphia: Temple University Press.

Romero, Mary. 1997. "Life as the Maid's Daughter: An Exploration of the Everyday Boundaries of Race, Class, and Gender." In Mary Romero, Pierrette Hondagneu-Sotelo, and Vima Ortiz, eds., *Challenging Fronteras: Structuring Latina and Latino Lives in the U.S.* New York: Routledge.

Rossi, Alice S. 1970. "Status of Women in Graduate Departments of Sociology." *American Sociologist* 5 (February): 1–12.

Rossi, Alice S., and Ann Calderwood, eds. 1973. *Academic Women on the Move.* New York: Russell Sage Foundation.

Rubin, Lillian B. 1976. *Worlds of Pain: Life in the Working-Class Family.* New York: Basic Books.

Rubin, Z. 1973. *Liking and Loving.* New York: Holt, Rinehart, and Winston.

Ruddick, Sara. 1989. *Maternal Thinking: Toward a Politics of Peace.* Boston: Beacon Press.

Sachs, A. 1994. "Men, Sex, and Parenthood in an Overpopulating World." *World Watch* 7, no. 1: 12–19.

Sachs, Wolfgang. 1999. *The Development Dictionary.* London: Zed Books.

Saimon, Fumi. 1990. *The Art of Loving.* Tokyo: Kenkyujo. (In Japanese.)

Sartre, J. P. 1948. *The Emotions.* New York: Philosophical Library.

Sassen, Saskia. 1988. *The Mobility of Labor and Capital: A Study in International Investment and Labor.* New York: Cambridge University Press.

———. 2003. "Global Cities and Circuits of Survival." In Barbara Ehrenreich and Arlie Russell Hochschild, eds., *Global Woman: Nannies, Maids, and Sex Workers in the New Economy.* New York: Metropolitan Books.

Sassoon, Anne Showstack, ed. 1987. *Women and the State.* London: Hutchinson.

Schachter, Stanley. 1964. "The Interaction of Cognitive and Physiological Determinants of Emotion States." In P. H. Leiderman and D. Shapiro, eds., *Psychological Approaches to Social Behavior.* Stanford: Stanford University Press.

Schachter, S., and J. Singer. 1962. "Cognitive, Social, and Physiological Determinants of Emotional State." *Psychological Review* 69: 379–99.

Schachter, S., and L. Wheeler. 1962. "Epinephrine, Chlorpromazine, and Amusement." *Journal of Abnormal and Social Psychology* 65: 121–28.

Schaevitz, Marjorie Hansen. 1984. *The Superwoman Syndrome.* New York: Warner Books.

Schafer, Roy. 1976. *A New Language for Psychoanalysis.* New Haven: Yale University Press.

Schaffner, Laurie. "Deviance, Emotion, and Rebellion: The Sociology of Runaway Teenagers." Honors thesis, Sociology Department, Smith College, 1994.

Scheff, Thomas J. 1973. "Intersubjectivity and Emotion." *American Behavioral Scientist* 16 (March–April): 501–22.

———. 1977a. "The Distancing of Emotion in Ritual." *Current Anthropology* 18, no. 3 (September): 483–91.

———. 1977b. "Toward a Sociology of Emotion." Mimeographed. Santa Barbara: University of California.

———. 1983. "Toward Integration in the Social Psychology of Emotions." *Annual Review of Sociology* 9: 333–54.

Scheper-Hughes, Nancy. 1993. *Death without Weeping: The Violence of Everyday Life in Brazil.* Berkeley: University of California Press.

Scheper-Hughes, Nancy, and Carolyn Sargent, eds. 1988. *The Cultural Politics of Childhood.* Berkeley: University of California Press.

Schoeck, H. 1966. *Envy: A Theory of Social Behavior.* New York: Harcourt, Brace and World.

Schor, Juliet. 1992. *The Overworked American: The Unexpected Decline of Leisure.* New York: Basic Books.

———. 1998. *The Overspent American: Upscaling, Downshifting, and the New Consumer.* New York: Basic Books.

Schwartz, Felice N. 1989. "Management Women, and the New Facts of Life." *Harvard Business Review* 1 (January–February): 65–76.

Schweder, Richard A., and Robert A. LeVine, eds. 1984. *Culture Theory: Essays on Mind, Self, and Emotion.* Cambridge: Cambridge University Press.

Seeley, J. R. 1967. *The Americanization of the Unconscious.* New York: International Science Press.

Segal, L. 1990. *Slow Motion: Changing Masculinities, Changing Men.* New Brunswick: Rutgers University Press.

Sells, Lucy. 1975. "Sex, Ethnic, and Field Differences in Doctoral Outcomes." Ph.D. dissertation. Sociology Department, University of California, Berkeley.

Sen, Nabaneeta. 1999. "The Wind beneath My Wings." *Indian Journal of Gender Studies* 6, no. 2 (July–December).

Sen, Soshitsu. 1981. *What a Beautiful Woman.* Tokyo: Shufutoseikatsush. (In Japanese.)

Sennett, Richard, and Jonathan Cobb. 1993. *The Hidden Injuries of Class.* New York: Norton.

Shahan, Lynn. 1981. *Living Alone and Liking It.* New York: Stratford Press.

Shapiro, David. 1965. *Neurotic Styles.* New York: Basic Books.

Sharpe, Rochelle. 2000. "Nannies on Speed Dial." *Business Week,* September 18: 108–10.

Shiotsuki, Yaeko. 1970–71. *Introduction to Rites of Passage,* vols. 1–3. Tokyo: Kobunsha. (In Japanese.)

Shore, Bradd. 1996. *Culture in Mind: Cognition, Culture, and the Problem of Meaning.* New York: Oxford University Press.

Shott, Susan. 1979. "Emotion and Social Life: A Symbolic Interactionist Analysis." *American Journal of Sociology* 84 (May 1979): 1317–34.

Sidel, Ruth. 1990. *On Her Own: Growing Up in the Shadow of the American Dream.* New York: Viking Press.

Simmel, Georg. 1950. *The Sociology of Georg Simmel.* Translated and edited by Kurt H. Wolff. Glencoe, Ill.: Free Press.

———. 1990. *The Philosophy of Money.* Edited by David Frisby. London: Routledge.

Simon, Rita J., Shirley M. Clark, and Kathleen Galway. 1967. "The Woman Ph.D.: A Recent Profile." *Social Problems* 15: 221–36.

Simonds, Wendy. 1992. *Self-Help Culture: Reading Women's Reading.* New Brunswick: Rutgers University Press.

Simpson, Richard. 1972. *Theories of Social Exchange*. Morristown, N.J.: General Learning Press.

Singelmann, Peter. 1972. "Exchange as Symbolic Interaction: Convergences between Two Theoretical Perspectives." *American Sociological Review* 37, no. 4: 414–24.

Sirianni, Carmen. 1991. "The Self Management of Time in Post-Industrial Society." In Karl Hinrichs, William Roche, and Carmen Sirianni, eds., *Working Time in Transition*. Philadelphia: Temple University Press.

Sivard, Ruth Leger. 1985. *Woman, A World Survey*. Washington, D.C.: World Priorities.

Skolnick, Arlene. 1991. *Embattled Paradise*. New York: Basic Books.

Slater, P. 1964. "Social Limitations on—Libidinal Withdrawal." In R. L. Coser, ed., *The Family*. New York: St. Martin's Press.

———. 1966. *Microcosm*. New York: John Wiley.

———. 1968. *The Glory of Hera*. Boston: Beacon Press.

———. 1971. "Passionate Love." In B. L. Murstein, ed., *Theories of Attraction and Love*. New York: Springer.

Smelser, Neil. 1959. *Social Change in the Industrial Revolution: An Application of Theory to the British Cotton Industry*. Chicago: University of Chicago Press.

———. 1963. *The Sociology of Economic Life*. Englewood Cliffs, N.J.: Prentice-Hall.

———. 1998. *The Social Edges of Psychoanalysis*. Berkeley: University of California Press.

Smith, Allen C., III, and Sherryl Kleinman. 1989. "Managing Emotions in Medical School: Students' Contacts with the Living and the Dead." *Social Psychology Quarterly* 52, no. 1: 56–69.

Smith, Pam. 1988a. "The Emotional Labor of Nursing." *Nursing Times* 84: 50–51.

———. 1988b. "The Nursing Process Revisited." Paper read at the Medical Sociology Group of the British Sociological Association Conference, York, England.

———. 1992. *The Emotional Labour of Nursing: Its Impact on Interpersonal Relatedness, Management and the Educational Environment in Nursing*. Houndsmills, Basinstoke: Macmillan Education.

Smith, Thomas Spence. 1992. *Strong Interaction*. Chicago: University of Chicago Press.

Solomon, Robert. 1973. "Emotions and Choice." *Review of Metaphysics* 27, no. 7: 20–41.

Sono, Ayako. 1971. *For Whose Sake Do You Love?* Tokyo: Bungeishuju. (In Japanese.)

Sorrentino, Constance. 1990. "The Changing Family in International Perspective." *Monthly Labor Review* 113: 41–58.

Spock, Benjamin. 1976. *Dr. Spock's Baby and Child Care*. New York: Pocket Books.

Sprout, W. J. H. 1952. *Social Psychology*. London: Methuen.

Stacey, Judith. 1990. *Brave New Families: Stories of Domestic Upheaval in Late Twentieth Century America*. New York: Basic Books.

Stack, Carol. 1974. *All Our Kin: Strategies for Survival in a Black Community*. New York: Harper and Row.

———, with Linda M. Burton. 1994. "Kinscripts: Reflections on Family, Generation and Culture." In Evelyn Nakano Glenn, Grace Chang, and Linda Rennie Forcey, eds., *Mothering: Ideology, Experience and Agency*. New York: Routledge.

Stanislavsky, Constantin. 1965. *An Actor Prepares*, trans. Elizabeth Hapgood. New York: Theater Arts Books.

Starker, Steven. 1989. *Oracle at the Supermarket: The American Preoccupation with Self-Help Books*. New Brunswick, N.J.: Transaction Books.

Steinem, Gloria. 1986. *Outrageous Acts and Everyday Rebellions*. New York: Signet Books.

Stern, Daniel. 1985. *The Interpersonal World of the Infant: A View from Psychoanalysis and Developmental Psychology*. New York: Basic Books.

Stone, Deborah. 1999. "Care and Trembling." *American Prospect* (March–April): 61–67.

Styron, William. 1951. *Lie Down in Darkness*. New York: Modern Library, Random House.

Suzuki, Kenji. 1982. *How to Be Considerate of Others*. Tokyo: Kodansha. (In Japanese.)

———. 1983a. *How to Be Considerate of Others II*. Tokyo: Kodansha. (In Japanese.)

———. 1983b. *A Story of Womanliness*. Tokyo: Shogakukan. (In Japanese.)

———. 1984. *Tenderness Makes Women Beautiful*. Tokyo: Kodansha. (In Japanese.)

Swanson, Guy E. 1965. "The Routinization of Love: Structure and Process in Primary Relations." In Samuel Z. Klausner, ed., *The Quest for Self-Control: Philosophies and Scientific Research*. New York: Free Press.

Swanson, Guy E., and Daniel Miller. 1966. *Inner Conflict and Defense*. New York: Schocken.

Swidler, Ann. 1973. "The Concept of Rationality in the Works of Max Weber." *Sociological Inquiry* 43: 35–42.

———. 1986. "Culture in Action: Symbols and Strategies." *American Sociological Review* 51: 273–86.

———. 2001. *Talk of Love: How Culture Matters*. Chicago: University of Chicago Press.

Tannen, Deborah. 1990. *You Just Don't Understand*. New York: Ballantine Books.

Tavris, Carol. 1993. "Beware the Incest-Survivor Machine." *New York Times Book Review*, January 3.

Thoits, Peggy A. 1985. "Self Labeling Processes in Mental Illness: The Role of Emotional Deviance." *American Journal of Sociology* 91: 221–49.

———. 1989. "The Sociology of Emotions." *Annual Review of Sociology* 15: 317–43.

Thomas, Marlo, and Friends. 1987. *Free to Be a Family*. New York: Random House.

Thompson, E. P. 1974. "Time, Work-Discipline, and Industrial Capitalism." In M. W. Flinn and T. C. Smout, eds., *Essays in Social History*. Oxford: Clarendon Press.

Thorne, Barrie. 1987. "Re-visioning Women and Social Change: Where Are the Children?" *Gender and Society* 1, no. 1 (March): 85–109.

———. 1993. *Gender Play: Girls and Boys in School*. New Brunswick: Rutgers University Press.

———. 1998. "Selected Bibliography on the Sociology of Childhood." Unpublished manuscript, Center for Working Families, University of California, Berkeley.

Tolich, Martin. 1988. "Doing Emotion Work: The Similarities and Differences between Manual Supermarket Checkers and Hochschild's Airline Flight Attendants." Paper presented at the Pacific Sociological Association, Las Vegas, Nevada, April.

Tolstoy, Leo. 1966. *War and Peace*. New York: Norton.

Tomkins, S. S. 1962. *Affect, Imagery, Consciousness.* 2 vols. New York: Springer.

Trice, Harrison M., and Janice M. Beyer. 1993. *The Cultures of Work Organizations.* Englewood Cliffs, N.J.: Prentice-Hall.

Trilling, Lionel. 1972. *Sincerity and Authenticity.* Cambridge: Harvard University Press.

Tronto, Joan. 1993. *Moral Boundaries: A Political Argument for an Ethic of Care.* London: Routledge.

Tucker, Robert, ed. 1978. *The Marx-Engels Reader,* 2d ed. New York: Norton.

Tung, Charlene. 2000. "The Cost of Caring: The Social Reproductive Labor of Filipina Live-In Home Health Caregivers."*Frontiers: A Journal of Women's Studies* 21, nos. 1–2: 61–82.

Ungerson, Clare, ed. 1990. *Gender and Caring: Work and Welfare in Britain and Scandinavia.* New York: Wheatsheaf.

United Nations Research Institute for Social Development. 1996. *Working towards a More Gender Equitable Macro-Economic Agenda.* Report of conference held in Rajendrapur, Bangladesh, November 26–28. Geneva, Switzerland.

United States Department of Labor Statistics. 2001. "Employment Characteristics of Families in 2000." In *Demographic Characteristics of the Labor Force* (Annual Report), tables 4–6.

Useem, Jerry. 2000. "Welcome to the New Company Town." *Fortune,* January 10: 62–70.

Uttal, Lynet. 1993. "Shared Mothering: Reproductive Labor, Childcare, and the Meanings of Motherhood." Diss., University of California, Santa Cruz.

———. 1996. "Custodial Care, Surrogate Care, and the Coordinate Care—Employed Mothers and the Meanings of Childcare." *Gender and Society* 10: 291–311.

———. 1998. "Communities of Care." Paper presented at the Work and Family Conference, Boston, November.

Van Buren, Abigail. 1981. *The Best of Dear Abby.* New York: Pocket Books.

Van Maanen, John, and Gideon Kunda. 1989. "Real Feelings: Emotional Expression and Organizational Culture." *Research in Organizational Behavior* 11: 43–103.

Van Manen, Max, and B. Levering. 1996. *Childhood Secrets: Intimacy, Privacy, and the Self Reconsidered.* New York: Teachers College Press.

Varley, A. 1996. "Women Heading Households: Some More Equal than Others?" *World Development* 24: 505–20.

Veblen, Thorstein. 1914. *The Instinct of Workmanship and the State of the Industrial Arts.* New York: Viking Press.

———. 1948. *The Portable Veblen,* ed. Max Lerner. New York: Viking Press.

———. 1979. *The Theory of the Leisure Class.* New York: Penguin.

Vedral, Joyce L. 1993. *Get Rid of Him.* New York: Time Warner.

Ventura, Michael. 1991. "Someone Is Stealing Your Life." *Utne Reader,* July–August: 78–81.

———. 1995. "The Age of Interruption." *Networker,* January–February: 19–31.

Vickers, Jeanne. 1991. *Women and the World Economic Crisis.* London: Zed Books.

Waerness, Kari. 1978. "The Invisible Welfare State: Women's Work at Home." *Acta Sociologica Supplement* 21: 193–207.

————. 1984. "Caring as Women's Work in the Welfare State." In Harriet Holter, ed., *Patriarchy in a Welfare Society*. Oslo: Norwegian University Press.

————. 1987. "On the Rationality of Caring." In Anne Showstack Sassoon, ed., *Women and the State*. London: Hutchinson.

Wallerstein, Judith, and Sandra Blakeslee. 1989. *Second Chances: Men, Women, and Children a Decade after Divorce*. New York: Ticknor and Fields.

Walster, Elaine. 1976. "New Directions in Equity Research." In L. Berkowitz and E. Walster, eds., *Advances in Experimental Social Psychology*, vol. 9. New York: Academic Press.

Walters, R. H. 1966. "Implications of Laboratory Studies of Aggression for the Control and Regulation of Violence." *Annals of the American Academy of Political and Social Science* 364: 60–72.

Ward, Kingsley. 1983a. *How to Be Considerate of Others II*. Tokyo: Kodansha. (In Japanese.)

————. 1983b. *A Story of Womanliness*. Tokyo: Shogakukan. (In Japanese.)

————. 1989. *Letters of a Businessman to His Daughter*. Tokyo: Shinchosha. (In Japanese.)

Warner, Stephen R., David T. Wellman, and Lenore Weitzman. 1977. "The Hero, the Sambo, and the Operator: Reflections on Characterizations of the Oppressed." Paper delivered at the American Sociological Association, Denver, August 31.

Weber, Max. 1958. *The Protestant Ethic and the Spirit of Capitalism*. New York: Charles Scribner.

————. 1963. "'Objectivity' in Social Science and Social Policy." In Maurice Natanson, ed., *Philosophy of the Social Sciences*. New York: Random House.

————. 1966. *The Theory of Social and Economic Organization*. New York: Free Press.

Weitzman, Lenore. 1985. *The Divorce Revolution: The Unexpected Social and Economic Consequences for Women and Children in America*. New York: Free Press.

Wellman, Barry, et al. 1997. "A Decade of Network Change: Turnover, Mobility, and Stability." *Social Networks* 19, no. 1: 27–51.

Wellman, Barry, ed. 1999. *Networks in the Global Village*. Boulder, Colo.: Westview Press.

West, Candace, and Don H. Zimmerman. 1987. "Doing Gender." *Gender and Society* 1: 125–51.

White, Lynn K., and Agnes Riesmann. 1992. "When the Brady Bunch Grows Up: Step-, Half- and Full-Sibling Relationships in Adulthood." *Journal of Marriage and the Family* 54 (February): 197–208.

Whyte, William H. 1956. *The Organization Man*. New York: Simon and Schuster.

Wikler, N. 1974. "Sexism in the Classroom." Unpublished manuscript, Sociology Department, University of California at Santa Cruz.

Wilensky, Harold. 1964. "The Professionalization of Everyone?" *American Journal of Sociology* 70 (September): 137–58.

Williamson, Marianne. 1993. *A Woman's Worth*. New York: Random House.

Winnicott, D. W. 1965. *The Maturational Processes and the Facilitating Environment*. New York: International Universities Press.

————. 1986. "The Theory of the Parent-Infant Relationship." In E. Peter Buckley, ed., *Essential Papers in Psychoanalysis*. New York: New York University Press.

Wong, Sau-Ling. 1994. "Diverted Mothering: Representations of Caregivers of Color in the Age of Multiculturalism." In E. Glenn, G. Chang, and L. Forcey, eds., *Mothering: Ideology, Experience, and Agency*. London: Routledge.

Wood, Leonard. 1988. "The Gallup Survey: Self-Help Buying Trends." *Publishers Weekly* 234 (October 14): 33.

Wouters, Cas. 1987. "Developments in the Behavioural Codes between the Sexes: The Formalization of Informalization in the Netherlands, 1930–85." *Theory, Culture, & Society* 4, nos. 2/3: 405–27.

———. 1995. "Etiquette Books and Emotion Management in the Twentieth Century, Part 1: The Integration of Social Class." *Journal of Social History* 29: 107–24.

Wrigley, Julia. 1995. *Other People's Children*. New York: Basic Books.

Zedek, Sheldon, et al. 1992. "Affective Response to Work and Quality of Family Life: Employee and Spouse Perspectives." In Elizabeth Goldsmith, ed., *Work and Family: Theory, Research and Applications*. London: Sage.

Zelizer, Viviana A. 1994. *The Social Meaning of Money*. New York: Basic Books.

———. 1996. "Payments and Social Ties." *Sociological Forum* 11, no 3: 481–95.

———. 2000. "The Purchase of Intimacy." *Law & Social Inquiry* (Fall): 2000.

Zerubavel, Eviatar. 1991. *The Fine Line: Making Distinctions in Everyday Life*. New York: Free Press.

Zlotnik, Hania. 1999. "Trends of International Migration since 1965: What Existing Data Reveal." *International Migration* 37, no. 1: 22–61.

INDEX

Abarbinel, Alice, 251
academic careers, 227–54; clockwork of, 236–38; in Cuba, 248–50; discrimination against women in, 230–32; family and culture of, 242–44; female role models in, 233–36; social psychology of, 238–42; withdrawal of women from, 232–33
acting, 91–92, 119. *See also* deep acting
Adams, Margaret, 55
adult personality stabilization, 37
advice books, 13–29; cool modern, 14–16, 19–26, 199; countertrends in, 28–29; gender codes in, 46–56; Japanese, 58–72; male rules of love in, 26–28; traditional, 16–19
affirmative action, 227–28, 243, 247–48
African Americans, 124, 163, 168–70, 227, 271n2
age discrimination, 238
Agee, James, 172
aggression: displacement of, 80; drives and, 92
Aid to Families with Dependent Children (AFDC), 216
Alcoholics Anonymous, 15
alienation, 119
Allport, Gordon, 77
altruism, 33; narcissistic, 156
ambivalence, 41–44; in colonized-colonizer syndrome, 155–58
American Medical Association, 249
American Sociological Review, 240
anger, 119; expressions of, 84; framing rules for, 99; management of, 133; power hierarchies and displacement of, 85–86
Anglo-Saxons, 169
anxiety, 92, 120, 121

appreciation, 105
appropriateness of feelings: situational, 94; types of, 82
Ariès, Philippe, 192–93
artisanal family, 3, 31
Art of Loving (Saimon), 71
Astin, Helen, 230
Asylums (Goffman), 7
attribution theory, 79, 174
Aunt Erma's Cope Book (Bombeck), 68
Austen, Jane, 26
Australia, 215
authoritarianism, 15, 19
authority: husband's, challenging, 18; Japanese versus American tones of, 70–71; male, mannerisms of, 50–51; traditional spheres of, 14
autonomy, 22, 23
Averill, James, 89

Bales, Kevin, 259n13
Bane, Mary Jo, 161
bargaining, cultural, 60
Bautista, Princela, 187
Bautista, Rowena, 185–87, 191, 193, 195, 197
beauty, oppressive norms of, 159
Beauvoir, Simone de, 20–21
Benedict, Ruth, 90
Bernard, Jessie, 230
Best of Dear Abby, The (Van Buren), 356n4
"Beware the Incest-Survivor Machine" (Tavris), 15
Bible, 15, 18, 19, 48, 50, 54, 144, 211
Bielby, Denise, 15
birth rates, falling, 215
black power movement, 236
blended families, 162

Text:	10/12 Baskerville
Display:	Syntax
Compositor:	BookMatters, Berkeley
Printer and binder:	Maple-Vail Book Manufacturing Group
Indexer:	Ruth Elwell